IN ON THE JOKE

In On the Joke

IN ON THE JOKE

THE ORIGINAL QUEENS OF STAND-UP COMEDY

SHAWN LEVY

THORNDIKE PRESS
A part of Gale, a Cengage Company

Copyright © 2022 by Shawn Levy.
Thorndike Press, a part of Gale, a Cengage Company.

ALL RIGHTS RESERVED
Thorndike Press® Large Print Biography and Memoir.
The text of this Large Print edition is unabridged.
Other aspects of the book may vary from the original edition.
Set in 16 pt. Plantin.

LIBRARY OF CONGRESS CIP DATA ON FILE.
CATALOGUING IN PUBLICATION FOR THIS BOOK
IS AVAILABLE FROM THE LIBRARY OF CONGRESS.

ISBN-13: 979-8-8857-8313-2 (hardcover alk. paper)

Published in 2022 by arrangement with Doubleday, an imprint of The Knopf Doubleday Publishing Group, a division of Penguin Random House LLC.

Printed in Mexico
Print Number : 1   Print Year : 2023

For Mickie and Jenny and Mary and
Lulu and Paula and Fanny and Alina
and Amy and Shannon

CONTENTS

CONTENTS

AUTHOR'S NOTE

For years, the most important women in my life — my daughter, Paula, and my partner, Shannon — have reminded me that the books I've written have been a manly lot, and they've cajoled me, in their ways, to write about a woman. And for some time, I've tried to make that happen, without ever quite hitting on the right idea at the right time. The concept for this book was, finally, both, and I am so grateful to have an opportunity to show the women who matter most to me that I hear and see them.

There are already several worthy histories of comedy and of women in comedy that deal, at least in part, with some of the figures and some of the era I've written about. (I especially recommend *We Killed* by Yael Kohen, *Seriously Funny* by Gerald Nachman, and *The Comedians* by Kliph Nesteroff.) But none hits *exactly* the target at which I've aimed: the rise of women as stand-up comedy stars during the period between, say, World

War II and 1970. As valuable and instructive as I found these and several other books on similar subjects, I recognized a gap in the bookshelf, in the historical record, that I could fill.

But, still: Why, in this age of #MeToo and #TimesUp, should a man take on the task of writing about a group of women *at all*? I asked myself that question often as I was starting out and continually as I was working.

Well, perhaps because one remembers best the thunder one heard in one's youth, I've got a real feel for and obsessive interest in the popular culture of the years between Pearl Harbor and Watergate. This subject sits right in the middle of my wheelhouse.

And imagine getting the chance to research, analyze, and write about Moms Mabley, Minnie Pearl, Elaine May, Phyllis Diller, and Joan Rivers, to visit Harlem and Greenwich Village and North Beach and Las Vegas in their heydays, to track a show-biz story that was sitting right out there in all its details but hadn't yet been gathered up and nailed down. Of *course* I wanted this gig.

The women in these pages are heroes. Each had the notion to enter a career in which there were virtually no female role models, mentors, or colleagues to emulate or be taught by — or at least none whom she knew of. Each created her own path, unaware, in the main, that other, similarly driven women were doing more or less the same thing, more or less at the same time. Each persisted despite social, professional, and even familial doubt, discouragement, resistance, and hostility. And each attained moments, if not decades, of success, sometimes only among insiders, but in several cases in the larger society — and, in a few, with truly iconic impact.

I've tried to present their lives and their work with accuracy, empathy, and appreciation, to see them as ordinary women as well as popular entertainers, to understand them in the contexts from which they emerged and indicate their deserved places in the history of comedy, of women in entertainment, of American popular culture.

I am in awe of every single one of them.

INTRODUCTION

In October 1983, the Friars Club, that bastion of American comedy royalty, held a roast of comic legend Sid Caesar at the Sheraton Centre Hotel in Times Square, one of those ceremonial functions at which show-biz insiders gather to drink and eat and smoke and make wicked, vicious fun of their guest of honor, all to raise money for their often-in-financial-need club or, in flush times, for charity.

Comedian Buddy Hackett was the roastmaster, and such Friars icons as Henny Youngman, Jack Carter, Dick Capri, and Jackie Vernon joined in the mockery of the honoree, which was, as at every such roast, decidedly vulgar and outrageous. Some two thousand men laughed appreciatively, and among them, as Hackett confirmed to a newspaper the next day, was not one single woman: "Women? There were no women at the roast. They're not allowed. There was a time when they weren't even allowed into the club[house]."

Mixed into the throng were some guests of club members, people who weren't entertainment professionals but who were happy to spend a goodly sum for the experience of being among a constellation of comedy stars and listening to raunchy jokes for a few hours. One of these was Phillip Downey, a slender, dapper, quiet, mustachioed fellow who was maybe a little pale for a guy from Southern California but who blended in like any other civilian at one of these wingdings, laughing at the bawdy jibes, saying a few polite hellos and goodbyes, and mostly spending his afternoon looking all around the room as if awestruck at the spectacle. Nobody seemed to have made note of him when he arrived, when he got up to visit the restroom, when he left.

But the next day, he was the talk of the Friars.

Phillip Downey didn't exist. Underneath that wig and mustache and tailored suit and demure manner was Phyllis Diller, a comedy legend of more than two decades' standing but someone who, simply by virtue of her gender, could not be admitted to the Friars as a member or be permitted to attend one of the club's stag parties/roasts without resorting to subterfuge.

"I've always wanted to eavesdrop," she told the *New York Post,* which ran a front-page

14

photo the next day of Phyllis in her Downey drag exiting a Sheraton Centre men's room. "It was the funniest, dirtiest thing I ever heard in my life."

Two years would go by before the Friars, as if shamed into it, made Phyllis the focus of a roast of her own (there was an even bigger turnout than for Sid Caesar's tribute), and another year would pass before they offered her membership in their ranks, making her the first woman ever admitted to their self-appointed comedy pantheon.

It wasn't an honor that she needed. For more than twenty-five years, Phyllis Diller had been a household name across America and, indeed, the English-speaking world, a star of nightclubs, theaters, television, movies, Broadway, even classical concert halls. She was rich, famous, widely imitated, and still working actively as she approached seventy — indeed, she was the most well-known and wealthy comedian in the room the day Phillip Downey snuck into the roast.

But there was a great sense of justice finally being done as she was anointed by her peers and granted a place among them. It was as if not only *a* woman had earned a place in the highest ranks of American comedy but as if *women in general* were seen as deserving of such recognition. Phyllis Diller had broken ground by attending a Friars roast, if in disguise, and by carrying on in her craft and career until the Friars had no choice but to acknowledge her as one of their own. But then, Phyllis Diller was one of a handful of women in comedy who had broken ground, blazed trails, knocked down doors, and made careers and legends for themselves regardless of the opinions of men. As in so many aspects of her career — indeed, in having a career as a comedian at all — she simply would not be denied.

That pretty much sums up the history of women in stand-up comedy, particularly the early history, when the women in these pages rose as more or less the first women to think that they could (duh) be as funny and sharp and entertaining as male joke tellers and who chose to pursue careers at it. They worked alone for the most part, both in the sense that they were almost all solo performers and in the sense that, in many cases, they didn't know about one another or see one another as doing the same thing as themselves. They faced the indifference, puzzlement, naysaying, and sometimes enmity of agents, managers, impresarios, audiences, critics, fellow performers, even their families. And yet they persisted, persevered, pushed forward, making their way ever farther and higher, if only incrementally, and clearing space not only for themselves but for the women working alongside them *and* for the women who followed them in the curious business of making people laugh for a living.

By the late 1960s, when several of these women were fully established in their careers, the idea of a woman standing up and telling jokes no longer seemed freakish or outlandish within show business or among audiences. There was still *a lot* of work to be done (indeed, even today it needs doing and redoing, in comedy as in so many other fields). They didn't get the same opportunities as men, or as many of them, or anything like equivalent pay. But the precedent had been set. The women in these pages didn't really have any antecedents or models they could point back to and say, "I'm like her." But with their lives and their bodies of work, they established a baseline that later generations of women comedians could use as a starting point for their own fledgling careers. Individually and as a never-really-united group, they created space for a form of expression — women telling jokes — that American popular culture had never truly accommodated until they demanded it be recognized and that continues to grow in size and impact to this day.

Today you look around the landscape of comedy and you see women ascendant, if not preeminent — women of all types, styles, ages, sensibilities.

Today we have Amy Schumer and Sarah

Silverman and Tiffany Haddish and Hannah Gadsby and Ali Wong and Leslie Jones and Mindy Kaling and Tig Notaro and Chelsea Handler and Jessica Williams and Samantha Bee and Chelsea Paretti and Jacqueline Novak and Jenny Slate.

Today we have legends living and working and joking among us: Mo'Nique, Rita Rudner, Tina Fey, Whoopi Goldberg, Margaret Cho, Kathy Griffin, Wanda Sykes, Ellen DeGeneres, Paula Poundstone, Roseanne Barr.[*]

Today we have women doing comedy specials on streaming TV and headlining Las Vegas show rooms and moving from comedy clubs and podcasts to movies, sitcoms, talk shows, and book deals.

Today one of the most acclaimed series on television, *The Marvelous Mrs. Maisel,* is the story of a woman breaking into stand-up comedy at the dawn of the sixties. (Another excellent series, *Hacks,* shines a light on the situation of women in comedy today.)

Today it's indisputable: there has never been more — or, arguably, better — comedy by women. In fact, the only reason not to call today *the* Golden Age of Women in Comedy is the likelihood that women comedians will continue to rise and proliferate and redefine

[*] Indeed, some legends, like Elayne Boosler and Lisa Lampanelli, have explicitly retired, though they no doubt still have their chops.

the art of stand-up in times to come. The real golden age might yet be on the horizon.

Maybe that's why it can feel so absurd to recall a day when this once seemed impossible, when women were deemed unsuited for stand-up comedy, when the very idea of a female comedian seemed, to the eyes of the men who ran show business and to most audiences, to be a joke in and of itself.

But that was the truth of it. From the days of vaudeville until the dawn of color TV, a funny woman who wanted to tell jokes was faced with a brick wall — and not the kind you stood in front of at an improv comedy club. Female comedians were not only rare, they were actively discouraged. Club owners, agents, TV talent bookers, rival comedians, entertainment critics: none of them wanted to see a woman tell jokes, and, really, most of them seemed to believe that women simply weren't funny, full stop. A woman on a stage in front of a microphone was, they reckoned, there to sing, maybe dance, maybe take off her clothes. If she was funny, that was spice to the act, not the point of it.

Take one noted power broker's analysis of why women couldn't be as successful at comedy as men:

> A woman is feminine, a woman is not abrasive, a woman is not a hustler. So when you see a gal who does "stand-up" one-

liners, she has to overcome that built-in identification as a retiring, meek woman. I mean, if a woman comes out and starts firing one-liners, those little abrasive things, you can take that from a man. . . . The only one who really does it is Joanie Rivers, who's had, I think, great success with being a stand-up comedian. . . . I think it's much tougher for women. You don't see many of them around. And the ones that try sometimes are a little aggressive for my taste. I'll take it from a guy, but from women, sometimes, it just doesn't fit too well.

Which hateful misogynist said this? And in what prehistorical epoch?

Try Johnny Carson, the single most powerful creator of comedy stars in the history of show business, and in *1979*, when the Great Stand-Up Comedy Boom was in full swing and the likes of Phyllis Diller, Elayne Boosler, and, yes, *Joan* Rivers, whom he had more or less introduced to the world, were among the most popular stand-up comedians in the nation.

Or how about this, in the year 2000, from another comedy legend who once held the keys to one of the nation's highest-rated TV broadcasts?

A woman doing comedy doesn't offend me, but sets me back a bit. I, as a viewer, have trouble with it. I think of her as a producing machine that brings babies in the world.

That would be Jerry Lewis, the comedian and movie star whose annual telethon in support of the Muscular Dystrophy Association was one of the hottest bookings in the biz for the first fifteen years or so of its life, which began in 1966.[*]
Or this, from the pages of *Vanity Fair,* in 2007?

Why are women, who have the whole male world at their mercy, not funny? Please do not pretend not to know what I am talking about. All right — try it the other way (as the bishop said to the barmaid). Why are men, taken on average and as a whole, funnier than women?

[*] Never one to put down his shovel when finding himself at the bottom of a hole that he himself had dug, Lewis added, in 2014, "It bothers me. I cannot sit and watch a lady diminish her qualities to the lowest common denominator. I just can't do that." And, what the hell, in for a pound, a year later: "Seeing a woman project the kind of aggression that you have to project as a comic just rubs me wrong. I mean, you got some very, very funny people that do beautiful work — but I have a problem with the lady up there that's going to give birth to a child, which is a miracle."

That was polemicist Christopher Hitchens, launching into some twenty-eight hundred malignantly unfunny words to attempt a *biological* explanation for his theory of women's lack of humor.

Or — last one — *this*?

> I don't like funny women. I come out of that generation where a woman should be beautiful and sexy and a wonderful flower attached to a man, even though my whole life has been the antithesis of this. To this day, you don't expect a woman to be funny. . . . Nobody likes funny women. We're a threat. I don't like funny women. I don't think I'm funny. I think I'm witty.

That would be, of *all* people, Miss Joan Rivers, still rising to the height of her fame and career, in 1981 and, to be fair, *maybe* telling the readers of *Playboy* what she thought they wanted to hear.

How did we evolve from such neanderthal ideas about women and humor to the current day, with its rich female comedy culture?

Step by painstaking step, as it turns out.

(Before we continue, though, a few words from Ms. Tina Fey in response to the preceding. In her brilliant 2011 memoir, *Bossypants,* she wrote:

> Whenever someone says to me, "Jerry

22

Lewis says women aren't funny," or "Christopher Hitchens says women aren't funny," or "Rick Fenderman says women aren't funny. . . . Do you have anything to say to that?" Yes. We don't fucking care if you like it. I don't say it out loud, of course, because Jerry Lewis is a great philanthropist, Hitchens is very sick, and the third guy I made up. Unless one of these men is my boss, which none of them is, it's irrelevant. My hat goes off to them. It is an impressively arrogant move to conclude that just because you don't like something, it is empirically not good. I don't like Chinese food, but I don't write articles trying to prove it doesn't exist.

(A few years later, asked *again* about whether women had a disadvantage when doing comedy, she politely seethed: "The only disadvantage women have is [we] have to keep fucking answering the question of, 'Is it hard and are women funny?' The men don't have to answer that question. That's the only impairment.")

To arrive at an age when women stand-up comedians would be considered a normal thing, American culture and American show business had to metamorphose, sometimes in sync, sometimes leapfrogging each other.

Some of the struggle had to do with the

very nature of stand-up itself. To speak of stand-up comedy is to speak of a very specific art form: the solo artist, armed only with a microphone and a store of wit, energy, jokes, and nerve, facing an audience, telling jokes, making trenchant observations, spritzing one-liners, engaging with the public directly in a performance as daring as that of any tightrope walker, escape artist, or test pilot.

Johnny Carson wasn't entirely wrong. Stand-up is not for the meek. It combines writing and performing and moxie in a way best suited to the most confident, aggressive, presumptuous, even arrogant personalities. Comedians operate under the assumption that their observations on life and the world are not only humorous but essential. They take the stage with chips on their shoulders, with something to prove, almost looking for a fight. They probe at their audiences, measuring their mood, adapting their acts to the temperature of the room. When they fail, they are said to have "died" or "bombed." But when they succeed, they have "killed," their audiences have been "slain," everyone in the room "died laughing": aggression exemplified.

The stand-up comedian answers to a punch list of responsibilities unique in popular culture. He or she must be funny, most of all, but also fresh, original, relatable, economical, rhythmic, topical, timely, and adaptable. A stand-up act requires the approving response of an audience several times a minute, as compared to a singer, who has three to five minutes between anticipated rounds of applause, or an actor, who can go an hour or more without a peep from the crowd. ("I can die every fifteen seconds," sighed veteran comedian Minnie Pearl.) And a stand-up is, by convention, subject to the harassment of a bored or unamused audience or, indeed, any individual audience member; we can't imagine shouting down a singer or a dancer or an actor in the middle of a performance, but a stand-up, even a world-class name, is open to the scourge of heckling whenever he or she has a weak moment.

The scrutiny to which stand-up comedians are subject is both ongoing and personal. Watch a lousy comedy sketch (or play or film) and you can blame the script or the director or the ensemble for the failure. Watch a lousy comedian, and there is one and only one person upon whom to pin your disapproval. The stand-up rises and falls on his or her own strength or quality or lack thereof. And it's a minute-by-minute thing: A comic sketch or play or film can start slow and build, and an audience will go along with the development, submitting to the narrative and remaining patient in hope of a payoff. A comedian's performance, ranging in scale from a "tight five," as it's known in the trade, to a sixty-plus-minute concert, has to provide snap after crackle after pop for the whole of its running time. Whether at open mic in a bar, as a featured performer in a nightclub, or as a headliner in an arena, a stand-up has to provide laughs from start to finish or die from lack of impetus. A comedian, like a sculptor working with an irreplaceable piece of marble or a golfer trying to win a major championship, can't afford many poor strokes.

All of these qualities of the art could seem, to someone steeped in antiquated and patriarchal ways of thinking, to be somehow "inappropriate," or "unbecoming" for a woman, somehow "unladylike" — characterizations so absurd and offensive in and of themselves that merely typing them feels like succumbing to the most thick-skulled sort of misogyny. But prior to the spread of feminism in the 1960s, at the time the women profiled in these pages were scrapping to build their careers, these were the dominant notions in the minds of the gatekeepers of show business *and* the audiences whom they served. A woman alone on a stage was expected to be pretty and to sing, maybe dance. If she did comedy at all, it was with a man or as part of an ensemble. And she certainly didn't deploy an arsenal of one-liners or zetz any hecklers in the audience. If you believed all that — and these were widely held beliefs — then you couldn't imagine a woman stand-up comedian, and you would have missed some truly brilliant performers.

It wasn't that audiences and show-biz poo-bahs thought women weren't funny per se. Women have made successful careers in comic acting from the days of Mabel Normand and Marie Dressler in silent movies through the likes of Carole Lombard, Irene Dunne, and Myrna Loy in screwball comedy films, to the emergence of Lucille Ball, Carol Burnett, and Mary Tyler Moore on TV — among many, many others. For just as long, women have performed Jane-of-all-trades acts combining comedy (often sketch comedy) with singing and dancing on the live stage (and, later, radio and television) in the vein of Fanny Brice, Mae West, Martha Raye, Pearl Bailey, and, early in their careers, women who eventually turned fully to stand-up such as Moms Mabley and Jean Carroll.

Never, however, in these earlier days were funny women permitted to be *women,* to talk about their lives, their troubles, or their places in the world in the way male stand-up comedians did regularly. On the rare occasions when a woman was seen primarily as a comedian and not as a comic actress or singing comedienne, the culture forced her into narrow, constricting, undignified roles, neutralizing her gender, her sexuality, her perspicacity, or all three. For women to be accepted as comedians, they had to be constrained or distorted in such a way that the womanhood was bled out of them. They could be ditzes, cute but featherheaded in the vein of Gracie Allen, a brilliant comedian who worked for decades alongside her husband, George Burns, and got most of the best jokes in the act while he served more or less as her straight man. Or they could infantilize themselves outright as the great vaudevillian Fanny Brice did when she adopted her Baby Snooks persona, dressing as a child, speaking babytalk, and entertaining audiences with impish stunts in response to the adult world. They could act older than they were, as the comedian Jackie Mabley did in the 1940s, calling herself "Moms," dressing as a granny in a housecoat and slippers, and affecting the demeanor of a woman decades older than her actual forty-odd years. Or they could act foolish and rustic, as the college-educated Sarah Ophelia Colley did in her late twenties when she adapted the persona of a sunny, wide-eyed, man-crazy country gal whom she named Minnie Pearl. But what they could *not* do was walk out on a stage looking like an ordinary (or, in the manner of men who told jokes in tuxedos, elegant) woman from anywhere in the world and talk in plain, comic terms about the things that people like them — that is, *other ordinary women* —

might recognize as true and funny: husbands, children, housework, shopping, air travel, or any number of the quirks of everyday life that affected men and women equally but which show business and popular audiences seemed to think that only men could address. If they wanted to be funny, in short, they had to, in some way, deny their womanhood.

Ironically, it was the emergence of stand-up comedy as a distinct art form that made it possible for women (as well as members of various minority groups) to find wide acceptance as comedy stars. Comic monologues have been part of popular entertainment forever. At the start of the twentieth century, vaudeville (and its raunchy kid brother, burlesque) presented a wide variety of entertainment genres, and comedy — often in skits, often blended with singing, dancing, and novelty acts — was a big part of the draw. Comic entertainers in vaudeville often did double duty, performing their own acts *and* serving as emcees, even if they were part of a team or ensemble in their principal endeavors. In that way, they often became standouts, recognized not only for their prepared material but for their offhanded, adlibbed reactions to unforeseen moments onstage or in the audience.

(Importantly, vaudeville and burlesque were mirrored in culturally segregated portions of the culture: the so-called Chitlin' Circuit of all-Black shows presented to almost entirely Black audiences; the Borscht Belt of Jewish entertainers performing in resort hotels in the Northeast, and, later, Florida; and the Grand Ole Opry, home to what was originally known as "hillbilly" entertainment and then, after World War II, as country. Those subcultures had their own comedy stars, some of whom, as we shall see, went on to broader careers.)

Vaudeville was, history tells us, killed off by the rise of radio and talking movies, but its essential structure persisted on the airwaves (radio and then television) as the variety show. Too, many comic vaudevillians morphed into comic actors in film or on radio, continuing, in most cases, acts and personae they had introduced on the vaudeville stage.

By the end of World War II, the nation's vaudeville circuits almost entirely ceased to function. But as those opportunities evaporated, others bloomed. Nightclubs, which offered intimate, scaled-down shows for a sophisticated urban clientele, began to grow in importance. By the late forties, every city of reasonable size was home to at least a few such venues, places where grown-ups could go to eat, drink, and watch a performance that was a little more bijou and deluxe than whatever was at the local movie house (or on radio or TV) on a given night. Nightclubs of-

fered shorter, less diverse programs; a vaudeville show might consist of a dozen or more
acts, a nightclub three or four. And the acts
were smaller: comic ensembles were win-
nowed down to small teams or, in many
cases, solo performers — modern comedians,
essentially, "working in one," in the parlance
of the trade. So widespread was this latter
phenomenon, and so new, that *Variety,* the
font of so much show-biz jargon over the
century of its publication and influence,
began to use a new term for it — "stand-up
comedy" — in 1950.[*]

By the fifties, stand-up had taken on the
form we recognize today: the loner at the mic
telling jokes and stories, spewing one-liners,
sometimes riffing off the audience either as a
premeditated strategy or as a form or reaction or even in self-defense. In cities such as
New York, Chicago, Miami, San Francisco,
Los Angeles, and the newly prominent gambling and entertainment destination Las
Vegas, prestigious nightclubs presented
comedians who were already well known
from television and radio. At the same time,
those cities were home to cabarets, lounges,
cafés, and so-called "discovery clubs," smaller
venues where lesser-known or outright unknown new talent performed, often without

[*] The phrase didn't appear in most dictionaries for
another fifteen years.

salary, in hopes of building a following or being discovered by a manager or agent — perfect breeding grounds for new comedy talent.

And then, as so many other aspects of the culture did, stand-up comedy changed from something standardized, impersonal, and traditional into something experimental, idiosyncratic, and revelatory. The jokes told by such old-timers as Milton Berle, Bob Hope, and Henny Youngman might have been told by anyone (or, as those stars and their peers almost always performed material supplied by professional gag writers, anyone *with money*). But in the 1950s, just as the groundbreaking practice of method acting demanded that actors look into themselves to mine truths, just as rock and roll disrupted performance norms of popular music, a new type of comedy based in political commentary, personal psychology, spontaneous improvisation, and an attitude of cynicism and even hostility toward the status quo emerged. In New York, Chicago, San Francisco, and select points in between — and on LP records, the emergent platform in home entertainment — new comedians, almost always working from material that they themselves had written, appeared seemingly in a giant wave, turning stand-up comedy from a form of amusement into a form of self-expression, consciousness raising, even social critique.

They were a distinctly diverse group — political satirist Mort Sahl, theatrical monologist Shelley Berman, hipster firebrand Lenny Bruce, quirky ironist Bob Newhart, and surreal madman Jonathan Winters prominent among them. But they were lumped together by commentators and critics as the "sick comics" — *Time* magazine actually ran a cover story with that name in 1959, labeling them "sickniks" — as if their attempts to somehow personalize their material signaled mental derangement. And there was something else unique about this generation of comedians: it included Black performers such as Dick Gregory and Godfrey Cambridge, and it included (or would soon include) such women as Moms Mabley, Elaine May (with her partner Mike Nichols), and Phyllis Diller. As a generation, they would establish new standards of originality and idiosyncrasy in the field.

It may have been a sign of "sickness" in some eyes that women were being allowed the same chances as men to be funny or fail in the effort. But as the early history of women stand-up comedians demonstrates, those who persevered and made places for themselves in the field were anything but frail or debilitated. Where doors creaked ajar, they kicked them open; where management was willing to take a chance, they made themselves irreplaceable; where the spectacle of one woman telling jokes drew in curiosity seekers, they came to constitute an array of can't-miss acts just as varied and diverse as any selection of male comics.

There were, of course, caveats and conditions. While some women were able to force their way to the first rank of comedy stars by the end of the 1960s, they still seemed to do so within brackets. Phyllis Diller, Totie Fields, and Joan Rivers didn't present themselves in the same clownish guises as earlier funny-women, but they nonetheless took onstage personae that circumscribed their femininity, that set them apart from quote-unquote "normal" women: the manic harridan, the vainglorious fat girl, and the desperate neurotic, respectively. Their stage faces were more ordinary than the characters that Moms Mabley and Minnie Pearl embodied, they acknowledged their roles as wives and mothers, but they were still set off from the "ordinary" by qualities that made them ill suited for "regular" lives. There were biographical and psychological bases for those differences — internal truths behind those performative masks — and, perhaps not coincidentally, Phyllis, Totie, and Joan all experimented with plastic surgery (indeed, Phyllis and Joan became famed devotees of it) and were frank and public about their desire to attain a state of attractiveness that they didn't feel in their younger days. So, yes, they each found a way through the glass ceiling, but each left something personal, feminine, and real behind in the effort, and each tried to reclaim it, even if only superficially, later on.

To chronicle the rise of women in comedy is to focus on a specific moment in history, from the rise of stand-up as a distinct practice through the emergence of "sick" comedy in the late fifties, when the shape of comedy became clear and fixed in a way that has been maintained for more than a half century. Since that metamorphosis, since the women in these pages made their distinct and individual impacts, the path for younger women who aspired to careers in comedy has become clear: how and where you had to work, what a woman's comedy act looked like, aspects of stagecraft and career management, the specific venues and practices and styles and subjects that were available to mine and utilize, and so on.

Some definitions are in order. In these pages, stand-up will be considered as distinct from comic acting as practiced by the likes of Mae West, Lucille Ball, Carol Burnett, Shirley MacLaine, Gilda Radner, and Kate McKinnon, geniuses all, but geniuses working with the luxury of scripts and fellow cast members and well-rehearsed characterizations and scenes. It will also be considered distinctly from the art of performers whose acts are chiefly musical and who might best be labeled *comediennes,* women such as Sophie Tucker, the bold and bawdy "Last of the Red Hot Mamas"; Anna Russell, who cleverly spoofed classical music; Ruth Wallis, a singer and songwriter famous for her risky double entendres; or such entertainingly funny musical theater performers as Ethel Merman, Carol Channing, Pearl Bailey, Doris Day, and such latter-day inheritors of the tradition as Bette Midler.

Because of the way stand-up comedy, especially women's stand-up, evolved from vaudeville and associated entertainments to the modern ideal of the art, the notion of a stand-up *can,* as a matter of history, include women who used music as a vehicle for comedy and told more jokes than they sang songs, women who performed monologues in character (the French word for them, *diseuse,* would be helpful if it weren't so obscure), and women who performed semi-improvisatory sketches, especially in the late 1950s, when the techniques of comic improv were radical new inventions in entertainment. And thus, because of the specific moment of their rise (and, in several cases, their falls), some women who combined comical singing with the new sorts of comic energy have made the cut, as have some women who didn't necessarily work alone but whose contribution to the evolving art of comedy was so specific and influential as to demand that they be recognized and included.

And so we begin with a handful of women whose careers originated in vaudeville and its cognate platforms: Moms Mabley, Jean Carroll, and Minnie Pearl. We will take a side trip to consider a group of women whose acts combined comic song with norm-shattering exploration of the bounds of free speech and good taste: Belle Barth, Pearl Williams, and Rusty Warren. Another aspect of the comedy revolution, the rise of improvisation, will be represented by the story of Elaine May. And the triumph of women in what was unmistakable as modern stand-up comedy will be explored in the stories of Phyllis Diller, Totie Fields, and Joan Rivers, the last of whom, more than any of the others, synthesized everything that came before her: the traditional rat-a-tat style of the Borscht Belt and the male nightclub comic; the daring (and, indeed, raunch) of the after-hours bawds; and the warts-and-all confessional style of the "sick" comics.

This book is an assemblage of biographies, a selection of lives that don't necessarily connect like a jigsaw puzzle but rather lie side by side, sometimes overlapping, sometimes with gaps between them, to create a collage. The intent is to show what it took to create a culture in which women could be allowed to pursue careers as stand-up comedians. Today, that notion is a commonplace. But when these women began their careers — and, in some cases, even when they retired or died — the very idea was a matter of puzzlement and consternation. Thanks to their fortitude, we are in a far richer place. And we've had more than a few real laughs in getting here.

ONE:
THE PHILOSOPHER

When I look out on an audience, they belong to me as my own children. We all have little weaknesses. I been insulted. I been called names. But I don't get angry. I feel sorry for ignorance in any form. And I'll try to help them.

— 1961

If you wanted to stick a proper name on women's struggle to be accepted as stand-up comedians in American show business, you could call it "Moms Mabley."

Jackie "Moms" Mabley began her comedy career not long after World War I, performing in all-Black shows for all-Black audiences on an all-Black vaudeville circuit (sometimes even in blackface, more on which soon), and she ended it in the 1970s, as a staple on TV, the star of a feature film, the spokesperson in several national ad campaigns, and a head-liner at venues such as Carnegie Hall, Yankee Stadium, and the Fabulous Forum alongside the likes of the Jackson 5, the Temptations,

Smokey Robinson, Aretha Franklin, Ray Charles, and Tina Turner.

She was born in North Carolina in the nineteenth century to a family that included former slaves, and she died a suburban New York homeowner who wore minks and diamonds, was chauffeured around in her own Rolls-Royce, and was invited to the White House to discuss civil rights.

She had logged forty years in show business before someone thought to capture her comedy act on records, and another seven before someone put her on TV, and she wound up selling millions of albums and appearing regularly on national variety shows and as a presenter at the Grammy Awards.

She was billed as "the funniest woman in the world" for decades before she was able to carve a path out of the narrow lane of Black show business and cross over to the quote-unquote "mainstream," becoming popular with white (and, impressively, youth) audiences at an age when a lot of entertainers would be thinking about retirement — an overnight success, as it were, in her sixties and seventies.

She was a lifestyle groundbreaker, who favored man-cut suits off-stage and the company of chorus girls, who often accompanied her as travel companions. She was a crackerjack gambler, hustling jazz musicians and stagehands in games of pinochle and

Spanish Pool checkers. Onstage, she broached profanity and sang suggestive parodies of popular songs and spoke openly of sex and of political topics such as racial equality.

In short, she woke up every morning for decades facing impossible odds of racism, misogyny, prudery, dismissal, and doubt, and she went out and stood alone in front of a microphone and created her own legend by making people laugh with the sheer force of her wit and her sensibility. If there was ever a woman who made her own luck out of raw, audacious willpower, it was Moms Mabley.

The ability to pursue her quixotic ambition to be a professional entertainer despite the twin disadvantages of being Black and a woman was part of a particularly confident, upbeat, and resilient character instilled in her as a child. She was born Loretta Mary Aiken in Brevard, a mountain town about thirty miles southwest of Asheville in western North Carolina. It was, as she recalled, a bucolic setting, small and airy and uncommonly tolerant. "To tell the truth," she said in 1961, "there was no segregation where I was born."

The histories and genealogies of rural families of this era can be hard to pin down reliably. Dates and timelines disagree with one another; spellings on government forms can be irregular;[*] and there are often gaps with no documents of any kind. What's more, the stories that do get passed down (particularly those shared by Moms, who tended toward fancies and reveries) aren't always consistent or verifiable.

Some things, though, we can assert for sure. Loretta's father, James P. Aiken, was born a free man in 1861, the son of Benjamin Franklin Aiken and Mary Jane (Rhodes) Aiken, who had several children each from earlier marriages that had ended in their spouses' deaths. The Aikens were prosperous, and James carried on the family's good fortune, entering into various business enterprises, establishing himself as one of the town's top merchants. According to his daughter, "He had the only white barber shop, the undertaker shop, a grocery store, a dry goods shop" as well as "a house and a plot for all his children." Aiken was considered a significant man of the town, enlisting in the volunteer fire department, a position that carried prestige and was considered an honor.

In 1884, Aiken, who already had two children, married Daphne Bailey Keyth. Seven years later, in 1891, she died soon after giv-

---

[*] In her first appearance on a federal census form, the three-year-old girl's name is recorded as "Loretter."

ing birth to their only known child together. Aiken very quickly married again; his bride, Mary Magdaline Smith, daughter of Pink and Emiline Smith, was, at age fifteen, some fourteen years his junior. With his new wife, Aiken continued to grow his family — a total of ten children over the subsequent eighteen years, seven of whom would survive birth. Loretta would fall right in the middle among those surviving siblings, arriving in the Aikens' large home, complete with servants, on March 19, 1897.*

By her own accounts, Loretta was a happy child. The house was comfortable, there was sufficient food and clothing, and she had extended family all around her, giving her a sense of safety and security. "I wasn't born in any log cabin," she boasted. "I was born to a prominent family in North Carolina." Such was her contentment that she thought the world ended in the mountains of the Pisgah National Forest that formed the horizon west of Brevard, at the point where the peaks met the sky, and she never imagined life beyond it. "The mountains were very high," she remembered, "so high that we grew up think-

---

* There would be reports claiming that she was born in 1894, and many more that claimed she was born sometime *after* 1897, but she appears as a three-year-old in the 1900 federal census and a thirteen-year-old in the 1910 census.

ing that on the other side everything drops off into eternity."

In particular, her grandmother and great-grandmother, who lived with the family, were inspirational guiding spirits. "My great-grandmother was a grandmother in slavery, and my grandmother was born during slavery," she said. That great-grandmother, according to Loretta, "lived to be 117, and her words were like gold nuggets. . . . She used to tell me stories about slavery. She would always say to me — she couldn't say my name Loretta — she would say, 'Retta, you are freeborn. There's a world out there, and I want you to go out in it.' " Grandma, too, had lessons to share. "My granny was a slave," Loretta remembered. "She was never sold or nothing. But she was a slave. . . . She told me, 'Child, you look into that fireplace and see the future in those flames, 'cause you're gonna see the *world* like your granny never did.' "

That future would come fast enough, and on the heels of several painful episodes. On August 25, 1909, Jim Aiken and his older brother, Lawrence, raced to the scene of a conflagration in their roles as members of the volunteer fire brigade. The town's fire truck carried a boiler to generate pressure and force water through hoses, and on that hot day the boiler exploded, killing both Aiken brothers. Mary found herself a widow at twenty-four,

44

with six children of her own, three more from her late husband's previous marriage, and Jim's last child due that fall.

By then, Loretta was on her way to becoming a mother herself. In various tellings, she said she was raped by at least two grown men while living in Brevard, as early as the age of eleven, and she was impregnated by at least two of her rapists, one of whom was, she said, the town sheriff. Both of those children were put up for adoption, leaving no traces in historical records. Years later, their mother would recall that she served as a wet nurse to a well-to-do white family when she was "about 14" and nursing a baby of her own. "I loved that baby like my own baby," she said of the white girl she nursed. "I sacrificed my own baby Lucretia sometimes. I would say, 'You're a big strong baby, but Lois is weak and sick. Now don't cry, and save some of that milk for little Lois.' "

Mary broke up the Aiken family home sometime after 1910. She found a new husband, George Parton, who worked as a waiter at Union Station in Washington, D.C., and by the 1920 census she had moved north with him and added yet more children to her large brood.[*] For a time, Loretta joined

---

[*] Estimates of the number of full and half-siblings to whom Loretta could lay claim range from eleven to sixteen.

Mary, but she couldn't abide Parton, and she ran away from home, and once again was preyed upon by a man. As she told it, "I was in Buffalo, New York, and, as young girls do who run away from home, got in a little situation." That situation resulted in another child: Yvonne, born in 1917.

In that desperate moment, pregnant and on her own, Loretta sought divine counsel to steer her through her confounding life. "I got on my knees . . . and prayed to God to open a way. And I don't know if you've ever heard a voice like that or not, but something said to me, 'Go on stage.' "

Divine or not, this wasn't a completely random inspiration. Back in Brevard, she recalled, she had taken part in local theatricals. "I used to star in a lot of church plays," she said decades later, "and I was always the funny one. So why not try it for a living?"

As fate would have it, the home in which she was staying was next door to a boardinghouse that catered to entertainers. One of them, a singer and dancer named Bonnie Bell Drew, noticed Loretta hanging around and struck up a conversation. "She asked me was I in show business," Loretta later remembered. "And I said, 'No.' And she said, 'Well, you should be. You're pretty. You're beautiful.' Well, I didn't know how the Lord would answer my prayer, but she says, 'Tonight, throw your clothes over the fence.' " And so,

46

accepting this offer to run away again, she joined the troupe the next day as it headed off for Pittsburgh. There, as she bragged in the *Pittsburgh Courier* decades later, she marked "The first time I set foot on a stage." She may have appeared alongside the celebrated hoofing-and-singing duo Buck and Bubbles (John Bubbles would later become a breakout star). As she recalled it, she was given a role in a sketch called "The Rich Aunt in Utah," and the audience ate up her performance.

Her initial stage career was short-lived. She returned to North Carolina to have her baby and fell under the sway of an older man. James A. Hall was a preacher seventeen years her senior when Loretta met and married him at the insistence of her stepfather. She had two daughters by him, Christina Lucheria Hall, born in North Carolina in 1917, and Bonnie Bell Hall, born on Leap Day in Baltimore three years later.

It was 1920, and Loretta Aiken Hall, just twenty-three, had borne five children, three of whom — Yvonne, Christina, and Bonnie — she would claim for the rest of her life. "I had those girls young," she later admitted. "I asked God how I could support 'em, and God got to me to tell me to do it in show business." She wanted to take another shot at the stage, and her mother could sense the young woman's determination to make her own way in the world: "You're too much like me not to do something," she said. This time, Loretta made a more systematic effort at a career. She hitched a ride with a traveling minstrel show that took her to Cleveland, where she once again caught on with a vaudeville troupe willing to give a comely young woman a crack at the stage.

As she recalled, the show was led by the vaudevillian and sometime prizefighter Tim Moore, who would go on to fame in the role of Kingfish in the deeply racist *Amos 'n' Andy* TV series. And she would appear in it under a new name. No longer would she go by Loretta or by Aiken or Hall. She rechristened herself Jacki (later Jackie) Mabley, taking the name from a fellow performer, Jack Mabley, with whom she'd briefly been an item onstage and in life. "He took a lot off me," she said repeatedly over the years, "and the least I could do was take his name."

The stage on which the emerging Jackie Mabley learned her craft and launched her half-century-plus career was part of a Black vaudeville circuit known as the Theatre Owners Booking Association. TOBA had launched in 1920 and served as an entertainment pipeline for Black theaters across a broad swath of eastern, southern, midwestern, and southwestern states. It was composed entirely of Black performers playing before almost entirely Black audiences at theaters owned, mainly, by white businessmen, and it skipped the biggest cities — New York, Chicago, Washington, Philadelphia — where larger, more profitable independent theaters could afford to book better-known acts and mount shows of their own.

Like a lot of vaudeville enterprises, TOBA gradually collapsed in the early 1930s under the twin pressures of the Great Depression and the advent of talking movies. But while it was in existence, it provided a training ground for some of the most talented, entertaining, and influential performers of the twentieth century. Among its alumni was an extraordinary array, some of whom were established headliners who traveled only briefly on the circuit, others of whom learned their profession as TOBA troupers: singers Bessie Smith, Ethel Waters, and Josephine Baker; musicians Fats Waller, Count Basie, Louis Armstrong, and Cab Calloway; comedians Mantan Moreland, Dewey "Pigmeat" Markham, and Lincoln Perry (aka Stepin Fetchit); and all-rounders like Sammy Davis Jr., who was barely out of diapers when he first appeared on a TOBA stage.

TOBA wasn't as well funded as the primarily white vaudeville outfits. The salaries were lower, the transportation and accommodations more scattershot, the theaters less well appointed. It was a grueling circuit that demanded entertainers perform in as many as thirty shows a week and travel more or less nonstop, starting a route in one city, say, Washington, D.C., then spending as much as eighteen months going from place to place before finishing in, say, St. Louis. It was for good reason that the entertainers who worked for the outfit joked that TOBA stood for "Tough On Black Asses." (It was also commonly known as the Chitlin' Circuit.)

It was, however, a superb training ground for the bigger time. According to Jackie, "It taught young people how to be entertainers. Both in character as well as ability. . . . You had to do everything and learn everybody's parts; in case somebody takes sick, you get right in there and do their part. You had to sing, dance, and talk. That's what was so great about the TOBA: It taught you how to do everything and do it well. They perfected you in whatever category that you were best in." And that perfecting was *work*. As she later recalled, "You talk about rehearsals — honey, we rehearsed before shows, between shows, and after shows!"

TOBA also had high standards for its performers as people as well as entertainers. As Jackie remembered of her seniors on the circuit, "I had listened to those people and watched them carry themselves as ladies and gentlemen. And if you didn't get it right in that TOBA time, your punishment was you had to go over it again. I don't care how great

50

the audience thought you was, if you didn't know how to carry yourself, you had to go over that circuit again."

In compensation for this grueling routine, Jackie Mabley was paid $12.50 a week,[*] which served as both salary and expense money. And when she proved herself an apt student of her craft and a crowd-pleasing entertainer, she was given a raise. "When I got raised to $15 I thought I was rich! Oh boy!"

She may not, despite her youthful naivety, have been well paid, but she made her name. She was first noticed in July 1922 when playing in Cincinnati. Teamed as Mabley and Broadway alongside a female impersonator who went by the stage name Bobbie Broadway, she did some singing, some dancing, and "a line of chatter," according to a *Billboard* reviewer who caught the act the following month in Shreveport. The critic seemed not to care for the pair but conceded that they "picked up enough applause to warrant calling it an 80 per cent act." Fair enough. But there was a disturbing note to the review, passed over as a matter of routine but inconceivable from a century's vantage: Jackie Mabley, though unmistakably a Black woman, performed "under cork" — that is, she had used the ash from the burnt end of a

* Approximately $182 in 2022.

cork to make herself up in blackface.

It boggles the mind, but such was the deep-seated and systemic assignation of certain stereotypes of speech and behavior to Black skin that even people born with it had to accentuate their blackness when performing professionally, whether before integrated or all-Black crowds. The spectacle of white performers adopting the guises of Blacks through the use of makeup was so commonplace that Black performers themselves were compelled to do the same so as to be seen as "legitimate" entertainers.

The American roots of blackface trace back to the early nineteenth century, when whites co-opted the songs, dances, speech patterns, and prejudicially stereotyped behaviors of Black men and women, enhancing the charade with blackface paint, exaggerated lips and eyes, disheveled costumes, and kinky-haired wigs. A character in blackface was generally understood to be lazy, stupid, cowardly, obsequious, and immoral, driven by superstition, libido, and avarice, incapable of speaking proper English, and childishly eager to please the crowd. Known as minstrels, these performers proved immensely popular.[*] By the 1840s, full-on minstrel

[*] One of the most prominent minstrel stars was Thomas D. Rice, a white man from Manhattan, whose 1828 song and dance "Jump Jim Crow"

shows, with multiple performers all appearing in blackface, were the most attended and celebrated popular entertainments in the United States.

After the Civil War, actual Black performers began to emerge from barns, churches, tent shows, and other ad hoc venues and perform before paying audiences, both mixed and all-Black. And, by the reigning customs of minstrelsy, in order to take the stage at all, they had to don a mask that white performers had invented in order, simultaneously, to mock and steal from Blacks. That is, to be perceived as performers and not as themselves, to be *permitted* to perform, early Black professional entertainers were compelled to take the stage in blackface.

The social and psychological degradation and cost of blackface seems impossible to tabulate.* And the fact that it persisted into the twentieth and even twenty-first century as a form of comedy or (deeply wrongheaded) tribute as practiced by, among others, Sophie Tucker, Al Jolson, Eddie Cantor, Bing

---

would supply a name for legislated policies of racial segregation and suppression.
* Spike Lee's satiric 2000 film *Bamboozled* poignantly depicts the pain felt by contemporary Black entertainers forced to wear blackface to further their television careers.

Crosby, Shirley Temple, Judy Garland, and Fred Astaire is a matter of endless confusion, horror, and despair.

But arguably the most pernicious legacy of minstrelsy and blackface was that it forced Black performers to inhabit grotesque caricatures of themselves. Some of the most celebrated entertainers on the TOBA circuit and its predecessors, in vaudeville, on Broadway, and in film, wore blackface or enacted exaggerated stereotypes of Black speech or movement. The legendary Bert Williams, considered the finest comedian of any race in the early decades of the twentieth century, broke many color lines, yet he still performed in blackface for most of his career, which ran from the 1890s until his death at age forty-seven in 1922. Following him, other Black performers wore blackface on stage and film, including headliners such as John Bubbles, Bessie Smith, Pigmeat Markham, Mantan Moreland, and, before he rebelled against the practice, Bill "Bojangles" Robinson. Jackie Mabley, a neophyte with no name or clout, had no choice but to follow the demeaning practice.

"Under cork" or otherwise,* Jackie continued to perform on the TOBA circuit until at least mid-1923 — she appeared in passing in

* References to her appearing onstage in blackface would continue periodically until 1930.

54

a review of another Shreveport performance as a "soubrette" (a coquettish young woman) who earned from the crowd "a fair hand." And then, once again, someone reached out with a foster instinct.

In this case, her fairy godmother was actually a pair, Butterbeans and Susie, a husband-and-wife team who were big enough stars to play on bills with white vaudeville acts. A lot of old-time entertainers are described as "beloved," but the name seems truly to fit Jodie Edwards, aka Butterbeans, and his real-life wife Susie. As a pair, they performed together until the 1960s, combining singing (often comic or suggestive songs), a bit of Susie's dancing, and a lot of knockabout marital comedy. They were popular enough to release dozens of records in the twenties and thirties, including the risqué numbers "He Likes It Slow," which they cut with Louis Armstrong's Hot Five, and their biggest hit, "I Want a Hot Dog for My Roll."

As Jackie remembered her fateful encounter with the pair:

> We were going from Dallas, Texas to Port Arthur. And Butterbeans and Susie came to me after the show and said, "Girl, who are you and where are you from? You are sensational! You're the whole show! How much is Boudreau [the regional TOBA boss] paying you?" And I say, "$15." And they

said, "Ain't that a shame. Well, after the next show, you put in your notice and quit." And they wrote Mr. Boudreau in New Orleans. They were headliners. And they booked me from New Orleans to Chicago to the place that used to be here called the Monogram Theatre. And they booked me at $90 a week.

In November 1923, Jackie was on the bill with Butterbeans and Susie in Cleveland. She headed east with the pair, appearing multiple times with and without them around New York in 1925.

She may once have been a country girl who thought the world ended at the horizon she could see from her Granny's knee, but when she got to New York, Jackie Mabley became herself. For the next fifty years, though she would travel widely and for long spells, though she would always boast of her Brevard roots, though she would sometimes claim that Baltimore, Washington, D.C., and Cleveland — in all of which she had family — were like homes to her, she would be a New Yorker down to her bones.

In those early years, she performed at Harlem nightclubs and theaters such as Connie's Inn, the Alhambra, the Lincoln, and the Lafayette, then the premiere Black venue in the country. She was featured on a bill of Black folk, gospel, jubilee, and popular songs presented at the Ambassador Theater on Broadway in 1926. She developed a lifelong love of New York Yankees baseball. And she began to become something other than the pretty young thing who was preyed upon and left with children by opportunistic men.

Jackie had arrived in Harlem at one of the most propitious times possible. The Roaring Twenties were in full swing — the stock market was booming, and Harlem, the nation's capital of Black culture, was undergoing what came to be called the Harlem Renaissance. It was a time when Black writers, musicians, and artists were working simultaneously, at a high pitch, feeding off one another's energy and inspiration, pushing for new freedoms and new expressive idioms, and attracting the appreciative attention of downtown (that is, *white*) audiences and critics. Some of the names associated with the moment still ring powerfully: authors Zora Neale Hurston, James Weldon Johnson, and Jean Toomer; musicians Duke Ellington, Fletcher Henderson, Lena Horne, and Fats Waller; artists Romare Bearden, Jacob Lawrence, and James Van Der Zee. Many of them likely saw the shows in which Jackie performed, and at least one of them, the poet and journalist Langston Hughes, became a lifelong fan of her work.[*]

_____
[*] She even appeared as a character in his poem

In the midst of this cauldron of creativity and relative liberty (if not libertinism), Jackie Mabley began to find her truth as a performer and a woman. She had often been singled out in reviews as a crowd-pleasing entertainer, but it was usually in the context of a teamed act, usually opposite a man, which included a little singing, a little dancing, and a little humorous chatter. ("I didn't know I was a comic until I got on the stage," she said in 1967.) By the end of the twenties, she started to appear more frequently without a partner, and her act became increasingly focused on comedy. She still sang, but it was usually parodies of contemporary hits (often with bawdy new lyrics), or comic novelty songs, or racy numbers, or in imitation of well-known singing stars of the day (she could do both Bessie Smith *and* Louis Armstrong). In July 1927, as part of a revue at the Lafayette Theatre, she "had to respond to six calls for encores," according to the *New York Amsterdam News.* Three months later, she received this rave notice in the same newspaper:

> Particular mention must be made of Jackie Mabley. This young woman is one of the

---

"Projections," an account of a dream of racial integration.

ablest performers on the stage. Her humor is irresistible. For fully ten minutes she had the audience rocking with laughter. She sings and she talks and she dances in a manner which cannot be described, but which makes the audience just go wild. Will Marion Cook [a renowned composer, violinist, and bandleader] told the reviewer some time ago that he regarded Jackie Mabley as one of the best comediennes of all times — white or colored — and that at least one noted producer of successful plays will soon engage her.

Presently, she was appearing throughout the Northeast, the Midwest, and the mid-Atlantic region in a variety of miscellaneous revues with come-on, catch-all names such as *The Devil's Frolics, Harlem Vanities, Adam and Eve in Harlem, Sidewalks of Harlem,* and *Rhapsody in Black.* And as her experience grew, so did her billing. In Philadelphia in 1929, an ad declared, "She Made All New York Laugh." The following year, at the Lafayette, she was billed as "inimitable." For another performance, she was billed as "the Black Ace of Joy." And in 1930, when she was at Harlem's Alhambra Theatre, the ad stated, simply: "JACKIE MABLEY — You All Know Her."

Or did they? Triangulating from a number of

accounts and photographs, the onstage Jackie Mabley was presenting herself as a kind of knockabout trickster, never quite glamorous, not exactly a showgirl, but often paired with a man in comic situations. Despite her stage presentation, she was, she later reflected, attractive: "Honey, when I was startin' out, I was really somethin'. Man, talk about somethin' sharp? I was really sharp back then, and built like a brick. . . . I was *built.*"[*] But she seems to have been finished with men, at least romantically. From the late twenties on, she would be photographed offstage dressed in men's tailored three-piece suits, with her hair slicked down in a masculine fashion (Murray's Superior Hair Pomade was her dressing of choice) — she even sent out Christmas cards with photos of herself thus accoutred. She was frequently seen in the close company of attractive young women — one of her steady traveling companions/ dressers was said by a gossip columnist to be so beautiful that she could have been a starlet. She was described in newspapers as wearing trousers, as being "mannish," as getting hassled in the streets for dressing in men's clothes. She may even have worn drag onstage, as evidenced by comments in the *Inter-State Tattler,* a

[*] The ellipses in that original surely take the place of the unprintable-in-a-daily-newspaper word *shithouse.*

60

Harlem weekly that covered arts and current affairs, in which a critic who was identified as "V. E. J." repeatedly carped, neither delicately nor kindly, on her ambiguous gender identity:

> "Jackie Mabley defies the audience to tell whether the person is he, she, it, *or* the 'old lady.' I haven't found out yet."

> "Jackie Mabley back again so soon? And the column has not yet found out what you are? However — he — she — it — does nice work and quite unique. Must make the discovery this time. See you in 'Church' — backstage."*

Backstage, Jackie might very well have been discovered in the close company of a young woman. Moms was never out as queer, not in the modern sense, but most show folk around her knew her truth. As recalled by Norma Miller, a dancer who knew her in the thirties and forties, "She and I shared a dressing room for two weeks — she and I and her

* In a bizarre echo of this stuff, a 1972 column in the *Washington Sunday Star* dedicated to readers' questions took this one from "N.R." in Mahwah, New Jersey: "Could you please settle an argument? I say Moms Mabley is a man and they say she is a woman." The answer: "Sorry, dad, but the inimitable Moms is a woman."

girlfriend. She was real. I mean, she was Moms on stage, but when she walked off that stage, she was Mr. Moms, and there was no question about it. We never called Moms a homosexual. That word never fit her. We never called her gay. We called her Mr. Moms."

It wasn't only a backstage thing, either. She was a familiar face in bars that were known gathering places for queer women, particularly the Log Cabin Grill in New York (where she occasionally performed on the bill) and the Club Madre in Washington, a so-called "Jill joint" owned and operated by Odessa Madre, a colorful figure known as "the lady Al Capone" and "queen of the Washington underworld" for the substantial figure she cut as a kingpin in the worlds of drugs, prostitution, illegal gambling, and after-hours nightclub operation. Moms was said to be a decades-long friend of Madre (who flaunted her girlfriends around town); an oft-told tale of Washington nightlife involved Moms being present one night when police raided one of Madre's clubs and somehow getting the key to a nearby theater so that the displaced partiers could meet there to continue their revelries.

Whether going by "Jackie" or "Mr. Moms," she was known as well for a few other stereotypically masculine pursuits. She liked to hunt and fish. She was a big boxing fan — in the fifties, she would visit Sugar Ray Robinson at his mountain resort training camp, telling reporters on the scene that she considered him her godson. And she was a famous backstage gambler, particularly noted for a fondness for blackjack and pinochle and, most especially, for her mastery of a checkers variation called Spanish Pool, at which she was good enough to hustle money out of big-band musicians and stagehands.[*] And, of course, her determination to forge her own career as a stage comedian without being part of an act with a man was in and of itself a declaration of female empowerment and independence.

Strangely, despite her insistence on being her own woman and her apparent preference for female companionship, Jackie found herself briefly wed, sometime in the 1920s, virtually by accident, to comedian Leroy White, with whom she occasionally worked on the TOBA circuit. As she told the story decades later:

> Any man who was caught in the room of
> a girl in Macon [Georgia] had to marry her.
> And I was ill, and Leroy, the comic on the

[*] In an obituary of checkers champion James Searles, it was cited as a point of pride for him that he bested Moms at the game, but she insisted that the match wasn't fair as he took too long to move.

show, came in to see how I was feeling. And somebody got to fighting at the hotel and the cops come in. And of course they went into everybody's room. And they said, "What are you doin' in here?" And he said, "Well, she's sick, and I came to see how she was doing." And they said, "Well, you either marry her or go to jail." So they called in a preacher and married us. No license, no birth certificate, no nothing. And we were married!

By all accounts, they simply walked away from this civic version of a shotgun wedding, with no claims on one another. "They just parted and said no more about it," reported the *Baltimore Afro-American* in 1937.[*]

Jackie Mabley was coming into her own as the 1930s dawned, but outside of a revue or vaudeville show there was no ready place for her to appear. Stand-up comedy didn't really exist yet — the technical term then used for someone who did what she did was "monologist," and one of the very few widely recognized practitioners of the craft was Will Rog-

[*] At the time of her death in 1975, another possible husband, Ernest (Pops) Shearer, who had died the previous year, was mentioned in a few press reports. His name appeared in no records or articles about her during their presumed time together, though.

64

ers, the folksy "cowboy philosopher" who couldn't have been more different in mien, manner, or content from Jackie. She had found her metier, but the world wasn't quite ready for it. So she kept working, mainly in New York but as far afield, apparently, as Hollywood, from which an ad for a gig in Philadelphia in 1930 declared her "Just Back."[*]

In 1931, she appeared on Broadway in *Fast and Furious,* an all-Black comedy revue written largely by Zora Neale Hurston but with at least one sketch, "Scene on 135th St.," credited to Jackie. The show, presented at the New Yorker Theatre (years later, the famous disco Studio 54), cost some thirty to forty thousand dollars to produce.[†] It starred a teeming cast of Harlem-based performers and was meant to present a window on Black life for white audiences. But it was too scattershot and miscellaneous a program (with thirty-seven scenes/acts) to hit the mark. *Variety* found it "spotty" and complained that the "show lacks laughter a lot." But that was practically a rave compared to the review by the famed critic Brooks Atkinson that ran in

---

[*] There is no reliable record of her appearing in a film made at that time, though she has been identified as part of the cast of a 1922 silent comedy called *Spitfire* in which she *may have* performed the comical stunt of falling off a horse.

[†] Roughly $567,000 to $756,000 in 2022.

The New York Times, which was astonishing in its condescension and outright racism: "Most of the singing is no more than a blood-curdling yell, shot through a sun-burst of gold teeth, and some of the dancing is ugly. . . . When the material is hackneyed, when the performers are fat and clumsy, the animalism of Negro entertainment is lumpish and unwieldy." The show was only performed seven times downtown before moving up to Harlem and the Lafayette, where it enjoyed a longer run and greater appreciation.

The following year, Jackie was back downtown in another revue, *Blackberries of 1932,* which opened in early April 1932 at the Liberty Theatre on Forty-Second and closed that same month after twenty-four performances. Despite her participation in these failed shows, Jackie's reputation continued to grow; when she appeared in Washington not long after the fiasco of *Fast and Furious,* a columnist in a Baltimore paper effused over her:

Twicetimes the little heavyweight cutie — now watch her blush — who is called Jackie Mabley — and more than twicetimes — did she send staid sophisticated Washington down in tears — natural tears — but they came because she was making them laugh so hard. . . . When better comediennes come, or are made — take it from us, Jackie

Mabley will be dead. She is the most natural comedienne ever seen on any stage. How *Fast and Furious* folded up with folks like Jackie in the cast is more than I can see. Undoubtedly, they didn't have any more like her to go along with her.

Back in New York, she made her first verifiable film appearance: a small role in *The Emperor Jones,* a loose adaptation of the Eugene O'Neill play about a Black American railroad porter who escapes prison after being convicted of murder and flees to a Caribbean island, where he sets himself up as a demagogue. The film, shot entirely in Queens and on the beaches of Long Island, starred the great singer and civil rights icon Paul Robeson in the title role, which he had played onstage. Jackie played Marcella, the operator of an illegal Harlem nightclub/casino/brothel; she has two brief appearances, dressed in a mannish suit, flirting with Robeson and breaking up a fight. She claimed to have improvised the role ("The people had written a thick book with all these lines," she said of the adaptation of O'Neill. "Now how can a white man write lines for a Harlem landlady? I saw it live. I knew what [was] true. They didn't.") The film has come to be recognized as a milestone of Black cinema, but at the time the critical and commercial reception was disappointing.

■ ■ ■ ■

The consensus at this moment might have been that Jackie Mabley was a talented and crowd-pleasing entertainer in a specific mode for which there was no readily defined platform. And then a platform manifested itself, finally affording her a stage where she could hone her craft, make her name, and establish a little fiefdom for the next three-plus decades of her life and career.

The Apollo Theatre on 125th Street was built in 1914 as Hurtig and Seamon's New Burlesque Theater, presenting Black performers to segregated, whites-only audiences until the early 1930s, when it fell into disrepair and closed.* Impresario Sidney Cohen reopened it in January 1934 as the Apollo Theatre with a new all-races-permitted policy for audiences. At the time, Harlem's chief venues for Black patrons were the Lafayette and the Harlem Opera House, both of which regularly booked Jackie, and she remained loyal to them for a while after the Apollo opened. But in April 1934, in a revue called *Jazzmania,* Jackie took to the renovated theater's stage for the first of a literally

---

* Indeed, several of the most prominent venues in Harlem, including the famed Cotton Club, didn't admit Black audience members, even when the performers were, to a one, Black.

68

uncountable number of times. Until she quit performing — that is, until she died — the Apollo would be her home base, and it would be estimated that she performed there more often than any other comedian or other woman in the theater's history.*

It is impossible to overstate the contribution of the Apollo Theatre to Black American culture, which is to say American culture, which is to say *culture,* full stop. For decades, some of the most influential popular artists of all time used the fifteen-hundred-seat theater as their home base or their New York pied-à-terre, a clubhouse where they could count on big, appreciative audiences that included fellow performers, from living legends to up-and-comers. The Apollo reigned as the premier showcase for Black entertainers from the big band era to the rise of soul and R & B through the heydays of funk, disco, and even early hip-hop. Its Hall of Fame came to include such icons as Louis Armstrong, Aretha Franklin, Charlie Parker, Little Richard, James Brown, Smokey Robinson, Stevie Wonder, and Patti LaBelle, all of

* She would say in interviews for decades that the theater's longtime owner, Bobby Schiffman, son of the man who bought it after Sidney Cohen died, was her best friend in show biz, and he was one of many show folk who referred to her as his "other mom."

whom played the theater scores of times. And its weekly amateur night — when unknowns from the neighborhood and, indeed, the globe, got a shot on the famed stage — was a cultural institution that introduced dozens of new acts to the world, among them Ella Fitzgerald, Sarah Vaughan, and Jimi Hendrix. In addition to being an entertainment staple of Harlem, the Apollo served as a beating heart for its community, hosting political rallies, fundraisers, even memorial services. Other cities with large and influential populations of Black performers had their capstone theaters: the Howard in Washington, the Regal in Chicago, the Earl in Philadelphia, the Royal in Baltimore. But there was only one Apollo, and it loomed so large over Black American popular culture that it seemed to belong to the world as much as it did to New York.

For all it afforded as a platform and a stage and a steady source of income, working at the Apollo was a grind. Performers appeared as often as five times per day, with only a single day off each week — a murderous work schedule compared to eight shows per week on Broadway or the two-shows-a-night routine of most nightclubs. It was no wonder, then, that although she quickly became a mainstay of the Apollo, Jackie never stopped touring or trying her luck at other spots around New York. She was booked as a headliner at the Ubangi Club and the Plantation Club, both in Harlem. She toured all over the Northeast and Midwest (she studiously avoided going any farther south than Washington, D.C., for many years). And she performed in boy-girl acts with several notable comedians, including Dusty Fletcher (who popularized the comic song "Open the Door, Richard") and Sam Theard (who wrote and popularized the songs "(I'll Be Glad When You're Dead) You Rascal You" and "Spo-Dee-O-Dee").

But the bulk of her work was as a solo at the Apollo, which put her in the dead center of Black popular entertainment from the 1930s through the 1970s. In those early years, she played on bills with the premier entertainers of the era, including Bessie Smith, Louis Armstrong, Ethel Waters, Bojangles Robinson, Fats Waller, the Ink Spots, Pigmeat Markham, her old patrons Butterbeans and Susie, and bands led by Duke Ellington, Count Basie, Cab Calloway, and Chick Webb. She was in an all-female show featuring the International Sweethearts of Rhythm, an all-woman big band. She even appeared alongside the Scottsboro Boys, the Black teenagers who had been falsely accused of rape in 1931 and subjected to a series of racially rigged trials, brutal imprisonments, and spells on death row; their case was an international sensation, and when a series of appeals and retrials resulted in the acquittal of four of them, they toured Black theaters in 1937 with a combination of inspirational testifying and a theatrical reenactment of their ordeal.[*]

It was a thriving career, but it had an obvious and insurmountable ceiling on it: namely, Jackie Mabley could only get so far as an entertainer because she was 1) Black, 2) a woman, and 3) a comedian and not a straight singer or dancer. She also offended some audiences. As early as 1930, she was taken to task in the press for her liberal use of the word *damn,* and two years later, a commentator noted that she "tells the dirtiest jokes without causing offense." As the years passed, her wisecracks and songs about sex and her use of coarse language were used against her. She was still telling jokes that raised reviewers' eyebrows in 1936, when Louis Lautier, one of the deans of Black journalism, and the first Black reporter ever accredited as a member of the White House press corps, sneered, "Scallions to Jackie Mabley, the comedienne, for her version of 'Two Old Maids,' a new low in suggestive parodies being sung to audiences including kids. Wonder

[*] In 2013, the state of Alabama, where the Scottsboro Boys' trials had taken place, posthumously pardoned those in the group whose convictions had not been reversed decades prior.

what would a teacher say if a pupil saw her listening to Jackie and the next morning asked her how she liked that number!" A few months later, his scorn hadn't waned. In a column item entitled "Things I'd Like to See in 1937," he wrote: "Jackie Mabley kept in a livery stable and out of the theatre [sic]." Later that year his colleague columnist Ralph Matthews, published a letter from a reader in Washington, D.C., who moaned, "Pigmeat Markham and Jackie Mabley can be top-notch laughmakers without profanity or smutty jokes, but they seem to take a sadistic delight in pouring forth such trash."

She had a robust defense of her language and subject matter: "My audience helps me make up my program," she told the *Afro-American.* "Sometimes the audience is in a jovial mood and anything goes. It's times like that that I go the limit and get all of my naughty stories off my chest. But sometimes the audience is sophisticated and snooty and easily shocked; that's when you have to be discreet so that nobody will be offended. But I don't pull my punches often, because if people are too stuck up to enjoy a good laugh, they ought to stay home and let the other folks enjoy themselves."*

* The idea that her material was "ribald" would follow her for decades. Compared to her later contemporaries, though, she was a pussycat.

There were no naughty words to be heard in her next significant venture, 1939's big-budget stage musical *Swingin' the Dream,* inspired by a swing jazz version of *The Mikado* that had made waves the previous year.[*] *Swingin' the Dream* was a massive production, a jazz-influenced adaptation of Shakespeare's *Midsummer Night's Dream* featuring the Benny Goodman Sextet as the pit band, Agnes DeMille as the choreographer, sets inspired by Walt Disney drawings, and a cast that would include Louis Armstrong as Bottom, Butterfly McQueen (then on screen in *Gone with the Wind*) as Puck, Afro–Puerto Rican actor Juan Hernandez as Oberon, blues singer Maxine Sullivan as Titiana, and Jackie as Quince. It was a wildly expensive production — estimates ranged from \$100,000 to \$300,000[†] — and it was staged in the Center Theatre, a gargantuan thirty-seven-hundred seat sibling to the larger Radio City Music Hall, which stood on the next block.

Swingin' the Dream was many things: a romp on Shakespeare; a showcase for Goodman, Armstrong, and Sullivan; a mini jazz concert; a jitterbug dance show; a choral

[*] Another influence may have been Orson Welles's famed 1936 all-Black version of *Macbeth* (aka *Voodoo Macbeth*), which was parodied regularly by comics, Jackie included.

[†] Roughly \$1.84 million to \$5.592 million in 2022.

presentation; and a celebration of (mostly) Black art and entertainment. It was also a stupendous flop. The reviews weren't exactly scathing. In *Variety, Billboard,* the *New York Times,* and the Black press, there was much appreciation of the music (the standard "Darn That Dream" debuted in the show), the dancing, many of the performances, much of the comedy. But the unanimous opinion was that the thing didn't cohere: it was three or four or five things, not one, and felt to the *New York Amsterdam News* like "a vaudeville show and not a play." As for Jackie, that same critic opined, "Miss Mabley, a fine comedienne when permitted to sneak in her side-splitting ad libs, seems particularly lost in reciting a script from which there can be no deviation." She was, in effect, straitjacketed, but not for long: *Swingin' the Dream* closed in early December after a mere thirteen performances. It would be the last time Jackie came close to starring in a proper downtown show ever again.

But it wasn't the last time she would appear on the actual Broadway. In late 1941, the Ubangi Club moved from 125th Street in Harlem to a spot between West Fifty-Second and Fifty-Third Streets on Broadway, with a policy of bringing the best uptown performers to downtown audiences. Among the first was Jackie Mabley. Or, rather, Jackie "Moms"

Mabley, as she was billed for the first time in her career.

At age forty-three (and, to be fair, perhaps already a grandmother, with all of her daughters married by that summer),[*] Jackie had fully developed the stage persona by which the world would come to know her: Moms, a sharp-eyed, cantankerous, plain-speaking older woman who suffered no fools, wore housedresses and floppy hats (often over a wig, which was, often, red) and slippers, wasn't afraid of salty language, and had an eye for irony and hypocrisy and a sweet tooth for gin and for the company of young men. As a fireside philosopher, Moms commented on men, children, sex, politics, contemporary fashions in music, clothes, courtship — the whole gamut of human experience. The character was a mask: the wardrobe like a clown's suit, the slow, raspy-voiced delivery, the countrified speech, and, in later years, the decision to perform while seated in a chair and without her false teeth. You felt as if you were sitting in her kitchen, listening to her pontificate while she cooked. The character also freed her from the obligation to tell joke-jokes. Oh, she had them, lots of them. But Moms's discourse was more freeform than rat-a-tat. In some of the earliest surviving footage of her stage act, she warns her audi-

[*] By 1949 she was claiming four grandkids.

ence, "Moms don't know no jokes. . . . But I can tell you some facts."

A lot of the humor of her act was based on contrasts: the wizened old gal with the lively libido and fondness for the bottle. She would shuffle onto the stage, slowly, a bit disheveled, maybe talking to herself, or hushing the band or the crowd, and she would wander up to the mic (in later years, she took to sitting in an easy chair), and she would begin her discourse with a humble "I got somethin' to tell ya . . ." — a wise, weary impatient granny to all the world, even while still in her forties.

She would, invariably, talk about men, complaining about the difference between suitors of her own age and the fellows she really hankered for. As she said a million times, "The only thing an old man can do for me is bring me a message from a young man." She compared having sex with an old man to "pushing a car uphill . . . with a *rope,*" she complained that an old man she was once forced to marry was hit with a grain of rice at the wedding and passed out, and she declared, repeatedly, "A woman is always a woman, but a man's only a man as long as he can."

In a typical bit, she bemoaned a romantic offer she'd recently received: "Old washboard-face mildewed man had the nerve to come around backstage and ask me can he see me home? I said, 'Damn, you can't see *period.'* " It was a chore, she confessed, her appetite: "I'm old, and I need youth, and it's very expensive." But when it was satisfied: Wow. Teasing one of her bandleaders, she said, "Let me tell you girls somethin'. George took me home the other night and kissed meeeeeeeee. My big toe shot up in the air just like that!"

The Moms character was truly one of the most inspired comic inventions of its time, becoming as familiar, at least to Black audiences, as Jack Benny's cheapskate persona or, later, Rodney Dangerfield's disrespected schlub were to whites. But it wasn't entirely an act. Indeed, despite her reputation for sometimes surprising offstage behavior, a native motherliness in her real-life character was evident to her show-biz colleagues and was the source of the nickname Moms. As she said later, "The show people gave me that name, of both races. I don't know why, but even when I was young they would bring their problems to me to settle. They would get away from home and not be able to get back, so I would help send 'em home. Or I would put on a pot of something for those that didn't have much money, and I would see that they were fed. So they named me 'Moms.' "*

* It's worth noting here that despite her reputation as being a motherly presence to her fellow showfolk,

78

She took that same foster attitude with her onstage, greeting her audiences by calling them her "children," as if embodying her own beloved granny, dispensing wisdom as she cooked over an open hearth. She had a decades-long gag about being asked by world leaders for their advice — a way of mixing political jokes in with her homespun schtick. She would refer to presidents and their wives by their first names, as if they were kin, and talk about how she'd teach 'em some sense. (When the Eisenhowers were in the White House, she would say something like "Last week Mamie called me up, you know? I said, 'Listen, Mames.' She said, 'Yes Miss Mabley . . .' ") It was charming and genuinely groundbreaking: She discussed race relations, economics, and politics at a time when virtually every other comedian (almost every single one of whom was a man) stuck to jokes about their mothers-in-law or taxes or whatnot. As she once put it, "I just tell folks the truth. If they don't want the truth, then don't come to Moms. Anybody that comes to me, I'll hip 'em. I don't say anything I don't mean." Between the death of Will Rogers in 1935 and the rise of Mort Sahl in the mid-1950s, Moms Mabley was just about the only

---

her biological daughters were all raised by her own mother or her sisters.

comedian in America offering pointed opinions on current affairs. That she was Black and a woman made her originality and daring trebly remarkable.

In some regards, Jackie had been crafting the Moms character for twenty years, ever since she first drifted out of boy-girl acts and into her own specialty as a solo monologist. She was noted early on for her clownish stage clothes and her chatter, which was more like cracked folk wisdom than setup/punch line joke telling; eventually, weary of trying to maintain stage partnerships, realizing that singing and dancing weren't truly her calling, she simply dropped everything except the straight-talking old gal persona. As she later explained, there was a concept behind the act, even in her very earliest days as a professional entertainer when she was, in her words, "letting granny grow. . . . I had in mind a woman about 60 or 65, even when I first came up. . . . She's a good woman, with an eye for shady dealings. . . . She was like my granny, the most beautiful woman I ever knew. She was the one who convinced me to go make something of myself. . . . She was so gentle, but she kept her children in line, believe that."

None of which is to say that Moms wasn't hip. In fact, at around the same time that she was fully embracing the persona in which she would become famous, part of the act was making fun of herself by using hepcat lingo while presenting herself as a frumpy old granny. The *New York Amsterdam News* described her as playing "the old-school type of comedy in which she is the ragged urchin dazzled by modern life's progress," adding that she was able to get the best of her fellow comics "under the sheer weight of shrewd 'jive' talk." She had a catchphrase, based on a novelty song that she performed: "Ketch On" ("Do you ketch on?" she would ask audiences.) She had an ongoing joke about famed jazzbo Cab Calloway being her boyfriend. And she would win big laughs with such cool patter as "Put this jive in your back pocket, man, until I get back. I'm going downtown to see the man, and I have no time to shake your hand."

Even with success in midtown at the Ubangi Club,[*] where she appeared on and off for several years, Moms, as she was almost always known in newspapers from the mid-forties on, wasn't able to cross over to a full career in front of white audiences. She was making a comfortable living, with steady bookings at the Apollo, a regular circuit of appearances that ranged from Washington,

* Later rechristened Club Ebony with the same policy of bringing Harlem entertainers to a spot where white audiences were more apt to see them.

D.C., Baltimore, Philadelphia, and Atlantic City to Pittsburgh, Cleveland, and Chicago. (When she could be convinced to perform below the Mason-Dixon line, she was always sorry she had assented: "I wish I could find that so-and-so who wrote 'I Wish I Was in Dixie,' " she was quoted as saying. "I'd cut his dam [*sic*] throat!") She was able to afford a comfortable home and a staff including a driver and a secretary — often assumed in gossip columns to be her romantic partner — and to bring her family to visit her in the city. Her mother, Mary Parton, lived for a while in Cleveland, and then in the Baltimore/D.C. area; in late 1943, Moms brought Mary and her own daughter Bonnie to New York for a slap-up vacation of shows, shopping sprees, and dinners out. (Mary would die three years later, at age seventy-one, when she was struck by a mail truck on New Year's Eve near her home in Washington.)

She herself traveled on vacations for much of the year — favoring spots where she could gamble, go to the horse races or prize fights, or simply relax. In April 1944, she wrote a letter to the *New York Amsterdam News* to sing the praises of Hot Springs, Arkansas: "Feeling wonderful after having these baths. I'll be ready to hit the ball soon. . . . Everybody is here. You should see the glamour girls falling out at races in their animal covers, from cat to mink. But there are very few show people here, although many should be to get the creaking out of their bones." (Note that creaky-boned Moms had only just turned forty-seven at the time.)

That same month, in a survey of fifteen hundred troops in the Pacific Theater of World War II, Moms was one of three comedians whom servicemen told a reporter for the *Chicago Defender* that they would wish to see perform for them. Importantly, it was a survey of *Black* servicemen only. Virtually no white audiences knew who Moms was, a failing decried by the influential columnist Billy Rowe just a few years later. As he seemed to believe, she was not a bigger star because, whether in her skin or in her art, she was, bluntly, too Black:

> One of the greatest comedians of the vaudeville stage, the thing which has kept Jackie away from B'way [*sic*] and the commercial radio channel will forever remain an American tragedy. It is something closely allied to that dilemma which keeps us in constant fear of another body of marching youths going out to become armed men. The luck which has been showered on others who flit across the screen and the great stages of our country, allowed them to filter out to where the air waves begin, is not theirs by right of a better talent, but a lighter pigmentation.

In June 1948, the truth of Rowe's observations would be borne out. NBC Radio announced that it would soon premiere a program originating in Harlem's Savoy Ballroom that would replicate an evening's entertainment at that famed venue and would feature such mainstays of Harlem entertainment as Moms and the veteran comedy team Miller and Lee. Guest stars would include Lena Horne, Sarah Vaughan, the Ink Spots, and Louis Jordan. And the name of this groundbreaking all-star entertainment? *The National Minstrelsy Show.* It wasn't just a title, either: according to the press release for the show, it would "combine the technique of the minstrel show and the follies."

From the moment the show was announced, the Black press was torn against itself. On the one hand, there were very few opportunities for authentic all-Black entertainment to appear in the white entertainment mainstream. On the other hand: *Minstrelsy? In 1948?* "I am not opposed to the title for the planned NBC show but the show itself," went one response. "Use of the threadbare stereotype of the colored minstrel shows either a lack of understanding or a lack of taste. NBC and (Savoy owner) Moe Gale should know better, or they should ask somebody." The NAACP demanded meetings with NBC and received the unusual privilege of being allowed to review scripts and to name a writer to oversee revisions (poet and newspaperman Langston Hughes — a fan of Moms's — got the job). The show was delayed for three weeks while the controversy roiled in the press, and it finally debuted on July 28 under a new title: *Swingtime at the Savoy.*

Despite the protest, negotiations, and rewrites, the show perpetuated the most invidious racist imagery imaginable. Miller and Lee did straight-up minstrel routines of the sort that were the norm a half century prior, and Moms performed a tribute to Bert Williams, singing one of his hit tunes, "He's a Cousin of Mine," in an imitation of his voice (which, as Williams died in 1922, very few listeners would recognize). There were some positive responses to the program — Billy Rowe praised Moms's impression of Williams and bemoaned the fact that the show's heavy hand with scripting and editing allowed her "only a limited opportunity to exhibit [her talent] to advantage." But *Swingtime at the Savoy* aired for only five weeks before NBC pulled the plug entirely, and it would be years before a national network would attempt an all-Black show again, either on radio or the newly emerging medium of TV.

That same year found Moms in two feature

films that were released only to theaters in Black neighborhoods: *Killer Diller,* a lifeless comedy about a missing girl, starring Dusty Fletcher and Butterfly McQueen, that was little more than an excuse to present a full stage revue featuring, among others, Moms and the Nat King Cole Trio; and *Boarding House Blues,* an even shaggier picture with Moms playing a woman named, yes, Moms, who runs a boardinghouse for show folk and another miscellany of Black variety artists showing up to perform their specialties: singing comedian John "Spider Bruce" Mason, the dancing Berry Brothers, and, again, Dusty Fletcher.

These films were shot and staged in New York by an outfit calling itself All-American Pictures, which seemed to care nothing about scripts, sets, performances, cinematography, editing, or any other of the fussinesses of moviemaking. Even at seventy or eighty minutes of running time, they are work to sit through, memorable chiefly for the opportunity to see Moms and her colleagues performing — in many cases in the earliest or *only* surviving footage of their acts.

In *Killer,* Moms tells a few jokes and sings "Don't Sit on My Bed" (which is more single-entendre than you'd think). Later, she's seen backstage getting ready for a second appearance, donning hairnet, wig, and hat (and, more importantly, as she's leaving her dressing room: "Where my teeth?"). In *Boarding House* she has actual scene-scenes: presiding benignly over her household and her "children," as she calls her boarders, growling at the evil landlord, and imitating a gypsy fortune-teller (complete with indeterminate put-on accent). Again, she gets a stage solo, telling a few comic stories and doing some tap dancing, a charming bit that she caps by beaming at the audience and boasting, "Made it!"

Needless to say, neither *Killer Diller* nor *Boarding House Blues* gave Moms entrée with a wider — that is, *whiter* — audience. The following year, she appeared, perhaps for the only time, at a Greenwich Village nightclub, the original Café Society, and, according to an almost hostile (and subtly racist) review in *Variety,* flopped: "Her patter routine is so-so in an indigo vein. . . . She uses that Broadway Rose getup which bowls 'em over in the Apollo but is slightly depressing in a nitery."

But she kept striving for that bigger audience. That same year brought her first recording, a novelty single for Columbia Records in which she and Pearl Bailey had a merry time with a loose rendition of Louis Jordan's "Saturday Night Fish Fry." It was a jukebox hit that even the *New York Times* took note of, calling it "full of pep." It didn't, however, perform well enough on the charts to win her a place in the larger world of show biz.* Back to the Apollo, her reliable circuit of clubs — she was now ranging as far as Los Angeles — and the world of all-Black entertainment she returned.

As it happened, her reign at the Apollo would be the means through which she finally broke out as a crossover star. It wasn't, however, predictably, a speedy thing. In early 1956, the famed record producer and talent scout John Hammond† decided to record a live album of a typical night at the Apollo for the adventuresome Vanguard Records. It was something of a novelty disc, in that it would feature professional acts such as Moms, impressionist George Kirby, and the Count Basie band (uncredited for contractual reasons) along with the real treasure: selected performances from the theater's famed amateur nights. Released in the spring with liner notes by Langston Hughes, it was well received critically: *Variety* called it "effervescent and noisy," while *Billboard* declared it "one of the most entertaining disk [*sic*] programs of the year" and "one of the most important

* On the strength of it, she signed a deal with Aladdin Records that resulted in no releases.
† Discoverer and/or early booster of, among others, Count Basie, Billie Holiday, Benny Goodman, Bob Dylan, Aretha Franklin, and Bruce Springsteen.

documents dealing with 20th century show business." The Black press reviewed it positively as well, in particular Moms's contribution, which constituted the longest track on the second side of the record. According to the *Pittsburgh Courier,* she so "dominate[s] this waxing that one is barely aware of the tremendous background scoring. . . . It takes the listener right into the 125th St. emporium . . . and leaves him or her breathless from laughter."

The record didn't sell much, but it found an audience of aficionados who likely hadn't heard of Moms previously. Comedy was changing, albeit subtly, and in the places where it overlapped with underground culture and the nascent taste for "authentic" roots music (blues, folk, gospel, jazz), something like a "raw" recording from the Apollo had real cachet. Among the hipsters who were captivated by Moms's performance on the record was the beatnik parodist/comedian Lord Buckley, who would ask a friend to play it whenever he visited and would sigh his wish that he could create an act for himself more like hers.

As a cult item, *A Night at the Apollo* stayed alive in the memory of the right people. By the late fifties, comedy albums had started to become big sellers throughout the business, in the form of both big-label LPs (comedians Mort Sahl, Bob Newhart, and Shelley Berman enjoyed megasellers) and under-the-counter "party records" that often pushed the edges of propriety and even the law with raunchy, profane humor. Moms was never outright potty-mouthed; she was merely suggestive. But she was kin to other comedians, particularly Redd Foxx, with whom she had toured when he was still billed as Detroit Red, who freely spouted four-letter words and who was making a name with underground LPs.

There had been adults-only comedy records for decades, and there were even a few artists who had national reputations for their "sophisticated" and "risqué" material, including a patrician cabaret pianist named Dwight Fiske, who recorded outrageous 78 rpm discs, and comic singer Ruth Wallis, whose material was considered so scandalous that she had to create her own label to distribute it. But the national craze for party records really took off in the mid-fifties, when 33 rpm LPs became the new standard and there were enough pressing plants for LPs that a no-frills operator could get records manufactured cheaply, often by using after-hours crews working on overnight shifts. A string of fly-by-night outfits emerged to meet the demand for LPs laced with dirty jokes, often operating under multiple names so as to avoid legal prosecution and, in some cases, to hide money from tax collectors and even the performers on the records themselves. Foxx, who released literally dozens of these albums under the aegis of several record labels, was becoming widely known on the basis of material that might get him arrested if he were to perform it in public; at best he could promote his work in nightclubs in Black neighborhoods, where enforcement of local decency ordinances was less strict than in other areas. But Moms, performing on the sanctioned side of naughty, seemed capable of not only cutting records that would sell but actually going out and selling them to big crowds.

That, at least, was the thinking at Chess Records, a Chicago label run by white Jewish immigrants and dedicated to the work of Black American musicians including Chuck Berry, Muddy Waters, Bo Diddley, Howlin' Wolf, and John Lee Hooker. Chess was seeking to expand into the spoken-word LP market, and management assigned producer/ scout Ralph Bass the task of finding comedians. His wife, Shirley Hall, had danced in a troupe that performed with Moms some years prior, and she suggested Bass look Moms up. He listened to *A Night at the Apollo* and made his way to New York to see if she was interested in recording a full LP.

Moms wasn't sure. She hadn't been paid *at all,* apparently, for the Vanguard LP, and, now past age sixty, she was wary of offers of pie in the sky. But she had acquired a manager in the past few years, Joe Glazer (who also managed Louis Armstrong), and with his approval, she agreed to do it. She happened to be appearing at the Tivoli Theatre in Chicago in January 1960 on a bill with the Duke Ellington Orchestra, and Chess recorded her there.

A few months later, her first comedy LP, *The Funniest Woman in the World: Moms Mabley Onstage,* appeared in stores and started selling well, based in part on Bass's inspiration to select a few choice bits from it and compile a 45 — a spoken-word comedy single, in effect — and release it to radio DJs and in jukeboxes. The record wasn't a runaway smash, but it was repackaged and rereleased several times over the coming years, with the title slightly tweaked and the cover art updated; in time, it went gold. Chess immediately planned another album — capturing a performance at the Uptown Theatre in Philadelphia — and released it in early 1961 as *Moms Mabley at the UN.* That one was a much bigger hit, cracking the *Billboard* Top Forty and boosting sales of the previous LP. A third record, *Moms Mabley at the Playboy Club,* was recorded that summer and released before the end of the year. There would be *four* LPs in 1962, including an appearance on *Comedy Night at the Apollo,* and two more the following year.

She was a smash. Mercury Records lured

her away from Chess with a lucrative deal and continued to pour out new records: two in '64, one each in '65 and '66, three in '69, and one in '70, while Chess regularly mined her early releases and some previously unreleased recordings to issue new product for more than eight years after she'd left the label. As all of this activity might indicate, starting in 1961 and running through 1971, Moms would have at least one album in *Billboard*'s end-of-the-year Top One Hundred *every single year.*[*]

No doubt her sales were boosted by the unusual savvy and frankness in her material. Speaking openly — and humorously — about race relations in the early 1960s made her one of the nation's most daring popular artists. She would ease into her condemnations of Jim Crow, of conditions in the South, of the pernicious effects of racism, and she would always couch them in humor. But her observations were pointed and explicit.

She'd typically warm to the subject with a joke: "A lotta old men sayin' 'Times ain't like they used to be,' and I say 'I'm damn glad of it. Who wants times like they used to be?!' "

* That said, she was perennially outsold by such men as her fellow Apollo veteran Redd Foxx, not to mention Bill Cosby and such white comedians as Bob Newhart, Allan Sherman, Shelley Berman, and team of Mel Brooks and Carl Reiner.

Then she'd get a little feisty: "They want me to go down to New Orleans," she said. "It'll be Old Orleans before I get down there. The Greyhound ain't gonna take me down there and the bloodhounds run me back, I'll tell you that!" And then, frequently, she'd have a story to tell, a joke that was as damning as it was amusing: "I just come back from down there. . . . I didn't wanna go. . . . But I went down there and I tried to pass . . . for anything except what I was. . . . I was ridin' along in my Cadillac, you know, goin' through one of them little towns in South Carolina, passed through a red light. One of them big cops come over to me: 'Hey, hey, woman! Don't you know you went through a red light?' I say, 'Yeah, I know I went through a red light.' He say, 'Well what you do that for?' I say, ' 'Cause I seen all you white folks goin' on the green light, I thought the red light was for us!' " Almost nobody else — man or woman, Black or white — was telling jokes like this. It was no wonder that there was a growing audience for her work.

It would be worth wondering, nonetheless, just *who* was buying all those records. Moms was still appearing almost exclusively in front of nearly all-Black audiences in East Coast, mid-Atlantic, and mid-western cities. She had not appeared on national radio since 1948 or on national TV *ever,* and her film appearances were barely seen and virtually forgotten. So, in one sense, her horizons hadn't been appreciably affected by her recording career. Yes, there was a vogue for comedy records, which was why Chess signed her in the first place. And yes, a handful of black stand-up comedians were crossing over to play before large white audiences: Bill Cosby, Dick Gregory, and Godfrey Cambridge (needless to say, men all). But their success didn't explain why Moms, without a national media platform, was becoming a cult sensation. In her *sixties.*

Apparently, Moms was tapping into a new phenomenon in entertainment: namely, the growing influence of young people. Something about the spectacle of an old lady in a no-fuss outfit dispensing tart truths with a soupçon of double entendres about sex and booze struck a chord with a generation who truly could have been her grandchildren. And the feeling was mutual: Moms really did seem to feel a bond with youth audiences, as if she saw in the rising spirit of the generation that would embrace and fuel the civil rights movement a version of her own teenage restlessness and hunger. She treated them like peers. "The time to hip a child is the minute that it's born into this world," she would explain. "The first words you say to that child — it's like a blank record, ready to be hip or be a square for the rest of its natural life." And if some of her advice was geared to grown-ups

("Love is just like a game of checkers. You sure got to know what man to move. 'Cause if you move the wrong man, he jump ya!"), some of it was just plain common sense: "We tell those children, 'You be careful. Watch the lights!' Damn the lights. Watch the cars! The lights ain't never killed nobody."

And she really did connect with the young crowd. "My best audiences are youngsters," she told the *Pittsburgh Courier.* "They understand me. They dig me. I'm too fast for the old folks, but the young ones, I adore them because, believe me, I understand them. There ain't nothing dirty in what I say to them. I just speak facts, and when I get up there on the stage, they ain't goin' to hear nothin' they don't hear every day on the street."

The proof was in the bookings. Moms was still appearing at such places as the Apollo with the heroes of older generations: Duke Ellington, Count Basie, Ella Fitzgerald, and so forth. But she was also appearing with younger acts and was often the only performer over (indeed, *well* over) age thirty in a given show, sharing stages with early R & B outfits like the Flamingos, the Dells, the Olympics, and the Capris, and, in time, such emerging stars as Aretha Franklin, Marvin Gaye, Smokey Robinson and the Miracles, and Gladys Knight and the Pips. In 1959, she had played a week in Philadelphia on a bill with a bunch of acts appealing to teens and was seen by an audience of over forty thousand.

The gigs, too, were becoming bigger, more prestigious, better paid. In June 1962, she headlined a midnight show at Carnegie Hall that also featured the Cannonball Adderly sextet and singer Nancy Wilson. ("She brought down the house and had the customers crying for more," per the *New York Amsterdam News*.) In Cleveland, she played to three thousand people at the Music Hall. She appeared at the Shrine Auditorium in Los Angeles with jazz pianist George Shearing and on the bill of a civil rights benefit at the Apollo that included performances by Tony Bennett, Thelonious Monk, and Sonny Rollins. In 1964, she was the first nonmusician to take the stage at the Newport Jazz Festival, soon after which she toured several midwestern cities with Motown hitmakers the Supremes.

During this flurry of activity, as her appearance fees sprang beyond the $5,000 per week mark[*] and her record royalties mounted with similar speed, she began to live far more grandly than she ever had. In September 1962, she purchased a home in Westchester, north of New York City, right next door to singer Laverne Baker, with whom she fre-

[*] Approximately $43,000 in 2022.

quently shared the bill. She acquired automobiles — among her fleet, eventually, would be a Cadillac and a Rolls-Royce, both driven by a liveried chauffeur. She cut down her work schedule to a few months a year and took long vacations; she spoke of plans for a two-month trip to Africa. And she was starting to be taken seriously in the press; *Ebony* magazine ran a feature story on her in August 1962, virtually the first time that "respectable" publication mentioned her. The lengthy interviews she granted to the Black press, a more and more frequent occurrence, were syndicated nationwide — albeit *only* in the Black press. (She made headlines inadvertently in April 1966, when she was appearing before an audience of three thousand at the City Auditorium in Columbia, South Carolina, and a man with a pistol took a few potshots at his wife and her friends. "Man, I was so scared that you can't print what I was thinkin'," she cracked.)

She had been in show business for something like fifty years. She sold records, lots of them. She drew big crowds. She was a favorite of at least three generations of audiences. And after years of joking about giving counsel to American presidents, she was actually invited to the White House, in June 1966, to attend a conference on civil rights. The one thing she didn't have, though, was the recognition of the vast audience of white Americans. If they didn't own one of her records, or if they hadn't attended one of her shows, they simply did not know who Moms Mabley was.

That changed after March 1967, when Moms, just turned seventy, made her TV debut on *The Merv Griffin Show,* a nationally syndicated program watched by predominantly white audiences. Griffin was genuinely broad-minded in his booking policies, often introducing acts from the outer margins of show biz, and he was sincerely appreciative of Moms, inviting her back for a string of return engagements throughout the rest of the year.

The following month, she made her national network debut on an hourlong special on ABC. Produced by Harry Belafonte, hosted by Sidney Poitier, and entitled *A Time for Laughter,* it featured a panoply of Black comedy stars: Redd Foxx, Dick Gregory, Richard Pryor, and Pigmeat Markham among them. Moms appeared in a single sketch, as the sardonic housemaid of Godfrey Cambridge and Diana Sands, an upwardly mobile Black couple who've just purchased a home in a white suburb and are desperate to avoid any stereotypes of Black behavior. Critics didn't make much of the show, which was heavily scripted and diligently edited to avoid the sorts of spontaneous wit that was Moms's sweet spot. But she nevertheless made an impression, and her TV bookings became more frequent and more visible.

In October 1967, she made the first of at least six regular appearances on *The Smothers Brothers Comedy Hour,* the iconoclastic CBS variety show. She was a guest on singer Pat Boone's variety show, and she appeared on Merv Griffin's first late-night national network broadcast in August 1968, alongside comedian Woody Allen, New York Jets quarterback Joe Namath, and New York mayor John Lindsay. The following year saw her make the first of three visits to *The Ed Sullivan Show* as well as take part in a PBS roundtable program on Black humor entitled *On Being Black: Laughing to Keep from Crying.* She appeared on talk shows hosted by Johnny Carson, David Frost, and Dick Cavett and variety shows hosted by Pearl Bailey, Flip Wilson, and Melba Moore. She played opposite comedian Mantan Moreland as the main character's feuding aunt and uncle on *The Bill Cosby Show.* And she appeared on at least two of Jerry Lewis's Labor Day Telethons for muscular dystrophy.

At the same time, she was getting some of the most impressive live bookings of her lengthy career: another visit to Carnegie Hall in June 1968 with South African trumpeter Hugh Masekela; a spot in the Randall's Island Soul Festival in New York that same summer; and appearances at such gigantic arenas as the Fabulous Forum in Los Angeles with Aretha Franklin, Madison Square Garden in New York with the Temptations, and the Spectrum in Philadelphia with Ray Charles. In June 1969, in what must have been a pinch-me experience for her, she played *Yankee Stadium,* the home of her beloved baseball heroes, along with the Isley Brothers and the Ike and Tina Turner Revue in a concert that was filmed for a documentary, *It's Your Thing.* Later that summer, she appeared at the now-famous Harlem Cultural Festival. The following year, she played ten nights at the Greek Theatre in Los Angeles with the Temptations and in a massive show at Braves Stadium in Atlanta with Aretha Franklin.

And there was more: She was featured in national print ads for Ballantine beer and Kool-Aid. She had a *Billboard* Top Forty hit with her straightforward rendition of Dion DiMucci's paean to slain heroes of progressivism and civil rights, "Abraham, Martin, and John," adding a verse to include Bobby Kennedy. (In a genuinely moving performance, she sang it on *Playboy After Dark* at the prompting of her fellow guest Sammy Davis Jr., whom she had known since he was a toddler and who had begun to do impressions of *her* in his own stage act now that *his* audiences, mostly white, knew who she was.)

She was given the key to the city of Cleveland in 1971 at a cockeyed press conference at which she repeatedly declared, "Everybody likes me except old women." (Perhaps, but after a chance encounter at around that time, Phyllis Diller, the most successful female stand-up comedian in show biz and middle-aged herself, took Moms on a shopping spree for some high-fashion offstage clothes.) In 1972, she appeared with the Jackson 5 at a concert in Atlanta to commemorate Martin Luther King's birthday, cohosted TV's daytime *Mike Douglas Show* for a week, and made her debut at Manhattan's Copacabana, still one of the most prestigious nightclubs in the country. (Amazingly, a *Variety* reviewer, dismissing her performance, declared that she really belonged at "her homebase, the Apollo Theatre in Harlem, where *her racist humor* finds a comfortable base" [emphasis added]. Some barriers, apparently, still would not fall.)

She was seventy-five years old and a bigger star and a wealthier woman than she had ever been. There wasn't a single thought in her head of slowing down, taking a step backward, retiring. Perry Diller, Phyllis's son, a financial analyst who was asked to look into Mom's affairs, says, "I told her, 'Moms, you can pull the oars out of the water any time.' But she was scared of losing everything and she was determined to keep working." She was reaping the justified rewards of a lifetime of endurance. From her new position of success and comfort, she could reflect back on the better part of a century and see how far she had come. Black entertainers had been systematically shut out of opportunities, she declared: "I don't care if you could stand on your eyebrows," she told the *New York Post,* "if you were colored you couldn't get no work at all" in white venues. Now, with her face on TV regularly, she felt a shift in her own mood. "When I started doing TV," she said, "instead of looking at the audience as my children, I looked at the world as my children." She confessed, though, that her good fortune may have come a bit too late for her and such colleagues as Redd Foxx truly to appreciate it: "Now that we've got some money, we have to spend it all for doctor bills."

In 1973, she began what might have been her greatest adventure yet, starring in a feature film, *Amazing Grace,* about a cantankerous but wise Baltimore granny who learns about the corruption of a Black candidate for mayor and tries to reform him before he can harm the city. It was an independent film, appearing at a time when Black-themed movies were enjoying their widest popularity, produced and written by Matt Robinson and directed by Stan Lathan, both of whom had connections to *Sesame Street* (Robinson was the show's original Gordon character) and *Sanford and Son,* the hit TV sitcom that starred Redd Foxx. Moses Gunn was cast as the dodgy candidate, Rosalind Cash as his alcoholic wife, and a few of Moms's old stage chums were given roles as well: comedian Slappy White, actress Butterfly McQueen, and, remarkably, Lincoln Perry (aka Stepin Fetchit), who was still performing in minstrelish fashion in his eighties.

The film was shot primarily in Philadelphia in the fall and early winter, but production was halted when Moms collapsed on set and was rushed to the hospital suffering from heart failure. She had emergency surgery, and a pacemaker was installed, three weeks after which, ever the trouper, she returned to the set and finished her work.

Unlike her films of the late forties, *Amazing Grace* would receive a proper national release in theaters in both Black and white neighborhoods. United Artists, which had acquired distribution rights from Robinson, planned a slow national rollout, not unusual for the time, starting in Pittsburgh in June 1974, spreading around, and climaxing with a New York premiere in November. Moms, Slappy White, and Stepin Fetchit were shuttled around the country to drum up business, making personal appearances and speaking to the press.

Alas, despite the considerable goodwill

generated by this publicity tour, particularly in the Black press, the film received generally negative reviews, even as critics recognized Moms's unique presence in it. "The movie sort of shambles along," wrote Vincent Canby in the *New York Times*, while noting that it "treated [Moms] like a holy relic" and that "we laugh along with [her] in appreciation of her implacable, firmly unbudgeable stand in favor of common sense." In the *Los Angeles Times*, Kevin Thomas called it "patently — very, very patently — make-believe" but seemed heartened to say that it was "invaluable as a film record of a key show business figure." *Variety* was less enthusiastic, suggesting that the film would face "rough sledding" commercially and taking a moment to note that there were touches of racial caricature in it that made it difficult to watch: "White audiences . . . may feel extremely embarrassed, as if by laughing at some of the gags they will be considered racist. Similarly, younger militant blacks [*sic*] could find a lot of stereotypes. What to do?" It was a prescient question, as borne out by a review in the *New York Amsterdam News*, perhaps the nation's most prestigious Black newspaper, in which James P. Murray called the movie "a sluggish, unsatisfying, and often embarrassing failure." Worse, he said, "in the guise of humor, many of the images — particularly evident in the cameo portrayals by Stepin Fetchit and Butterfly McQueen — are nightmarish throwbacks to the worst of the 1930s and 1940s. If *Amazing Grace* had been produced by whites, the reaction would be nothing less than outrage. Since it has been in fact presented by young Black filmmakers, the reaction can only be expressed in terms of one emotion: hurt."

You don't need to be racially sensitive to be hurt by *Amazing Grace,* which is nearly as clumsy a movie as were the films Moms made in the forties. And yet, it isn't entirely without charm. There are several scenes of Moms puttering around her home, talking to herself, doing chores, beseeching Jesus, and so on. Throughout the film, her body physically changes — there are clearly scenes shot before her illness and scenes shot after. And there is a touching valedictory quality to her final monologue, a meandering scene in which she cleans a bowl of green beans and then drops it on the floor, all the while talking aloud about the lessons the audience should take from the movie it has just seen. Like most of *Amazing Grace,* it is ham-fisted, yet there is a verisimilitude to it — you feel as if you are spying on the actual Jackie Mabley in her own home — and it's actually quite dear.

In the spring of 1974, Moms appeared, as she had the previous year, as a presenter on the televised broadcast of the Grammy Awards. Walking out on the arm of the hip and dashing Kris Kristofferson, she cooed, "Eat your heart out, Tom Jones!" She turned to Kristofferson to tell him, "I'm crazy about that song you wrote . . . 'Help Me Make It Through the Night.' If you can make it for a half-hour, it'd be alright with me!" He couldn't stop laughing: "You're too real for all this, darlin'!" When they finally got around to announcing the award they were there to present, she needed a moment: "I never could work with my teeth," she said, turning around and putting a handkerchief up to her mouth to perform a little dentistry on herself. Kristofferson broke down laughing again: "You're a woman after my own heart," he told her, and, "Hey, give us a kiss here!" And she did, right on the smacker. A few moments later, as they read off the list of nominees, she lost the thread of the script, causing him to moan, haplessly, "You just stole my cue." She came back immediately with "That ain't all I'm gonna steal." The eventual winners, her old chums Gladys Knight and the Pips, were shown sitting in open-jawed amazement. It was a truly epochal pop moment.

In 1975, though, at her next Grammy appearance, she was far more subdued, with some of the mettle clearly lost to her continued delicate health and, indeed, her age. A few weeks after the Grammys she turned seventy-eight. She gave little thought to slowing down — "Moms will never retire," she told a reporter the year before. "As long as I live I will never be too old to make people happy." In early April, she was in Washington, D.C., to appear at the grand reopening of the Howard Theatre, the city's premier Black performance house, a venue where she had made people laugh for more than fifty years. At the end of the month, she was booked for a week of shows at Mister Kelly's, Chicago's top nightclub for comedians; just the summer prior, she had enjoyed a long and lucrative maiden run at the spot. But that second gig was postponed when she became ill at her home in New York and canceled all her pending bookings. (It should be noted that her hospitalization and pacemaker hadn't stopped her from smoking; video of her *Amazing Grace* press appearances show her puffing away despite her frail health.)

That April illness lingered into May, six weeks in all. For most of the time, she was a patient at White Plains Hospital near her home. She rallied a few times, and even left the hospital once to visit seniors at a nearby community center alongside some other old-time Black entertainers. That was her last public appearance. On May 23, 1975, she passed.

The tributes came from high and low, near

and far. The nation's Black newspapers ran articles in which men and women on the street spoke of meeting her, seeing her perform, or listening to her records, often shared with them by their parents. In an editorial, the *Chicago Defender* wrote of her unique role in Black American culture, "She was a consummate artist whose jokes, though slightly risque at times, were never out of good taste. They were the reflections of her life, a life that knew at an early age all the vicissitudes and melancholy that Black men and women experience." Comedian Dick Gregory commented, "She just finally lived in the past 10 years. It should have been 60." Gregory, Slappy White, jazz legend Charles Mingus, and singers Wilson Pickett and Arthur Prysock were among the many entertainers who canceled shows elsewhere to be in New York for the funeral at Harlem's Abyssinian Baptist Church, to which Moms had belonged for decades. A throng of five hundred filled the sanctuary, and they filed past an open silver casket leaving flowers, including orchids flown in from Paris especially for the occasion. A trumpet played a muted solo of the tender ballad "My Buddy." And the church's pastor, Dr. Samuel Proctor, choosing for his sermon the biblical verse "A merry heart doeth good like medicine," praised Moms for her ability to "take sorrow and disappointment and lift something out of it, to put it on a screen somewhere and sit back from it and have a hearty laugh to keep it from destroying us."

Even in death she found a way to delight her public. A few days later, in a *New York Times* article about Harlem's long-running illegal lottery, aka "the numbers," an anonymous operative in the racket said, "The other day, when Moms Mabley was buried, we took a beating, because it seemed like just about everybody in Harlem played 769, the number for death in the dream books, and it came out. We paid off 600-to-1, just like always, and people came up to me and said, 'Moms givin' her children new shoes from beyond the grave.' "

Ironically, when details of her estate were revealed, it was discovered that not all of her *actual* children were as well provided for. Her home, other real estate holdings, cash, and personal property were estimated at a value of $500,000, and there was another $90,000 in stocks and bonds.* In a will dated January 15, 1974, Moms made bestowals to her daughters Bonnie and Christine, her sister, Marjorie, her nephew Charles, and her niece Minghnon. Deliberately excluded from her will, though, was her oldest daughter, Yvonne Lipscomb, then fifty-eight and living on dis-

* Approximately $2.4 million and $433,000, respectively in 2022.

110

ability insurance in Buffalo, New York. Yvonne claimed that she and her mother had fallen out because she had failed to visit Moms after her heart attack episode of two years prior — she said she was simply too ill and too poor to travel to Westchester — and there was bad blood in the family as a result. It had mended, though, she claimed, by the time of Moms's death. "She used to call me every night and tell me how much she loved me and how much she wanted me to be down in New York with her," she said. "I believe she had every intention of changing her will, but she never got around to it because she kept getting weaker and weaker." Her sisters confirmed that some of the securities in Moms's estate were earmarked for Yvonne, and the story of family strife drifted out of the headlines.

In the ensuing decades, Moms Mabley was perennially celebrated as a pioneer, an iconoclast, a legend. She was among the twenty-five performers who made up the Apollo Theatre Hall of Fame inaugural class in 1986. Several nightclub acts and shows were built around her life, humor, and commonsense wisdom, most notably *Moms: A Praise Play for a Black Comedienne,* written by Alice Childress and starring the veteran actress Clarice Taylor (best known for her role as the title character's mother on *The*

Cosby Show), which ran for more than 150 performances off-Broadway in 1987 and later toured the country to generally appreciative reception.

She also, inevitably, inspired imitators and disciples, two of whom achieved some fame and success while Moms was still alive and working.

Hattie Noel did every conceivable thing a Black woman could do in show business in the first half of the twentieth century. She sang and danced in vaudeville, both on the TOBA circuit and on various less-organized tours. She appeared on Broadway and in Hollywood studio films (she was said to have narrowly lost out on the role played by Hattie McDaniel in *Gone with the Wind*). She was a radio sensation (briefly), a nightclub entertainer, a performer in USO shows during World War II, and a straight singer of blues and popular standards onstage and for a major record label. She broke new ground for Black entertainers in the West, particularly in Las Vegas, where she appeared before the famed Strip was so much as a gleam in Benny Siegel's eye. She performed with Louis Armstrong, Count Basie, Bessie Smith, Bojangles Robinson, Eddie Cantor, Joan Blondell, and Al Jolson. Most astoundingly, she put a ballet tutu on her considerable frame and danced for a team of Walt Disney Studios animators who were executing motion studies and sketches while preparing the famed dancing hippo sequence in *Fantasia.*

But through all of this work, she made only a minor name for herself, her profile as an entertainer so low that the Black press that followed her career didn't always agree on whether her surname was Noel or "Noels." Only in 1961, at age sixty-eight, when a Los Angeles record label that specialized in risqué comedy albums recorded her for an LP of naughty jokes, did she achieve genuine fame (or, perhaps, notoriety). Three years later, she stopped working altogether, living until 1969 in Southern California, her death not noted in either show business trade newspapers or the Black press until several months after the fact.

Hattie's career in comedy began after her acting days ended and after she released several unsuccessful comic/suggestive songs on the MGM and Blue Records label, including such numbers as "Put Some Glue on That Mule" (1948), "Hot Nuts — Get 'Em from the Peanut Man" (1949), and, on a 1956 LP with comedian Billy Mitchell, "Mama Likes to Take Her Time," "Come Get Your Hot Dog," and "Play with Your Yo-Yo."

All of these were recorded under the auspices of trumpeter, bandleader, and record producer Dootsie Williams, the last of them on his own self-dubbed label, DooTo.[*] Williams had an eye for popular trends, and he recorded several early rock and roll and R & B records. In the late fifties, when spoken-word comedy records gained in popularity, DooTo created a bona fide star in Redd Foxx, whom Williams had discovered performing at the Brass Rail nightclub in downtown Los Angeles. Foxx's albums — filled with profanity and explicit sex talk, recorded in front of howling live audiences — numbered in the dozens after only a few years with DooTo. Even though they were sold under the counter (the language on them made contraband in many locales), they were massive hits, and Williams was inspired to release more such material. When he saw Moms Mabley making a splash with her albums on Chess, he remembered Hattie and offered her yet another chance to relaunch her career in a new guise.

Although Hattie had long been recognized as a performer with a comic touch, she was never a comedian, that is, a monologist who stood alone on a bare stage, without singing

---

[*] Originally named DooTone, it was, until the rise of Motown in the 1960s, generally regarded as the largest Black-owned label in the music business, with its own music publishing division, pressing plant, and recording studios, giving real credence to its slogan, "Supremacy in Negro entertainment."

or dancing, and told jokes. Nevertheless, Williams arranged for her to perform live at Doo-To's studios in South Los Angeles, with a friendly (and well-boozed) crowd on hand to provide laughs and hoots as Hattie spritzed them with ribald jokes provided by writers under contract to the label.

The stuff was undeniably raunchy. Just a sampling gives a sense of her comedy act. Straightaway she acknowledged her ample size, adding a bit of spice: "I got the same damn thing that those skinny gals have, only I got a damn sight more of it! And it's all mine, ain't none of it false. It's real!" She spoke of a beau who drove her to a romantic spot before making his moves: "He had nerve enough to ask me, 'Baby, you got a cherry?' I say 'Hell yes, but it's been pushed back so damn far you can use it for a tail light.' " In another story, he took her out golfing: "That son of a gun kept my hole filled up so much, I never did get a chance to tee off!" She sparred with her audience, telling a woman in the crowd, "Uncross your legs: you chokin' the hell outta yourself," and roasting someone else with "Your old man beat his meat in a flower pot and raised a bloomin' idiot!"

The result, edited together with obvious gaps and sutures, was *The Whole of Hattie Noel,* a record filled with suggestive and downright dirty jokes told with gusto to a delirious, whooping audience. DooTo released it in late 1961 (at virtually the same time that it released an album of Martin Luther King Jr.'s speeches). A second LP, *The Bold Hattie Noel,* essentially identical in tenor, recorded under almost exactly the same circumstances, followed just a few months later, ballyhooed by press releases from DooTo claiming that Hattie was outselling both Moms Mabley *and* labelmate Redd Foxx, an assertion that there was no way to verify. Before another year had passed, a third LP was issued: *The Tickled Soul of Hattie Noel.* When DooTo moved to a larger headquarters in 1963, Hattie did another recording session, part of a full lineup of underground comedians that included Rudy Ray Moore, who would become famous a decade later as the blaxploitation film star Dolemite.

Hattie didn't tour to promote these records. DooTo had a finite budget for such niceties, the company's production stream was usually running at full capacity, and she was, by the time of these unlikely successes, some seventy years old and too tired to endure the rigors of the road. She played a few dates around Los Angeles, and she gave interviews to the Black press defending the provocative nature of her material. "I contend that there is no such thing as a dirty joke," she frequently said, expanding philosophically, "If I were sacrilegious, or if I dealt in mean racial humor, then I'd be a dirty comedienne. But I deal with life, with things people do, and say, in their daily lives. . . . Some people say sex is dirty, but how can sex be dirty when if it wasn't for sex none of us would be here?"

When the public appetite for comedy LPs started to wane, DooTo put out a few more Hattie Noel records. Her last new release for the label was in 1964 (there would be reissues and repackagings later on), and that was also the last time, apparently, that she performed onstage.

If Hattie Noel wasn't eager to be labeled as a dirty comic, there were younger women willing to bear the standard. LaWanda Page was a dancer from the Midwest who was working at nightclubs and strip joints around Los Angeles in the late sixties, when she was in her late thirties; her act included literal pyrotechnics — she lit cigarettes with her fingertips — and she was billed as "the Bronze Goddess of Fire." At one of her gigs, Page was told she had to perform in sketches and bits with the house comedy act as well, and thus she teamed up with the team of Skillet and Leroy on an intermittent basis for the next several years. Their act was raw, filled with profanity and sexual humor, and on the strength of her gusto with such material, Page was signed to Laff Records, a small-time L.A. label that specialized in raunchy comedy records. Her first album, *Mutha Is Half a Word*, was released in 1970 and sold well enough to occasion two follow-ups: *Back Door Daddy* (1972) and *Pipe Layin' Dan* (1973). (Say what you might about the quality of Laff's product, they let you know exactly what you were getting.)

Despite the fact that her act, as evinced by her records, was irredeemably obscene by any standards, Page was scouted for an acting job by representatives of *Sanford and Son,* the NBC sitcom starring Redd Foxx. At first she demurred, saying she couldn't work with scripts, but Foxx, as she explained, was willing to "take me home for the weekend and help me with the lines." The tutelage was so successful that she was cast as Aunt Esther, the sanctimonious, Bible-thumping, handbag-swinging, insult-slinging nemesis of Foxx's Fred Sanford. The role defined the rest of Page's life. She played Aunt Esther in forty-eight episodes over the show's six seasons, as well as in several short-lived spin-off series, and, more or less, in a series of performances as cantankerous grannies, maids, and neighbor ladies in films and TV series until her mid-seventies, cemented in the public mind as a righteous Bible-thumper after having drawn attention with arguably the most obscene material any woman comedian ever recorded.

After Moms Mabley died, her legacy continued to inspire Black women to follow her to the stage in careers as stand-up comedians and comic monologists. In particular, two famously successful entertainers explicitly cited their debt to her and took up her mantle as gimlet-eyed, hard-talking truth tellers: Wanda Sykes, whose feisty, raspy (and openly queer) stage persona owes something to Moms;[*] and Whoopi Goldberg, who rose to fame as a theatrical monologist specializing in inhabiting marginalized characters, including, at the very beginning of her career, Moms Mabley herself. Over the decades, Goldberg often talked about revisiting Moms in a one-woman live show or making (and even starring in) a feature film about Moms's life, finally producing and directing a compelling documentary, *Whoopi Goldberg Presents Moms Mabley,* that aired on HBO in 2013. It was, for many viewers, their first taste of the remarkable Moms.

As a child of the nineteenth century, Loretta Aiken believed that if she were to go beyond the mountains that formed the edge of Brevard, North Carolina, she would drop off into eternity. And as the star of one of the most unlikely show business success stories of the twentieth century, she transformed herself into Moms Mabley and lived out exactly the fate that she imagined: she dared to leave her

---

[*] She actually performed as Moms in a small role in an episode of *The Marvelous Mrs. Maisel.*

small hometown, and she carved out a slice of immortality for herself.

TWO:
THE PRO

I didn't think of it in terms of competing. It never occurred to me that only men were supposed to talk. I didn't say, "My God, I have to go out there and do battle against the male species." I knew I was funny, and I just did it.

— 1991

Jean Carroll was so far ahead of her time that she was ready to retire from show business when something resembling her time finally dawned.

In the mid-1940s, twenty-plus years into a career of dancing, singing, and doing comic sketches, Jean began performing stand-up comedy in what would be recognized as a modern style: alone in front of a microphone, well dressed, appearing more or less as herself, tossing off one-liners about ordinary life in a form meant to amuse the widest audience possible. There wasn't even a name for what she did when she started doing it; "comic monologist" remained the preferred nomenclature through her early career.

From the start, no matter what they called her act, Jean was recognized, appreciatively, as the female analogue of such notable jokesters as Milton Berle, Bob Hope, and Henny Youngman — and, moreover, as the only woman in mainstream show business who could be so described. Starting in the early 1940s, and for two decades thereafter, she worked top nightclubs and theaters in New York, Chicago, Miami, Las Vegas, and Britain; she starred in her own TV sitcom; she released a comedy LP; she made literally dozens of appearances on Ed Sullivan's popular TV show; she showed up innumerable times to perform at benefits and telethons for a variety of causes. Her husband was, by any measure, one of the most powerful men in the world of entertainment, running one of the biggest talent agencies in the business *and* serving as Dean of the Friars Club, the living pantheon of comedy. She was funny, she was attractive, she was elegant, she was hardworking, and she was even enmeshed in a juicy tabloid scandal and trial. You could not devise a more apt formula for household-name-level success.

Yet Jean Carroll was never quite a star-star, never quite known to millions, and she backed away from the spotlight in the mid-1960s, tired of the road and the grind, uninterested in pursuing modish trends, just when a handful of younger women comedians were emerging. She had some health concerns at the time she quit the stage, but by and large she was vital and engaged. She kept homes in Manhattan, upstate New York, and Miami. She owned racehorses and regularly attended the seasons at Monticello and Gulfstream raceways. She oversaw a wide and deep portfolio of investments. She had a foster hand in the lives of her extended family. She was, by all accounts, a live wire: gardening, swimming, playing bridge and Scrabble, kibitzing with friends, dominating her household virtually up until her death in 2010 at the age of 98.

She was truly a grand dame, self-made and respected. But as a headliner and, more than that, a pioneer, she was largely forgotten.

The small group that remembered her, however, did so powerfully. She made a lasting impression, for instance, on at least one of the more famous funnywomen who followed her. Lily Tomlin would forever recall growing up in Michigan and being transfixed by Jean's TV appearances, and she always mentioned Jean appreciatively when asked to name her youthful influences. "She was the only woman I've ever seen standing up and telling jokes, just like the men did," Tomlin recalled. "When I was 10 and putting on performances for the people in my building, I'd end the show by telling a bunch of 'husband jokes' taken straight from Jean on Ed Sullivan." But few others remembered the sole woman who stood very near the center of American comedy for more than a decade, an ironic outcome for someone who pulled herself out of obscurity to perform at some of the most celebrated venues in all of popular entertainment.

Jean Carroll's story ranges from the sagas of early-twentieth-century immigration to the frontiers of Las Vegas show rooms, from amateur nights in neighborhood movie theaters to live coast-to-coast television, from the anonymous ranks of vaudeville troupes crisscrossing America to the top of the marquee at the Copacabana, the Palace, the London Palladium. It's a tale of resiliency, talent, opportunity, a little bit of romance, lots of hard work, and persistence — oceans and oceans of persistence. And it's a reminder of just how hard it was for a woman of unique gifts and ample opportunities to forge a path in a field so stubbornly seen as the province of men.

In her prime, from the end of World War II until the early sixties, Jean Carroll cut a unique figure in comedy, dressed impeccably in fine gowns, flashy but tasteful jewelry, sometimes a mink or gloves, her hair and makeup always done just so. "If you couldn't do it in a ball gown, she wasn't there," recalled her granddaughter Susan Chatzky, who remembered Jean's closet full of dresses labeled "Expressly made for Jean Carroll by Neiman Marcus." Jean was modern, sophisticated, sharp-brained, sharp-tongued. When she first appeared on television, at virtually the birth of the medium, she was working strictly in the mode of the well-known male counterparts to whom reviewers and audiences perennially compared her, speaking about ordinary life in a manner that anyone — *especially* the women in the audience — could recognize. On the one hand, what she was doing was familiar: a gusher of broadly comic stories and one-liners. On the other, because she was an elegant woman making humor out of the ordinary circumstances of a woman's life, she was utterly one of a kind.

Milton Berle, to whom Jean was often compared, remembered, "Jean used to make them scream. . . . She played to who she was, and that's why the material counted." Lily Tomlin put it this way: "Other women doing comedy were scatterbrained, fat, or homely. Jean was very attractive. She was in control but not aggressive. She was her own person, and she was funny. Standing up and talking about their family was something you'd see only men doing. You never saw a woman comedian with that kind of command. But she was good-natured and light-hearted."

Jean's signature routines were absolutely

reminiscent of the work being done by male comics, but they unmistakably came from a woman's perspective, which made them her own. Her material, which she almost always wrote for herself, was personal but universal, her delivery assured, saucy, and rapid-fire: as archetypal a stand-up routine as you would ever see.

She joked about a no-good old boyfriend: "He was a real sport. Money? Money meant nothing. He didn't have any. . . . And manners? I've seen people eat with their hands before, but not soup!"

She made light of her husband: "The thing that attracted me to my husband was his pride. I'll never forget the first time I saw him, standing on a hill, his hair blowing in the breeze — and he too proud to run and get it!"; "He told me, 'Tonight you are really going to enjoy yourself!' And I said, 'Why? Are you leaving me?' "

She spoofed domesticity: "People are never satisfied. Lawyers wanna be doctors. Single men wish they were married. Married men wish they were dead."

She put a torch to the idea of being a doting mother, describing her relief when company finally left the house "and I could hit my own kid."

She could construct a grand-scale aria combining all her themes of household woe, such as this classic bit:

I'll say to my husband, "Honey don't you think you should have a little bite to eat?" and he says "Sure." I say "Whattaya want?" He says, "Make anything." I say, "Whattaya want?" And he says, *"Anything."* I say, "What kinda 'anything'? Which 'anything'?" Because anything you make, it's not the "anything" he wanted. "What do you want?" "Anything." So I go to my kid, my rotten kid, and I say "Honey, how about some food?" She says, "Alright, I'll have a little something." I said, "I'm not cookin' two separate meals this afternoon!"

And in one of her most famous routines, she mocked pushy saleswomen: "I said to the girl, 'What's the size of the dress in the window?' She says, 'It'll fit you.' I said, 'Well, what is it? A 10? A 12?' She says, 'It's your size. Take it. This dress was *made* for you.' I didn't even know I was gonna be in the neighborhood, but she made a dress for me!"

Yet even though her act was comprised of familiar nuts and bolts, it was nevertheless regarded as if in parentheses, as if the mere idea of a woman doing stand-up — typically seen as an aggressive, cutting, masculine discipline — made her a novelty. She was never a comedian; she was always a *woman* comedian.

In the fall of 1964, Jean took the stage of *The Ed Sullivan Show,* as she had done and would continue to do many times, and had a brief exchange with the host:

Sullivan: "It's so wonderful to have you back on the show again, and I wanna congratulate you. You've taken off a lot of weight, your hair's different, everything about you is different."

Jean: "You really think so?"

Sullivan: "Uh huh."

Jean: "Wait'll you hear the jokes!"

Sullivan: "Now don't tell me you're gonna be picking on your husband again."

Jean: "Well, who do you want me to pick on — Alan King's wife?"

Sullivan: "No, but he's such a nice little guy. (*Turns to audience.*) You people really should see him."

Jean: "Who? My husband they should see?"

Sullivan: "Yeah."

Jean: "*I* should see my husband!"

Sullivan: (*Walking away.*) "Oh, stop!"

It's silly, staged repartee, designed and rehearsed to segue into her act, but there's a lot going on. For one, Sullivan is, as ever, leaden in his delivery, mushmouthed and uncertain of his timing and locution and what to do with his hands, while Jean is sparkly, bouncy, quick-witted, poised, all smiles. There's also Jean's appearance, over which Sullivan makes so much fuss. A full ten months after the Beatles' titanic debut on the show, and after such rising women comedians as Totie Fields and Phyllis Diller had taken the same stage in their characteristic over-the-top attire and personae, Jean, always impeccably turned, is a figure of a soon-to-vanish era, her hair in a stiff flip, her outfit a plain skirt-and-jacket ensemble, her jewelry simple; she's elegant, but fashionwise she's walking up a down escalator. Most telling, though, is the banter about the subject matter of Jean's routine. There's unmistakable condescension in Sullivan's suggestion that it's unbecoming for Jean to criticize her husband. And there's a genuinely subversive tweak in her retort, implying that he would never make such a comment to a male comedian; Alan King, like any other man, was permitted to mock the women in his life without being second-guessed.* She gets on with her act, husband jokes and "rotten kid" jokes and all, and she does well: big laughs. But she's had to do so while still elbowing her way to her due place. Forty years into

* Years later, Carroll would claim that King stole a bit of her act, to which charge King shrugged his shoulders and said, "I stole from everybody when I was a kid, so I could have stolen from Jean, too. If I stole her routine, I owe her one."

her career as a professional entertainer, and she still has to scrap.

But, then, even more than she was born to tell jokes, Jean Carroll was born to scrap Or, rather, Celine Zeigman, as she came into the world, was so born — in Paris, on January 7, 1911. The family wasn't French. Her parents, Max and Anna, were Jews who'd fled Russia for the U.S., making a few stops along the way. Max worked as a baker; Anna tended to their growing family, which, with the arrival of Celine, known to her kin as Sadie, consisted of three girls. In early 1912, Max emigrated to the U.S., and Anna and the girls followed a few months later, unremarkable pinpricks among the millions of Yiddish-speaking Jews who had passed through Ellis Island since the 1880s.

The family moved with Max's work opportunities: upper Manhattan; Englewood, New Jersey; New Britain, Connecticut; the Bronx. Celine attended school and, quickly recognized as an apt pupil, was promoted at an accelerated rate, finishing the eighth grade, as she later recalled, at age ten.

By then, two things had caught her eye and ignited her characteristic determination. The first was Max's brutal treatment of Anna. "He was a baker," Jean remembered, "but he was also a drunk," who was physically and emotionally abusive toward his wife. "I gotta stop him," the young girl thought. "What can I do to save my mother?" She set her mind to remaining free from any such treatment. "I was only eight years old, but I made up my mind at that moment that never, ever, ever in my life would I be beholden . . . to a man . . . or to a woman, but mostly to a man. NEVER would I be subjected and accept what he was doing to my mother." The second thing she observed had to do with money. Even at a young age, Celine understood that her father's brutality was enabled by his financial dominance of the household. "If you brought home the pay, you ruled supreme." And she would soon discover a way to make money of her own: with her sharp brain, her fearless moxie, her talent for mimicry, and her big mouth.

Goaded by an older sister into trying out for the school play, she not only won a role but she was cast in the lead and given scholarships for dance and elocution lessons. She was steered toward amateur contests at neighborhood theaters near her home, winning small cash prizes even when management had seeded the pool of contestants with professional ringers. Still not a teenager, she negotiated for better pay from exploitative theater owners — and often got it. She even learned to deal with hecklers: When she was brought back onstage after one amateur night success, a shout came from the balcony, "Oh no, oh no! You stink!" to which she replied, "Nevertheless, I have an encore!" to a big laugh. The combination of paid appearances and amused audiences made her begin to consider seriously a career in entertainment.

There remained the business of her name. Celine, or Sadie, Zeigman wasn't an option: too foreign, too *Jewish.* When she was taking the stage at a theater in the heavily German Yorktown section of Manhattan, the announcer asked her name, and when she told him, he replied, "Oh no . . . all the German bundts are right here . . . they'll kill you. You're Jean Carroll."*

Even though she was only eleven, Jean was enrolled in high school, where she was set up by a job placement office with a clerical gig that paid ten dollars a week at a time when her family's rent was eight dollars a month. This money, coupled with her stage earnings, allowed her to liberate her mother. Along with her two older sisters and the two broth-

---

* The name was hardly inspired: at roughly the same time, on tiny stages around the country, a number of young women calling themselves Jean Carroll were at work, including a dancer, a singer, a stripper, a tattooed lady, and a drag queen; until the comedian Jean Carroll became a familiar name in the show business trade papers, their varied careers of the 1920s and '30s would create some ironies and confusions for a researcher.

ers who'd been born since the family's arrival in the United States, Jean found a new home where Max was not welcome. He would wander in, insinuating that as a man he could rule this new domain as he wished, but his daughter, the new family breadwinner, would have none of it. "I said, 'No, you won't. You're not moving into this house. Not ever again. Not ever.' " As she later put it, "I went from age 11 to age 40. I really never was a child."

At more or less this time, Jean was noticed by a talent scout for the Shubert Organization, who offered her a career. Anna, assured that her daughter would receive some schooling in addition to her education as a singer, dancer, and stage pro, agreed. And so, in February 1922, at the age of 11, Jean Carroll made her professional debut in faraway Brooklyn as part of a musical revue entitled *Midnight Rounders.* The show toured neighborhood theaters in the New York area, and Jean, given solo numbers to sing, was noticed by *Variety,* which described her variously as a "petite ingenue" and "a pretty blonde dancing soubrette."

After a few years of performing as part of a large ensemble, fourteen-year-old Jean quit the troupe she'd been working with and, with a girl named Pearl Saxon and a pair of young men, formed a song-and-dance outfit of the kind known in the trade as a "flash," a high-energy unit that would perform for five or ten minutes on a vaudeville bill among as many as a dozen other acts. In this looser format, Jean began to mix some comedy in with her singing and dancing. "I'd tell the band, 'Wait! Wait! I've got something to tell the people.' And I'd walk down to the footlights: 'You know what happened? I went into this restaurant,' or whatever."

Her ability to think on her feet was particularly useful when she and Saxon were abandoned by their male cast mates, who absconded not only with their salaries but with their sheet music *and* their costumes. Not long after that, Jean was touring with a band in New Jersey when the bandleader snuck off with the act's money. Characteristically, she claimed to be unfazed by these incidents: "Nothing shook me. I'd have taken a job washing dishes to make enough money to get back home."

Always insistent that she not be dependent on anyone else, Jean began to work in a smaller act, a boy-girl tap-dancing routine with Carl Shaw, a comic "tanglefoot," that lasted about a year. Soon after, she was teamed with Jules Edward Lipton, who performed under the name Saranoff the Violinist and with whom, in an act called "Saranoff & Carroll," she served mainly as a dancer.

Then, in the spring or early summer of 1930, at age nineteen, she got a real break. She was passing time backstage, strumming a ukulele, when comedian Marty May, who was at the top of the bill, approached her.* "You know something," she recalled him saying, "you're really a talented girl, and you're really funny. How would you like to work with me?" It would be a real coup: higher billing, a bigger salary, and the chance to do more than just dance. She gave notice to Saranoff, and by July 1930, she was performing in Chicago with May.

May, twelve years her senior, had a real pedigree in vaudeville. A comic/musician in the vein of Jack Benny (to whom he was often compared, not necessarily favorably), he told jokes and played fiddle and trumpet and often served as emcee for revues in which his fifteen-minute-or-so act was billed as a highlight. His act with Jean was composed of a bit of his patter, a bit of back-and-forth between the two of them, and a bit of singing and dancing by her, with him accompanying on the violin, as the finale. It all changed one evening when May teased her with an ad lib that hit her a little too hard: "I was so hurt I told him off right on stage: 'I don't think you

* For what it's worth, in April, 1930, the U.S. federal census found Jean and May both listed as lodgers at an Oklahoma City boardinghouse.

135

should say those things about me!' I blubbered with tears in my eyes. The audience howled. So I turned around and told them off, too. After the performance, Marty said I did great. He insisted I go on the next show with him and do the same thing. 'Say anything that comes to your mind,' he advised."

With time, her participation in the joking increased. "Nothing was written," she recalled. "Marty used to talk to me on the stage, and I would answer whatever came into my head, and this developed into a little style of naivete. I became a little bit of a patsy." In fact, she was playing what was known in vaudeville as the "Dumb Dora" part: the ditzy girl whose misunderstandings and inanities provide comic fodder for the frustrated or bemused fellow beside her, a sort of act that reached its apogee in the team of George Burns and Gracie Allen (and, with a little modification, later on in Lucille Ball and Desi Arnaz).

At first, they were known as "Marty May & Company," though she was the entire "company" and many reviewers cited her contributions as the highlight of the act. When she protested that she deserved equal prominence, they were billed in trade ads as "Marty May Being Annoyed by Jean Carroll." From mid-1930 to mid-1934, they crisscrossed the nation: Los Angeles, San Francisco, Denver, Kansas City, Chicago, Akron, Baltimore,

Philadelphia, Atlantic City, New Haven, and points between, as well as venues all over the New York area, including such premier houses as Manhattan's Capitol, Roxy, and Palace theaters.

Alongside a significantly larger star, Jean began to make a name, first for her singing and dancing, then for the comic stage act that she devised with May. Time and again reviewers singled out Jean for praise. Often, they noted that she was attractive, a trope that trade publication critics — invariably men — returned to again and again over the years. But they found much to praise, as well, in her comedy gifts:

"A clever comedienne on her own."

"As comedienne and as hoofer a soubrette of demonstrated effectiveness."

"Good at Dumb Dora comedy and better at dancing."

"The Carroll line and personality seemed to have special appeal for the Fox clientele, and everything she said or did was hotsy-totsy with them."

"A pretty lass who manages to get a rather new slant on her Dumb Dora material and who contributes a fast and excellent tap at the end, stopping the show cold thereby."

"Miss Carroll's chatterbox style remains chiseled and to the point. On looks and manner, she's there."

"An ideally mated couple for this type of comedy — the man a picture of nonchalance and the gal gabby-mouthed. Laughs were plentiful and the applause was okeh."

By the time of that final review, though, May and Carroll were fraying. She had gotten the more prominent billing she sought, but she wanted better pay: half of the earnings, precisely. Per her account, May balked and she replied, "You worked by yourself before. You did very well. You can go back to doing that. . . . I'm grateful that you did ask me to work with you, but I still have to think of myself and my contribution to the act. . . . I'm making a proposal. You can turn it down. . . . You still can go back and do your Marty May act." He wouldn't budge, and she left him, as *Variety* reported, to "essay a comedy act of her own."

This was, at the time, madness. There were hardly any women working even *semi*-comic solo acts, and those who were — Fanny Brice and Sophie Tucker, most prominently[*] — were better known for their singing than for their comedy. But Jean was buoyed by her success with audiences and critics. Earlier that year, in a column in *Billboard* entitled "Possibilities," Jean was touted as a likely prospect for Hollywood: "Apronmate of Marty May. . . . an attractive, cute looking and shapely brunet [*sic*]. Musical films would suit her best, since she's a good hoofer, can handle a song well, and is also a pleasant comedienne. Her speaking voice and looks, however, plus her ability to handle lines, make her a possibility for other roles, too."

That sort of press could turn a young performer's head, and it seems to have done so to Jean's. But she may have had another reason for wanting to leave Marty May: her heart had, apparently, been turned as well.

Bud and Buddy, they were called, a couple of young dancers originally from the East New York section of Brooklyn, where, in 1925, still in their early teens, they were discovered in a rehearsal studio. Signed by RKO, they hit the vaudeville circuit, crisscrossing the nation doing two-a-day shows. The money was pretty good; Buddy remembered that he

[*] Moms Mabley, working strictly in Black entertainment, would have been unknown to Jean and her audiences.

was getting fifty dollars a week, more than half of which he sent back home to his folks. But by 1929, he was on his own, dancing as a solo, a mere eighteen years old. A solo act meant, of course, solo billing, and just as Celine Zeigman had learned when emcees wanted to know what to call her, Buddy discovered that his birth name — Benjamin Zolitan* — wouldn't work in show biz. He continued to dance as just Buddy, and one day he was announced with the fanfare "and how he can dance!" In that banal little accolade he decided that he'd found his full stage name. Henceforth, he would be introduced as "Buddy Howe dances . . . and how!"

Howe's specialty was a staircase dance, which was pretty nifty business but not exactly novel. He knew he needed to add something, and he found it on a beach in Chicago, where he saw a portly fellow amusing people with some comic patter. Howe learned his name was Leonard Lubinsky and asked if he'd consider joining him in an act. The fellow agreed to give it a try, rechristened himself Jack E. Leonard, and began a lengthy career as one of the first insult comics in the business (he once introduced Don Rickles at a Friars Club roast as "a man who's been doing my act for about 12 years").

* In some official forms, such as the 1940 federal census, his family name is listed as "Zalkin."

Leonard joined Howe and a dancer named Alyce McLaughlin in a singing-dancing-comedy troupe that toured the RKO circuit for three years. During those travels, in 1933 or so, they appeared on a bill with "Marty May & Company." Howe got a gander at the "company" — that is, Jean Carroll — and found himself smitten. As she later put it, "He made a comment to Jack that he thought I was the funniest and the cleverest and the bah bah bah . . ." She had an eye on him, too, but when she watched as he bossed his fellow performers around during rehearsal, she was not favorably impressed. "He was asserting his supremacy," she recalled, "and I didn't like that." When they finally met, her opinion shifted once again. Leonard and Howe paid her a social call, she said, "and this Buddy was nice. He was pleasant, he was gentle, and he wasn't trying to show his insecurity by being Mr. Big." After the ice had broken, she was in the wings watching him perform, and "My heart went blip-de-blip, and I thought, my God, I'm in love with that boy."

Before they went their separate ways, a fateful moment: "He got up and came towards me," she remembered. "I could tell that he was going to come over to try to kiss me or something . . . I put my hand up and I said, 'Listen, I don't like men. I have no respect for most men. I don't like them. I didn't like

141

you when I met you. But I like you now. I like you a lot.' "

Less than a year later, in September 1934, Jean was performing solo in Toronto on a bill with Howe and his troupe, and the two of them started to work on an act together.

Crucially, *she* would be the star of their new enterprise. As Howe remembered, "Jean wrote us an act and taught me to read lines. I had never done any lines before. Jean was very experienced. She was also a good writer who knew the business." Whatever the power dynamic was between them offstage, their professional relationship was clearly defined: she did the writing, she got the laughs. "Jean could dance, sing, and do a little of everything," Howe said. "But she was essentially a comedienne. . . . I was lucky enough to find a girl who could write material that was so distinctive that they had to play us I was strictly a straight man."

They debuted the new act at the Palace Theatre in Chicago in February 1935, as "Carroll and Howe." Jean had finally earned top billing.

And they were, per *Billboard,* socko:

Jean Carroll and Buddy Howe deuced it. Jean opens with a song and is interrupted by Buddy and they go into comedy talk. Most of the chatter is good, made even better by Jean's delivery, but there are quite a

142

few antiquated gags in the assortment. Buddy does a clever acrobatic dance, and after some more talk they both do a song and double-tap routine. Two bows.

Within six weeks, they brought the act to *the* Palace Theatre, on Broadway in Manhattan, where, again, they scored:

> Forte is comedy, and in the hands of Miss Carroll it's made very delectable. Howe is a good performer, but in foiling for Miss Carroll he's overshadowed by her grand work. . . . Miss Carroll, making a nice figure, has a gift of gab.

There were more bookings in Chicago, New York, and points between, as well as the state fair circuit. In the spring of 1936, *Variety* finally caught the act: "This is a new comedy team for vaudeville and shows promise, especially the wacky femme. She's of the dumb-dora school, but with a rather new delivery, if not so new jokes. She's a looker besides. . . . This pair can go places."

And they did just that: They went to the altar, in fact, marrying at Howe's parents' home in Brooklyn in June 1936, and then, the very next day, to Glasgow, Scotland. In the United States, Carroll and Howe were always overshadowed by the fame of Burns and Allen, the sine qua non of boy-girl comedy acts. In the U.K., on the other hand, they were soon to find pastures entirely their own.

Great Britain provided Carroll and Howe with a dreamlike honeymoon. They premiered at the Glasgow Empire in late June and went on to play dates in Edinburgh, Liverpool, and Birmingham. They debuted at the London Palladium and were a smash: "a peach of a comedy talk and tapping turn that is both original and snappy" said *Billboard,* while *The Stage* declared, "Their chief appeal is because of their exceptionally smart patter," adding "Miss Carroll has a delightful air of knowingness." They were booked for multiple appearances in the venerable show palace. *Variety,* catching them a few months later, agreed with the general consensus: "Act is good for a succession of calls and bows and must be ranked among the greatest hits of recent importations." They received several offers to stay and continue working, but they returned to the United States at the end of the year.

It's worth noting, not two years into their partnership, how prominent Jean's part in the act was. She was the attractive one, the clever one, the exceptional one, the shining one. Buddy Howe was an apt sidekick who added some fancy footwork to the act — which was not, by anyone's reckoning, the thing that made them special. Of course, the critics didn't know that Jean was the one writing the routines, nor did they make mention of the fact that she had, effectively, turned the traditional boy-girl act around: Howe was the additional entertainment, the dancer; and she, whether people knew it or not, was the brains.

Howe certainly knew it. Speaking of one of Jean's most famous routines — the bit about the pushy saleswoman — he revealed just how creative his wife was:

We were playing Loew's State . . . and Jean went across the street and saw a blouse she liked in a shop window. A woman came out and asked Jean, "Do you like the blouse?" Jean said, "It's nice. What size is it?" The woman said, "Come in and try it on." Jean said she didn't want to try it on, she just wanted to know the size. Now that's all there was to it. When Jean came back and told me about it, I said, "Yeah, it must've been a funny incident." Well, this is true. She went out there and it was the opening thing in the act. She did ten minutes on it, and I just stood there with my mouth open. It was born on the Loew's State stage. I didn't know what to say or do.

That was the essence of the act: she wrote, she improvised, she got the laughs, she got top billing, and he was her handsome, dancing rhythm section, responding as he had been instructed to and standing stock still waiting for the routine to resume. As he remembered, "If she wrote, 'When are you coming to dinner?,' that's what I said every show, exactly as written. If she changed the words — I was gone."

By January 1937, they were able to resume working in England, and they spent an entire year touring the country to the same enthusiastic receptions — critical and popular — that had previously met them. They scored successes wherever they appeared. And that included, for the only time in their career, the big screen.

That year they shot a bit of their stage act for a theatrical short film. Declaring itself the presentation of "Another Famous Comedy Act," the two-minute movie opens on Howe sitting at a café table, nattily dressed and alone. Jean, also well attired, comes breezing in with quick, mincing steps. He stands to welcome her, but he's vexed.

Howe: "Hurry up, will you? What's the idea of making me wait?"
Jean: "I can't help it. I was talking to a man out there. You know, that man out there, he almost gave me an automobile for nothing."
Howe: "Whattaya mean, for nothing?"

Jean: "Really! It's true!"

Howe: "It is . . . ?"

Jean: "Yes. He was out there, and it was a beautiful car. I walked up to him, and I said, 'Are you the owner of this car?' He said, 'Yes.' I said, 'Well, I like it very much. Give it to me?' He said, 'No!' "

Howe: "He said, 'No.' So you almost had an automobile for nothing . . ."

Jean: "Sure! Imagine if he'da said yes!"

It's not exactly Noel Coward, but it's charming, and it plays just as you'd picture it: Him dubious and squinting; her bright-eyed and quick-talking and perky; him finally burying his face in his hands, incredulous with the inanity that is his burden to bear.

Their roles are clear, and the differences between them stark. He's handsome and smiling and stiff, she's chipper and vivacious, her voice a birdsong of intonations and giggles, her hands aflutter. Where he comes off as wooden, she is a font of energy — her eyes, her posture, her facial expression changing with every moment. The pep seeps out of the bit when the camera focuses on him or pulls back to take them both in. They're both young and attractive and polished, but as with Burns and Allen, it's clearly the girl who is the star.

Carroll and Howe were booked to play British theaters through September 1938 as part of a touring revue, but politics and the talk of impending war intervened in their plans. In February of that year, the Labor Ministry ordered them to leave the country, despite their solid contractual commitments.

Back in the States, they worked and traveled ceaselessly: New York, Syracuse, Boston, Atlantic City, Philadelphia, Baltimore, Cleveland, Chicago, Miami, and Atlanta, where they helped avert a panic when a fire broke out in the wings of the theater and they did twenty-five minutes, allowing management to clear the house without a stampede. On a few occasions, Jean added duties as emcee of the entire bill to her workload, and she proved to be as good in the role as you would expect, unless you were somehow expecting that a bright woman with two decades of stage experience couldn't handle such a job, as a *Billboard* reviewer seemed to think: "Most unusual was Jean Carroll, emcee, who handled this job as adeptly as any man and with better results than many. She seems to be very much at home as emcee, handling the intros and keeping the customers at ease."

By then the act had evolved. Rather than end with Howe's razzle-dazzle dance routine, it ended with Jean doing imitations of famous trumpet players Louis Armstrong and Harry James blowing their horns. It was a popular bit, much commented on in reviews, and continued proof that she was the more original and better received of the pair.

The trumpet routine would become particularly popular in the next phase of their career. Carroll and Howe joined the USO's program to bring entertainment to servicemen, touring military bases in, among other places, Maryland, Illinois, and Missouri. Writing about her year with the USO for *Billboard,* Jean estimated that they performed more than two hundred shows around the country, enduring conditions worse even than those they'd been subjected to in vaudeville. She expressed gratitude, though, for the opportunities that came their way as a result of their efforts. When they resumed their normal touring, she said, "in each town, a number of uniformed men stopped back to see us and tell us that they came in to see the show because they remembered the act from camp."

Not long after this article appeared, the war changed the fortunes of Carroll and Howe forever. Buddy Howe, age thirty-three, was drafted into the army. In July 1943, they performed together in Chicago, the closing act on the bill. "Their comedy turn never had more snap," said a critic for *Billboard,* noting that "Jean Carroll should have no trouble landing some lucrative dates as a comedienne." The next time they performed, it was almost as that critic had foreseen, but with a twist. In late September, Jean was appearing solo at Camp Grant, outside of Rockford, Illinois, when she called Private Buddy Howe up from the audience to perform his part in their act in his uniform.

He would spend the next two years at Camp Lee, south of Richmond, Virginia, never going overseas to see action. She would go on to remake herself as a solo comedian. And, as fate would have it, a mother — a daughter, named Helen, was born to them in October 1944.

From the fall of 1943 until the spring of 1946, much of that time with a baby daughter to take care of, Jean was more or less on her own — professionally and domestically — not at all an unusual predicament during wartime, when so many men were away. But Jean was just about the only Rosie on the home front doing her riveting onstage with jokes — and without a straight man to keep things moving.

In those earliest months, she had to teach herself how to do a comedy act by herself. "I stood for hours and hours in front of the mirror," she recalled. "I would lampoon the different radio shows, especially the giveaway shows . . . and I sang and I did imitations." In particular, she used a stopwatch to achieve the kind of rapid-fire patter she'd seen male comics perform.

The result, at first, was something of a

hybrid. In her first years as a solo, Jean performed some songs straight and some with the lyrics comically rewritten; she did parodies of pop culture staples and imitations of well-known stars (including the much-admired Harry-James-playing-trumpet bit); she told comic stories and one-liner jokes; she experimented with Yiddish dialect and suggestive — never vulgar — material. Often, she served as emcee for an entire program of disparate entertainers, increasing her stage time, her need for material, and, of course, her salary. It also forced her to point out to the audience when her *own* time on the bill came, "Now this is my regular act."

She played Louisville, St. Louis, Baltimore, Newark, Philadelphia, Boston, Cleveland, Washington, D.C., Chicago, and, most of all, New York, where *Variety*'s "New Acts" column caught her in March 1944:

Jean Carroll is a singing comedienne who . . . . proved a smash here, largely with a rep of double entendre lyrics and dialog. Possibly a little too crude for class spots, she's a cinch for the regular vaude stands. . . . She drew some heckling comments following lines such as "Do you get stiff in the joints?" and "He tried to get under my skin". . . . In short, corny but commercial.

Notably, the *Variety* notice made no men-

151

tion of the fact that Jean was doing comedy per se, as if the musical part of her act, which made it familiar in the vein of Fanny Brice and Sophie Tucker, was the occasion for the jokes. Indeed, another critic felt as if the comedy was holding her back: "Miss Carroll sang one number straight, showing a nice voice. . . . More singing and less mugging, particularly to emphasize punch lines, would help the act." But Jean seemed headed in a different direction: a few weeks later, in Philadelphia, *Variety* implied that the balance of her act had tipped more toward jokes: "Jean Carroll, now doing a single, is also amusing in a monologue a la Milton Berle. Gal knows timing. Couple comic parodies on pop songs help nicely."

By 1946, she seemed to have made comedy the focus of the act and learned to shape it for the audience for which she was performing. In February, she was booked into the Chez Paree, one of Chicago's premier nightclubs. Both *Billboard* and *Variety* caught her act, both thought she was terrific, and both noted that it was out of the ordinary that she was a woman essentially performing as a straight-up comedian, with just a bit of singing thrown in:

"Jean Carroll is a bit unusual, as she is a top-flight comic in a field almost monopolized by males. Gal delivers some meaty material for bistro patrons. Bulk of the material dips into the blue,* but that's where nitery patrons get their biggest kicks."

"Jean Carroll, femme raconteur, is a show-stopper. Unusual (for a gal) line of risque ditties, plus her poke-fun-at-herself angle — although she is a cute-looking trick with a load of acsexories [*sic*] — intrigue the payees. . . . A swell act."

Jean had discovered a creative direction that produced quality work *and* pleased audiences, whether in large theaters or intimate nightspots. She also had acquired someone to help steer her career. Buddy Howe was discharged from the army in early 1946 and came to Chicago to reunite with her during this booking — but not, they both recalled years later, onstage. "Jean was already doing

* The use of "blue" or "working blue" as a synonym for indulging in obscenity is a curio of the vaudeville era, when representatives of the various touring entertainment circuits would monitor shows and report back to headquarters about which acts were popular, which weren't, and which performed material that violated the conventional standards and practices of decency; if a performer was guilty of that last infraction, he or she would receive a letter in a blue envelope detailing the transgression and warning against further instances of it.

a single," he said, "and doing so well it seemed foolish to do a double again. Show business had changed a lot, and I was a little older, and, to be very honest about it, she was too good." As she remembered, she wanted to have him rejoin her or to stop performing altogether: "He told me, 'I held you back. You could have been one of the biggest stars.' I said, 'I'm not interested.' I wanted a marriage. 'With the money you're making,' he said, 'how can you pass it by?' "

And thus encouraged, she continued her career as a solo comedian, and he did what legions of discouraged entertainers had and have always done: he became an agent, joining the Chicago office of General Amusements Corporation, a talent-booking agency. Howe would never again dance professionally — or read lines as his wife's straight man. And, incidentally, Jean Carroll was guaranteed representation for the rest of her career as Howe rose in the agency and in show biz in general.

For a solid year after he left the army, Buddy Howe worked for GAC in Chicago. He and Jean made the family home there, but she traveled frequently for work, appearing very often in New York and venturing as well to Milwaukee, Baltimore, and Washington, D.C. Together, they were facing an entertainment landscape that seemed to be in constant flux.

154

Vaudeville, where they had made their bones, had all but died in the war. There would continue to be vaudeville-like programs of multiple, varied acts in the coming ten to fifteen years, but they were chiefly to be found in what were known as "presentation houses," large movie palaces that offered live — if relatively brief — entertainment along with feature films. Another new vein was nightclubs, intimate venues in big cities that had risen in popularity and importance with the decline of big bands (another casualty of war) and the shift toward more cabaret/performance-style entertainment. A third new trend was the growth of the Borscht Belt, the hotels around upstate New York and parts of New Jersey and Pennsylvania that were morphing with the postwar economic boom into full-scale resorts complete with name entertainment — in particular, comedians, and even more in particular, *Jewish* comedians. A fourth innovation was the rise of commercial air travel, which meant that there was more work for top-name entertainers, most notably in Miami and the newly emergent destination of Las Vegas. And, perhaps most of all, just on the horizon as the war ended, there was television, a world-changing innovation that would powerfully impact Howe's business, Jean's career, and the course of the next decades of their professional and personal lives.

It might seem that the agglomeration of so many changes would result in doors opening wide for everyone in the industry, but Jean was hard for the entertainment world to figure out: a solo performer, a woman trying to make her way in a specialty that was almost entirely the domain of men, with neither examples of proven success in front of her nor a cadre of peers alongside her to help pave her path. In almost everything she did professionally after World War II, she was either the first or the only or, often, both. There were perhaps two other women whom you could call straight-up comedians — not singers-who-joked, not comic actresses — working with anything like the same level of recognition: Moms Mabley on the Black show-biz circuit and Minnie Pearl in the world of country entertainment. But Jean — because of her marriage to a powerful agent, because of her talent, because of her bona fides as a vaudeville trouper, because she worked inside the mainstream of American show business, because she was white and from a city in the Northeast, and because of her indomitable drive — would stand apart from and ahead of these others. And she had to claw and kick and keep her chin up at every step forward she took.

The thought of how hard she had to fight was never far from her mind. "A sense of humor has no sex," she told a columnist. But the problems confronting her as a woman were ever present, on and off the stage: "If the male comics don't eat you alive, there's always a chance that the audience will. When it comes to poking fun, most men, in and out of show business, think getting laughs for a living just isn't ladylike." After nearly thirty years, she knew exactly what a female comedian was up against: "There seems to be a subconscious resentment toward a woman being funny. In fact, the minute she walks on stage she can almost feel the audience daring her to make them laugh."

She had a number of theories as to why this was, having to do with a male-dominated society wanting women to appear dignified, respectable, domestic, motherly, and proper. She understood that she presented audiences with a conundrum by not dressing or speaking in a deferential manner. She insisted on elegance, confidence, intelligence — all of which, she explained, were hard for audiences to accept. "Men in the audience instinctively resent listening to anything clever by a woman, particularly if she appears poised and well-dressed," she would say. "And the women resent her too, because they are afraid the men will listen to her. It's a kind of jealousy in them. They keep thinking how nice it would be if they were up there on the stage and had all those men listening to them. Both the men and the women sit there as if grimly daring you to make them laugh."

Over the years, she developed a few strategies for dealing with the obstacles that lay before her simply because she was a woman. She would, she said, start by choosing the easiest target: herself. "The task is to get them to feel superior to you, to overlook the fact that you are feminine, and then to be so funny that they forget your sex altogether. You have to do it fast, too — in the first two minutes. And they can seem like a long two minutes." She would also, she explained, pick a member of the audience as her target — not for jokes or ridicule but rather as a gauge of whether or not she was getting through: "I usually pick out the toughest-looking man I can see. You know, the guy in the third row with the sneer on his face. If I can get him to crack a smile, I know everything is going well."

That said, she was extremely judicious about the sorts of material she used. Though she was accused early in her career of telling risqué jokes, by the time her act was fully mature, she was outspoken in her aversion to bawdy humor. The routine of a woman comedian, she insisted, "must be selected with the utmost care. If she uses 'blue' lines or attempts to impersonate male characteristics, it's considered undignified." And there were other limits defined by gender: "I can joke about the foibles of my sex, as long as I

158

leave men alone. I can be as funny as I'm able about the gullibility of women shoppers, but I don't dare make the same sort of gibes about their husbands."

In short, she said, she had a harder job than any man telling jokes: "Unlike a male comic, who needs only to be funny to get laughs, a comedienne has two obstacles to overcome. In addition to good material, she has to knock down 'the wall of resistance' built up in the minds of men that 'women aren't funny' and, more important, that women 'shouldn't be funny.'"

It was hard enough, at any time, to make a career by making people laugh, even if you were genuinely good at it. And Jean Carroll *was* good at it: the reviews and the surviving film clips prove it. But being a woman, as she understood and made abundantly clear, meant that she had to work twice as hard, be twice as gifted, and make twice the effort of her male peers to ingratiate herself with employers and audiences, and all, in most cases, to get half as far — and that was provided that she was lucky.

As it happened, Jean had both good fortune and good support. Howe steadily built his name as an agent. And she made her name as a woman telling jokes — a stand-up comedian when there still wasn't a name for that particular specialty. As a "comedienne" or a female "comic" or "monologist," she toured constantly, emceeing (and performing) shows at presentation houses, Catskill resorts, state fairs, and nightclubs. In those first years as a solo, she appeared in Chicago, Baltimore, Washington, D.C., Montreal, Toronto, Minneapolis, Miami, the Borscht Belt hotels, and, most often, New York, where she and Howe moved permanently in the spring of 1947 after he was transferred there by GAC.

If Jean had been a man, this combination of rising success, new opportunities, a next-of-kin in the agenting business, and her domestic situation in one of the capitals of show business would surely have made her a star. But time and again, reviews of her shows, even positive ones, would address her as if in single quotation marks, with grudging appreciation and many caveats. To wit:

"Customers are accustomed to male funsters. Consequently Miss Carroll finds the going a little bit tough."

"Perhaps it's the novelty of a gal comic that puts extra hop on what from a male funny-man would be ordinary. . . . Whatever it is, she gets 'em with very little."

"One of the few femme comics who can give

vigor to a funny line as well as toss off material with casualness."

There's a lot of praise for her, even in the most dismissive reviews; *Variety* could dish out a pan, and she never really got one. But there was a reluctance, too, to speak about her in the same way that similar performers — Milton Berle and Henny Youngman, say — were lauded in the same pages for doing, more or less, the same things.[*]

Ever waging an uphill campaign, she seemed finally ready to score with the big time in the summer of 1948, when GAC got her one of the most prized bookings in show biz: a gig at the Copacabana, the premier nightclub in New York City and one of the small stages that could launch a performer into true national stardom. Jean wasn't the headliner; that would be singer Morton Downey.[†] But she was in a spotlight that everyone in town would be aware of. And

[*] And this isn't even to mention what they were paid. Berle would soon sign a contract with NBC guaranteeing him $200,000 per year for the next thirty years, whether he had a TV series running or not — a retainer, in effect, of about $2 million annually in today's terms.

[†] Later to be known as Morton Downey Sr. when his son and namesake gained fame as a snarling right-wing TV talk show host in the 1980s.

while it's true that Buddy Howe was becoming influential in putting talent on the Copa stage, it's equally true that Jean earned her place in the famed nightclub on her own merits, as this review from *Variety* attests:

Here's a comedienne who from here on should ring the bell in important quarters. She is a cinch for any rostrum in town. She works like a man, in fact her race track tout stuff is a bit reminiscent of the Jackie Miles technique, but fundamentally her personality is distinctive and her own. The overtones of Berle, Miles, et al are more suggestion, certainly not carbon copies. . . . Her monolog is a blend of mimicry and straightforward gagging. The buying-a-dress routine is a gem. The racetrack stuff punchy although the constant references to the Racing Form, etc. more become a Joe E. Lewis than a femme. As a monologing comedienne she's a rarity in or out of niteries. That she holds them in this bistro is doubly to her credit.

Again: a really positive review, but, also again, those qualifiers that Jean could not *not* hear: "She works like a man. . . . more become a Joe E. Lewis than a femme. . . . a rarity." It was an endless litany of left-handed compliments, and it overlooked the singularity of her work and career. As was said of

Ginger Rogers, she did everything Fred Astaire did "backwards and in high heels."[*] Jean may have been preternaturally determined to stomp to the top of her business in those heels, but it was going to be a fight.

In the months after the Copa gig, she went on to engagements in Philadelphia, Pittsburgh, and Boston, and even though she was well received, she was still treated as an oddity. Nevertheless, by November her star had risen sufficiently that she got to do a few minutes at a "Night of Stars" gala at Madison Square Garden in honor of the newly formed nation of Israel, a big fundraising benefit for the United Jewish Appeal. Slated to follow Lucy Monroe, a famous singer of the "Star-Spangled Banner" (and direct descendant of President James Monroe), who that night sang the Israeli national anthem, "Hatikvah," Jean stole the show, declaring, "I've always been proud of the Jews, but never so proud as tonight. Because tonight I wish I had my old nose back." Recalled Buddy Howe, proudly: "A solid five-minute laugh. The biggest laugh you ever heard, 20,000 people screaming."

Before long, Jean was playing to an even bigger crowd — the whole nation, in fact, or

[*] Remarkably, this trenchant observation is credibly believed to have been coined by cartoonist Bob Thaves in his *Frank and Ernest* comic strip in 1982.

at least those early adopters with television sets tuned in to the electronic age's version of vaudeville, namely the variety show, and more specifically *Toast of the Town,* the talent showcase hosted by Broadway columnist Ed Sullivan. The show had launched in June 1948 and quickly become one of the most popular programs on the air. Jean appeared twice in January 1949, while she was engaged in a high-profile run at the Paramount Theatre in Times Square, and she was well received both times.

This *had* to be her moment: a hit in nightclubs and big theaters, a hit on TV, a hit at Borscht Belt hotels, a hit even at charity fundraisers. In March 1949, Jean was named the Female Comedy Discovery of the Year by the National Laugh Foundation (Dean Martin and Jerry Lewis shared the male prize). The following year, *Billboard* named her one of its "New Stars" and spoke of the $2,000 a week she was commanding for bookings.[*] There was talk of her getting her own TV series; Buddy Howe had even shifted roles at GAC to begin focusing on booking variety acts on television — that *had* to be an ace in the hole.

But it just never happened.

From the time she was declared the female

---

[*] Equivalent to more than $22,000 in 2022.

comedy find of the year through the fall of 1953 — a full four and a half years — Jean Carroll got virtually every break and opportunity show business could accord her. She played prestigious nightclubs such as New York's Latin Quarter and Chicago's Palmer House. She was booked at Manhattan's Paramount and Capitol theaters, arguably the nation's premier presentation houses. She debuted on the Las Vegas strip and continued to appear at the biggest hotels in the Catskills. She toured extensively. She returned to London and was warmly received onstage at the Palladium and on TV. Her stateside television appearances included guest spots on popular variety shows hosted by Milton Berle, Perry Como, and Jack Carter, and CBS television tested her as the host and star of a live variety show, a pilot episode of which aired in April 1951.

Late the following winter, she was afforded one of the great platforms in all of show business: a run at the Palace Theatre in Times Square, the Parthenon of vaudeville, still going strong even as television had deeply eroded the audience for live entertainment. Following no less than Judy Garland, who had broken box-office records with old-fashioned two-a-day performances, Jean, supporting the top-billed act, operatic tenor Lauritz Melchior, received some of the best reviews of her career, even when, as ever, they included some slight sniffing about her gender:

"Jean Carroll scores the top laughs . . . [with] funny material and excellent diction. Her modus operandi is unusual for a femme. She can project patter in a hard-hitting style that would do credit to a male comic. She will prove to be an important comedienne in legit musicals as she has in niteries, vaude and video. What's more, she's a funny dame with looks."

"Jean Carroll is the best femme comic since Fanny Brice."

"Miss Carroll does not hurt her cause by being lovely to look at and by enunciating like an elocution teacher. In addition, she carries on a line of patter, first about her husband and later about a day at the track that is nothing short of hilarious. Her timing is faultless and the laughs follow each other in almost unending succession."

Buddy Howe and his colleagues at General Artists (the new name of General Amusements) trumpeted her successes in full-page ads in *Variety*, and they generated interest and bookings. But whether the issue was a hesitancy on the part of the public to embrace a female comedian fully or something about

166

Jean's act (a distinct possibility, as even positive reviews tend to mention her doing some of the same set pieces again and again), she seemed to be running at a furious pace only to stay, more or less, where she was — a rung or two short of true stardom.

TV came calling again. In November 1953, Jean debuted on ABC, the smallest of the three national networks, in *Take It from Me* (aka *The Jean Carroll Show*), a sitcom about a wisecracking suburban housewife with a distracted husband and a stereotypically modern daughter. The show's big gimmick was that Jean would periodically turn to address the audience and offer comic observations in a sort of stand-up routine — breaking the fourth wall as George Burns did in *his* sitcom. One difference was that Burns spoke *around* the stories in the episodes, whereas Jean spoke *during* them — literally turning from her fellow performers in the middle of a scene to speak to the camera. Another difference was, alas, the quality of the thing. Jean herself was well received: "one of the best-looking gal comediennes on TV [with] a brassy kind of charm which wears well because she underplays it" (*Billboard*); "she can put across a gag line with crispness and elan, and her sense of timing is extremely good" (*New York Times*); "her intonation and her grimaces are gems of comic invention" (*Variety*). But almost every critic complained that the show was subpar, the writing in particular.

Take It from Me debuted on November 4, but it never really launched. At the end of December, the network announced that the show would cease airing after a few more weeks. There was some lip service given to the notion of reviving the show in an improved form, but *Take It from Me* had never found its footing or its audience.

Critics didn't blame Jean, almost universally declaring that she deserved better scripts. She agreed heartily with that — she had always written her own material previously, but she had no part in the scripts that were handed to her. What's more, she wasn't shy about voicing her opinions about the indifferent material. Told that she couldn't "dictate to the network," she replied indignantly, "The hell I can't!" By her account, ABC didn't cancel as much as she quit it. "My future in television is on the line here," she recalled telling her producers. "It's my show, and I'm dictating my own life — and I don't want to do this show any more!" Indeed, the whole thing had soured for her. "I'll never, never undertake a live weekly series again. . . . I'm not interested in working that hard. The line of least resistance is what I'm looking for. A panel show, for instance, or just keep doing what I'm doing, making 10 or 12 guest appearances a year."

She wasn't kidding. TV — at least as she experienced it — was holding her back: "I was making much more money, anyway, just doing my stage act." And she added, poignantly, that there was an irony in her pretending to be a homemaker in a sitcom when her career stood in the way of her long-standing wish to be just that: "All I really wanted was to stay home and be a wife and mother."

That, too, however, was harder than it seemed.

"He was my soul mate," Jean said of Buddy Howe. "But he was a control freak. I couldn't stand his constantly criticizing me." Actually, according to family members, it was even worse than that. "Their marriage was respectful but not great," said Susan Chatzky, one of the couple's two granddaughters. "They kept separate bedrooms and bathrooms. He was famously unfaithful. They separated, and she dated at the time."

Normal enough. But that separation involved a fracas that made for sensational headlines and even a trial — if not exactly a clear account of events.

Per the official record, the following facts were undisputed by all parties.

In early 1950, Jean was playing a nightclub date in Pittsburgh when she met Robert McHale, an engineer who was seeking investors for an industrial project in Venezuela. He told Jean that if she gave him $100,000 it could turn into $1 million or more. She agreed to invest $5,000 — and only on condition that she get 25 percent of the profits of the venture or have her $5,000 refunded if it foundered. A series of meetings ensued, in the course of which the failure of McHale's project was made known. McHale, estranged from his wife, Dorothy, a former fashion model and mother of four, visited Jean at her apartment in New York and at her summer home in Wurtsboro, New York, where he was doing some repair work in partial repayment of her lost investment.

In October 1950, Jean, McHale, and their spouses met for dinner at the Pick-a-Rib restaurant on West Fifty-Second Street. Dorothy used the occasion to declare her suspicion that McHale and Jean had been carrying on an affair. She had hired a private detective to trail her husband, she said, and he had caught McHale at Jean's home at three a.m. Dorothy claimed that McHale had paid the detective $150 to keep the matter quiet, and eventually, a total of $850 in hush money. McHale responded that his wife was crazy — that she had previously been institutionalized, in fact — and that he was planning to divorce her, even though she was seven months pregnant. The conversation grew heated. Dorothy struck her husband.

From there, the stories differ.

According to Dorothy, upon seeing McHale struck, Jean kicked *her* and then slapped her head. According to Jean and Howe, voices had been raised but no physical contact was made. In any case, the dinner party ended, but the drama — and conflicting accounts — did not. Two months later, according to Dorothy, a week before the birth of her fifth child, she was resting at her mother's home in Pennsylvania when she received a late-night phone call from an allegedly drunken Jean, who bragged that she had been sleeping with McHale — was with him that very moment, in fact. As Dorothy put it, Jean went on to demand that she divorce McHale and when she refused declared, "I'm coming down to kill you." Jean's retelling was quite different. According to her, her relationship with McHale was strictly professional, and she only met with him in the presence of her husband. She never touched Dorothy at their calamitous dinner meeting, and she never called her or threatened her. But, she said, Dorothy called *her,* threatening to go public and ruin Jean's reputation unless Jean paid her $25,000. "I checked on your reputation, and it is quite good," Jean claimed Dorothy told her. "It must be worth $25,000 to keep it good." When Jean refused, she claimed, Dorothy lowered her demand to $10,000 and then lowered it again to a sum that would cover her legal fees.

There the matter stood: two contrasting versions of events.

In July 1951, Jean was due to make another appearance in Pittsburgh, where Dorothy had filed a complaint against her. Local authorities were prepared to serve her with a warrant. But someone at the district attorney's office blabbed to the press that they were looking for Jean, and, thus alerted, she skipped town ahead of being served.

Eventually, Jean was subpoenaed in a civil suit filed by Dorothy, who claimed physical and emotional damages and sought $25,000 in restitution. In March 1954, the matter came before a jury of eight men and four women in the State Supreme Court of New York, both women and their spouses testifying to their versions of events. Jurors learned that Jean and Howe had separated in 1951 — the second such hiatus they had taken in their eighteen years of marriage — and that the McHales had divorced in 1952 and Dorothy had remarried and was going by the name of her third husband, Varian. After two days of evidence and one hour of deliberation, jurors declared Jean innocent of all of Dorothy's charges. Jean left the courtroom joyfully. "The whole thing was fantastic," she told reporters. "I knew I'd be vindicated. I am very happy."

Jean, ever indomitable, brushed it all off,

returning to work, playing dates in London, Reno, Atlantic City, Chicago, St. Louis, the Catskills, and Las Vegas, where she was put under contract at the Sahara Hotel. She shot a TV pilot in Chicago — again, no dice — and continued to appear at charity galas. Buddy Howe had gotten involved in the campaign against cerebral palsy, and she appeared regularly at fundraisers and telethons for the cause. Indeed, even though they had separated and endured a crazy tabloid rumpus, they still worked together, traveled together, and were seen regularly in public together. In February 1956, with little fanfare, columnist Walter Winchell reported, "Jean Carroll's reconciliation with husband Buddy Howe ended a 5-year estrangement." Whatever happened in their household after that would stay private and between them.

In 1956, Jean was still essentially the only woman doing straightforward stand-up comedy in the most visible platforms of American show business. On the strength of her name, her talent, and her sheer novelty, she began a regular relationship with *The Ed Sullivan Show,* which afforded her a steady showcase for the next ten years on one of the most popular programs on television.[*] Through the

[*] There are reports that she earned as much as $10,000 per appearance, but accounts differ.

next ten years, she would pop up on Sullivan's stage upward of twenty times, often warmly received but never really striking major sparks. (It appears that many of Jean's bookings were made at the last minute; Buddy Howe's work as an agent alerted him whenever Sullivan had a cancellation, and he would offer Jean as a reliable replacement.)

Jean wasn't crazy about Sullivan. She complained that he got upset when she appeared on other programs, that he would capriciously limit the time allotted to her act at the last minute ("Just before I'd go on, he'd whisper in my ear to cut four minutes"), and that, most criminally, in her mind, "He really had no great sense of humor. He never said anything funny, ever." He treated her dictatorially, she said, insisting, for instance, that she repeat a joke that his wife liked but that Jean had performed on his show just one month prior. "I'll come to your house one day and do it for [her]," she recalled telling him, but he insisted that she do it on the air, after which, she said, "I'd get all kinds of criticism because I was doing the same old routine." Eventually, Jean said, she came to see her appearances on this most hallowed of stages as just another job: "I did my show, I took my shopping bag, and I went home." (This was no exaggeration, per Jean's daughter, who remembered that her mother "would finish cleaning the house, and then take her gown and shopping bag with her shoes and makeup and go to work.")

The touring continued — Chicago (once warming up for Nat King Cole), Atlantic City (once with Carl Perkins), Las Vegas (once with Marlene Dietrich), Miami, Philadelphia, Reno, Pittsburgh, and, as ever, various spots around the Catskills and New York. But the gigs were less frequent and the hullabaloo not quite as loud. In 1960, she released an LP; entitled *Girl in a Hot Steam Bath* and composed of bits that were familiar to viewers of *The Ed Sullivan Show,* it sold only modestly well. That spring, she returned to London, where she'd always been a favorite, and enjoyed such successes at the Palladium and on televised variety shows that she was offered a TV series of her own — a twenty-six-episode sitcom at a reported fee of 50,000 pounds.[*] But Jean demurred for, she explained, three reasons: "(a) I am not desperate for money; (b) I don't like leaving my 16-year-old daughter alone in New York; and (c) I am frankly beginning to get very tired of hearing myself talk."

Increasingly, that was her mantra: family meant more to her than work. She *seemed* to want to do the British show, but she presented the producers with a few demands that appeared like poison pills designed to

[*] Approximately $1,159,000 in 2022.

kill the deal — namely, that the series shoot in the summer so that her daughter could be in London with her during production *and* that her daughter be cast in the role of the teenage daughter in the show. As she told a reporter, "I'm too much in love with my family to keep going away from my home. My husband and 16-year-old daughter are dead-heat for first place, and I just don't want to travel around any more. The only date I want are those on home ground — and not more than a mile away from where I live. Yes, I still love show business, but I love my family more."

She stayed true to her word. After her London appearances in October 1961, she rarely appeared more than a car ride away from one of her homes in Manhattan, Miami, or upstate New York. She took the stage regularly for benefits — cerebral palsy, Tay Sachs disease, the March of Dimes, the United Jewish Appeal. And she spent more time at home with her daughter, Helen, known as Robin in family circles, much as Jean herself was a Celine whom everyone called Sadie.

According to the family, Helen was having a difficult go of her teen years, and Jean, like so many parents of that era, had few skills when it came to dealing with such troubles. She did what she could and what she was advised to, and she tried to soldier on through her career. "I used to have to go on stage and be funny when my heart was breaking," she later recalled, "or when I was sick, and I'd have to force myself." In 1963, Helen, barely nineteen, married, and she would ultimately have two daughters of her own. But Jean took over the rearing of the girls — who would grow up remembering, among other things, that Grandma spent some time each day alone, writing, and was not, failing a house-on-fire emergency, to be disturbed.

In her fifties, with four decades in show business, Jean more or less allowed her career to evaporate. She would no longer tour, no longer try to conquer television, no longer push. She didn't so much walk away as fade. "I was making pots of money," she later said. "In clubs, I could name my own price. But I just didn't care for the business. I had stopped laughing at my own jokes. All I wanted was to be treated like an ordinary wife whose husband sends her to Miami for a winter vacation."

She did just that, appearing only occasionally and usually in the name of some charity, becoming more familiar among the crowds at her favorite race tracks and boutiques than to variety show or nightclub audiences. She and Howe were well off, with investments in, among other goodies, a Miami Beach hotel, a steak house on Long Island, shares of Monticello and Yonkers raceways, even a Picasso on the wall of their Park Avenue apartment. Their financial prospects remained rosy as Howe's professional ascent continued. He became president and chairman of the board of GAC in 1966 and, two years later, merged the agency with Creative Management Associates into an even bigger entity, International Creative Management, for which he would serve as an executive or board member until 1980. In 1964, when writer/director/producer Harry Delf died, Howe replaced him as Dean of the Friars Club, an executive position (as opposed to the strictly titular position of Abbott, usually conferred on a celebrity) that he held for seventeen years.

In 1968, Jean made one of her very last public appearances, playing a small role in director Robert Aldrich's Hollywood grotesque *The Legend of Lylah Clare* — a film about show business devouring itself. In a joke that few people outside the Friars Club would appreciate, she played the wife of a talent agent.

That same year, with her mother, one of her sisters, and a niece all fighting cancer, she herself suffered a coronary episode that hospitalized her and gave her a perfect excuse to walk away from her career for good.

The work of making people laugh day in, day out had, she later explained, become too much: "You're cried out. Then you walk on stage, and your eyes look like two big red onions. All that's going on, and you have to be funny."

In retirement, Jean was anything but idle. She golfed, she went to the races, she skied and ice skated, she played handball and cards and Scrabble, she shopped, she oversaw multiple homes. She was a significant figure in her extended family, not only helping to raise her granddaughters but seeing after her many nieces and nephews, several of whom she paid to put through college, still the family breadwinner and adjudicator that she first became as a young girl. She was a generous sovereign, but she had her limits and wasn't afraid to wield a verbal sword. "People were legitimately afraid of her sharp wit," remembered her granddaughter Susan. "She said what she wanted to, always."

She and Buddy Howe divided their time among their homes right up until his death in 1981, after which she continued to do so on her own, following the sun from New York to Florida and back again, driving herself in her own car both ways into her eighties. Touchingly, she was known by people she met not as Jean Carroll, famous comedian, but as Celine Howe, her legal name.

That didn't mean that she forgot who she was or what she'd done. As she watched a number of women ascend to careers in comedy in her wake, she understood that she had cleared a path for them. Now and again, one of those who followed her reached out to reintroduce her to audiences, but she wasn't interested in nostalgia. In 2006, though, aged ninety-five, she consented to be interviewed for a documentary about her life* and to be the honoree of a special program at the Friars Club, where she was feted by, among others, Lily Tomlin, Joy Behar, Rita Rudner, and Jerry Stiller and Anne Meara.

Not long after that epochal evening, Jean was living year round in Westchester County, where she died on January 1, 2010.

Under the headline "Jean Carroll, 98, Is Dead; Blended Wit and Beauty," the *New York Times* noted that she was "widely credited with having blazed the trail for legions of female stand-up comics who came after her."

As her granddaughter said, "It was not lost on her, what she had accomplished. She loved that she did that."

Or as she herself put it on that last night in front of a microphone at the Friars Club, "I had no idea that I was so good! You think I'm joking. I'm not joking. I had no idea that I would make the impact that I obviously made."

She simply shoved open every door that was in front of her, determined to make her way,

* Entitled, "Jean Carroll: I Did It Standing Up," it has never been released.

180

never pausing to think that those doors would be open to other women with wit, moxie, and ambition like hers. Just as it never occurred to her that only men could talk or be funny, it never occurred to her that she was anything less than entitled to stand alone in front of a microphone and make the world laugh.

THREE:
THE SUNFLOWER

I didn't complain or whine or ask for any favors or special treatment because I was a woman. I took the rigors and changes just like the men. I came from hardy stock, and I think my heritage of the rugged ancestors on my father's side served me well.

— 1980

In 1964, VISTA,[*] the domestic version of the Peace Corps, the program created to provide economic and social assistance in the developing world, began sending volunteers into disadvantaged communities of the United States. As it happened, just as with the Peace Corps, many VISTA volunteers had little firsthand knowledge of the areas they served, so VISTA instituted a program of seminars to give them insight into the worlds they'd be entering. In 1966, with many VISTA volunteers serving the Appalachian region of the

[*] The acronym stands for Volunteers in Service to America.

American South, that training included a presentation by Sarah Cannon of Nashville, who spoke on the subject of "the culture of country people," something that she, a native of a town of barely a thousand souls in the Duck River Valley of central Tennessee, knew intimately.

It's likely that none of those volunteers were familiar with Mrs. Cannon, who was active in social and charitable circles around Nashville and in the doings of her alma mater, Ward-Belmont College, one of the most esteemed finishing schools for young women in the region. She was a fine recreational tennis player and golfer, she traveled extensively with her husband, a pilot, and she was a gracious hostess at whose dinner table one might encounter any number of entertainment celebrities and even her next-door neighbor, the governor of Tennessee.

But, no, Sarah Cannon was not famous.

On the other hand, her alter ego might have been familiar, if only slightly, to her audience. Sarah Cannon, you see, was Minnie Pearl, the cheerful, ditzy, man-crazy country girl who, for more than twenty-five years, had been regaling audiences with tales of her family, her adventures in chasing down "fellers," her encounters with the occasional city slicker, and daily life in her tiny rural hometown of Grinder's Switch, Tennessee. Wearing handmade dresses, black Mary Janes, and a wide-brimmed straw hat with a price tag hanging off of it, and invariably greeting audiences with a boisterous cry of "How-DEEEE! I'm just so *proud* to be here!," she was a sunbeam and a comfort, never changing even as the world around her aged and weathered.

From 1940 until 1960, even with Moms Mabley and Jean Carroll forging significant careers, even with women popping up and telling jokes in front of microphones in nightclubs in New York, San Francisco, Miami, and Chicago, Minnie was the most famous woman doing stand-up in the nation, even if she mainly worked in Tennessee and the big shots in the media industries of New York and Hollywood hadn't even heard of her.

If they *had* ever encountered her, they may not have even *understood* her. Minnie spoke to her audience the way its members spoke to one another: in country terms, using country dialect, speaking of country manners, values, and customs. An excerpt from her work, printed in her *Grinder's Switch Gazette* in the 1940s and in *Minnie Pearl's Diary*, published in 1953, gives a sense of what she sounded like and what she joked about. Speaking of a big party thrown in her hometown, she said,

Right off Brother had to show off. Uncle Nabob says that runs in our fambly — like big feet and buck teeth (ever member of our fambly kin bite a pumpkin through a rail fence). Brother wuz abraggin about his strength — said he had the strongest hand-shakin grip of any feller thar. So Lem Teppin offered to shake hands with him. Lem won. Brother wound up with a thumb and one wide finger. Along about midnight some old girl started hollerin' "Let's play kissin games — let's play kissin games" — jest kept on hollerin — my throat's so sore I can't hardly swaller today. They drawed a circle in the floor and a girl would stand in the circle and the fellers would have to kiss her or pay a fine. I made $11.34. Buster Owens still owes me 6 cents — says he'll pay me come Sa'dy.

More familiarly, she joked about her looks. She identified as an old maid, one of the few gals in her town without a "feller," and she blamed her homely appearance for her fate: "When they passed around looks I thought they said 'books,' and I said, 'Gimme a funny one!' "; "I passed a man on the street the other day, and I said to him, 'Didn't you give me kind of a funny look?' He said, 'Lady, you've got a funny look but I didn't give it to you' "; "A feller told me I looked like a breath of spring, and that always sounds good. Well, he didn't use them exact words. He said I looked like 'the end of a hard winter' "; "I ain't two-faced. If I was, I'da worn the other one tonight."

But, then, to hear her relations tell it, marriage was no great shakes. Take the afore-cited Uncle Nabob, betrothed to Aunt Ambrosia and none too pleased with his lot. "Uncle Nabob says that getting married is like getting in a tub of hot water. After you get used to it, it ain't so hot," she would recount, and then go on to talk about his proclivity for drink: "Uncle Nabob only takes a nip when he's nervous. And it's not his fault he's such a nervous wreck." One night, when he was out drinking and Aunt Ambrosia wanted to teach him a lesson, she put on a Halloween mask and leapt out from behind a bush when he was returning home past midnight: " 'Boo! I'm the Devil!' " she shouted at him. And Uncle Nabob said, " 'Well, shake hands with your kinfolks. I married your sister.' "

Between 1941 and 1964, Minnie was a mainstay — arguably *the* mainstay — of the weekly radiocast of the Grand Ole Opry, one of the nation's most listened-to programs before the advent of television. The meat of the Opry was music, but several of its principal performers included gags in their acts, and Minnie, a straight-up comedian who occasionally dabbled in music, broke up the show a couple of times a night with comic bits and monologues and sometimes served as emcee. When she joined the Opry, it was a four-hour show airing on Nashville's powerful WSM station, which produced a signal that could be heard from the Atlantic to the Rockies; one of the middle hours was carried on the national NBC Radio Network, meaning it could be heard coast to coast. As a result, more people could catch Minnie's act on a single Saturday night than might see Moms or Jean Carroll in an entire year's worth of live appearances. Later, from 1969 on, Minnie was a significant member of the cast of TV's *Hee Haw,* a hugely popular sketch comedy variety show that inverted the Opry formula by focusing mainly on humor and mixing in music for variety. And during all those years, from before Pearl Harbor until after Woodstock, Minnie appeared scores of times every year at state fairs and county fairs, outdoor arenas, and conventions, entertaining audiences as large as forty and fifty thousand at a time, sometimes doing multiple shows a day.

Throw in dozens of national TV variety show and talk show guest spots, a couple of film appearances, some LP comedy recordings, and even strings of franchised fried chicken and roast beef restaurants bearing her name and likeness, and it's clear that until the massive popularity of Phyllis Diller and Joan Rivers, no other woman working strictly as a comedian had anything like Minnie

Pearl's fame.

And yet Minnie Pearl seemed always to have an asterisk next to her name, much like that $1.98 price tag that ever dangled from her flowered hat. Working in the field of country music — or, as it was called by the poo-bahs of show business for decades, "hillbilly" or "redneck" music — she worked in what was considered a sidebar industry, a *genre.* Her audiences may have been massive, her Opry costars — Roy Acuff, Hank Williams, Patsy Cline, Marty Robbins — may have sold millions of records, and the goodwill she personally generated may have seemed infinite. But she thrived in a forum that the gatekeeping writers and editors of *Variety* and *Billboard* and the big daily newspapers held at arm's length, as if with clothespins. She was the most visible woman comedian in the country for more than twenty years, and she was nonetheless regarded by the nation's arbiters of taste as a curiosity, a freak.

Country artists understood this dynamic. They considered themselves outsiders, ordinary people with more in common with their audiences than with the stars of Hollywood or the majority of national radio or television. They joked that "Nobody likes us but the people," and they called themselves hillbillies among themselves (but woe betide the outsider who used the term without smiling). They happily played towns that the big names wouldn't dream of visiting. And they reveled not only in the adoration of their audiences but in the fortunes they made while entertaining them. Nashville generated its own music industry of recording studios, talent agents, song publishers, and, of course, via the Opry, radio and TV shows; the country music industry even created its own awards shows and hall of fame. And when the culture around the music finally got its due recognition from the likes of the *New York Times,* Minnie Pearl, as ever, was smack dab in the center. In 1957, when that paper ran a feature story declaring that "hillbilly" music was henceforth to be known officially as "country," Minnie got the last word:

> Minnie Pearl, *doyenne* of the country field, was asked when hillbilly becomes country music. She laughed loud and long, gently patted the sumptuous blue mink stole she was wearing at the moment, and declared, "Hillbilly gets to be country when you can buy one of these!"

But there was a second asterisk. To her loving audiences, Cousin Minnie Pearl was as real as could be, but she was, in fact, a *character,* created and worn by a woman who wanted to be an actress but who stumbled on comedy as a means of getting onstage, a woman who became so identified with her signature creation that she could actually go about the world passing unknown as herself when she was offstage.

In a story she loved to tell on herself, she recalled being in a grocery store and passing a casual acquaintance who seemed for a moment unable to place her. In an instant, the penny dropped for the other woman and she declared, "Oh, Minnie Pearl! I didn't recognize you: You weren't smiling!" And that was the truth. Life might rain on the woman who created her, but Minnie Pearl knew only sunny days.

As Sarah's real-life husband, Henry Cannon, once said, "Minnie's never lost a relative," to which Sarah, somehow always both herself and Minnie at the same time, added — tellingly, in the third person — "Isn't it a wonderful thing to think that she'll never have a tear on her face!"

Upon learning that Minnie Pearl was a character and not a person, you could be forgiven for thinking that Grinder's Switch, too, was as real as Avonlea or Yoknapatawpha County or Lake Wobegon* — which is to say, not real *at all*. But there actually *was* a

---

* The last of which it directly inspired, by the by, per that town's bard, Garrison Keillor, who grew up, obviously, listening to the Grand Ole Opry.

Grinder's Switch. It wasn't a place, exactly — it was literally a switch along a railroad line about three miles outside of Centerville, Tennessee, a tiny town approximately sixty miles southwest of Nashville that had barely a thousand residents when Sarah Ophelia Colley was born there in October 1912.

Even though Centerville had no paved streets in 1899 when Thomas Kelly Colley and his wife, Fanny (*née* Frances Tate House) arrived to begin their married lives, their little family prospered there. Thomas's lumber business, based just across the Duck River, was sufficiently successful to sprout a hamlet known as Colleytown where its workers resided, and the family's gracious, custom-built home, known as the Gables, had the largest library in town and one of its few pianos. Fanny, an educated woman from Franklin, a well-established city twenty miles south of Nashville, was active in her church, in women's groups, and, as a musical accompanist, in amateur theatricals. The Colleys were respected citizens and, it happened, politically and socially progressive. "Daddy was a yellow-dog Democrat," Minnie recalled, "which, Mama said, was somebody who would vote for a yellow dog if it was on the Democratic ticket"; Fanny herself was a suffragette and a civic leader who took a role in fundraising for the town's schools.

By 1912, the Colleys already had four

daughters, aged between seven and thirteen — and were themselves fifty-five and thirty-seven — so Ophelia, as the family knew her, always believed that she was an unplanned surprise. As if to celebrate this one last baby, the family indulged the child. The older girls promenaded her through town in costumes and fancy dresses; when she was a toddler of eighteen months, they encouraged her to wander into their music lesson recital. A few years on, barely five, she appeared as a featured singer and piano player at World War I bond rallies. When she fell under the spell of (silent) movies and declared an interest in becoming an actress, Fanny let her take "expression" lessons from a local woman after school, though she drew the line at allowing her to play the piano in the local theater.

By the time she was in high school, Ophelia (the family shortened it to "Phel," rhyming with *steel*) was known around town as a card and a performer. She was, per her own description, a gawky, coltish girl with bad skin and hair, a girl who, by her mother's counsel, would have to rely on a sense of humor to draw beaux. Her first big stage laugh, she recalled, came as a teenager, when she was enlisted as a last-minute entrant in a beauty contest; she milked the crowd's confusion at her being there *at all* for its comic potential, strutting and preening with an ironic air. At the time, she agonized — "I thought, 'Oh Lord, just let it be over and I'll *never* let myself get into something like this again.' " Even the assurance of friends that she had stolen the show didn't console her. She didn't want to make people laugh: she hoped to attend the American Academy of Dramatic Arts in New York and major in drama and escape the heartache of being the girl everyone thought was a hoot but no boy wanted to kiss.

One of her great pleasures came in the summertime, when a representative of the Wayne P. Sewell Production Company would arrive in Centerville to stage a fundraising play for the PTA. The company sent young women — fledgling actresses or vacationing teachers — to small towns for two-week stays, during which they would cast, rehearse, and mount one of a repertoire of plays and revues, casting local notables (bankers, fire chiefs, schoolmarms) in lead parts, filling the stage with choruses and dance lines of children, and splitting the profits from ticket sales with the host organization. Ophelia took part in these spectacles avidly, and she would follow the young directors around, asking endless questions of them as if they were celebrities. It was her first taste of show business, and she was drunk on it.

During her senior year of high school, the stock market crash of 1929 dealt a mortal blow to her father's business and investments, meaning she would have few choices for further education — none of which involved New York. Her parents offered her two years at Ward-Belmont College, the most fashionable finishing school in Tennessee. There was some consolation in the reputation of the school's drama department, which was headed by the stately Miss Pauline Sherwood Townsend, a grande dame who had attended the New England Conservatory and was renowned as much for her knowledge of the theater as for her lessons in elocution and bearing; a Ward-Belmont alumna (and they were a well-known breed) invariably presented herself with bearing, poise, and diction directly influenced by Miss Townsend.

If she had felt self-conscious in a high school beauty pageant in her hometown, where she was well liked and popular, Ward-Belmont made Ophelia Colley feel *truly* like an ugly duckling and a rube. Her classmates, who came from as far away as Texas and, yes, New York, had traveled the globe and spoke casually of whole worlds that a girl from Centerville could only have read about — and then only because she happened to live under the roof of the town's largest library. It wasn't a *Mean Girls* situation: nobody picked on her or asked why she didn't have a fur coat or a selection of gowns and matching shoes. But she felt painfully out of place, completely outclassed, and deeply homesick.

It didn't help that her chief social weapon, humor, seemed to be failing her. An autobiographical sketch she wrote for her English class was returned to her with dozens of corrections to her spelling and grammar and, worse, this note from the teacher: "I perceive you've been given the idea that you are funny. *You are not.*" She kept to herself and took to spending hours alone in a lounge that had a piano in it, playing popular tunes and comic songs in an effort to buoy her spirits. One afternoon, banging away and singing in full voice, she turned around only to find that she had an audience of upperclassmen. Aghast, she immediately stopped, only to be encouraged to continue. The older girls took her in, showed her the ropes, helped her emerge from her shell. At the end of the year, though she wasn't in the graduating class, she was honored in the school yearbook as Most Humorous.

After she graduated, Ophelia returned to Centerville, where the family were still struggling with the collapse of its fortunes. She opened a small drama and elocution studio, and she applied to the Wayne P. Sewell Company, hoping to become one of their traveling play directors. They accepted her.

And so it was to Hendersonville, North Carolina, and not Broadway, she headed in the summer of 1934. She was put through a boot camp for new directors, learning not only the repertoire of shows (most written by Sewell or his wife, actress Hettie Jane Dunaway) but also the craft of directing amateur performers, the rudiments of choreography (she had a knack for tap dancing), the basics of bookkeeping, and some of the tricks of staging shows in small towns that were crushed by the Depression and not necessarily inclined to spend precious time and money on amateur theatricals. (Among the tools used to impart this latter set of skills was immersion in Dale Carnegie's lessons in positive thinking and making friendly impressions; the Sewell girls were salespeople as much as anything else.)

She began her career as a director that autumn in Valdosta, Georgia, making ten dollars per week and developing a variety of useful extracurricular skills as a single woman on the road in the 1930s — navigating the egos of small-town big shots, teaching amateurs how to sing, dance, and act, balancing tiny budgets, fending off lechers, and so on. In each town she visited, she was given room and board by the sponsoring organization, and she was expected to make herself a staple of the community: attending church services, soliciting ads for the show program, selling tickets, planting the seeds for a return show in a year or two.

She was so good at the work that Wayne

Sewell offered her a job training new staff at the company's Atlanta headquarters, a position that she began in 1935. Thereafter, she spent the summer months supervising instruction for a total of one thousand or so recruits, then she would hit the road for eight or nine months of itinerant show productions all over the South.

In January 1936, Ophelia took a train to Cullman, Alabama, a small mountain community at the southern end of the Appalachian range, to put on a show. She arrived in a blizzard and found that there was nobody there to greet her, much less lodge her or help her get started with her work. She heard about a family up the mountain who took in boarders, and, arriving at their shack of a house, found it presided over by a woman of indeterminate years who spoke in the folksiest manner possible and was happy to accommodate a traveler. In the coming days, Ophelia took meals with these plain country folk and learned their life stories ("I've had sixteen young'uns and never failed to make a crop," the matriarch boasted), and she was transfixed. They were plain and decent and generous with the little bit they had, and Ophelia was actually moved to tears when she departed for her next assignment and the woman of the house said, "Lord a'mercy, child, I hate to see you go. You're just like one of us."

The woman's optimistic and loving and openhearted manner stuck with Ophelia, and she began to imitate her, mimicking her hostess's voice as a tool of persuasion while directing amateur actors or selling print ads to shopkeepers. In time, she began to think of the voice as a character, distinct from either herself, Ophelia, or its inspiration. A story about this fictional woman bloomed in her head — a hometown, a family, a set of personal traits — and a moniker. "I named her Minnie Pearl," she recalled, "because both names were country names I had heard and loved all my life." The next time she was in Centerville visiting her parents, she told them about the mountain woman in Alabama and gave them a little taste of Minnie Pearl. They laughed appreciatively, and her father gave her a golden nugget of advice: "You'll make a fortune off that some day, Phel, if you keep it kind."

Thomas Colley wouldn't live to see Ophelia follow his advice. In March 1937, when she was on the road in eastern Tennessee, he died, aged eighty, of heart failure. In the coming years, his widow tried to hold on to what was left of his lumber business and their home, and Ophelia continued to work for the Sewell organization, but she was losing her appetite for the traveling, the hustling, and the low wages.

In early 1939, a woman whom she had met while organizing a show in Aiken, South Carolina, invited Ophelia to perform as Minnie at an upcoming banquet, offering her twenty-five dollars and travel expenses. Ophelia accepted, but there was a dilemma: she had always performed Minnie as a voice only; there was no Minnie costume. So she headed to a thrift store with a concept in mind: "I dressed her as I thought a young country girl would dress to go to meetin' on Sunday or to come to town on Saturday afternoon to do a little trading and a little flirting." She found an inexpensive yellow organdy dress, some white leather sandals, matching white stockings, a "tacky straw hat," and some flowers to plop on top of it, and voilà: for less than ten dollars, from head to toe, Minnie had her look.[*]

The costume was a catalyst. "I felt myself moving outside of Sarah Ophelia Colley into Minnie Pearl," she recalled. "I felt more uninhibited than I ever had felt doing her

[*] The dangling price tag — perhaps *the* symbol of Minnie Pearl — came to her some three years later, when she bought some artificial flowers for the hat just before a show and didn't notice that she'd left the tag on them until it flopped down midperformance . . . and got a huge laugh. She was so gratified by the accident that she made it a permanent part of the act.

before, but it was more than that. I *became* the character. It was the first time I had ever really changed places with her, and it gave me a wonderful sense of freedom I hadn't had before."

That summer it became clear that the business of mounting amateur theatricals in tiny towns was reaching an end. People everywhere were getting their entertainment from radio and phonograph recordings. Ophelia returned home to live with her mother and to the life she'd always feared: a spinster of twenty-eight whose sisters had all married and whose dreams of a life on the stage had come to naught. With no joy at all, she set up an after-school recreation center in town and earned some extra income as a private dance and drama teacher.

She was increasingly resigned to her humble situation when the local Lions Club asked her to put on a fundraising play for them. She decided to mount a revue that would feature Minnie Pearl as its centerpiece and would include local notables in the roles of Minnie's brother, sister, aunt, uncle, and fella.★ Come the night of the show, it all went off according to plan, but the featured speaker for the evening was delayed in arriving and

★ This would be, she later noted, the *only* time in more than fifty years that Minnie appeared onstage with the characters from her stories.

so she vamped at the end, approaching the microphone on her own with a big "How-*deee*! I'm just so proud to be here" and a litany of unrehearsed but tried-and-true cornball jokes and stories.

One week later, she got a call from someone claiming to be from the Grand Ole Opry radio show in Nashville. He had heard from an acquaintance about a girl in Centerville who did a hilarious country humor act. Would she be willing, he asked, to come audition for a chance to appear on an upcoming program?

Decades on, she would confess that she hadn't been a fan of the Opry. "Most country music stars dream about being on that revered stage for years before they get there," she said. "But I had never thought of it one way or the other except that I didn't particularly like the music." She had heard the show, she recalled, because her father, who *did* like the music, had been in the habit of listening to it from not long after its first appearance on the air in 1925. Originating as a Saturday-night "barn dance" show featuring a loose collective of regular performers and guest stars, it was initially aimed at spreading word of the National Life & Accident Insurance Company, which happened to own radio station WSM (which took its call letters from the firm's motto, "We Secure Millions"). By

1940, the Opry was a cultural institution of a size to rival anything in show business, airing weekly for four hours and drawing a live audience from Nashville and well beyond. It had made superstars of a galaxy of homegrown musical talents and was the foundation of an entire subculture of American entertainment, catering to rural audiences that not only consumed but, because so many listeners became musicians themselves, produced the homey music that was the chief attraction of the show.

Ophelia arrived at the WSM radio studios and auditioned for the Opry brass. They liked her, but they had a quibble. Minnie Pearl was a wonderful character, but Sarah Ophelia Colley was an educated, cultivated young woman; would audiences suss her out, smell a fake, and feel cheated or even mocked? "I explained over and over," she recalled, "that I was dead serious about the act and had no intention of making light of country folks, whom I *loved* and of whom I was a part." They agreed to give her a shot, but they weren't taking any major risks: She would take the stage at 11:05 p.m., in the final hour of the four-hour broadcast, well after the nationally aired portion of the show had ended. The audience would consist of the live crowd at the War Memorial Auditorium[*] and

[*] The *Opry* wouldn't move into its famous Ryman Auditorium home until the following year.

whoever was tuned in to the local WSM broadcast.

On a November night, she stood in the wings in her Minnie Pearl garb and was overcome with anxiety. She might not have cared much for the Opry, but this was a genuine job in show business, a prospect she had all but given up on. Taking note of her obvious apprehension, Judge George Hay, the show's creator and announcer, gave her a bit of advice that, like that of her father, shaped the rest of her career: "Just love them, honey, and they'll love you right back." She went out, she did her brief set, which included a bit of comic singing, and she left, headed back home. She asked her mother, who'd been in the audience, how she thought it went, and Fanny Colley, wanting to be encouraging, replied, "Several people woke up."

A few days later, another call from Nashville: Would she like to do another show on Saturday night? They stipulated that she'd have to do new material and that she'd have to submit it for review on Friday, so she went into the office with her pages. When she announced herself at the front desk, the receptionist declared, "Am I ever glad to see you!" and went into a back room to fetch a mail sack containing more than three hundred letters that listeners had sent to Minnie Pearl. Overwhelmed, she toted the bag with her to the production office, where, straight up, they offered her a job. She'd get ten dollars a week and the services of a writing staff to help her keep up with the amount of new material she'd have to generate.

And there it was: Two weeks prior she was a barely employed after-school care provider in a small town, and based on a few minutes of work, she had been granted a position that would make her a household name for the next fifty years.

It wasn't a dream fulfilled, not exactly. For one thing, she had aspired to the stage, to drama, and here she was doing comedy in Nashville — and *country comedy* at that. Country was, as she had assured her Opry bosses, part of who she was; but it was a part that she had sought to shed. Indeed, reverting to her Centerville self after years of hoping to transcend it seemed to her, at the time, an admission of defeat. As she once put it, "I realized I didn't have the talent to be an actress, so I settled for second-best." (Years later, she had a much more sanguine — indeed, a much more *Minnie Pearl* — take on her path: "I was country," she recalled, "but I was kicking against it the whole time. My whole idea was to get away from the country, not knowing that the country was going to be my salvation.")

Her Ward-Belmont education and her years with the Sewell agency may have primed her

204

for a different kind of career than the one she had stumbled onto; but nothing could have prepared her for the strange culture of the Opry. She had to find a place among the show's family of performers, who could be, despite their fame, rather shambolic in their approach to their profession. She had to grow accustomed, as well, to having two people, in effect, to inhabit — Ophelia and Minnie. She had to learn how to play weekly shows with new scripts (written by Opry staffers with her significant input). And she had to learn to cut loose, to let Minnie blossom both inside her and onstage.

The latter, especially, was a struggle. "When Minnie first started out," she recalled, "she was quiet and gentle and nice. She didn't scream, she just talked." In retrospect, the idea that a comedian needed to be immersed fully in a comic persona would seem obvious to her, but Ophelia had to learn a hard lesson before she truly inhabited the character she created. In late 1940, when she'd been with the Opry — that is to say, when she'd been a professional performer — for about a month, Roy Acuff, the reigning King of Country Music and the Opry's biggest star, asked her to join his touring show at a salary of fifty dollars per week. At the time, the Opry, famous as it was, was nobody's main job. Musicians would perform their act on the air on Saturday night, then hit the road for a week of moneymaking gigs before rolling back into Nashville in time for the next Saturday radio show. And as much as the Opry felt like everybody's Saturday-night get-together, those road shows were where artists truly connected with the public that supported them with record sales and loyal fandom.

Touring with Acuff was a massive opportunity — not only a significant financial boost but a chance to really cement Minnie in the public consciousness. But she simply wasn't up to it. She had to perform a far longer set than she did on the air — twenty minutes or so — and she didn't have enough material. Worse, she hadn't yet fully committed to her character. She hadn't imbued Minnie with the brashness and confidence to win over an audience. She could do it for a few minutes at a time, with most of the crowd invisible on the other end of radio waves, but she couldn't do it in the big, packed arenas that Acuff's tour visited. And, worse yet, she *knew* it: "I still wasn't ready to divest myself completely of my own personality and become a silly character," she remembered. "I wasn't ready to give up sex appeal and a feminine image to be a clown."

Acuff was patient. He saw how well audiences liked Minnie on the Saturday-night Opry broadcasts, and he was a savvy enough showman to know that there was something endearing in her. But he couldn't figure out how to unlock it. One night they were eating at a truck stop and listening to the jukebox, when Ophelia got up and started doing a comic jig to the music. Acuff saw the spark that was missing from the act.

"Now, why don't you do that on the stage?" he asked.

"Oh, that's too silly," she replied. "I couldn't do that."

"Minnie," he said, "you have to realize that you *must* be silly. Don't ever be embarrassed to give them a good show."

She knew he was right, but she didn't yet have the key to open herself up. A few weeks later, he let her go.

She continued to work the Opry and to expand Minnie's breadth, deepening her commitment to the character, amplifying her voice, even letting her do a little of that comic dancing. Then, in the summer of 1941, Pee Wee King, an Opry mainstay in the thirties, returned to the show and took a liking to the maturing Minnie. He invited her to join his road troupe at the same fifty dollars per week that Acuff had paid. King was a far brasher and more colorful performer than the courtly Acuff, and from the start Minnie felt more comfortable — and perhaps less cowed — in his company. Seemingly day by day, she found her way as a performer.

As the summer season wound down, King's

revue was offered the chance to tour with the Camel Caravan, a massive operation sponsored by the Camel cigarette company that involved several troupes of entertainers in different regions of the country performing shows at military bases and nearby cities. It was a combination morale booster and advertising gimmick: there were pretty girls along for the tour who handed out free cigarettes to servicemen, and Ophelia agreed to chaperone them, for which she was paid fifty dollars per week on top of the fifty she was getting from King.

They were on the road on December 7, when the Japanese air attack on Pearl Harbor meant the United States would go to war, and the following night's show was rough. The servicemen in the audience had enlisted — or, in many cases, been drafted — in peacetime, and now they were to engage in a live war, and they weren't all happy about it. The air was thick with tension. A couple of fellows in the crowd wanted no part of Minnie or her cornball schtick and let her know it: She was being heckled for the first time in her career, and she couldn't handle it. She fled before her act was done, literally in tears. Backstage, she was confronted by the show's emcee, who told her bluntly that she was being unprofessional, that she owed her audience a show, that she was asking for heckling by dint of asking to be laughed at, and that she'd better develop the tools to fight back. Ever an apt student, Minnie would never succumb to hecklers again.

By the summer of 1942, Minnie had performed before more than three hundred thousand servicemen in the United States, Panama, and Guatemala. At the beginning of that year, she had been added to the nationally broadcast hour of the Opry, a promotion that occasioned yet another lesson in stagecraft. The NBC people — and the William Esty advertising agency, which supervised the show for its sponsor, Prince Albert tobacco — didn't at first care for Minnie, echoing the initial fear of Opry brass that audiences wouldn't accept her because she was, as they saw it, inauthentic. But now that the Minnie persona had been fleshed out, they wanted it bigger and bolder. As she recalled, "Those people from the William Esty Agency in New York came down, and one of 'em said, 'Why don't we scream the "Howdy," and let the audience holler back?' I didn't like that idea at first, but the response was just tremendous. So she got a little more brash that way." And she would greet audiences with that call-and-response for another half century.

For the next six years, Minnie appeared almost every week on WSM and NBC Radio and made some two hundred or more live appearances per year at tent shows, fairgrounds, high school gymnasiums, civic auditoriums, and anywhere else country people went to see a show. And it was rarely in big cities. Occasionally, the performances — mini-Opry affairs with a musical headliner, Minnie, and several other acts — would pop up in metropolitan areas: Detroit, St. Louis, Dallas, Atlanta. When they did, they filled big arenas. More often, though, they would appear in smaller towns — Dearborn or Independence or Galveston or Macon — and in rustic venues. From her Nashville base, Minnie began mailing out a monthly newsletter, the four-page *Grinder's Switch Gazette,* sharing tales of her make-believe hometown and its inhabitants, who had become as familiar to her audience as members of their own families; at its height, it had a few thousand subscribers. She had imitators — a comedian named Pinky Pepper was billed during his brief career as "the male Minnie Pearl" — and her catchphrase, "I'm just so proud to be here," was quoted by politicians and other notables throughout the South.

She didn't, however, have competitors.

Although there were several men on the circuit who did country comedy, they were primarily musicians such as Grandpa Jones and the Duke of Paducah, who added humor to their playing as a bit of showmanship; only one straight-up comic, Rod Brasfield, worked the Opry and its related touring circuits in those days, and he was often teamed with Minnie in scripted boy-girl bits. The one other woman who did comedy in a country vein, Judy Canova, a vaudevillian who sang and danced and played guitar, was working in radio sitcoms and Hollywood movies by the time of Minnie's rise. She was a star but she never was a stand-up comedian. Minnie was a one-off, rather miraculously, a woman standing at the microphone and telling jokes, and perhaps that uniqueness added to the true love audiences seemed to have for her. She became known to one and all as Cousin Minnie Pearl, and her arrival on the stage or behind the microphone felt, to her vast and appreciative audiences, like a tonic.

Those audiences were turning up in some unlikely places. In September 1947, the popular Texas singer Ernest Tubb, along with the singing Short Brothers, Minnie, and a few other musical acts performed two shows in two nights at, of all the honkytonks in the world, New York's Carnegie Hall. It was a gamble for the promoters and a trip into the unknown for the performers, and it turned out to be a smash. Both shows were sold out, resulting in a gross upwards of $12,000.* They followed with a pair of shows in October at Constitution Hall in Washington, D.C. — another hit. Moneymen in New York were taking notice of the phenomenon (still referred to as "hillbilly" or, in the *New York Times* — which didn't review the Carnegie Hall shows — as "folk").

There was talk of a Grand Ole Opry–inspired revue on Broadway. That never happened, but if it had, Minnie would have been part of it, and she would have stood an excellent chance of a big payday — not because she was such a big attraction, but because she had acquired a business manager earlier that year. After more than six years of working for the Opry and its various touring arms on the basis of verbal agreements and contracts organized by the Opry's own artist bureau/agency, Minnie's career would be overseen by Henry Rolffs Cannon, whom she had married in February 1947 after just a few short months of courtship.

She hadn't seen it coming. No matter how man-crazy Minnie may have been, Sarah Colley[†] had both feet on the ground and two

---

* More than $140,000 in 2022 terms.

† Outside of the family home, she would be known as Sarah offstage all her adult life.

very clear eyes when it came to men. She'd traveled on the road as a Sewell producer and as a performer since 1935, and she was single all that time (as she recalled later in life, she hadn't had her first kiss until she was at Ward-Belmont). She dated in Nashville — often on double dates with her roommate, a secretary in the Opry offices. And she hinted in later years at a couple of romances. But she seems genuinely to have been focused mainly on her work, and she never talked about any specific relationships of any length or depth. As she put it, "I was a pretty normal old gal. I didn't sit in a corner. . . . I was young then and had a very good figure. And while there were certainly opportunities, they weren't as common as one might believe. . . . To say that I had overwhelming temptations night and day would be inaccurate, because I was not a glamour girl by any means."

And then she got set up with Henry Cannon, an Air Force buddy of her roommate's fiancé. Cannon, a Tennessee native who was building a charter airline service, was a bit of a dude, with smart suits and a smooth line of palaver. Sarah had seen him around town in the company of a string of dates, and she wasn't especially impressed, not least because she'd been in show biz and seen plenty of slick fellows of his type.[*] And then, one night

[*] And, perhaps too, because he was five years her junior.

213

in December 1946, when she was on a date, Cannon convinced her to ditch the fellow she was with and spend the evening on the town with him, which, to her own surprise, she did. When he brought her home that night, he gave her a kiss and delivered as slick a line as she'd ever heard, onstage or off: "Baby, after the Lord made you he sure must have buffed his nails."

Then he started talking about marriage. Again, to her surprise, she found that the idea sounded pretty good. There would have to be a trip to Centerville to get the approval of Fanny, who had come to depend on her baby daughter's financial support and company. But when Cannon met her, he turned on the charm: "Mrs. Colley, I have heard all my life that you were one of the most beautiful ladies who ever came out of Franklin. I know now that they were right." That iced it. They were married barely two months after that first kiss, on a Saturday afternoon in February a few hours before the bride took the Opry stage as her alter ego.

From the time of their marriage, Henry managed all of Minnie's business affairs, which were becoming increasingly robust and lucrative. As she put it years later, "I am Sarah Cannon . . . but we are selling Minnie Pearl. It's a product just like a jar of peanut butter, and about that exciting!" She briefly had her own Saturday daytime show, *The Minnie Pearl Saturday Social,* on local radio. She continued to tour regularly (Henry's airline business expanded as he flew his wife to her gigs and her costars began to recognize that planes beat the hell out of station wagons as a means of getting around). She could hit fifty-plus fairgrounds in a single summer, in addition to several dozen one-off shows during the weeks in between Opry broadcasts. In 1949, her travels included a USO tour of American military bases in Europe. The following year, she signed on to the Hadacol Caravan, an honest-to-God traveling medicine show comprised of an all-star team of country stars such as Hank Williams, her former boss Roy Acuff, and such national entertainment celebrities as Mickey Rooney, Bob Hope, Milton Berle, Judy Garland, Jimmy Durante, and Chico Marx. Hadacol was pure snake oil, offering as its chief medical benefit the fact that it had alcohol in it. It was popular for a while, especially in the dry counties of southern and midwestern states, and the Caravan enjoyed two summers playing to massive crowds in rodeo arenas, fairgrounds, and baseball stadiums (admission by proof of purchase of the product, to wit a boxtop) before the company went bust in 1951.

Didn't matter to Minnie. That same summer, she played at the Cotton Bowl in Dallas on a bill with bluegrass master Bill Monroe before forty-three thousand people (who had paid a whopping fifty cents admission). The following year, she was back in New York, this time playing a nightclub on the roof of the Hotel Astor along with singer Red Foley; the gig was meant to kick off a rotating series of Opry performances in a fixed big-city locale, and while that first booking went over pretty well (*Variety* praised Minnie as having "a good style for the genre" and being "an excellent yodeler"), the novelty of the shows failed to grab Manhattan audiences, and the series ended within a month of its launch. As *Variety* put it, "Each of the cornfed entertainers felt he had been taking a cut by coming into New York. They declared that they could go out on one-night stands and clean up considerably more."

That was pretty much true. The Opry, and country music, didn't need New York or Hollywood to be successful. By the early 1950s, most of the major music recording labels had offices and studios in Nashville, NBC was planning on adding some live televised programming of the Opry to its still-popular Saturday-night radio show, and a small independent production company was filming Opry stars in color for short features that played in the nation's theaters.* For Minnie

* It was a quirk of *Opry* culture that these films did better *outside* of the South and Midwest because

216

personally, opportunities continued to abound. She was signed by RCA Victor for a series of 45 rpm records, about half of which were duets with the comic banjo player Grandpa Jones (none sold particularly well, and the deal dissolved after its initial three-year term). She released a book of stories about Grinder's Switch, *Minnie Pearl's Diary.* She grew so famous that she was feted on *This Is Your Life,* the popular TV show that surprised celebrity guests by walking them through their lives via unannounced appearances by people dear to them; Minnie's mother, Fanny, her four sisters, and friends from Centerville, Ward-Belmont, and the Opry all showed up at NBC's Burbank studios for the charming episode.

All of the financial successes of Minnie's career allowed her and Henry to buy a series of increasingly grand homes in and around Nashville. (They would not, despite both their hopes, fill it with children. Without ever getting into details, Minnie would later state, quite plainly, that they were unable to conceive and that they chose — again, with no

---

people in those regions had so many opportunities to see the same entertainers in person, whether in venues near their homes or by driving to Nashville (the *average* commute of *Opry* audience members was estimated to be 650 miles one-way).

explanation — not to adopt.) The first was a relatively modest affair right in town, but after a few flush years they moved into the tony Brentwood community just outside the city limits, buying a home next door to the official mansion of the governor of Tennessee, who, regardless of political party, was always invited to dinner at the Cannons' and given permission to use their tennis court.* The house became famous. Several times a week, buses that drove tourists around to see the homes of their favorite Nashville musical stars would be greeted by Minnie — sometimes in stage garb, sometimes in civvies — who loved to give fans a personal thrill, as well as a glimpse of a way of life that in no way resembled that of Grinder's Switch.

And that, more or less, is how it went for fifteen or so years. Minnie appeared regularly on the Opry — the radio and television versions — and became perhaps *the* most commonly familiar face of what was becoming one of the great institutions of American popular culture. She made thousands of live appearances, including one, in 1959, at Madison Square Garden before an audience of Rotarians in New York for their annual

* The Cannons were conservative Republicans and, in time, on friendly terms with Richard Nixon and his attorney general, John Mitchell.

convention, and twice again — in 1961 and 1966 — at Carnegie Hall. Minnie released a couple more books and records, including straight-up comedy albums on a variety of small labels.* Minnie appeared in a few films, sometimes as herself, adding a bit of comedy to a country revue, and twice in proper roles: as the matriarch of a family involved in the titular scrap in 1965's *Forty Acre Feud,* and as a preacher trying to save the soul of a reckless young country singer in 1966's *That Tennessee Beat.*† Minnie appeared more frequently on noncountry television: alongside talk-show host Merv Griffin, on variety shows hosted by country singer Jimmy Dean, balladeer Steve Lawrence, trumpeter Al Hirt, and more. And Minnie (or, frequently, Sarah

* In 1966 she had a surprise hit with a one-off 45, "Giddy Up Go Answer," a semi-sung, rather melodramatic riposte to Red Sovine's hit truck-driving ballad of the previous year, "Giddy Up Go." It marked her only appearance on the *Billboard* country charts, hitting as high as number ten in its three-month run and finishing the year at number seventy-eight overall.

† The latter story echoed her real-life relationship with the doomed Hank Williams, who was often put in Minnie's care when they were on the road together and he was caught in the downward spiral of depression, alcohol, and pills that took his life in 1953.

Colley Cannon) participated in charitable works: the March of Dimes, cancer research, natural disaster relief, and many others, often as a performer, but equally often as an organizer and board member. (In 1965 she joined the Country Music Association board of directors, a position she would hold for many years, and then, a couple years later, the board of the Nashville chapter of the National Academy of Recording Arts and Sciences — the folks who gave out the Grammy Awards.)

She had so much going on, in fact, that she was suspended from the Opry for an entire year, 1965, because she had failed to make the minimum twenty-six appearances on the show in the previous twelve months. (She was permitted to use the name "Opry" in billing herself during her hiatus, which ended when she signed a new deal stipulating twenty appearances a year.) As if to acknowledge how essential she was to the Opry in particular and to the culture of country music in general, the business started showering her with accolades: In 1966, she was named — and this is absolutely true — *Man* of the Year at the Country Music Association awards show, which had never considered, apparently, the possibility that a woman could rise to the acme of that field of show business, or what to do in the event, suddenly before them, that one did.

In April 1967, Henry was flying them back to Nashville from a live appearance, as he had done thousands of times previously, having built one of the largest charter flight operations used by country performers and serving as Minnie's personal pilot for nearly twenty years. ("I'm the luckiest gal in show business," she often said. "I married my transportation.") On this flight, though, the plane lost all power some 180 miles east of Nashville, with no airport nearby, and started to glide inexorably downward. Henry, cool as could be, told his wife to strap herself in and brace herself, and he looked for a place to put the plane down. He spied a stretch of roadside field and bucking the plane upward to prevent the gas tanks from exploding, brought it to a crash landing from which, miraculously, they both walked away. He'd been flying for nearly thirty years and had never experienced such drama. After that, he vowed not only never to pilot a plane again — a vow he kept — but to sell off his charter airline business.

The combination of age, weariness of traveling, and that air crash combined to make Minnie seek other means of making money as she approached middle age. The late 1960s were a heyday of franchise businesses, particularly those with celebrity names attached. Comic movie star/director Jerry Lewis licensed his name to a chain of movie theaters, Nashville songwriter Roger Miller (who wrote the hobo-themed hit song "King of the Road") lent his name to a string of motels, and the varied likes of New York Jets quarterback Joe Namath, baseball hero Mickey Mantle, singing cowboy Roy Rogers, and English character actor Arthur Treacher were the featured faces for strings of singles bars, country-style buffets, roast-beef sandwich joints, and fish-and-chip shops, respectively. Based on the nationwide success of Harlan Sanders's Kentucky Fried Chicken franchise, a Tennessee consortium thought a Minnie Pearl fried-chicken chain could catch on. A group headed by Nashville lawyer (and recently failed Democratic gubernatorial candidate) John Jay Hooker Jr. approached the Cannons in 1967 with a proposal to launch Minnie Pearl's Chicken restaurants and Minnie Pearl's Roast Beef houses, starting with a few local outlets but selling franchise rights nationally.* The business built *fast:* as many as sixteen hundred franchise agreements were sold and signed in the first

* At the same time, Hooker and his associates were in business with gospel singer Mahalia Jackson to open a chain of Mahalia Jackson's Glori-Fried Chicken outlets that offered a variety of traditional Southern soul food staples in addition to the titular product.

year of operation. Model franchises opened in Knoxville and Nashville, complete with personal appearances by Minnie in full stage garb, and in May 1968, Minnie Pearl's Chicken System Inc. made its debut on the New York Stock Exchange, with shares selling for twenty dollars at the opening bell and closing that first day at forty-two dollars; soon, the price was forty-eight. In the coming year, large chunks of stock sold multiple times in deals valued from $5 million to $25 million.

It was a success, but there was a problem. Unlike Kentucky Fried Chicken, which expanded slowly based on an actual chicken recipe and the model of an actual functioning restaurant, Minnie Pearl's Fried Chicken was an idea without a foundation. Yes, Minnie cooked fried chicken for herself and Henry and guests at home, but she was never a professional chef or restaurateur, and Hooker and his firm had never operated eateries of *any* kind. Many of the franchisees, given only rough instruction in how to cook the food and how to manage their locations, failed to keep the doors open; many others never opened or served a single meal. (The roast beef spots came and went fastest, but those chicken franchisees who *did* launch had trouble with the recipe; a shareholders' meeting of a firm that invested in the operation was given over to a lengthy debate over how to improve the chicken batter.) The big profits that had lured large holding companies to invest in thousands of shares of Minnie Pearl's Chicken System had been generated not by sales of chicken or roast beef but by sales of *franchises*. "Pyramid scheme" is perhaps overstating the case, but it really did seem that there were more licenses sold than dinners.

At least that was how it looked to the U.S. Senate and the Security and Exchange Commission, both of which took special interest in John Jay Hooker's businesses. In the course of investigating the chain, investigators discovered that only *1 percent* of the company's income in its first phenomenal year was derived from actual food sales, the rest comprising franchise fees, promissory notes, and loans. Minnie herself was subpoenaed to appear before a Senate committee in January 1970, a deeply embarrassing situation for someone who had engendered such goodwill in her country-gal-with-a-heart-of-gold persona.* By the end of the year, the holding company that owned most of the stock in the

* Later, in less fraught circumstances, she would testify in front of congressional committees twice, once as a witness in favor of adding a division on folklife to the Smithsonian Museum and once in support of WSM's petition to retain its special license for nearly coast-to-coast radio transmission.

enterprise had written off almost $24 million of its $25 million investment and reported to its shareholders that the current value of its holdings in the Minnie Pearl Chicken System was *one dollar.* Some aggrieved franchisees filed lawsuits against Hooker, the corporate entities he ran, and Minnie herself, but they received no satisfaction. By 1971, the company and its few locations had vanished, and Minnie Pearl's name came, at least in financial circles, to be synonymous with starstruck, blind-faith investment in pie (or fried chicken) in the sky. The Cannons had other investments — including a string of more than a dozen southern-style cafeterias and holdings in Angus cattle — but none bore Minnie's name, a name she never again lent to anything other than her own work.

Fortunately, audiences didn't seem to hold this fiasco against her. Indeed, in at least one significant regard, she was better known — and better loved — than ever before. In 1968, she almost got her own CBS sitcom, but the pilot proved a dud. The following year, she was one of the featured performers on a new country-themed show on CBS television. Entitled *Hee Haw,* it was heavily influenced by *Rowan & Martin's Laugh-In,* a madcap comedy program that trafficked heavily in the hippyish energy of the moment. *Hee Haw* was built on a similar format of fast, almost slapstick comedy bits, heavily scripted, all with country themes and settings (well, patently fake soundstage country settings), and it added musical performances by its co-hosts, singer/ banjo player Roy Clark and singer/guitarist Buck Owens, as well as guest stars from the full gamut of country music. The show was scheduled as a summer replacement for *The Smothers Brothers Comedy Hour,* which had drawn network censors' ire for its explicit anti–Vietnam War pronouncements; a more explicitly antithetical embrace of old-fashioned values couldn't be imagined. A big part of that sense of tradition was embodied in the presence of Minnie, who joined the show on its second episode and immediately became a regular cast member.

CBS ran *Hee Haw* for two seasons, then let go of the show, which immediately found a home in first-run syndication, where it thrived, uninterrupted, until 1993, filming more than six hundred new episodes.* And Minnie appeared in more than one hundred seventy of them, sometimes telling jokes, often in sketches with her old Opry pal Grandpa Jones and other country comedy regulars such as Junior Samples and George "Goober" Lindsey.

The Minnie of *Hee Haw* was, more or less,

---

* In 1996, it was revived for a single, unsuccessful encore season.

the Minnie of the Opry: countrified, goofy, and libidinous. It didn't matter that her audience was by now aware that her actual life was different from that of the persona she wore onstage. She had created a character so beloved that her fans wanted it frozen in time, even as, in reality, the woman evolved and matured. Twenty years on, she could still tell jokes about being a man-crazy country gal. Talking about a visit to New York, she said, "A man come up to me with a gun and he says, 'Gimme your money.' I says, 'I haven't got no money.' And he frisks me up and down, and he says, 'You haven't got no money, do you?' And I says, 'No, but if you do that again I'll write you a check.' "

Hee Haw filmed its entire year's season in Nashville in two chunks of four to six weeks, leaving Minnie free to make her regular Opry appearances and allowing her to tour when she wished to. And, yes, she was still touring. She had branched out since the mid-sixties, playing more frequent dates in far-flung locales such as Las Vegas, Reno, and Southern California, where she appeared at both Disneyland and its rival theme park Knott's Berry Farm. She was seen more than ever on TV; Dean Martin, a son of Steubenville, Ohio, was a particular, if unlikely, fan, and she turned up on his variety show several times. She also visited Johnny Carson (six times), Merv Griffin (eighteen times), Mike

Douglas (twenty-two times), and Joey Bishop (twelve times), as well as turning up on such TV staples as *The Ed Sullivan Show, The Carol Burnett Show,* and variety shows hosted by musical stars such as Johnny Cash, Dinah Shore, Jim Nabors, and Glen Campbell.

She was still a regular at the Opry, and in March 1974 she was one of the stars of the final performance at the decrepit Ryman Auditorium in downtown Nashville and again the following night at the new Opryland theme park and theater (among the performers in that inaugural show was a soon-to-resign President Richard Nixon, who contributed a bit of piano playing).

She had done everything, it seemed, but one thing that had, painfully, eluded her: although she had been nominated for admission to the Country Music Hall of Fame annually since 1962, the first time *anyone* had been admitted, she was still not a member.[*] Every year without fail, Minnie sat at the Country Music Awards while some man — or several men — entered the Hall, applauding with a smile on her face and a sunken feeling in her heart. She tried to rationalize

[*] Notably, the members of the Hall were almost entirely men. The only women admitted in its first dozen years were singer Patsy Cline, posthumously, and country music pioneers Maybelle and Sarah Carter, as part of the entire Carter Family.

what felt like a snub: "I thought they were going to bypass comics," she said. "I suspected that it had to be confined to singers and people who were connected to the music end of it." In October 1975, almost thirty-five years exactly after her nervous debut on the Grand Ole Opry, she was, almost reluctantly, in the audience once again for the CMA Awards show, certain that she'd be overlooked one more time. Her old friend, singer Tennessee Ernie Ford, was enlisted with presenting the identity of that year's inductees, and it turned out that there was only one: Minnie Pearl. He said, in part, that "no one exemplifies the endearing values of pure country comedy more," and he called her "the first country music humorist to be known and loved worldwide." The honor, and the standing ovation, brought her to tears.

For another decade and a half, with less travel but no less sunshine or ditziness, Minnie did her thing. She regularly appeared on cable TV's Nashville Network, where she had a long-running stint reading jokes submitted by viewers and choosing a favorite from among them. In 1979, she had a proper acting role (well, proper-ish), playing opposite Arthur Godfrey on an episode of *Love Boat;* for a time, she was the host of an annual country Christmas TV special. She popped up on seemingly every country-themed TV special or tribute show or awards program or, especially, telethon or fundraising event. In honor of her reliable and constant willingness to do charitable works, the Nashville Network initiated an annual award for community service by making her its first recipient and naming it for her, the Minnie Pearl Award. There was also a Minnie Pearl Parkway, a stretch of highway in her native Hickman County, where Grinder's Switch, still an actual railroad switch off an unpaved road, drew so many tourists that local officials removed all signs pointing to the place. In 1980, her next-door neighbor, Tennessee governor Lamar Alexander, declared October to be "Minnie Pearl Month," which was marked by a proclamation, a celebratory gala, and the release of a song, "Pearl at the Opry," by bluegrass singer Bob Wickline.

She still toured, though nothing like the way she used to: fewer and larger shows each year, on the bill with new generations of country stars who grew up on her comedy and were bigger (and wealthier) than anybody in the old Opry had ever imagined was possible. She appeared on a bill headlined by Kenny Rogers at the Silverdome in Pontiac, Michigan, in front of sixty-five thousand fans, and she played Major League Baseball stadiums in the South, Midwest, and Texas with Barbara Mandrell.

Her health became an issue. In her sixties,

she had taken ill a couple of times with what was deemed "exhaustion." In 1985, she was diagnosed with breast cancer and underwent two separate mastectomy operations, a few months apart; afterward, she became an outspoken proponent of regular mammograms for women, something that was considered too private to discuss by many people in her world (including, as it happened, her husband), but which she felt was vitally important. She eventually agreed to give her name to the Minnie Pearl Cancer Foundation.[*]

In 1989, she fell in her home and suffered a knock on the head, requiring a hospital stay of several days. In 1991, she signed on to do a ten-city large-arena tour of Opry stars headlined by Garth Brooks[†] and Ricky Skaggs, but that June she had a stroke and she was unable to fulfill her contract. The following year, to mark her eightieth birthday, the Nashville Network mounted a TV salute to her studded with stars from all the years of her half-century career. That summer, President George H. W. Bush, a bona fide

---

[*] With a similar instinct for helping those in need, she was one of very few country stars to appear at and lend her name to fundraisers for AIDS patients in the 1980s.

[†] Brooks's daughter, Taylor Mayne Pearl, was partly named for Minnie.

country music fan, awarded her a National Medal of the Arts, the nation's highest civilian honor for entertainers and artists; her class of co-honorees included blue-grass banjoist Earl Scruggs, actor James Earl Jones, operatic soprano Marilyn Horne, and film director Robert Wise.* Again, her lingering poor health prevented her from attending; Henry accepted the award in his wife's stead. Two years after that, she was enshrined in the National Country Hall of Fame.

In February 1996, at age eighty-four, she suffered the first of a series of strokes that put her in the hospital and culminated in her death in early March. Her funeral near her Nashville home was attended by a pantheon of country stars: Vince Gill, Wynona Judd, Reba McEntire, Hank Williams Jr., Chet Atkins, Ricky Skaggs, Garth Brooks, and Barbara Mandrell among them. There were performances by singers Amy Grant and Connie Smith, followed by a private burial service in Franklin, the town where her parents had met almost exactly a century prior. Some twenty months later, Henry, her

---

* Another would-be honoree, Broadway composer Stephen Sondheim, refused to accept an award from Bush and would wait several years before being given a medal by a president he preferred.

husband of just shy of fifty years, passed as well and was buried alongside her.

The Ryman Auditorium, where Minnie Pearl entertained for more than thirty years, fell into disrepair after the Opry moved to Opryland, and it was nearly twenty years before the country music community and the citizens of Nashville joined forces and resources to restore it. In 1994 it reopened, more beautifully appointed than it had been even back in its maiden days as a magnificent house of worship. It had, in fact, become a kind of secular temple, and in its new state, it was graced with reminders of its long history and the performers who had made it so special — its saints, in effect. Two of them in particular were canonized in bronze in the lobby, seated on one of the sanctuary's original pews, captured in animated, amiable conversation: Roy Acuff, the King of Country Music, and Minnie Pearl, his costar and friend of decades.[*]

Being cast in bronze was a fitting tribute, especially to Minnie, as she was, and would remain, singular in the world of country music and the world of comedy. There have always been country musicians with comic aspects to their personalities, from Uncle

[*] And, of course, an employee whom he once had to fire.

Dave Macon to Dolly Parton. But there has never been another country comedian, much less a *woman* country comedian, to rival Minnie in recognition or longevity. She almost never played an instrument, at least not seriously, and she rarely sang, and even more rarely without trying for a laugh. But for more than fifty years, with her corny humor, her never-changing costume, and her genuine love of her audience, she more or less *was* country music. Her father had told Sarah Ophelia Cannon that she might be able to do something with her Minnie Pearl character if she kept it kind. She did just that, and she did it in such a way that anyone who ever saw her could feel in their bones. For Minnie, comedy was community — yes, a community that she teased and mocked, but never, per her father's advice, without love, without the sympathetic eye of an insider, without the approval of the people who were the butt of her jokes *and* her best audience. And, really, you can't get more country than that.

FOUR:
THE BAWDS

I ain't afraid of anybody stealing my jokes:
Where are they gonna use 'em?
— BELLE BARTH, 1969

Back when only a handful of women felt
empowered to stand before a microphone
and tell jokes, a clutch of them indulged in
scatological humor coated with a veneer of
song. Some were bona fide musicians —
lounge pianists and singers who could belt
out standards if they wished but fared better
when they got a little rude or even downright
profane. They weren't many in number, and
they tended to appear in out-of-the-way
saloons and show rooms in certain big cities
and, especially, on the edges of resort towns.
In the late 1950s, a couple of new wrinkles in
traditional show business made it possible for
them to have bigger careers: the rise of
disruptive — aka "sick" — comedy, and the
advent of the so-called party record, which
allowed audiences to hear dirty jokes at home
while giving them the sensation of being in a

boozy, raucous club where anything went. It was a brief window, open only for the decade or so when something like an underground culture for adults could swim alongside family-centered entertainment. And in that window, a group of rowdy, saucy, bawdy women broke down barriers in comedy, even as they brought undeserved scorn and even legal peril upon themselves.

In November 1910, the rising vaudeville star Sophie Tucker performed a novelty tune called "The Angle-Worm Wiggle" onstage at the Pantages Theater in Portland, Oregon. Tucker, a robust twenty-four-year-old, born in Ukraine as Sofia Kalish and raised in Boston and Connecticut, had been singing professionally for about three years and was making a name for herself as a singer of suggestive songs, a lusty girl who enjoyed sex and wasn't shy about sharing the fact of her appetite.

For "The Angle-Worm Wiggle," Sophie wore four rings set with bright-green stones that would "glitter as I used my hands snakily up and down my body as I sang, producing, as I hoped, a naughty effect."

During the matinee performance on November 3, the desired effect was achieved, especially in the eyes of Lola Baldwin, one of the first policewomen anywhere in the United States, then serving as Portland's Superintendent of the Department of Safety for Young Women. Declaring the performance to be "the most loud and offensive" she had ever witnessed, she filed a criminal complaint against Tucker and the theater manager for "committing an act which grossly disturbed the public peace and grossly outraged the public decency." Policemen attending the evening show were not nearly as inflamed by the song as Mrs. Baldwin had been, according to the *Morning Oregonian,* which reported that the officers applauded the number along with the audience. Nevertheless, they arrested Tucker after the curtain fell.

Posting fifty dollars in bail, Tucker was permitted to take the stage again pending further inquiry. At the next day's matinee, she sang "The Angle-Worm Wiggle" once again, this time with Chief of Police A. M. Cox himself in the audience. After the show, Cox informed management that he would allow the show to go on as he had seen it, so outraging Mrs. Baldwin that she went to the office of Mayor Joseph Simon to file a second set of charges.

Tucker was delighted by the brouhaha, holding court with the press in the theater lobby. "I intend to fight the thing to the finish," she declared. "If Mrs. Baldwin thinks that by taking the bread out of my mouth and those whom I support, my mother and sister and brother, she is 'doing good,' she has a mistaken idea of what 'doing good' means." After a few more days of back-and-forth in the newspapers, District Attorney George James Cameron threw the entire matter out of court, upbraiding Mrs. Baldwin for making a frivolous complaint in the bargain.

"I was left sitting on top of the world," recalled Tucker, "with pages and pages of publicity and a line at the box office three blocks long."

For decades, Tucker would delight in such provocations, billing herself as "The Last of the Red Hot Mamas," singing suggestive lyrics, engaging in ribald repartee with her longtime accompanist, Ted Shapiro, and altogether turning on its head any and all stereotypes of large and, later, aging women as lacking in libido or in sexual opportunity. She always defended herself by insisting that her material wasn't about vice (that is, crime or immorality) but about sex (that is, love and fun). "I've never sung a single song in my whole life on purpose to shock anyone," she said. "My 'hot numbers' are all, if you will notice, written about something that is real in the lives of millions of people."

She was famous for spouting such apothegms as "I've noticed one thing, girls. You can store this in your dome: All the married men who run after me have skinny wives at home"; "Laugh, and the whole world laughs with you. Weep, and you sleep alone"; and

"From birth to 18, a girl needs good parents. From 18 to 35, she needs good looks. From 35 to 55, good personality. From 55 on, she needs good cash. I'm saving my money."

Whether or not Tucker was the last of anything was a matter of debate.[*] But she would turn out to be the *first* of a line of women who made their way as comic actresses and singing comediennes who pushed the edges of propriety with declarations of their sexual selves, even when, as in her case, the body in which that sexuality was carried didn't fit the beauty norms of the day. It was a remarkably empowered persona, not only rejecting the received notion that a woman couldn't claim desire and libido for her own but asserting that she would not let societal standards of attractiveness constrain her to a life without sex. Indeed, in word and manner Tucker embodied the notion that a big, beautiful woman offered more fun and pleasure to men than the slender girls who were

[*] In 1970, in the Continental Baths, a gay steamroom/bar/nightclub in the Ansonia Hotel on the Upper West Side of Manhattan, Bette Midler, who had spent three years on Broadway in *Fiddler on the Roof,* began to present a singing act that was laced with risqué song parodies and dirty jokes that she attributed to "Soph" but were far more the province of other women who took inspiration from Tucker.

held up as the ideal.

Sophie did have a significant contemporary, Mae West, the Brooklyn-born vaudevillian turned Broadway and movie star who was decades ahead of her time not only in declaring her sexual appetites but in writing and staging successful entertainments about them. She was born Mary West in 1893 and entered show biz before her teens. From her earliest days in vaudeville, where she was a renowned dancer of the provocative Shimmy, West trafficked in the risqué, a tendency that reached its apogee with the 1926 hit play *Sex,* which she wrote and starred in. Even though the show enjoyed almost four hundred performances, West was arrested and convicted on morals charges for her part in it and spent ten days in jail (wearing, she bragged, silk panties rather than the burlap undergarments that her fellow inmates sported). Her subsequent Broadway productions — *The Drag, The Wicked Age, The Pleasure Man, The Constant Sinner,* and *Diamond Lil* — cemented her in the public imagination as a woman of licentious appetites, and as soon as the movies could talk, Hollywood came calling for her.

West was never, exactly, a comedian, but her one-liners — "I used to be Snow White, but I drifted"; "Marriage is a great institution, but I'm not ready for an institution"; "You only live once, but if you do it right, once is enough"; "Too much of a good thing can be taxing" — had a pop and verve that indicate that she could have made a go at stand-up.

At any rate, there were a few other women willing to follow the template of gal-being-bawdy that Tucker and West introduced into popular culture and turn it into neither songs nor theater but something very like stand-up comedy.

The Pottymouth

Belle Barth could have been the picture of the stereotypical Jewish grandmother if it weren't for the things she said.

She looked the part: plump and frocked and bejeweled and made up and, we might imagine, fragrant. She was born in New York, she spoke fluent Yiddish, she summered in the Catskills and wintered in Florida, she had a big, wheezy laugh and a yippy little lapdog. She never had any children of her own, despite being five times married, but one look at her and you could well imagine her holding court in a living room decorated in old-world kitsch, doting on family members, enjoying family gossip, overseeing a big meal. If you ever had a glitzy, bubbly, extroverted great-aunt who hugged and squeezed you too eagerly and crowded you a little too much, that was Belle Barth.

But, in fact, Belle Barth was a performer with a career that, at its height, was built on shocking audiences with jokes and language that could make a mafioso wince. She took Sophie Tucker's brassy persona and amplified its grace into gonzo and its innuendo into, well, *out*-uendo (a joke she no doubt would have adored and expanded — lovingly and crudely). In her prime, Belle was downright notorious, getting arrested and fined for public indecency regularly at a time when the future First Amendment martyr Lenny Bruce was still striving to make a career out of coloring between the lines as a Borscht Belt comic.[*]

In 1953, she was brought before the Florida State Beverage Department, which oversaw nightclubs, and was warned about the contents of her show at the Good Hotel's Music Box room in Miami, an act that, per *Variety,* was composed of "special material with ad libs on the uninhibited side." She promised to behave, but a few weeks later agents of the department returned to the club, recorded

* Note should be made of Bruce's mother, Sally Marr, born Sadie Kitchenberg, a sometime comedian/emcee on the vaudeville, burlesque, and Borscht Belt circuits whose greatest claim to fame was discovering and nurturing younger acts — her son, of course, as well as Cheech and Chong and Sam Kinison.

her "lewd" act, and fined her and the club owner twenty-five dollars each.

Two years later, she was performing at the Sky Lounge in Philadelphia when she and her then husband, David Thorne, were arrested, along with the club owners, by no less than future Philly mayor Frank Rizzo, then a police captain, who hauled them in for "staging an obscene show."

In January 1961, while she was free on bail of $525 for "presenting a lewd show" at the Cloisters nightclub in West Hollywood, Los Angeles County sheriff's officers raided a warehouse where thirty-five hundred record albums of her act (as well as those of fellow potty-mouths B. S. Pully and Pearl Williams) were seized.

Later that year, she was packing audiences into Le Bistro in Atlantic City when local authorities hauled her and the club owner in front of the Alcoholic Beverage Control Board after its agents attended a show at which they witnessed "lewdness and immoral activity and foul, filthy, and obscene language and conduct in that a female performed for the entertainment of customers and patrons in a lewd, indecent, and immoral manner."

In December 1962, she was arrested in Buffalo for "tossing off cracks in her act that were 'downright filthy,' " per *Variety.* Out on bail, she told the press that she was forty-nine years old (she was actually fifty-one), that her real name was Annabelle Martin, and that "if it's breaking the law to make people laugh, then I'm guilty."

The acme of her career affronting public morals came when she was sued by two schoolteachers for $1.6 million for the "grievous mortification and mental anguish" they suffered from exposure to her act during a vacation to Florida; like most of the charges against her, the suit was summarily tossed.

What in the world could the plump little lady with the teased-up hair and the twinkling eyes have done or said to provoke such an onslaught of legal scrutiny? She sang, often adding profane twists to the lyrics of popular tunes; she engaged with her audiences, often on the basis of what she surmised to be their sexual habits; and she told jokes — which she labeled as "risqué" but which, truly, were filthy, especially for their time. "I give the people what they want, nice, dirty stories," she regularly said. In a typical show, she spritzed her act with such lines as:

"I eat lettuce. I figure if you eat like a rabbit . . ."

"I always say the most difficult thing for a woman to do is to act naive on the first night of her second marriage. She hollers 'It hurts,' and he's gotta tie his feet to the end of the bed, he shouldn't fall in and drown."

"What I got to eat you don't need teeth for."

"I'm sixty-five, I'm fat, and I can still take five guys a night. I pay them now, but that's okay."

"You ever hear about the girl who couldn't join a key club cause she didn't have a key so she joined a country club?"

"One prostitute talking to another prostitute says, 'I made a hundred dollars last night.' She says 'Gross?' And she says, 'No, Schwartz.'"

With one major exception, Belle Barth never played the big rooms. She was strictly a saloon performer, playing in front of rowdy audiences whose responses to her outrageous bits were an essential element of the fun. She thrived in vacation spots — not in luxury hotels or fancy show rooms, but in slightly shady spots down the road — and she appeared not in the dinner hour or even in the late show, but in the *after*-after hours, often winding up her last set as the sun rose. Another singer of ribald songs, Rusty Warren, recalled of Barth's long-running stint in Las Vegas in the sixties, "She worked at four o'clock. . . . the late, late, late shift." She was strictly for the party animals, the true night owls, the people out for a toot after tucking the kids and the squares into bed. In a culture that encouraged buttoned-down thinking and mass conformity, she was like a pressure valve, giving ordinary folks a chance to indulge their inner hedonists for the length of a nightclub show or, later, an LP record.

Belle Barth, future scourge of scolds, was born Annabelle Saltzman in New York City on April 27, 1911, the youngest of a brood of seven (or nine, depending on the source) born to a shopkeeper and his wife. Raised in East Harlem, she attended Julia Richman High School on Second Avenue before dropping out as an adolescent to hit the stage, belting out popular songs of the day, in English and Yiddish, in the full-throttle manner of Sophie Tucker, frequently accompanying herself on the piano. She found work in vaudeville and on the Borscht Belt circuit, and by the late 1940s, with almost twenty years' experience, began to appear as a featured act — with some indications that she had already begun to push the limits of generally accepted taste. Through the late forties and early fifties, she ventured as far as the Midwest, but she was most popular in the resorts around the Catskills, the Jersey Shore, and South Florida, especially Fort Lauderdale and Miami, where she was a sufficient draw as early as 1953 to have a regular nightspot named for her, one of several over the years.

By then, as her impressive rap sheet demonstrates, she had abandoned all pretense of propriety and had gone, as they said in the business, "blue" — that is, she was telling jokes about sex and booze and using profanity, often in Yiddish, throughout her act. Well, Belle proved a blue Belle indeed. Her arrests and fines tell the story of someone intent on pushing her act and her name to a certain level of notoriety. There had always been comic performers whose material skirted the edges of decorum for the sake of shock or recognition or even, it could be said, free speech, ranging from red hot mamas such as Sophie Tucker and Mae West to intellectual bohemians such as Dwight Fiske and Ruth Wallis, to raunchy burlesque-house comedians such as B. S. Pully. In the segregated world of Black comedy (less observed and, therefore, less policed by guardians of public decency), the likes of Redd Foxx, Pigmeat Markham, and even Moms Mabley were toying with the boundaries of obscenity, if they didn't plain burst through them. And an underground of new, freethinking comedians, with the famed free-speech martyr Lenny Bruce in the vanguard, was emerging in bohemian nightclubs and coffeehouses.

But even amid that impressive company, Belle stood out for a number of reasons. For one, she was a straight pianist and singer who could have, reviewers frequently noted, worked without the blue stuff and continued to enjoy a modest career. On the more outrageous end of her act, she covered some of Ruth Wallis's naughty ditties but also composed her own innuendo-laden material, frequently variations on popular and folk tunes. When she wasn't playing music, she told jokes (often with the most vulgar parts in Yiddish, perhaps in an attempt to slip them by censors) and bantered mockingly with her audience, making her act more like stand-up than straight singing, even comedic singing. And, of course, she was a white woman, unlike the majority of the other comics doing risqué material (and, for that matter, an avowedly Jewish white woman, at a time when most Jewish entertainers bleached their ethnic identities). She out-ribalded Sophie Tucker, she worked dirtier than Jean Carroll ever dreamed of, and she could play places that would never have welcomed Moms Mabley. It was a narrow niche, but it was hers.

After several years of pushing proprieties aside, Belle wasn't getting rich — earning perhaps $700 for a week's engagement[*] when the top acts were being paid tens of thousands — but she had an enthusiastic little cult, especially in her home base of Miami Beach, where a show room at the Saxony Hotel was

* Approximately $6,300 in 2022.

renamed Belle Barth's Pub and she held sway for several months on the trot each year. It was in that room in 1959, when she was nearly fifty years old and a forty-year veteran of the business, that Belle Barth's career finally took off. Under contract to the almost anonymous After Hours Records, she recorded several nights of her shows for a party record for the adult market.

It wouldn't be an exaggeration to say that After Hours more or less existed as a vehicle for Barth and her act. The label was run by a veteran music industry pro named Stanley Borden, who had founded Unique Records in the early fifties. After a few years, he sold the label to film and TV studio RKO and stayed on as general manager of what had become the music division of an entertainment conglomerate. But he went out on his own in the late fifties and got into the party record racket under the After Hours label, which he ran out of an office near Times Square. In addition to Barth, After Hours recorded Pearl Williams, another foul-mouthed mama of a certain age, and the similarly profanity-prone likes of B. S. Pully and the young Nipsy Russell.

The live recordings put out by After Hours and other party record labels were rudimentary from a quality standpoint. There was no apparent effort taken to ensure good acoustics in the clubs — the sounds of clattering barware and waitresses making the rounds were frequently evident — and the tracks lacked the shape and definition that were marks of professionalism on mainstream comedy records. But rather than prove detrimental, these crudenesses gave party records a you-are-there feel that made them truly suitable for playing at home during your own parties. They were designed not so much to be listened to as to provide ambience, to get the party started by priming the pump with the sound of *another* party that was apparently in full swing.

The recordings weren't entirely slapdash. As Borden explained, "You have to record the comic or comedienne fully enough so that you can substitute acceptable lines for the blue lines that the comic might use in the night club act. This takes considerable time and trouble, but it is the only way to make a suggestive record with taste." And, he insisted, the rawness of the in situ recordings was essential to their appeal: "You have to record it live with honest laughter, or else it falls flat on its face. Audience laughter gives enough time for a gag to get across. If you do the recording without an audience it's too tough to know how long to pause between gags." (Not taking chances, he had engineers cut out Belle's most incendiary profanities and sweeten the mix with bits of canned laughter; on some After Hours recordings, the same exact laughs could be heard repeated again and again after punch lines.)

This wasn't exactly production board magic, but it was effective, especially in the case of Belle's debut record, *If I Embarrass You, Tell Your Friends*. Released in 1960 at something like the high-water mark of the comedy record boom, the album consisted of two tracks of about twenty minutes each: side one labeled "Midnight Show," and side two labeled "4 A.M. Show" — a winking promise that the *really* dirty bits would be found there.

She began each track singing, with tremendous vigor, a takeoff on the old barroom standard "The Darktown Strutter's Ball":

I'm gonna line 100 men up
Against the wall
I bet 100 dollars
I can bang them all.
I banged about 98;
I thought my back would break.
I went around the corner, got an oyster
stew.
Came back, banged the other two.

And so on. She told her dirty jokes. Delicately fingering the piano, she mocked her age: "This box is older than mine!" She teased the audience during lulls in the laughter: "This is such a dignified group, I'm gonna commit suicide." She acknowledged

251

her reputation as a libertine: "How bad can I be? I'm on the Beach ten years and I only got two suspended sentences." And she admitted that her act was based on shocking the crowd: "I know clean stories. I don't make money with 'em, but I know 'em."

Obviously, it couldn't be played on the radio, nor was it intended to be. And the record stores that were willing to carry it usually didn't display it openly among the other comedy and novelty LPs. It was sold under the counter, or in shops in red-light districts that catered to the dirty magazine crowd. It was, as the 1961 warehouse raid in Los Angeles and an explicit ban on its sale by the Manhattan district attorney's office made clear, contraband. *Hit* contraband, to be sure. It would be hard to prove exact numbers given the ephemeral nature of After Hours. In fact, *Billboard* couldn't use its normal system to determine exactly how many records the label sold; as a result, its albums weren't included in the magazine's sales charts. But *Billboard* did make an educated guess in late 1961 that *If I Embarrass You* had sold seven hundred thousand copies — a massive hit. And the follow-up LP, *My Next Story Is a Little Risque,* had moved two hundred thousand units within just a few months of its 1961 release.

Borden was naturally delighted with these sales figures, especially since, as he conceded,

Barth's records had to be sold "through word of mouth." (He also noted that Barth and Pearl Williams outsold the male acts he'd recorded: "Women telling suggestive stories sell better than men doing the same thing," he told *Billboard*.) But the success drew a lot of the wrong sorts of attention. District attorneys in a number of jurisdictions actively snuffed out sales of party records, and crusading newspaper editors and district attorneys made examples of retailers and distributors, raiding stores and warehouses, confiscating LPs, and running multipart investigatory exposés that would even be entered in full in the *Congressional Record*.

Stanley Borden and After Hours responded to this legal onslaught by getting out of the party record business altogether. After Hours never released another record after 1962, and under a new label Borden switched over to instrumentals with a bump-and-grind aesthetic (the likes of *Music to Strip By* and *Music to Make Love By* among them). By 1963, he was focused on producing and importing nudie films and so-called mondo movies like *Around the World with Nothing On, Primitive Love,* and *It's a Sick, Sick, Sick World.*

Belle, however, continued along in her chosen style. Indeed, she was a rising star, making her way into classier spots at a reported salary of $3,500 a week, five times the price she commanded prior to *If I Embar-*

rass You. In March 1961, she was booked at Manhattan's Roundtable nightclub on Second Avenue and Fiftieth Street, her first New York City performance in some ten years. Barth did publicity, joking (or was she?) that she had always imagined she'd grow up to be a schoolteacher. The advance sales were so strong that her initial three-week run was extended to six.

And for their money, customers got Belle Barth declawed.

With her album banned outright and representatives of the district attorney's office keeping an eye on her, Belle played nice. She brought along her Miami-based lawyer Shirley Wolfe and sat her right up front on opening night so as to check whether or not telling a certain gag would constitute crossing the line. Under such scrutiny, Belle stayed clean, a spectacle which nobody in the crowd had come to see. Instead, they were offered "an expurgated edition of Belle Barth," according to *Variety,* which noted that "the audience reaction . . . was far from enthusiastic." She was visibly unnerved by the shackles and the tepid response. As the review noted, "A staid Belle Barth is an uncomfortable one. There were occasional hints of naughtiness and a forlorn plea . . . 'Can I tell a dirty joke?' " But she never crossed the line, "to the disappointment of a packed house."

The combination of a high-profile gig and

a verbal straitjacket seemed to have confounded her, and she could tell that she was squandering her shot. After the first show, Barth, Wolfe, and Roundtable management huddled to discuss how much they could unleash her for the late show, and there were indications that she loosened up as the engagement went on, but it wasn't by much. A reviewer for *Billboard,* catching the act later in the week, found it "Snow-Whiteish" and said "you could bring your 13-year-old daughter and not worry about Belle making her blush." A month later, *Variety* was back, and noted that Belle "took off many of the wraps, although its understood that she's keeping herself sufficiently in check to satisfy the State Liquor Authority and the Police Department." Business didn't suffer much; the club booked her for a four-week return engagement the following November. But her reputation for fearless ribaldry took a bit of a hit.

The acme of Belle's fame came in November 1961, when she performed at the classiest joint she'd ever grace: Carnegie Hall. Tickets for her midnight performance ran a spendy \$4.50[*] — a buck more than she'd ever commanded (a price that didn't, as in a nightclub, include drinks). Roulette Records, a legitimate label that had recently signed her

[*] Approximately \$39.50 in 2022 terms.

and recorded her at the Roundtable as the centerpiece of Laughtime, a new subsidiary devoted to comedy, planned to capture the night for a future release.

More than twenty-three hundred people were in attendance, and, just as earlier that year, they got a self-censored and even disgruntled Belle, who had apparently reached an accord with the auditorium's managers to skirt her spiciest material and seemed both resigned to and resentful of it. She did what she could do as a straight performer: her Sophie Tucker–inspired renditions of standards, a sing-and-clap-along version of "Hava Nagila," even a novelty number built around the Twist, the nation's top pop-music craze — an "embarrassing" bit, according to *Variety*. Naturally, the crowd expected more, and when it became clear that they weren't going to get it, they grew restless. "Open up!" came a shout from the audience, to which Belle replied, "Shut up!" Calming herself a bit, she explained, "This is Carnegie Hall, and you gotta have a little class." But, of course, nobody had come to see class, and there were walkouts as the show progressed.

What was meant to be a triumph turned out a catastrophe: "Miss Barth is not only kidding herself by putting on this sort of show," *Variety* concluded, "she's kidding her audience." Other comedians, even truly profane ones, would play Carnegie Hall in the coming years — Lenny Bruce, Moms Mabley, Godfrey Cambridge, Allan Sherman — and when the show-biz trades wrote about their shows, they always used Belle's high-profile flop as a comparison: a famously easy-to-leap low bar. She had faced the spotlight and blinked, and the arbiters of taste would not let her forget it.

The pattern became clear: When she did her usual act outside the most visible venues (and, in particular, outside of Manhattan), she found appreciative audiences. When she played the top rooms, she risked prosecution. And when there was big money on the table, she got nervous and reined herself in. South Florida continued to be good to her — one of her frequent refrains when she was performing elsewhere and curtailing her vocabulary was "I don't tell it that way in Miami Beach." And, naturally, Las Vegas eventually summoned her, surprisingly late in her career. She made her debut at the New Frontier in March 1963, appearing in a jam-packed room that had been expanded to accommodate demand for tickets even though she was playing three shows a night. A cadre of vice squad officers, sheriff's deputies, and gaming commissioners were at the first performance and, satisfied that she was behaving, left her to her devices. As a result, *Variety* said, "Her second show was spicier, and the third bawdier than the second." Eventually the authorities chose to ignore her altogether, and she settled into the groove that audiences recognized from her records and, indeed, had come out to enjoy. In time, the New Frontier renamed its show room the Belle Barth Room,* and she became one of the toasts of the Strip. At the end of April, she celebrated her birthday by racing from her final show, which ended at around 4 a.m., to the Sahara, where she joined Louis Prima on stage at *his* show, and then she rolled on to the Thunderbird, where the Dukes of Dixieland were still playing, and she threw herself into their act as well.

She had to rely on touring for her livelihood because somewhere in shuffling through labels and corporate entities, Stanley Borden and After Hours had failed to pay her royalties on her two hit records and Roulette/ Laughtime had released only the one recording from the Roundtable and failed to follow up other contractual obligations. In a lawsuit filed in February 1963, Belle's representatives claimed that they had never seen a sales sheet from either record label and estimated damages at a minimum of $10,000. (If she'd been with a regular company, even with a crummy deal, she would have made *a lot*

---

* Not, of course, to be confused with Miami's Belle Barth *Pub.*

more than that.)

She needed the money more than ever. The same editions of the trade papers that reported on the lawsuit she filed carried news of a lawsuit she had *lost*. A year previously, representatives of a variety of music publishers, the firms which owned the rights to the world's best-known popular songs, had banded together to sue Belle, Pearl Williams, Stanley Borden, After Hours, the companies that pressed and distributed their records, and the retailers that sold them for using twenty-one of their titles for indecent parodies without obtaining permission or making proper royalty payments. The plaintiffs had asked upward of one dollar per record sold — which could come to millions — even as Belle was claiming she hadn't received any royalties on any of them. It would be another five years before a settlement was reached.

Fortunately, even though she had peaked, she could still work regularly. There seemed to be a limit to her career, but there seemed as well to be a vigor to it. She continued to draw crowds in Miami Beach, in the rowdier clubs in Atlantic City, Philadelphia, and the Catskills, and, of course, in Las Vegas, where she entered into a long-term contract to appear in the lounge at Caesar's Palace soon after the casino opened in 1966. And her records — both reissues and new releases — continued to find audiences on a string of small labels: Riot, Laff, Laughtime, LOBO, and Ember.

She had, in fact, become something of a legend. Some of the most famous faces in show business began showing up to catch her at her most uninhibited; in one memorable spree, Frank Sinatra and Sammy Davis Jr. attended her late show in Miami, then went out drinking with her and ended up at a porno theater, where the owner screened a film for them and allowed them to dub their own dialogue and sound effects over it. She wasn't officially one of the boys; several accounts of Friars roasts at the time include references to jokes *about* Belle Barth, but she was never invited to participate or even to attend the events.[*] That last slight wasn't necessarily personal — it would still be years before women were admitted to the club or permitted to attend most of its functions. But there was a thick streak of hypocrisy in the spectacle of a bunch of men who had no qualms about using profanity in all-male company mocking a woman who dared traffic in that same sort of raunch. Belle's language per se wasn't beneath them — indeed, they reveled in it. It was she herself — a

[*] At one Friars event, Jack E. Leonard, spying Jean Carroll seated beside her husband, commented that he was pleased to see "Buddy Howe and his beautiful wife, Belle Barth."

woman who spoke the same words and told the same jokes — whom they disdained. She was, in a sense, no different to them than a sex worker — and even more laughable, in their obnoxious arithmetic, for being a matronly woman.

Belle understood very clearly where she stood in the comedy world and how narrow her lane was in it. She knew she was never going to be on Ed Sullivan or Johnny Carson, nor would she ever be a heartland darling like Rusty Warren, a younger, more conventionally attractive woman who did a similar act of raunchy singing but who kept it just clean enough to scandalize the squares and *not* draw legal scrutiny. Warren, it happened, was Jewish (her given name was Ilene Goldman), but unlike Barth and Williams, she used no Yiddish in her act and was no doubt taken by audiences for a Gentile. Belle used to call her "the Jewish shiksa" and was usually collegial toward her, but not always: in one club appearance in Pittsburgh, Belle apparently directed her "one unkind and tasteless remark" of the night toward Warren, who outsold her on vinyl and in nightclubs and whose record labels dealt with her on the up-and-up.

By 1966, popular culture had become permissive enough to give Belle another look on a prominent stage. In New York City, in particular, authorities had come to accept a certain amount of profanity in nightclubs, and she was booked at the Basin Street East on Lexington Avenue in midtown for ten nights. Perhaps because she still felt the sting from her previous gigs in the city, she played nice, and the gig wasn't a success. "Miss Barth is very much under wraps," lamented *Variety.* "There were some suggestive passages and gestures, but nothing compared to what has been her trademark." And then the reviewer got downright dismissive: "Let's face it — she's not a straight singer who can justify a $3 couvert [*sic*]. She has a rep for being a dirty diva, and that's what they come to hear. Anything else she dishes up is a disappointment."

The whole trip proved a similarly mixed blessing. While she was at the Basin Street she made one of her very rare television appearances, on Merv Griffin's syndicated talk show. This would normally be a big opportunity, but her episode aired directly opposite the broadcast of the Academy Awards, typically the most-watched TV program of the year. Even her big breaks seemed destined to fail.

She continued to tour her circuit of East Coast resorts and the Las Vegas Strip. During the Republican National Convention of 1968, her long-running engagement at the Eden Roc Hotel in Miami Beach did turn-away business. In late 1969 she toyed with the possibility of returning to Manhattan and opening a room of her own, an annex of the Roundtable; she did a few shows at Rodney Dangerfield's newly opened comedy club in a trial run. But nothing came of the talk, and the following June, while performing at Caesar's Palace, she took ill and returned to her Miami Beach home. In February 1971, two months shy of her 60th birthday, she died of cancer.

In her day, she had been notorious. Law enforcement officials and district attorneys awaited her visits to their towns with handcuffs and subpoenas at the ready, the most daring record retailers couldn't keep her work in stock, A-list comedians could get a laugh just by dropping her name, and literally hundreds of thousands of American homes had copies of her albums. But by the time of her passing, she had become a marginal figure. The culture had grown comfortable with what had previously been considered obscenity: movies and pop music spoke openly of sex and drugs, underground (and some aboveground) literature used profanity freely, and the likes of George Carlin and Richard Pryor were selling millions of records on national record labels with language and subject matter far more coarse and explicit than anything Belle had ever said. In time, she became a footnote to entertainment history, kept alive chiefly in the memories of the countless baby boomers who grew up learning dirty jokes from her records, which they'd snuck from their parents' collections and absorbed, snickering, in their bedrooms.

Belle Barth was the most famous of the bawds who followed the model loosely established by Sophie Tucker, but there were a number of similarly frisky comedians who aspired to her renown, one of whom truly rivaled Belle Barth in renown and longevity, if not quite notoriety, arrests, or, alas, record sales.

Pearl Williams was born Pearl Woolfe in New York City in 1914, and at least briefly attended Seward Park High School near her family's Lower East Side home, half a dozen miles from where Barth grew up. By 1940, she had been active as a singer in the belt-'em-out Sophie Tucker mode for at least a decade and had acquired a reputation for "spice-filled specialties" and "smutty songs."

Pearl was featured regularly at nightclubs and piano bars in Philadelphia, Atlantic City, and the resort clusters of the Catskill Mountains and the Jersey Shore, a plump, small woman who literally sat on telephone books on the piano bench and could sing credibly well in between the endless waves of blue stuff. She was plugging along on her circuit of nightspots when she was swept into the party record business by Stanley Borden and After Hours, who released her debut LP, *A Trip Around the World Is Not a Cruise,* in 1961. It sold well, if not as well as Belle Barth's albums, but it did enable her to record again, for Borden's other label, Surprise, and for such small outfits as Laff, Avan-Guard [*sic*], and Riot, which released two LPs that consisted of a side of Belle Barth and a side of Williams: *Battle of the Mothers* and *Return Battle of the Mothers.*

If it was a battle to see who could flaunt conventional decency most egregiously, Pearl would've won handily, at least based on the surviving recordings. She sang less, she used less Yiddish to hide her profanities, and she employed more one-liners than jokes:

"Definition of 'indecent': if it's long enough and hard enough and in far enough, it's 'indecent.' "

"Two broads are walking past a beauty parlor and one of them says, 'Gee, I think I smell hair burning,' and the other one says, 'Maybe we're walking a little too fast.' "

"A whore goes to a bank to change a $20 bill, and the teller says, 'Miss, this is counterfeit,' and she says, 'My god! I've been raped!' "

"You hear about the absent-minded mounted policeman? He jumped off his whistle and blew his horse."

"By the sea, by the sea, by the c-u-n-t."

"You hear about the guy who bought his wife a gold diaphragm? He wanted to know how it feels to come into money."

"Definition of a happy Roman: glad he ate her."

"Honey, I got no talent. I got guts: big balls."

On the basis of LPs filled with this sort of thing, in late 1961, Pearl followed Belle Barth into the Roundtable nightclub on Manhattan's Upper East Side, where she performed in front of a microphone like a stand-up and, under threat of the sort of police action that kept hounding Belle, kept her act mostly clean. Reviewing her opening, *Billboard* noted that "she was nervous, the audience was nervous, and every time the door opened, both she and the audience looked as though they were expecting visitors." Her albums were confiscated in the Los Angeles sheriff's raid of After Hours's Southern California warehouse, and the profanity in her act was cited as the cause when an Atlantic City nightclub where she performed had its liquor license reviewed. But she was never arrested, and she never became a synonym for "dirty jokes" as Belle Barth did.

In 1963, she ventured west, debuting at the Castaways hotel and casino on the Las Vegas Strip, and she let loose with what *Variety* called "some of the bluest dialog ever heard in Vegas. Some of the lines seemed to shock even the jaded musicians." But, again, where Belle Barth's shows were under the scrutiny of local authorities, Williams, following in her more celebrated colleague's wake, seemed immune to their attentions.

She returned to Vegas a few times over the coming years, but her spiritual home was back east: Philadelphia, Baltimore, Atlantic City, the Catskills, and, especially, again, Miami Beach, where she was a staple. Billed as "America's Uncultured Pearl," and dismissed by *Time* magazine as "a road company Sophie Tucker," she eventually found a permanent home, the Place Pigalle, a Miami Beach strip joint that offered some straight entertainment — lounge singers and risque comedians, mainly — along with the girls. Pearl performed there on and off for eighteen years, for multiple long-term engagements per year, finally retiring from the stage in 1983 at age sixty-nine, with more than forty-five years as a performer behind her.

She apparently never married. Rather, her family was, truly, the circle of troupers who kept the nightspots of South Florida kicking in the years when Miami Beach and Fort Lauderdale went into decline, before the Art Deco district of the former was revived into an internationally celebrated party strip. In 1987, she was celebrated at a formal gala as one of the region's "Golden Girls," a remarkable honor for someone who was best known for a vocabulary that could make a Las Vegas lounge musician blush. Four years later, she died of heart failure at her home, relegated to a paragraph-length obituary in *Variety,* her years as an obscene firebrand reduced to a quaint note in the history of a culture that had virtually erased the old-fashioned lines of decency she had once pushed against.

The Liberator

At the end of 1962, as was customary, *Billboard,* the journalistic bible of the music business, published its list of the top ten bestselling albums of the concluding year. In those pre-Beatles years, very little in the way of pop music ever appeared on those annual lists. In fact, the majority of the nation's most popular LPs were the soundtracks of musicals from the stage and screen and live recordings of comedians. In 1962, the sole item that could be considered pop or youth oriented was *Your Twist Party* by Chubby Checker and *maybe,* if you had a dated idea of youth appeal, the soundtrack to Elvis Presley's film *Blue Hawaii*. Otherwise, it was movie music (the soundtracks of *West Side Story* and *Breakfast at Tiffany's*), music from Broadway shows (*West Side Story* again), a concert record (*Judy at Carnegie Hall*), and a jazz record (*Time Out* by Dave Brubeck). Of special note that December were three titles that had also appeared in the year-end top-ten list the *previous* year: the original cast recordings of two Broadway hits, *Camelot* and *The Sound of Music;* and an album that had made headlines for being declared obscene and confiscated by Los Angeles County sheriff's officers in the raid of a warehouse: *Knockers Up!* by a singing comedian named Rusty Warren.

To reiterate: for two years running, Americans collectively coughed up significant sums of money to own recordings of a nightclub performance filled with double entendres about bosoms, penises, and sex acts. Even more amazingly, *Knockers Up!* was only one of *three* albums Rusty Warren had on the charts in 1961, along with *Songs for Sinners* and *Sinsational* (a fourth, *Rusty Warren Bounces Back,* her fourth LP, was released at the end of November, too late to make an impact in that year's sales tally). In less than two years, she had sold more than two million albums. Based on raw sales, Rusty was more or less in a league with such superstars as Frank Sinatra, Ray Charles, and Elvis Presley.

Of them all, Rusty's achievement was the most remarkable because, unlike her peers in that heady list, she sold all those records without benefit of radio play or television appearances, both of which were denied her because of the perceived naughtiness of her work (reviewing *Bounces Back, Variety* primly declared, "It should . . . be kept beyond the reach of the young and the sensitive"). She was a word-of-mouth sensation, a tireless touring entertainer whose doggedness and brazenness turned her into a big star not only despite but *because of* her reputation for trafficking in obscenity.

Warren, of course, was not the only woman who performed a singing-joking act laced with suggestiveness. But she was kind of a clean-dirty performer, speaking in an elevated, cultured accent, stringing along stories for five minutes or more so that when she got to the punch lines they felt like crescendos rather than firecrackers, singing and playing the piano with appreciable talent, aiming her wit at the idea of empowering the women in the audience, and almost always planting herself on the merely ribald side of obscenity. "We all did totally different things," she said years on in comparing herself to her more foul-mouthed peers. "While I talked about *sex,* they talked about *the act.* Pearl [Williams] would talk about how big his thing was. . . . Oy vey! I could no more do that than stand on my head. My stuff was for Mr. and Mrs. America. But women didn't discuss sex onstage then. My attitude was, What do you mean, women don't like sex? We liked it, we should talk about it." And so she did, to acclaim — if not notoriety — and fortune.

Rusty was born in New York City too, on March 30, 1930, making her at least fifteen years the junior of her fellow bawds, and adopted by Herbert and Helen Goldman, who named her Ilene and raised her in suburban normalcy in Milton, Massachusetts. One of the few things that the Goldmans knew about their daughter's biological parents was that her father was apparently a musician, and so they thought to encourage her along those lines. By the time she was six, she was playing the piano, and she continued to take lessons throughout high school, after which she enrolled in the New England Conservatory of Music, where she began by studying classical piano and was once among a score of pianists at the Tanglewood music festival performing a salute to Chopin under the baton of none other than Boston Pops maestro Arthur Fiedler.[*] In

[*] Eventually, her papers and ephemera found a home in the school's library.

time, Rusty switched from the school's classical program to its popular-music track and began to sing along to her own playing. By 1954, she had left the Conservatory and begun a career as a cocktail pianist, using a newly chosen stage name ("Rusty" being a nod to her naturally red hair; "Warren" for the street on which she was raised) and getting gigs through sheer moxie — walking into piano bars and nightclubs and hotel lounges and asking management if she could perhaps audition. Being musically accomplished *and* conventionally attractive, with a genuinely sunny disposition, she was able to secure work playing and singing standards in various venues in the Northeast, Midwest, Florida, even Los Angeles.

Her mind was too active to be content with just playing, so she began to fill the time between songs. "Something didn't satisfy me about just sitting at the piano," she recalled, "so I started talking." Audiences responded to her amusing patter, and she found that she could mix her musicality and her innate funny bone even further if she performed takeoffs on popular tunes. "One of my bosses asked me if I knew any parodies," she said. "He also said that he would give me more money if I would sing them along with my regular songs I started to buy them from places in New York that used to sell them by the page."

The combination of straight singing, parodies, and cheeky chatter brought her even more success and, more importantly, a proper manager. She had heard of a fellow named Stanford Zucker who steered the careers of several bands, singers, comedians, and lounge pianists. She wrote to him, and he agreed to catch her act in St. Louis. "I was scared the night he was going to come in," she remembered. "A little guy . . . very dapper. He sat and watched it and thought it was great. He said maybe he could do something for me the next time I came to the West Coast. Stop by his office." She did, and he signed her right up: "He had pictures made and I was with him until the day he died."[*]

Zucker was, in fact, able to get her quality bookings as promised. Soon after, she was working at the famed Crescendo nightclub on Sunset Boulevard, a spot operated by jazz and comedy connoisseur Gene Norman, who also ran a record label under the Crescendo name. Norman noted that audiences seemed to like Rusty's patter even more than her singing and playing. In the midst of the comedy boom that had made stars of Crescendo regulars Mort Sahl and Shelley Berman, he thought she could expand her ap-

[*] Which was, for the record, at age ninety-five in 1998, making theirs a collaboration of more than forty years.

peal if she emphasized the humor in her act over the music. As she recalled, he told her, "You're going to have to get up from behind that piano. The people by the doorway, they can't see you sitting down.' "

She was, by her own admission, "scared to death. Back then, that was my crutch: Banging the piano." But she adapted. Eventually, she became so adjusted to performing comedy that she hired a piano player and sometimes a drummer and bassist, working from the front of the stage in something more like a stand-up comedian's posture. But that was still to come. In the meantime, she was still a pianist/comedian who could amuse audiences with song parodies and slightly risqué banter.

Whatever she was doing, it wasn't highly polished. In its "New Acts" column in early 1959, *Variety* caught her at one of her mainstays, the Beach Club Hotel in Fort Lauderdale ("Fort Liquordale," she called it), and while the reviewer made note of the long run of big, appreciative crowds, he didn't join them in savoring the show: "Miss Warren has only lately switched to the raw and raucous. . . . Her approach to the whole man-and-woman business is as direct as a sidewalk hawker's bark, her repartee a monument to the lack of innuendo." The *Fort Lauderdale News* wasn't much more enthusiastic: "She leaves absolutely nothing to the imagination.

We enjoy some clever double entendre once in a while, but how single-entendre can you get?"

She trusted her instincts, though, and she had even had an encounter with a mentor, of a sort, to confirm them. Earlier that winter, she was playing at one of her regular stops, the Pomp Room outside of Phoenix, when one of her heroes entered her life, briefly but significantly. Sophie Tucker was in town, and a mutual acquaintance offered to take Rusty to the grand dame's hotel and effect an introduction. "She asked me to have lunch at her hotel," Rusty recalled, and Sophie, informed that Rusty regularly sang one of her signature tunes, "Life Begins at Forty," asked, "Why would I ever do that song when I was 24 years old? She also told me to be honest with my audiences, as they will know if you're lying, because audiences are smarter than you think they are, and they'll catch you on it every time."

And there was another bit of advice. Sophie taught Rusty to build an audience in advance of arriving in a town by sending postcards to the people who'd seen her there on her previous visits. Rusty started to follow suit, and her fan base grew. Eventually, she could get booked into a place like the Pomp Room for upwards of twenty weeks at a go if she wished,[*] avoiding the grind of the road but still playing before packed, eager houses.

During such a residency, Stan Zucker convinced Jerry Blaine of Jubilee Records to catch her at the Pomp Room, where she was billed as "The 'IT' girl of Phoenix . . . singing and playing those saucy songs and parodies . . . that will keep you in an uproar" and where, for a fee of $225 a week[†] (plus tips), she played four shows a night — hourly starting at nine p.m. — to turn-away business.

Blaine, a former bandleader and singer, had been running Jubilee for more than a decade and was known to take chances on new sounds and material. He got a load of how crowds responded to Rusty and knew he had something he could work with. His crew set up recording equipment in a storage room and taped several of her weekend shows, capturing the sound of Rusty in the wild, "complete," she told a newspaper at the time, "with spontaneous applause and customers' remarks." He recorded and released an edit of them the following year as *Songs for Sinners*. At a time when comedy records were selling big, the record did nicely. But nobody

[*] And, being as she bought a home near Phoenix, she apparently *did* wish.

[†] Approximately $2,000 in 2022.

— not Blaine, not Zucker, not Warren —
imagined what would follow.

It started in Dayton, Ohio, at Mike Longo's
Supper Club. Warren had long been aware
that although men appreciated the candor
and "naughtiness" of her act, the women in
her audiences seemed particularly energized,
as if being in the presence of another woman
who spoke openly about sexual pleasure allowed them to acknowledge their own desire.
During one evening's set, she began to pound
out a march on her piano, and she encouraged the women in the audience to stand up
and parade around the room while she
improvised a kind of talking-singing tune on
the spot, a number that became famous as
"Knockers Up!" Rusty began declaiming over
the beat, "Come on there, girls! Throw those
shoulders back, and get your knockers up!
Put a smile on the world's face! There we go.
Doesn't that make your navel tingle? I bet
when you go home you'll march right through
your living rooms!"

The "Knockers Up!" marching bit became
a set piece of her act, and she applied some
of the old Sophie Tucker magic to what she
was doing, creating a Knockers Up Club and
selling memberships that included official
certificates and pins. Soon the club's members began showing up at her shows literally
by the busload, housewives from small towns

making their way en masse to big-city clubs to revel with their new ringleader. Jerry Blaine sent out a recording team to capture her act for a follow-up to *Songs for Sinners,* and when he heard what was happening in those clubs he knew he had something sensational on his hands. In fact, he was going to name the next LP for the bawdy little novelty track that had launched all that enthusiasm: *Knockers Up!* As Rusty recalled, "They said, 'You wouldn't dare! How are you going to sell it? Where are you going to put it? No one is going to take it. Jerry says, 'Watch me.' "

It's worth noting that Jerry Blaine would go down in history most famously for his role in the record business payola scandals of the late fifties and early sixties. Jubilee was one of the labels caught paying disc jockeys and record retailers to favor their artists on the air and in stores in violation of broadcast and trade regulations. Be that as it may, his corrupt dealings with disc jockeys didn't affect sales of Rusty's albums, if only because her material couldn't have been played on the radio in the early 1960s even if Blaine had been willing to bribe people. But she definitely benefited from his relationships with retailers, who put her albums in the comedy section of their stores rather than hide them behind the counter along with records by Belle Barth and Pearl Williams.

Rusty was cleaner than those artists by a

discernible margin. "I didn't talk dirty," she remembered. "I was a lady and looked it, with the clothes and all. I said 'damn' and something — 'knockers' I'd say. But I never said 'f.' There were males who did that. . . . But I didn't." Her recorded act bore out her claims: she was *naughty,* yes, but never *profane.* "They talk about me and they whisper about me and they go right home and try it all out," she said of her audience, adding, "I only *talk* about things you *do* all the time!"

That narrow space in which she worked, the space between sex and vice, between innuendo and expletive, between PG-13 and R, was a gold mine. *Knockers Up!* debuted on the *Billboard* LP chart at number thirty on November 6, 1960. It stayed on the chart, uninterrupted, for all of 1961, becoming the number-six overall bestseller for the year, as it did for 1962, when it ended that year at number nine overall. In total, the album was on the chart for 181 consecutive weeks, selling well over two million copies. By the end of 1962, Warren's five LPs (the first pair were followed by *Sinsational, Rusty Warren Bounces Back,* and *Rusty Warren in Orbit*) had sold more than four million copies altogether.

Jubilee was, naturally, exultant. And Rusty was rich. Not only was she earning royalties on all those sales, she was touring constantly — as much as she cared to, and her weekly rate had skyrocketed from a couple of hundred dollars a week to a reported $7,500.[*] In 1962 alone, *Variety* made note of her appearances in Phoenix, West Hollywood, Atlanta, Pittsburgh, Minneapolis, Chicago, Milwaukee, Cincinnati, and Greensboro, North Carolina — and that was merely where they showed up to review her. She was such a strong attraction that clubs *near* where she was appearing would suffer dips in business and have to scramble for customers while she was in town. When she was performing in Dallas, Jacob Rubenstein, who owned a nightclub down the block from where she was playing, cheekily put a sign in his window that read

NOW APPEARING
on record
RUSTY WARREN

(Under his professional name — Jack Ruby — he would later become famous for something other than his sense of showmanship.)

Nobly, Rusty remained extremely loyal to the spots that had gambled on her when she wasn't a hit. Club owners like Mike Longo and his peers at the Pomp Room and certain niteries in Indianapolis and Anaheim got her at the old price, at her insistence, even when Stan Zucker told her she could charge them

* More than $65,000 in 2022 terms.

more. She could afford that sort of magnanimity, though, because, in a cunning bit of business, Zucker had, when drawing up a contract with Jubilee, included a clause that retained Rusty's ownership of the master recordings of her performances, meaning that, in time, she would own 100 percent of her own hit material. She couldn't be heard on the radio, she almost never showed up on television (and *never* on prime-time national shows), she even suffered the indignity of having a warehouse full of her records confiscated by Los Angeles law enforcement officers for their alleged obscenity in early 1961,[*] but for all that she was, going by sheer ticket and album sales, the most popular female comedian in the business. At the end of 1962, in the annual poll of the National Association of Record Merchandisers, she was named America's top comedy star.

For the audiences who flocked to see her, Rusty was clearly filling some sort of need: frank talk about sex and romance and marriage from the point of view of an unabashed woman. She recognized that the people who were coming to her shows were ordinary folks seeking a bit of release, and she saw that she

[*] Along, of course, with records by Belle Barth and Pearl Williams: many virginal ears were spared by that famous raid.

sold the most tickets in "any place that had a drinking crowd of fun-loving people. Resorts and places that had a large suburban population." Her act, she reckoned, danced expertly on the fine line between bawdiness and obscenity; her audiences could tear loose for a bit but never had to feel unclean or embarrassed. She was bringing taboo subjects into the open with a bit of fun, and the people who flocked to her shows and bought her records were evidence that she was fulfilling a need.

For some, though, her frankness was completely unacceptable, the crowds she drew deplorable. *Time* magazine decided to weigh in on the "Knockers Up!" phenomenon in a scathing, unsigned article under the headline "Barnyard Girl." It is, from the start, an absolute paradigm of condescension:

> Comedians often specialize. Some toy with national politics, others with the race problem. Rusty Warren's field is sexual intercourse. A squarely constructed red-headed woman in her middle 30s, with the hoarse voice and hearty manner of a call-house madam, she talks about sex in clear, unsubtle terms. Her joke vocabulary is full of colons and ova. . . . She is just another dirty comedian who deprives sex of all its grace and sophistication, while she claims

282

to be helping inhibited females to enjoy themselves.

And as for those females (that is, her loyal audiences), "Like Rusty, they all seem at home in a barnyard. They sit there and roar happily."

Rusty, having anticipated the *Time* article as a career booster, felt sandbagged and despondent upon reading it. "I could hardly believe it. . . . It implied that my audience was stupid. . . . I was in shock and cried for days," she recalled. "I yelled at my press agent and fired my public relations firm. I was so young . . . and so unprepared for an attack like this by the press, especially in light of the way my career was soaring." In time, though, she realized that the sneering article wasn't an attack on her but rather on the liberty and consciousness represented by her act and her fans' appreciation of it. "A woman doing material that was breaking down barriers and talking about sex was fair game for every reporter who had a typewriter. . . . I learned a valuable lesson when the *Time* article broke: Toughen up and learn to tune it out or get out of the business."*

* She needed tough skin. In 1964, a columnist in the *Chicago Tribune* declared hers "the dullest show thru [*sic*] which we ever struggled to keep our eyes

Throughout this time, Rusty remained un-married and childless; no matter how willing she was to speak about sex, she was unwilling and unable to tell the world that her prefer-ence was for women. And the combination of her frank talk, her physical charm, and her apparent rootlessness and availability made her something of a target for doggish men, particularly those in the business who might have been accustomed to getting sexual favors from women in exchange for career opportunities. In Fort Lauderdale, as the club was closing, a drunk from the audience ap-proached her, grabbed her breasts, and hissed, "Are these the things you've been talk-ing about?," only to find himself knocked to the floor and kicked in the balls. In Omaha, a club manager came upon her backstage and exposed himself, only to be rebuffed by her quick stage patter: "I said, 'What? Are you gonna do something with *that*? It's ridiculous looking.' His whole thing went flat again. It was over. . . . I started being Rusty and tried to get him with the jokes. I said, 'Am I going to get out of here or am I going to have to fight my way out?' He said, 'Ah, you're not

open. . . . She makes sex as appetizing as dish water heavily laced with rat poison."

worth it.' I said, 'Really, I'm not.' "

Even Jerry Blaine, her record label boss, had a go at her, with similar results. On the night she accepted the 1962 NARM award, "We stayed over at Jerry's suite," she remembered, "and he comes walking into the bedroom. . . . He says, 'You mind if I flop down here?' 'Yeah, whatever'. . . . I didn't pay any attention to him. He just laid there, and all of a sudden he says, 'Why don't we. . . . We're here, aren't we?'. . . . I turned over and looked at him, and I said, 'Do you really want to fuck up a million dollars for a lousy twenty minutes?' Well, he said, 'Ah, I guess not.' 'Yeah,' I said, 'put it down.' "

Perhaps because of the loosey-goosey nature of her shows, there were a curious number of violent and near-violent incidents at her performances. In Anaheim, she was making jokes about married couples when a man going through a divorce rushed the stage and someone shouted that he had a gun. In Detroit, she made a crack about the new cars that were being made, and a guy who had lost his job at Ford threw a glass at the stage, hitting her drummer. The wildest melee around one of her shows occurred at the Surf Club in Revere Beach, Massachusetts, a spot she visited every summer. One night during her July 1963 stand at the club, the owner was shot twice in the chest by a man who'd been able to rush the entrance because the front door had literally been torn off its hinges by crowds trying to get into the show. While this bloody fracas was aroar at the entrance to the club, Rusty carried on with her show inside; the crowd was so caught up in it that nobody was aware what was going on out front.

Sex, money, violence: it was only a matter of time before Las Vegas came calling for her. Rusty debuted as a headliner at the Dunes in late 1963. She made a new base for herself in the desert gambling mecca, buying a house there. After that, she spent about half the year on the road and half in Vegas, where she signed a long-term contract at the Aladdin, and the party seemed never to stop.

Jubilee kept the records coming: *Banned in Boston?*[*] (1963), *Sex-X-Ponent* (1964), *More Knockers Up!* (1965), *Rusty Rides Again* (1967), and a double dose in 1969: *Look What I Got for You* and *Bottoms Up.* The first of these were, like their successors, big sellers — all went gold — and Jubilee was so pleased that they even acceded to her request that they release an LP with straight singing, *Rusty Warren Sings Portrait on Life,* in 1964.

But 1964 was also the last year that any of these records wound up in the *Billboard*

---

[*] Illustrated, by the way, with images of crowds lined up outside the Surf Club in Revere Beach, where, as in Boston, she was never banned.

album charts. Like so many grown-up entertainers of the era, Rusty was a casualty of the youthquake occasioned by the arrival of the Beatles on American shores. People seemed to go overnight from buying comedy records to buying pop albums. And along with the cultural revolution, there was a sexual revolution in progress everywhere; performers who had once seemed risqué and naughty now gave off an unappealing scent of daintiness or lechery. "Knockers Up!" and "Bounce Your Boobies" may have been a hoot if you were a middle-aged housewife of the Kennedy era; if you were a bra-burning feminist of just a few years later, they seemed haplessly retrogressive.

This metamorphosis didn't kill off Rusty's career: she was still packing them in wherever she went and in her long-running home stands in Vegas. But it did mean that she had plateaued. The Knockers Up brigade was still a phenomenon, but it had crested with its heroine just shy of true stardom. Rusty would always have a place to play in Fort Lauderdale, Phoenix, Palm Springs, or Revere Beach, but the clubs were still only clubs; in Vegas she could appear for weeks, months, at the Aladdin (and, after a few years, the Riviera), but it was always in the *lounge,* not in the main show room. When the *New York Times* interviewed her during her run at the Latin Quarter in 1968 (they assumed it was her local debut, though she had played several Manhattan gigs over the years), she confessed that, in comparison to what was going on in the culture (the partially nude musical *Hair* was a smash hit on Broadway), she felt like she was "becoming a nun in my business."

Still and all, she was recognized by her peers as a professional and as a pioneer, particularly in Las Vegas. Fellow comedians and singers, especially women, would frequently pop over after their own shows to see her perform: Angela Lansbury, Totie Fields, Joan Rivers, Liza Minnelli, Pearl Bailey, Eydie Gormé, Belle Barth. Sometimes they would meet up for a drink and talk shop, trading tips and pointers, developing real friendships. "Joan Rivers was always nice to me," Rusty recalled of her Vegas residencies. "Phyllis Diller gave me her house when she was gone. I was there three times a year, and she let me use it. Totie Fields, she was younger. Her house was nearby. She'd come round." Indeed, Rusty had developed a habit of leaving her last show of the night, which might end around three or four in the morning, and heading to a nearby equestrian center, where she would take a sunrise ride; Totie felt close enough to her to ask her to mentor one of her own daughters in the sport.

She especially remembered going on a toot with Phyllis Diller in Chicago when they both happened to be performing there and they learned about an after-hours drag bar hosting a show in which performers imitated both of them.

The one who did Phyllis was, like, six-feet-tall and black. He did Phyllis with the wig and the gown and the screaming and cigarette. The whole nine yards. You know what Phyllis did? She had this full-length chinchilla coat, the most gorgeous coat. She takes the coat — and, you know, Phyllis likes to nip a bit — she took the coat and she threw it on the stage. The guy died! He took that coat and whipped that thing around him. Phyllis was broad shouldered. This guy wasn't particularly feminine; he was big, he was tall. . . . My guy was a short guy with a lot of balloons for boobs, and he did "Bounce Your Boobies" or one of those numbers. He loved it. All I could throw up was a white mink with a kelly-cream lining that said "Rusty Warren" on it.[*]

[*] This wasn't the last impression of herself Rusty would see, or the best known. In 1981, on the immortal SCTV, Catherine O'Hara put on a red wig and created a character named Dusty Towne, a brassy, not-quite-potty-mouthed nightclub singer hosting her own "Sexy Holiday Special" — a clear homage to Rusty.

Phyllis, of course, was a big star of movies and TV and the largest show rooms by then, and she could afford to toss furs around. But Rusty, to her good fortune, had been well protected by Stan Zucker throughout her career. The constant touring with little overhead, the ongoing sale of "Knockers Up!" merchandise (bar towels, mugs, shot glasses), and, of course, the record sales — it added up substantially. As the owner of all of her recordings, she was in a position to demand large royalty percentages, which brought in lots of money, and Zucker had her invest in some pretty savvy properties: shopping centers, office complexes, even cattle. She was among a group of show folk, including Barbra Streisand and Charlton Heston, who made tidy sums in (but of course) the bull semen market.

She supported herself in grand style, and she even made some news when burglars struck her Las Vegas home in late 1969 and made off with upwards of $100,000 in furs, jewels, and Christmas presents.[†] In 1971, when Jubilee Records went out of business, she retained outright ownership of her recordings and licensed them to Crescendo/GNP, the record label run by Gene Norman, the club owner who had years before insisted she get out from behind the piano and embrace the comedic aspects of her act. (She

[†] Approximately $710,000 in 2022.

was forever loyal to the folks who had helped her in her early days.) They continued to sell, mainly at her shows, which she performed in her usual haunts throughout the seventies and eighties. After appearing at an Atlantic City casino in 1990, she retired from show business at the relatively young age of sixty. She eventually moved from Las Vegas and bought homes in Southern California and Maui, becoming a lady of leisure, riding horses, golfing, swimming, playing tennis, traveling, spending her life beside a longtime companion, a woman whose existence she never revealed to her public.

She was happy to speak with the occasional journalist or fan who looked her up, posing for pictures, having a laugh, always signing autographs with her catchphrase, "Knockers Up!" — still the life of the party long after the party had ended. In time, her health and her financial resources waned. In 2019, a crowdfunding appeal appeared on Facebook, seeking to raise $27,500 to help defray her steep medical expenses. She lasted another two years, passing away in May 2021, in Orange County, California. Waiting for her back home, in a cemetery outside of Boston, in a neatly tended patch beside the graves of Herbert and Helen Goldman, a tombstone sat in the grass reading:

BELOVED DAUGHTER
ILENE F GOLDMAN
"RUSTY WARREN"

She would come home at last, having gone off in the world and made her mark, however improbably, however long ago.

Mr. Moms: Jackie Mabley flaunting her style, early 1930s. *(Author's collection)*

The old philosopher: Moms Mabley as the wider world came to know her. *(Photofest)*

Hattie Noel: The woman who did it all, some of it quite shocking. *(Author's collection)*

The elegant, witty, and overlooked Jean Carroll at the height of her career. *(Photofest)*

"Nobody likes us but the people": Minnie Pearl onstage at the Grand Ole Opry. *(Photofest)*

Sophie Tucker, the first and the last of the "Red Hot Mamas." *(Photofest)*

The very blue
Belle Barth, banging
one out. *(Photofest)*

Rusty Warren, who
coined the catchphrase
"Knockers Up" and
called herself a "sexual
philosopher." *(Photofest)*

Phyllis Diller, before she electrocuted her hair but after she adopted her singular, electric persona. *(Photofest)*

At her dilliest: Phyllis Diller in the green dress she wore while touring Vietnam in 1966. *(Photofest)*

Generous to
everyone but herself:
Jorie Remus.
(Author's collection)

Elaine May,
pioneer of improv
comedy, brilliant
to the point of
being resented.
(Photofest)

Mary Elizabeth Doyle and Hershey Horowitz, aka Anne Meara and Jerry Stiller. *(Photofest)*

"I'm Perfect": Totie Fields, determined to be a star. *(Photofest)*

Before and after
The Tonight Show:
Joan Rivers as a
wayward bride in a
staple bit and, just
a few years later, as a
full-fledged star and a
real-life wife. *(Photofest)*

FIVE:
THE POSITIVE THINKER

Being a woman, right away you walk out to almost total rejection. Almost nobody wants you to be a female comic, and they give you a lot of static just because of your sex. . . . Men have this silly, witchy, witch-crafty attitude that a woman who is a comic has lost her femininity. . . . I still had to go through the onus of that even though I was never unfeminine, because I'm a feminine person.

— 1968

When stand-up comedy got its first woman superstar, it was someone who, like many of her predecessors, presented herself as something other than show-biz feminine. Dressed in garish stagewear that at once embraced and parodied modern fashion, with hair like a cartoon character who's stuck a fork in an electrical outlet, her voice a cackle, her demeanor manic, her patter a firehose, she seemed a creature from another dimension. But her subject matter — her deficiencies as

293

a sex object and a homemaker; her husband's sloth and stupidity; the ghastliness of her in-laws; and the foibles of modern life, from the headlines in newspapers to the hemlines of skirts — made her both an ordinary woman and a comedian of the moment.

Yes, Phyllis Diller resembled the most famous male comedy stars in being able to rattle off perhaps ten or so jokes a minute (like Jean Carroll, she timed herself with a stopwatch), to build a set of five or twenty-five or fifty-five minutes out of carefully crafted one-liners and jokes and whole paragraphs, to create a comic character that was so distinct from an ordinary human being as to be something of a punch line (or calling card) in itself.

But she was also, more or less, exactly who she said she was: a suburban mother of five, married to a man ill-suited to family life, surviving on her wits and guts and charm, and, believe it or not, actually named Phyllis Diller. What was more, she had talents that she had to keep hidden until her career was fully established: she was a conservatory-trained classical pianist; she could legitimately sing; she was a gifted amateur painter; and she was an avowed acolyte of a philosophy of self-belief and personal growth that derived from the great American tradition of making something of yourself on the strength of your own determined willpower.

When she started out, she was well into her thirties and working in a chichi nightclub in San Francisco, unaware, almost certainly, of the likes of Moms Mabley, Jean Carroll, Minnie Pearl, and Belle Barth. When she finished, some five decades later, she was an icon, known to and beloved by millions. And all because she believed she could do it.

By her own account, Phyllis Diller should not have existed. In late 1916, Frances Driver (nee Romsche) of Lima, Ohio, age thirty-eight, went to see her doctor about some abdominal discomfort she was experiencing. Frances had been wed for eight years to Perry Driver, a local insurance salesman seventeen years her senior, and their marriage was childless. There seems never to have been any thought of starting a family: Frances suffered from rheumatoid arthritis, and Perry (the eleventh of twelve siblings) was so old that he had a brother who'd fought in the Civil War. When Frances's doctor began exploratory surgery for what he suspected might be an ovarian tumor, however, the couple's lives changed. The doctor left the operating room to tell Perry that his wife was pregnant, eliciting the reply "Leave it in!" The following summer, on July 17, the couple's only child, Phyllis Ada, was born — on a floor spread with newspapers, as she later told it, in the family home.

Being the only child of an older couple was a strange birthright. Phyllis had no built-in playmates — no siblings or cousins her own age — and so she found most of her socializing spent among old people (she joked that she spent more time at funerals than playgrounds). Many of her earliest memories involved following Frances around as she performed the labors expected of an ordinary housewife of the 1920s: cooking, cleaning, sewing (she made her own dresses and her daughter's as well), and, when the family repaired to a farm that they owned near town, rudimentary but necessary chores around the property. "She seemed to do the work of three people," Phyllis remembered. "She did her own housework, helped my dad in his business, worked for the church — and she always seemed to be running."

The farm was a getaway, even a folly. Most of the time, the Drivers lived right in the center of town, in an apartment that also housed Perry's insurance office and allowed Frances to serve as his secretary alongside her household chores. Frances could be gruff — Phyllis remembered that she answered the phone with the abrupt salutation "State your business!" — but she had a playful side. She loved music ("She even played the piano with those crippled hands," her daughter recalled), and she occasionally appeared in amateur theatricals around town. She encouraged creativity in her child: by six, Phyllis was taking piano and singing lessons (adding saxophone a few years later). Practicing her scales, she imagined herself on a stage in front of a grand piano, being adored by a theater full of people — a fancy that, in later years, she believed her mother secretly shared.

School came easily to her. She excelled academically *and* was the class clown. "I was an absolutely perfect, quiet, dedicated student *in* class," she recalled, "but *outside* of class I got my laughs." She loved the attention and friendships her joking around garnered. She imagined great things for herself.

Even a scarring childhood accident didn't quash her dreams. At age nine, during a summer in the country, Phyllis planted herself behind the wheel of her mother's Model T and slammed it into a fence post, breaking her nose, a calamity which there was no doctor nearby to remedy. Phyllis might have been crushed by this turn of fate, but Frances tried to buoy her with some hopeful, if a bit backhanded, advice, telling her daughter that she had "the kind of face people laughed at," Phyllis recalled. "She told me when I was young that I would never be pretty, like other little girls, and that I ought to take advantage of anything else I had. So she used to teach me jokes."

This slightly skewed counsel, unimaginable decades on, actually encouraged the girl. Her antics among her schoolmates became a calling card. She was invited to parties, she was a hit in student plays and talent shows — indeed, she often performed *better* on opening nights than she had in rehearsals, a born trouper who found herself lifted rather than cowed by the pressure of appearing in front of a crowd.

In the summer of 1934, after graduating high school, she left Lima to attend the Sherwood Conservatory of Music, a small private institution in midtown Chicago. She enrolled in classes in piano, harmony, theory, and, when it was discovered that she could hit C above high C, voice. What was more, she was exposed to the cultural riches of a big city: the jazz clubs, the museums, the classical music halls. She took classes in the humanities and sciences at an adjunct campus of Northwestern University; she dated young men from local colleges; she loved it.

She wasn't, however, convinced that she was destined for a career as a performing musician; she could recognize real talent, and she knew that she fell short. After three years, she decided to transfer to Bluffton College, a small Mennonite liberal arts school located in a small town some fifteen miles northeast of Lima. She intended to complete her undergraduate degree with courses in education, which would enable her to become a music teacher. But three years of Chicago had spoiled her for life on a tiny campus in rural Ohio. At Bluffton, she was a cutup and a discipline problem. She was caught smoking in her dorm room, and she gave her classmates an unforgettable laugh one evening by parading through the dormitory halls in the nude save for curlers in her hair, a belt around her waist, and a rose clenched in her teeth. As ever, she was a good student, but she clearly wasn't meant for the sort of quiet, devoted scholarship that Bluffton expected of its students.

It turned out not to matter. In addition to her antics, she had met a boy and fallen in love and would soon leave Bluffton College for another sort of life altogether.

Sherwood Anderson Diller was born in 1913, before the famed Ohio writer Sherwood Anderson published any of his works about small-town mores. But the writer would've been proud to have dreamed up Diller and his family. As Phyllis later recounted it, the Dillers were a big deal in Bluffton, founding and owning several profitable manufacturing concerns and reigning as the town's brightest social lights. Waldo, Sherwood's father, had created the family fortune but didn't live to enjoy it, driving his car onto railroad tracks in 1929, at age forty-eight, after suspicions arose that he had fathered a child with the sister of his wife, Maude. Waldo's death, however scandalous, was ruled an accident, and his insurance policy added to the family's fortune.

Phyllis met Sherwood some nine years after Waldo's passing at a party at the Diller family home, where Sherwood, though in his mid-twenties, was living after dropping out of two Ohio colleges and making an abortive trip to California, where he had expected to make a fortune. As Phyllis soon learned, Sherwood and the family were prone to exaggerated and costly hobbyhorses and, worse, had been gradually letting their wealth bleed away, refusing to invest it or grow it, not even by nurturing the businesses that Waldo founded. (One of Sherwood's sisters was a physician, according to Phyllis, who opened an office and refused to see patients.) They comported themselves, as she recalled, "with their noses in the air," lording it over Bluffton, refusing to acknowledge their calamities, spending their money heedlessly, and taking what they wished.

Well, what Sherwood wished was Phyllis, and she was game for it. He was, by her reckoning, a hottie, "boasting a terrific physique and the beautiful blue eyes. . . . I was immediately hooked." (As she later put it, "It was sort of a mating thing. I just took one look at him and I decided, well, This is the way I want my children to look.") They met when she hadn't yet turned twenty-one and was still enrolled in college, and they began dating straightaway. And more: "Before long," Phyllis recalled, "I lost my virginity. It was a matter of not being able to fight him off." And more yet: "Almost as soon as Sherry and I slept together, I became pregnant." Though friends in Bluffton warned her not to marry a Diller, Phyllis dropped out of school for good. In the spring of 1940, just two months before she would have graduated college, she and Sherwood eloped to Newport, Kentucky, and, in September 1940, their son Peter, named for Waldo Diller's father, was born.[*]

Phyllis and Sherwood moved into the Diller family home, and she began to practice the homemaking skills she'd seen her mother perform. Sherwood set himself up as a manufacturer of fluorescent light fixtures at a time when they were a new phenomenon. According to Phyllis, he was smart and had genuinely innovative ideas, but he suffered from the family's bizarre blend of hubris and introversion, which made them averse to dealing with strangers — including such necessary strangers as business suppliers and contractors and even *customers.* It wasn't long before Sher-

---

[*] By then, Phyllis had altered their marriage license, backdating it to November 1939, so that her parents wouldn't learn that she'd been sexually active before her wedding.

wood's lighting business foundered.

As Phyllis soon learned, the whole Diller ruse was crumbling. It was more than a matter of letting bills dangle; they were flat broke. And then Sherwood was saved by the war. In early 1942, he started work at the Willow Run bomber plane manufacturing plant near Ypsilanti, Michigan, rising from laborer to inspector. Phyllis, left behind to close up his dead business in Bluffton, followed with little Peter and set up house.

Whatever work ethic Sherwood may have had at the bomber plant, he demonstrated none at home, according to Phyllis. She cleaned, cooked, and saw to every household chore and errand herself. About the only thing he did at home, she said, was force himself on her for sex. Even though he showed her no affection and could refuse to support her in such harmless endeavors as singing in the church choir, he felt no restraint in exercising his libido. As she remembered (emphasis hers), "Sherwood was *lousy* at sex, the *world's worst,* just pumping away with absolutely no idea how to come. I felt like a trampoline. He'd want to jump on me all the time, and there were occasions when he'd get his way and a few hours later, I would deliver a baby."

Evidence supporting her complaint could be found in the speedy growth of the family. A second son — Perry, after her father —

was born to them in Michigan, but he lived only two weeks. In November 1944, they had another child, a daughter named Sally, whose slow development led to a diagnosis of irreversible brain damage; she would spend most of her life living apart from the family under supervised care.

The following year, as work at the bomber plant wound down, Sherwood got a position at the Naval Air Station in Alameda, on the eastern shore of San Francisco Bay. He drove off with the family's possessions, and Phyllis took the kids west via train. As soon as she arrived, she learned that Sherwood had managed to grouse or quarrel his way out of the job he'd been promised. The family were nevertheless permitted to move into an apartment complex built for naval workers and their families, a temporary community intended to last only as long as the war; the buildings were made entirely of wood, according to Phyllis, even the sinks and showers. In that grim setting, the family continued to expand. Another daughter, Suzanne, was born in March 1946, and a third, Stephanie, in October 1948. And while Phyllis gave birth to and took care of this brood, Sherwood, who *still* never helped around the house, managed to get hired for — and fired from — more than seventeen jobs: foundry worker, toy salesman, taxi driver, drill press operator, night watchman, and on and on.

It was awful. "I was very young," she said years later, "and life was not what I wanted it to be. I was right out of college and it wasn't the beautiful Prince on a White Horse. It was greasy sinks and crying children. And I thought, 'What have I done?' I was a disturbed person. I was fearful, scared." Her saving consolation was participation in community events. Even though she considered herself an atheist, she was active in a local church, becoming music director and putting on pageants and recitals with the organist, Howard Brubeck (older brother of the as-yet-unknown jazz great Dave Brubeck). She became so well known in her tiny circle that she was invited to sing at the Naval Air Station one Thanksgiving Eve and was given a live turkey as payment for her performance.

Little glimmers like that tended to arise in Phyllis's life and then slip away. In October 1948, her mother, Frances, who was widowed that summer when Perry Diller died at age eighty-six, presented Phyllis with an inheritance big enough to buy a place where she could live with her own family. Frances moved to California to join the brood, and she helped pick out a big old Victorian house in Alameda that included rental units. She also bought the family a green Nash sedan, and she and Phyllis larked about the Bay Area in it, the back seat full of kids, away from the grim air around Sherwood, whom Frances had come to loathe. (She encouraged Phyllis to speak to the reverend of the church where she volunteered to seek approval for a divorce; the minister decreed that unless Sherwood was beating or cheating on her, she was compelled to stay with him.)

This episode, too, was short-lived. Frances outlived her husband only by five months, dying in California in January 1949. Now Phyllis truly had no allies in the world. Her friends from Lima and from college were all back east, her parents were gone, and she was alone in California with four kids under age eight (a fifth, again named Perry, would arrive in February 1950) and a husband whom she characterized as "an agoraphobic sex tyrant who couldn't socialize and rarely held down a job." She had inherited the family farm and a sum of $30,000 after Frances died,* and Sherwood began to tear through the money, insisting on buying a house in a more prestigious part of town (for $17,500, cash), treating himself to a new car, and, inevitably, skating along by spending the family savings rather than holding a job. Presently, they were broke again.

It became clear to Phyllis that she would have to support the household by finding work. She applied at a cannery, a restaurant, and a few other spots advertising entry-level

* Approximately $328,000 in 2022.

positions, but she had no luck. She felt increasingly desperate. One despondent evening, she took out her Sherwood Conservatory of Music scrapbook and leafed through it, reminding herself of her onetime promise and her abandoned dreams. "It was too painful," she remembered. "It was a loss of hope. You know, 'Forget it.' Forget being smart, forget having any talent, forget dreaming about making something of myself." In utter despair she threw the scrapbook into the fireplace.

In late 1950, Phyllis donned her one professional-looking outfit and presented herself at the hiring office of the *San Francisco Chronicle,* which had advertised that they were looking for a copy boy. She was told that she wasn't right for the job, but there was a glimmer of hope: the *San Leandro News-Observer,* just south of Alameda, was expanding from a weekly to a daily and taking on staff. The paper happened to be owned by her neighbor (an ironic perk of living in a part of town that was too rich for her), and he instructed the news desk to give her an audition. She wrote an entire Christmas insert edition of the paper and was hired on at seventy-five dollars a week, one-third of which went to pay for a full-time maid and babysitter, freeing her up to become the women's editor of a small-town paper.

It doesn't sound like much of a launching pad, but that was precisely what she made of it. As she had done as a schoolgirl, Phyllis not only did what was asked of her — learning the beat, making contacts, teaching herself to type, hitting deadlines, coming up with new ideas — but she managed to spike her writing with her own brand of humor, drawing within the lines, as it were, but doing it with flair and levity.

Her grumpy editor in San Leandro didn't care much for Phyllis's wit, but she quickly found other bidders for her services. In June 1951, she was hired at an Oakland department store as an ad copywriter. Seven months later, she went to work for Oakland radio station KROW as a copywriter and publicist at one hundred dollars per week. She kept the job for two years, learning the broadcasting business and making a name for herself.[*] Two years later, she moved on to a San Francisco ad agency that specialized in fashion; not only was the job a ticket to the big city, but it got her noticed by columnists in the San Francisco newspapers, who occasionally quoted her bons mots. And *that* gig led her to an even better one: director of promotion and

[*] And befriending, among others, the poet Rod McKuen, who was at the time a late-night weekend disc jockey on the station.

merchandising for KSFO, the city's most popular radio station. A September 1954 article about the station in *Broadcasting* magazine featured her as the only woman in the station's hierarchy — and was, incidentally, her first appearance of any sort in a publication dealing with show business.

During this series of career transformations, perhaps even impelling it, was Phyllis's accidental discovery of a way of thinking that would change her life. In late 1951, while idling around a client's office, she noticed a book on a shelf with a title that intrigued her. *The Magic of Believing* had been published by Claude M. Bristol in 1948 with the intention of giving servicemen returned from the war a lens of positivity and self-enhancement through which to approach their new lives. Bristol had come to his principles after reading extensively about psychology and working for decades as a journalist. He first set them down in a pamphlet entitled *T.N.T. — It Rocks the Earth,* which he promoted with extensive lecturing. He put together his magnum opus, *The Magic of Believing,* only three years before his death.

His system was based on the idea that thought gives rise to action, intention to realization, belief to reality. He sometimes wrote in vague platitudes — "Thought is the original source of all wealth, all success, all material gain, all great discoveries and inventions, and of all achievement" — but he had a knack, too, for punchy aphorisms: "You have to think big to be big"; "To win you've got to stay in the game"; "We become what we envisage. . . . What you believe yourself to be, you are"; "It is the fear of doing wrong that attracts the wrong thing." And he offered specific ideas about how to put his theories into action: "You must have a mental pattern clearly drawn in your mind. Ask yourself, Where am I headed? What is my goal? Have I visualized just what I really want? If success is to be measured in terms of wealth, can you fix the amount in figures? If in terms of achievement, can you specify it definitely?"

Phyllis took these words as marching orders. She heavily annotated a copy of *The Magic of Believing,* and she read the highlighted passages repeatedly. She didn't have a plan, exactly — Bristol assured his readers that the *how* would follow the *what,* in any case. But she had specific aims: she made notes to herself about how much money she wanted to make; about owning a house with enough rooms for all the kids, for a library, a music room, an art studio; about realizing her dreams through a career in writing or music or humor. For the rest of her life, she would share Bristol's ideas with people, and she kept literally hundreds of copies of the book on hand so that she could press it on journalists, fans, friends, and anyone else whom she thought could benefit from its message.

In the first years she followed Bristol's precepts, she took two affirmative steps toward setting out on her path. In late 1952, she wrote a script, gained access to a model kitchen at an appliance showroom, and spent seventy dollars to hire a crew and shoot a short comedy film, *Phyllis Diller the Homely Friendmaker,* about her catastrophic mistakes in preparing a turkey. Wearing a cocktail dress and apron, she plucked the bird with tweezers, tried to stuff it through its neck, and left the giblets inside "because I didn't want to stick my hand up its ass." It turned out that the images and sound were out of sync, and her budget didn't allow for fixing the problem, so the film vanished. But a seed had been planted.

At more or less the same time, urged by a colleague who supported her ambition to become some sort of entertainer, she wandered into the Purple Onion nightclub in North Beach to catch a performance by a woman named Jorie Remus, whom her friend had particularly recommended.

Jorie Remus was too hip for the room before being too hip for the room was a thing, and almost even before there was a room worth being too hip in. She floated into San Francisco in the early 1950s enveloped in a world-weary air that spoke of men and booze and regrets and that seemed at once hard earned and deeply ironic. She was billed as a singer, and she had a repertoire of torch songs and ballads, but she rarely sang anything straight, and she rarely got through even parodic numbers without satiric remarks, scandalous confessions, and comic asides. In a smoky, creaky voice that was nearly a baritone, from beneath disheveled hair suggestive of sex and/or indifference, wrapped in slinky gowns and a feather boa of absurd length, she sat on top of a piano while her accompanist tried to perform their act straight and spoke to her audience as if they were the last people at a saloon and she felt comfortable unburdening herself of her woes.

In the manner of such saucy wits as Tallulah Bankhead, Dorothy Parker, Marlene Dietrich, and, perhaps most especially, Beatrice Lillie, she was dry and droll and gave an impression of having been all around the world and having had her share of ups and downs, mostly the latter — a vamp with a history and a dry, sardonic way of talking about it. She seemed cultured and sophisticated and fallen, like the oft-married younger sister of a wealthy family, maybe even one of your lesser royals. She gave every indication of having used men as much as having been

311

used by them, of surviving disasters — and hangovers — of her own devising, of having lived and squandered a very high life and resurrected herself from the ashes of a fire she herself had lit and come to the stage to tell all about it. And she was convincing: there appeared to be very little theatrical make-believe between the persona she was presenting onstage and the person she seemed to be off it. If what she was doing was an act, it was a deeply convincing one.

In fact, Jorie Remus was just as singular a character in real life as in performance. Born in Manhattan in 1919[*] as Marjorie Ramos, daughter of a dentist, she claimed to have gone to good schools in London and been groomed for a proper middle-class future but to have rejected it all for a more bohemian life. In her early thirties she found herself in Cannes, France, drinking with friends in a café and demonstrating her vocal talents. The manager offered her a chance to sing for money, and, in the spirit of what's-there-to-lose, she accepted. Years later, recollecting her start as an entertainer, she said, "I sang seriously the songs I now satirize. But anything I did brought smiles instead of swoons. I don't know what it was, but every number had 'em laughing."

* Her professional biographies put the date ten years later.

She may have been puzzled by the thought that she was funny, but she was savvy enough to go along with it. She continued to perform as a singing comedienne in Paris and London. And then she found her way to San Francisco, where she fell in with a crowd of kindred spirits, debauched and worldly bohemians who, among other tastes, both appreciated show business and abhorred its conventions, banalities, and clichés. Two of them in particular became good friends and helped her craft her act, writing jokes for her, providing her with some of what would become her signature stage business, and generally encouraging her to become ever more flamboyant, outré, and (though the world didn't know the word yet) camp. Lloyd Clark was a stylish and ostentatious "drama coach" and Barry (short for Barrymore) Drew was a booming, oversized barfly who lived on a houseboat and claimed to be related to the famed acting family of Barrymores and Drews but who was actually born Cyrus King Drew IV — a grand enough name, one would think, to make fictional connections to theatrical greats seem superfluous.

Jorie debuted at the hungry i, a nightspot on Columbus Avenue in North Beach favored by beatniks and bohemians and given over to jazz and folk music and poetry readings and offbeat comedians such as Mort Sahl, then igniting a revolution in comedy by joking about politics and social issues in the manner of a chum sharing opinions over a beer. In this setting, where the artifice of show business seemed tacky and passé, Jorie's schtick, however she came to it and whether or not it was authentic, carried an au courant, vital air. She knew show biz *and* she knew it was bullshit. She became an underground hit.

Indeed, such was her repute that when her booking at the hungry i expired, she was scooped up by a club just across the street, the Purple Onion, a smaller venue run by musician Keith Rockwell and his family. Despite its prime location in the middle of the city's nightlife district, and despite the crowd of gay men who favored it as a regular watering hole, the club was struggling until Jorie crossed Columbus Avenue and brought along her growing following. (Barry Drew was hired by the club as a talent scout and emcee.) Among those drawn to see her in this new setting was the city's premier newspaper columnist, Herb Caen, who found her delightful and told his vast readership so. Thus anointed, Jorie became a local sensation, putting the Purple Onion on the map and making a name for herself outside the somewhat insular world of North Beach.

The *San Francisco Examiner* described her stage appearance thus: "Perched atop the piano, she will suddenly lie back languidly as on a sofa; crouch like a cat above the alarmed pianist's head; or simply stand upright, perilously waving her arms." Her jokes, delivered in a slow, knowing drawl and Katharine Hepburn-ish diction, got a lot of mileage out of her alleged misfortunes with men:

"My entire outfit was given to me by an admirer . . . and I haven't spoken to him since."

"They say that gentlemen prefer blondes, but as you can see, I'm not taking any chances."

"I'm writing a book: 'Men, How to Say "No" to Them, or What To Do Until the Police Come.' "

And she did a somewhat shocking routine about her abuse at the hand of her longtime lover, Reginald:

"On Valentine's Day, I gave him a case of his favorite scotch, and he gave me a perfectly marvelous, handmade, heart-shaped bruise. . . . He would throw a teargas bomb into my room and then beat me up for crying. . . . I said, 'Reginald, don't you love me anymore? Tell me the truth. Give it to me straight.' Well, I shouldn't have said that. As soon as I was able to walk, on crutches, I went to him again. I was tired of playing games. I wanted to know the truth. Well, I wish I had kept my big mouth shut: I wouldn't have lost so many teeth."

Watching Jorie's schtick, which combined music and comedy in a way that she'd never seen before, Phyllis had a concrete thought: "If she could do it, then perhaps I could, too."

It wasn't a daft notion. She had a few years of experience under her belt writing humorous copy for print and broadcast, her witty one-liners had occasionally appeared in newspaper columns, and she was always able to make people laugh at the office, at parties, even at the laundromat. She wrote down comedy bits at home — she kept her manuscripts on top of an upright piano so that the kids wouldn't destroy her pages while they played around her feet. She'd done a few minutes of jokes — embryonic stand-up sets — at parties and a few functions like PTA fundraisers. And she kept reading Claude Bristol, girding herself, perhaps unconsciously, to take a leap of faith.

Ironically, it was the unambitious Sherwood who impelled Phyllis to embark on the next step. "My husband decided I should become a comedian," she said. "He almost nagged." It started as a kind of twisted praise, she recalled: "He would watch TV and think I was funnier than the comics on there. . . . So,

316

ever keen to bring out the cash cow in me, he kept pushing me towards a show biz career." And it could be more than mere suggestion: "There were times when I felt he almost whipped me mentally." But his intelligence and his search for easy money were a form of support. "He did a lot of great things for me," she conceded, "mentored me, pushed me, encouraged me." His motives may have been less than noble ("He's always wanted a product, and I'm the product," she would say), but his instincts about her were savvy, and he could see that she had a promising set of skills.

And he wasn't alone. One evening, Phyllis stopped with colleagues for an after-work cocktail in an Oakland bar and found herself chatting with the fellow next to her. He turned out to be none other than Lloyd Clark, drama coach for Jorie Remus. Phyllis revealed her ambitions to him and assured him that she wrote her own material, and he offered to help her with pointers — for a charge of five dollars per hour (always pressed for money, she ran a tab, which, good egg that she was, she eventually paid off with a bonus).

Clark helped polish her material and added musical parodies to her repertoire — as with Jorie, he was trying to craft Phyllis into a classic, if comical, cabaret comedienne — until they felt she was ready to perform for people she didn't know. And so she appeared at . . . the hospital of the Presidio Army Base in San Francisco, where the Red Cross organized entertainment for convalescents. Accompanied by her son Peter on banjo, she played for a grand total of four men, captive because they were in traction, who groaned at her act and complained, "Lady, stop! We're already in pain!" She had a second gig at the same facility — in the psychiatric ward (as she later said, "I guess they figured I had found my true audience").

Thus launched, she was undeterred. She performed at church halls, women's clubs, and charity benefits. She spent time among the bohemian crowds of North Beach, to whom Clark introduced her as his protégé. She landed a part in *Poets' Follies of 1955,* a comic revue written and staged by, among others, writers James Broughton and Weldon Kees. It actually got written up in the *New York Times,* which mentioned her as "Phyllis Dillard." Whatever. The important thing was what it all did for her. "When I went on stage," she recalled, "something snapped. . . . It made my other work seem unsatisfying."

Soon after, she and Clark agreed that she was ready to appear at the Purple Onion, which was about to lose Jorie, who was on her way, her fans all reckoned, to conquer New York. On a sunny February afternoon, Phyllis entered the tiny club to audition for the Rockwell family, who owned it, and they responded to her act by phoning for an order of Chinese food and eating loudly while she performed. Aside from sheer bad manners, their indifference was related to the fact that they'd already hired a replacement for Jorie: Milt Kamen, a dry-witted stand-up comic from New York who was emerging as a star among the rising class of offbeat new comedians. But Kamen came, found himself homesick after barely ten days, and left. Someone at the Purple Onion remembered Phyllis. They called her on a Friday morning and asked if she could open on Monday; she could have two weeks, they said. Of course, she agreed.

Phyllis wasn't the only performer who got a break through the offices — or, technically, the *absences* — of Jorie Remus. Indeed, Jorie's most substantial claim to popular memory was her generosity toward performers of lesser experience than her, to whom she unfailingly offered advice, encouragement, and even work.

One of these was a young Black cabaret dancer named Rita Johnson whom Jorie and Barry Drew saw at a club called the Garden of Allah. They bought her drinks after the show and asked her all about herself. Jorie invited Rita to a party at her home, where the young woman, recognizing no one, felt uncomfortable and ignored, until Jorie swept her up and introduced her around. Before long, Rita got past her shyness and felt as though "these whites were treating me as an equal."

Rita learned that Jorie would soon be leaving for New York and that the Purple Onion would need to replace her. She revealed that she herself had given notice at the Garden of Allah, and she mentioned that she could sing as well as dance: pop standards, blues, and calypso, a rage at the time. Jorie excitedly encouraged her to audition at the Onion: "You'll be a smashing success. I mean they will simply adore you."

A few days later, Rita auditioned, and everyone was convinced she was perfect. Lloyd Clark agreed to help her work to create an act and a stage presence more befitting a headliner. But there was the matter of her name. Rita Johnson sounded too ordinary, all present agreed. She revealed that her actual name was Marguerite but that her younger brother used to call her Maya. "Divine, darling!" Jorie replied. Everyone thought Maya was sufficiently enticing and exotic, but Jorie balked: "Do deliver us from performers with one name: Hildegarde, Liberace. No. She must have at least two names." The group was stumped: Maya *what*? And then Rita offered another tidbit: "My married name is Angelos." Jorie liked it, but Clark felt it was too Spanish and not at all representative of her or her act. "I've got it!" he declared. "Drop the s and add a u! Maya Angelou!"

And under that name, singing and dancing, before she did any of the myriad other things for which she would become an icon, Maya Angelou replaced Jorie Remus as the Purple Onion's main attraction. Indeed, she was on the top of the bill on March 7, 1955, when Milt Kamen's replacement, a woman whom Maya recalled as "a frowzy blond housewife . . . [with] a wardrobe of silly flowered hats and moth-eaten boas . . . [who] would not change her name because when she became successful she wanted everyone to know it was, indeed, herself," made her debut.

In front of an audience seeded with colleagues from KSFO, business associates, and other friends, Phyllis did her first truly professional show that otherwise ordinary night. If the performance had been recorded, it would be unrecognizable from the work that Phyllis became famous for. She looked exactly like the thirty-seven-year-old working mother of five that she was, in a simple, businesslike outfit with her hair straight and demure. It was the only look she knew: "When you've been pregnant for ten years, you don't go to nightclubs," she explained. "I looked exactly like what I was: the woman next door." She sang comic parodies of the yodelly pop tune "Indian Love Call" and passages from the opera *Ahmal and the Night Visitors* (once a music major . . .), and she imitated the elastic-voiced Peruvian singer Yma Sumac, who was then a popular novelty. She did bits with props. And she told jokes, some quite generic, some — those written for her by Lloyd Clark — quite hip and insidery. "You virtually needed a dictionary to understand my act," she recalled.

She gave it, quite literally, her all, and her audience, disposed to be friendly, encouraged her with laughter and applause and kind words. And then something happened that she couldn't have predicted: a great many of them stayed to see the second show. Problem was, *she didn't have a second show.* "I had only seventeen minutes of very weak material," she remembered, "just what I had used for the audition." She was planning to do the same thing over again, and she got a sick feeling when she realized that she simply couldn't repeat jokes to an audience that had just heard them an hour or so earlier. Even as a rank amateur she knew "there is no such thing as doing a second show with the same material." Somehow she ad-libbed her way through that second set, and she spent the whole of the next day preparing sheaves of new material so that she'd never get caught flatfooted again.

Thanks in part to the goodwill she'd engendered in her years working in public relations, her Purple Onion gig was mentioned several times in San Francisco newspapers. And those articles mentioned something notable: she had quit KSFO to focus exclusively on performing. "I found that agents considered me a dilettante as long as I had another job," she recalled. Drawing confidence from *The Magic of Believing,* she had given notice, making sure she had no safe retreat to fall back into. "It was my grand affirmative gesture," she explained. "I realized I couldn't go in as an employed copywriter, I had to go as an unemployed comic." Her boss at the radio station urged her to reconsider, to take a leave of absence. But she was resolute: "I don't want a leave of absence. Fill my job. I won't be back."

It was a canny prophesy. Those two weeks at the Purple Onion were extended again and again. Taking over the top slot when Maya was cast in a worldwide tour of *Porgy and Bess,* Phyllis played the club throughout 1955 and most of 1956 — eighty-nine weeks in all, a record for the club, earning sixty dollars a week[*] for six nights of work, four shows per night. Management tried to let her go a couple of times, once to give the stage to

[*] Approximately $525 in 2022.

young comic Dick Gautier,* who bombed, necessitating her quick return, and once just before Christmas to make space in the show for a musical act that was passing through the Bay Area for the holidays. ("I have five children," she replied when the club owners told her she was being let go, "and it's going to be Christmas at my house, too." They relented.)

She became a staple North Beach entertainer, profiled in newspapers, appeared on local radio and TV, even showing up at the grand openings of supermarkets. "I did anything and everything," she recalled, "to be out there, to be known, to be seen." And while she was making her name, she was evolving. Lloyd Clark worked up some material for her that capitalized on both her musicality and physicality. The most celebrated of these was "Ridiculous," a send-up of "Monotonous," a song about a bored sex kitten that Eartha Kitt introduced famously in the revue *New Faces of 1952* and that made her a star. Phyllis's version, which she performed in a black leotard, was about the absurdities of her life as a housewife and mother, sung and danced in broad parody, and it became a signature bit.

* According to her son Perry, Gautier always held a grudge against Phyllis and would bad-mouth and even heckle her for years.

Other, more gradual changes began to emerge in her act. Just as Clark had helped Jorie Remus present herself as a comic version of a woman-with-a-past, he wanted Phyllis to embody a kind of debauched, worldly demeanor, dropping tony allusions and speaking vaguely about her bygone high life. But, unlike Jorie, Phyllis had never traveled, been a socialite, tempted the dark side. She was very much a mother of five from Ohio trapped in a dirty house with a no-good husband. So increasingly, she wrote about *that,* tilting her act more toward what she actually knew. A typical string of one-liners was a litany of confessions on her lack of domestic savvy: "I can louse up corn flakes. I always serve 'em on the rocks"; "Last Thanksgiving I stuffed my first turkey. Took three weeks. Stuffed it through the beak, which some idiot left open"; "There just isn't enough room in our refrigerator for two pets. . . . because my ironing is in there"; and, most famously, "Housework won't kill you, but why take a chance?" Her audience — especially the female half — responded. "When my material stopped being chichi," she explained later, "when it became more talk and more centered in my world — home, children, family, sex, autos — then I picked up all the women." And *that* was where she found her true voice.

She had a signature bit, which she crafted

and recrafted for at least fifteen years, about what a poor driver she was — a string of one-liners ending with a truly deep laugh. A typical iteration: "I was once hit by a house. And my husband didn't believe it when I raced in and told him I was parked on top of a tree. . . . My husband can tell by the way I say 'Hello, sweetie' what make and model I hit. . . . I called the other day and said, 'Hello, darling,' and he said, 'Who is it?' I said, 'I've had a little accident at the corner of Post and Geary.' And he said, 'Post and Geary don't cross.' I said, 'They do now!' "

Chief of the things she wrote about was a comic version of her husband, whom she called Fang Face, because, as she alleged, he had "one long tooth"; "What would *you* call him?" she asked her audiences. Fang, as he was eventually known, had many of the flaws of Sherwood Diller, but they were exaggerated distortions of the real thing. She joked about his sloth, his poor hygiene, his stupidity, his drunkenness — jokes of the sort that male comics made about their wives but with a gender twist: "On our honeymoon night, I wore a peekaboo blouse; Fang peeked and booed"; "The only way I can get Fang out of bed in the morning is to wear a black dress and a veil, and sit on the edge of his bed and cry"; "Fang always felt that a marriage and career don't mix. That's why he's never worked"; "I've been asked to say a couple of words about Fang — how about short and cheap?"

And, perhaps because she feared being rejected as some sort of harpy for cataloging her husband's failings, she turned her zingers on herself — her inept housekeeping, her lack of sex appeal, her misfortunes with shop clerks and doctors, her bizarre taste in clothes: "When I go to the beauty parlor, I always use the emergency entrance"; "A peeping tom called me on the phone, hysterical, begging me to draw my shades. He said he was eating"; "I love to go to the doctor. Where else would a man look at me and say 'Take off your clothes'?"; "I never made *Who's Who* but I'm featured in *What's That?*" This wasn't exactly the sort of confessional, psychological comedy that was then coming into vogue: Diller's "mad housewife" persona wasn't based on genuine self-examination. Rather, like her comments on Fang, it was a reductio ad absurdum, a story that was real in *spirit,* if not necessarily detail, blown up to comic effect.

Of course, if she was going to market herself as a sexual turnoff, she couldn't slink about in formfitting outfits, much less leotards. As it happened, even with six pregnancies in ten years, even approaching age forty, she had, as she put it, "a good figure. And when I made a couple of figure jokes, they didn't work . . . because the audience could see my body." So she started to dress to fit her stage character. She adopted oversized, shapeless dresses, feather boas, crazy hats, and garish leggings, favoring loud, mismatched colors, rhinestones, sequins, and glitter. Before, she recalled, "I looked like a typical woman next door. But people don't have to visit a club to see the woman next door. I'd always thought that girls who wore sequins had bad taste, yet it wasn't long before I was sparkling like them, reflecting flight with a platinum-blond hairdo that was aimed at grabbing *everybody's* attention." Her days in advertising had honed her eye for fashion ("I was always chic," she would say), and she began to wear the most outlandish designs that she could find — actual designer clothes of the sort that might make you wonder "Who would wear that . . . and to what . . . and *why*?" (In the early days, she acquired her wardrobe by combing thrift stores. Later, as she began to make big money, she added many couture pieces to her closet, but much of her stage wear was bespoke, crafted for her by a small clutch of dressmakers, including one who became a punch line in her act, Omar of Omaha — an actual Nebraska designer whose real name was Gloria Johnson, and whom Phyllis eventually lured to California.)

Two other trademarks began to emerge: her laugh, a high-pitched cackle that could shatter a champagne flute and which became a signature of any Phyllis Diller imitation, and her overlong cigarette holder, the one stage prop that she continued to use for years after abandoning other such gimmicks. Both of them served the same purpose: she would laugh manically at her own jokes to goose laughter out of the crowd, or she would make an ash-flicking gesture with the cigarette holder as a kind of rim shot, letting the audience know that a bit was over. It was a way of instilling rhythm in the act, of priming the pump for the crowd's response, of goosing a titter into a guffaw. The laugh, she always swore, was authentic: her dad called her "the laughing hyena" even when she was a kid. She first employed it out of nerves: "I used to have to laugh so much to sell my lousy material," she confessed. But then it became like fuel, like a guitar lick or piano chord that she would return to again and again to punctuate her set and give it shape. The cigarette holder (complete with a wooden cigarette; she was never a smoker) began as part of Lloyd Clark's stage management — suggesting a louche, world-weary life — but then became a reliable tool in itself, another means for her to tease laughs out of a crowd, an orchestra leader's baton that at once imparted a look to her *and* gave her a means to conduct the audience's attention and responses.* It would be a few years before she came to fully incorporate and master these tools, but she first started experimenting with them in that epic run of shows at the Purple Onion. In the span of those twenty months, she morphed from Phyllis Diller, housewife and career woman, into Phyllis Diller, comedy original.

Inevitably, Sherwood horned in on the act, at least from a management standpoint. He let Phyllis work out the stagecraft — he rarely showed up at the Purple Onion, which he considered déclassé — concentrating instead on negotiating bookings, salary, perks, and so on. In 1957, when her never-ending run at the Purple Onion was winding down, she started to appear elsewhere in California: Lenzi's nightclub in Eureka, and several smaller nightclubs in Los Angeles, including the Bar of Music, the 881 Club, and a satellite version of the Purple Onion on Sunset Boulevard in Hollywood. In August 1957, the *Hollywood Reporter* reviewed her act at the 881 favorably, calling her "a stand-up comedian who works with a few props but mostly depends on a sharp tongue and an agile mind. . . . She is the kind of performer

---

* She dropped the cigarette holder bit permanently in the late sixties when young fans pointed out that she was inadvertently condoning smoking.

who is going to develop a fanatic and devoted clientele. She is a new artist of unusual potential."

Slowly, even with Sherwood in charge of management, breaks started to come her way. The cabaret singer–comedian Kaye Ballard caught Phyllis's act and phoned her contacts back in New York to tell them they had to give her a shot. In particular, she contacted Herbert Jacoby, owner-operator of the Blue Angel, the small but influential nightclub on East Fifty-Fifth Street in Manhattan that had developed a reputation for presenting exciting new and slightly bizarre talents in an intimate setting. Jacoby, a tall, gravel-voiced, vaguely sinister Frenchman, scoured tiny spots in Harlem and Greenwich Village and, yes, San Francisco's North Beach for undiscovered acts. The combination of an in-the-know clientele and an intimate room suited performers of limited experience and quirky originality. Negotiations with Sherwood resulted in a booking for the following January.

At the same time, scouts for legendary comedian Groucho Marx's TV game show *You Bet Your Life* found her a perfect candidate to stand beside the star, banter a bit, and maybe win some money. In January 1958, on a Hollywood TV set, teamed with an honest-to-God rocket scientist as her game-playing partner, she was a bundle of nerves, stammering, squirming, stealing glances at the famous host, more or less spilling out of her skin. Explaining that in addition to raising five children she worked as an entertainer, she was given a few minutes to do her act, and she bombed. "Trying to ensure that I didn't say anything too offensive," she remembered, "I just wasn't funny." Groucho gave her a curdled smile when she wrapped up ("He looked at me as if I was a turd" is how she put it), and she and her brainiac partner went on to blow the final question and leave the show with $500 of a possible $2,000 to split between them.

Her initial foray in New York wasn't much rosier. She first appeared at the Blue Angel on a bill headlined by another comedian, Shelley Berman, and she flopped. As she put it, "My delivery didn't work in that room. It was West Coast and it was much slower than that of the fast-talking East Coast Borscht Belt types." Recalled Will Holt, a musician who was also on the bill, "She bombed, bombed, bombed, night after night. . . . [but] after every show she would go back to her dressing room and pore over each piece of material — why this didn't work, and what went wrong with that. And she got better and better." (*Variety* was so unimpressed with her work there that they reviewed her as "Phyllis Dillen" and groused about her "rather forced material.") To be fair, her act at the time was littered with grimaces, grotesque gestures, and visual cues to the audience that more or less said "These are the jokes, folks: laugh!" — sometimes even *before* the punch lines. In time, she became more confident and her stage presence became streamlined, letting the jokes do the work, with the laugh and the cigarette flick taking on the role of signatures rather than pleas. But it would be a while before she felt settled enough to let go of all the extraneous mugging.

Her domestic situation was no less a work in progress. Even though she was commanding as much as $125 a week for club bookings, Sherwood wasn't bringing in anything on his own, and the bills were piling up faster than they could pay them. They were forced to sell their house to avoid foreclosure, and then to split up the kids: Peter had left home a few years prior, heading south to attend Hollywood High School and make a go of a music career, and the two youngest, Stephanie and Perry, were sent to live with Sherwood's mother and sister in an apartment in St. Louis, where they had moved after squandering the family's wealth back in Ohio. (Perry remembered it as hell: the Diller fortunes had so fallen that his grandmother and aunt lived "above a liquor store in a seedy part of town," and Amah, as he knew his grandmother, "didn't talk to me for three years; she just stared at me with those steely eyes.")

Sally and Suzanne joined their parents on the road, forgoing school and traveling from gig to gig on trains (Sherwood was too anxious to fly). Before long, they too were sent to live in St. Louis, leaving Phyllis and Sherwood on their own in, among other places, New York, where they survived in a ratty hotel room, making meals on a hot plate and washing dishes and clothes in a communal bathroom. Not only did Sherwood refuse to help with chores, he developed a new way to dominate his wife, suffering a string of panicked "heart attacks" in the hours before her opening nights or other potential opportunities; doctors never found a physical reason for his episodes, and one, who'd known the family for years, flat-out asked Phyllis, "Are you two having some kind of trouble?"

Still, she continued to work, with the help of a guardian angel of sorts, a New York agent named Irvin Arthur, an old-time show-biz type who helped her find bookings in small clubs without actually having a contract to represent her. When the Blue Angel gig elapsed, she moved downtown to One Fifth Avenue, a smaller and less prestigious spot. In the summer, she reunited the family in San Francisco, where the Purple Onion welcomed her back happily and she rented a big, if not exactly comfortable flat nearby. When school started up again, the kids returned to St. Louis, and she was back on the road: Mister Kelly's, the premier comedy club in Chicago (columnists called her "the weirdest, wildest yet" and " 'hip' and luna-tic"); No. 12 Carver in Boston ("Hilarious isn't a good word. . . . but it may serve while one catches a breath," said the *Boston Daily Record*); and, again, One Fifth Avenue.

And then a bit of magic struck. In the fall of 1958, she opened at a New York venue that turned out to be almost as well suited for her as the Purple Onion. The Bon Soir was much closer in atmosphere, in aura, even in configu-ration, to the Purple Onion than it was to the Blue Angel. Down a flight of stairs on a busy Greenwich Village street and reputedly owned by shadowy figures with connections to organized crime, it featured a tiny bar which, like that at the Onion, served a gay clientele who were something like the gatekeepers for the talent: if they liked you, they *really* liked you, and you continued to be booked until you wore out your welcome or, fingers crossed, got bigger, better-paying work else-where. It was what was known in the trade as a "discovery club," a place where you per-formed for exposure, which was worth more, at least potentially, than the meager pay. A regular booking at a spot like the Bon Soir was a sign that you were someone to keep an eye on.

This was where she hit her stride. The Bon Soir was hospitable to experimentation, outrageousness, and even silliness. The barside regulars appreciated Phyllis's campy self-presentation and jokes about being a misfit at the mercy of a boorish man. The audiences at the Blue Angel were adventuresome for uptown crowds; the audiences at the Bon Soir were adventuresome for *Greenwich Village.* It was the difference between a decaf and a double espresso. And it gave Phyllis a setting where her special talent could gel and emerge. Her act grew tighter, sharper, snappier. She was still singing a bit, still working a little with props, still over the top and willing to try anything, but it increasingly seemed of a piece, the workings of a single sensibility and not a pastiche of things that she had observed or been talked into. She would perform at the club several times a year until 1962, becoming something of its residing grand dame and signature attraction. (In September 1960, she shared her minuscule dressing room with the eighteen-year-old singer Barbra Streisand, to whom she offered advice on stagecraft, stage wear, and career management. The young singer didn't take Phyllis's advice about wearing cocktail dresses. But she *did* listen when Phyllis told her never to have her nose fixed, a bit of advice for which the not-known-for-her-magnanimity future diva would, for the rest of her days, express gratitude.)*

On the strength of her Bon Soir booking, which was eventually extended for three months, new opportunities emerged. She signed to do a comedy LP, recorded live at the club, for the small Microsonic label. Released in July 1959, *Wet Toe in a Hot Socket* didn't threaten any of the comedy albums that were then enjoying such prominence on national sales charts. But it was one of the first released by a woman, and it helped continue to spread her brand. She appeared on network TV again that summer, taking part in a one-off NBC special about the foibles of modern marriage entitled *I Take Thee.*

Then she got the break of breaks: In October, she auditioned for NBC's *Tonight Show,* then hosted by Jack Paar, the sometimes acerbic host who projected a kind of erudite worldliness and had a proclivity for bringing unusual new acts to the nation's attention,

* In 2001, when Streisand received a lifetime achievement award from the American Film Institute, Phyllis was a featured speaker. As Phyllis reminisced about their Bon Soir days, Barbra repeatedly rubbed a finger against her nose and pointed at Phyllis, acknowledging this canny counsel.

particularly oddball women, such as the comic actresses Hermione Gingold, Peggy Cass, and Dody Goodman. A shot on Paar was a lightning bolt. Phyllis could launch from discovery clubs to the big time in the span of a single night.

What was remarkable is that, according to her own account, she got the gig through sheer persistence, and not even hers, but that of Harold Fonville, her piano player at One Fifth Avenue. Phyllis had been begging the show's bookers to consider her, and they kept telling her that her act wasn't for them. But Fonville, per Phyllis, "called the Paar show staff daily until, in complete desperation and to be rid of him forever, they said, 'Bring her down this afternoon and we'll audition her in the office.' " She was booked for that very night's show. "That's all it took," she remembered. "One minute my material wasn't right, the next it was perfect."

Performing live on TV before a big, packed theater and a nationwide audience, she pulled out all the stops, providing a greatest hits version of her not-quite-five-year-old career: the mad housewife jokes; the cackle; the cigarette holder; the glittery dress that she slipped out of to reveal the leotard in which she performed "Ridiculous"; a crazy fright wig, which startled the host. "This isn't hair," she told him. "It's nerve endings."

Paar could be prickly, but he howled with

laughter and showered her with sparkling praise. When she launched into "Ridiculous," he sat with mouth agape and watched, apparently unable to believe what was unfolding before his eyes. "When it ended," Phyllis recalled, "*time stood still.* All of the people onstage and in the audience were seemingly in shock, and there was a moment when nothing happened before the whole place exploded. I knew it, everybody knew it: this was important; this was a happening."

It *was* a happening, and what happened next was *everything.* Paar's staff immediately booked her for return appearances, practically on a monthly basis. She would perform on the show more than twenty-five times before he ceased hosting it in March 1962. She became so accustomed to it, in fact, that she used it, as she had the Purple Onion and the Bon Soir, as a laboratory, changing her act gradually, dumping the props, cutting the songs, and sharpening her image as a straight, rat-a-tat joke spieler, a stand-up comedian in the metier familiar to anyone who'd ever seen such kings of one-liners as Milton Berle, Bob Hope, or Jack Benny. She had always worked hard, she had always (at least since reading Claude Bristol) believed in herself, and she had never quit, no matter what sort of obstacles or rejections were thrown at her, but have no doubt about it: Phyllis Diller was *made* by Jack Paar's *Tonight Show.*

Almost as soon as her first Paar appearance aired, she was immediately scooped up by personal manager Irving Siders, who helped hone her act and choose worthwhile bookings, and by agent Leonard Romm at General Artists Corporation (home, of course, to Jean Carroll and her mega-agent husband Buddy Howe), who lined up a string of gigs for her. She got bookings to perform all around the country, in towns she'd never played and venues whose proprietors had previously rebuffed her inquiries about show dates; in some towns, there were even bidding wars for her services,[*] which were now routinely priced at $1,000 per week and up.[†] She became a personality, profiled in major magazines and newspapers. She became the subject of *other comedians'* jokes — namedropped by men as a shorthand for a ghastly harridan. She was imitated by drag queens

---

[*] Including, as it happened, San Francisco. Though she was always loyal to the Purple Onion, where her salary had risen to $2,000 per week, she was lured to its rival club, the hungry i, which was willing to pay her *$3,000* per week. It might've been a dicey situation, but she handled it with such candor and integrity that both clubs felt well treated. In fact, the Purple Onion put up a sign outside telling folks that they could see Phyllis at the hungry i.

[†] Approximately $9,000 in 2022.

and impressionists.

She went to Hollywood for a screen test at Paramount Studios, which was directed by none other than superstar comedian (and soon-to-be film director) Jerry Lewis; the hope was that she'd be cast in a sitcom, *Permanent Waves,* about women in the navy. The experiment was a bust: "My screen test was lousy," she recalled. "I didn't know how to prepare for a scripted test and didn't have the skill to handle as many props as required. I had to shave a man while doing lines. It was abominable." As the show never took off, it was just as well. GAC *did* manage to get her cast in director Elia Kazan's sexually daring melodrama *Splendor in the Grass,* a cameo role in which she played famed Prohibition-era nightclub hostess Tex Guinan, whose trademark phrase upon greeting patrons was "Hello, suckers!" On vinyl, she jumped from the tiny Microsonic label to Verve, one of the hippest companies in the biz and home to a number of hot young comedy talents, including Jonathan Winters and Shelley Berman. She made her stage debut in a legitimate drama, appearing in a summer stock production of the psychological drama *The Dark at the Top of the Stairs* in a string of suburban New York theaters (producers billed her as "Jack Paar's greatest discovery"). She was booked on *The Ed Sullivan Show,* one of TV's few outlets bigger than Paar's show, and she was, as on Paar, a smash.

It wasn't all roses and champagne. She struggled with some of GAC's management ideas, particularly as they tried to move her from nightclubs to show rooms and theaters. In late 1959, she was booked at the Fontainebleu Hotel in Miami, then equal to the biggest venues in Las Vegas for top-tier entertainment. Not only was the room significantly larger than she was used to, but she felt cowed by its deluxe aura. She ditched her wild-woman costumes for an evening gown and tried to do her usual routine while looking, incongruously, like a socialite; she bombed so badly that management asked her to forgo the evening's second show and, indeed, the remainder of the booking, sending her back to New York with her tail between her legs. Not long after that, she appeared in another inaptly chosen venue in Washington, D.C., and, again, laid an egg, only to learn that Bob Hope, one of her comedy idols and ideals, the man she referred to as Rapid Robert for the machine-gun joke-telling style that she tried to emulate, was in the audience. She tried to slink out, but he sought her out and, to her amazement, praised her.

"You're sensational," he said.

"Oh, dear. You just saw me bomb."

"Yeah, but I've seen you quite a few times

on the Paar show, and you're great."

She left in a daze, encouraged despite the evidence of the night's failure: "If Bob Hope likes my work, I must have *something*."

Increasingly, the world agreed. In a lengthy review of one of her Bon Soir residencies, the *New York Times* ranked her among the "first-rate performers in demand across the country" and gave a lengthy account of her act, her appearance, and her thoughts on comedy. "Her delivery is staccato," the paper noted:

> She makes two or three salient and funny comments . . . and then, like [Bob] Hope, keeps tacking gag after gag on it; just when you think the subject is exhausted, she will toss out the funniest line of all. She uses her husband as a scapegoat, in the same way that many male comics use their wives. . . . She accompanies her jokes with guffaws, large shrugs of the shoulders, staggers of dismay and horrible grimaces. She is not averse to hanging out her tongue and popping her eyes in gargoyle effect. Miss Diller explains the scarcity of her type of comedienne by pointing out that the work requires tremendous stamina, a thick skin, the courage to buck stiff competition in a predominantly male field and a speed that discourages hecklers and dispenses with the unladylike necessity for putting them down. "I don't have hecklers," she says. "My

timing is so precise, a heckler would have to make an appointment to put a word in."

And those appointments were increasingly scarce, even at her new $5,000 per week asking price. By the end of that year, she was so much in demand that the Blue Angel, where she had flopped just three years prior, had her back. In March 1962, she made her debut at the Copacabana, New York's most prestigious nightclub, appearing on a bill headlined by singer Tony Bennett. In May, she headlined a show at Carnegie Hall during a weekend dedicated to Verve Records artists. In September, she was back in San Francisco, and not in North Beach, where she'd made her name, but at the Fairmont Hotel, arguably the most elite venue in the city and, at that point, the only one in her own hometown that could afford her. It was a banner year: When it was over, she reckoned that she had earned more than $260,000* — another of her Claude Bristol–inspired dreams realized.

In another of the year's amazements, she was profiled in the *Saturday Evening Post* by the future bestselling author Alex Haley. Some six years prior, Haley, then stationed in the Coast Guard in San Francisco, had approached her during her epochal booking at the Purple Onion and asked if he could write

* More than $2.15 million in 2022 terms.

about her. "Honey," she told him, "I'm not big enough yet that a magazine big enough to do me any good would want my story, and if I were, you're not big enough yet as a writer that they would want you to write it." She suggested that he try back in a few years' time. When he showed up at one of her hungry i gigs, a rising writer with an assignment from a national magazine, she was delighted. "Baby, we made it!" she shouted as she leapt from her chair to greet him. "I'll never forget it," Haley remembered. "We met in the middle of her dressing room hugging each other." (He actually stayed with the family, which was spending some time vacationing on Barry Drew's houseboat in Sausalito; Perry Diller remembered bunking with Haley and realizing, for the first time in his life, that his mother was a star because a real journalist was writing about her.)

There were a number of reasons for her steep rise to success. Chief of them was that she was good at what she did: she was genuinely funny, not to mention quick-witted, hardworking, and dedicated to the craft of comedy and to forging a unique comic identity. She had also arrived at a time when the landscape of stand-up comedy had opened to make way for a variety of voices and styles that had never been popular previously: the so-called sick comedy/sicknik revolution of the late fifties that allowed for political satire (Mort Sahl, Lenny Bruce), psychological nuance (Bob Newhart, Shelley Berman), improvisation (Mike Nichols and Elaine May), and, for the first time, really, stars from the ranks of Black entertainment (Dick Gregory, Godfrey Cambridge, Moms Mabley). Phyllis wasn't really doing anything quite so modern — her rat-a-tat style was derived from Bob Hope and Henny Youngman, her jokes dealt with plain domesticity and ordinary life in the way of, say, Alan King — but she was coming at *everything* from a woman's perspective. Yes, she was hard on herself *as* a woman, but she was equally hard on the man in her life and her kids and the people and institutions who made her daily routine a merry hell. That she worked in what might be termed a masculine style — aggressive, relentless, punchy — may have helped put her over. But the main thing that she brought to the comedy stage was the unvarnished perspective of a run-of-the-mill (if, perhaps, out-of-this-world) American housewife of the postwar era. In and of herself, she was a novelty. (That said, her male peers were moving faster, to bigger paydays and more opportunities; comedy was still a man's game, even as Phyllis raised herself, admirably and steadily, toward the top of it.)

Throughout this period, Sherwood accompanied his wife on the road, to TV bookings, to business meetings. He had business cards made announcing himself as her manager and identifying himself as the real Fang. But he couldn't be with her *all* the time — there were family responsibilities, for one thing, and his fear of flying was a genuine curb on his ability to keep up with her hectic schedule. He spent a good deal of time in St. Louis, or, rather, Webster Groves, a tony suburb about twelve miles to the southwest, where Phyllis's earnings were put to use in 1962 to reunite the family in an eleven-room Victorian home filled with furniture that she found at thrift stores (some genuine antiques, even, for which she paid bargain prices). It may have seemed an out-of-the-way spot, but it was actually convenient, midway between the coasts and not terribly far from many of the cities where she was in high demand: Chicago, Cleveland, Cincinnati, Houston, and Pittsburgh. And, of course, Sherwood's family was a short drive away, which made *his* life easier, perhaps, if not Phyllis's. (She had added two more characters to her act: Moby Dick, an overweight, overbearing mother-in-law, and Captain Bligh, a bossy, contentious sister-in-law — any resemblance to people to whom she was related by marriage being strictly coincidental, of course.)

And while Sherwood stayed at home, Phyllis continued to tour and, as it happened, to spend time with other men. Years later, she confessed, without offering details, "I'd had my one-night stands on the road, which were all accidents." But that summer, while performing in a stock company version of the musical *Wonderful Town* in Chicago, she fell into something more than an accidental one-time romp. Also in the production was Warde Donovan Tatum, a tall, blue-eyed actor and singer with broad shoulders, a baritone voice, and a wandering eye. Cast opposite this strapping specimen, Phyllis felt a powerful attraction: "Within a couple of days the two of us were in the sack," she said, adding, "he was . . . *very* good at sex" (emphasis hers). Tatum, who performed as Warde Donovan, wasn't much of an actor, but he really could sing in a big-chested, braggadocious fashion. Like Phyllis, he was married. And, like Phyllis, he was, apparently, smitten. They spent as much time in each other's company, intimate and otherwise, as they could, flying off to trysts whenever possible, barely even sneaking around; they went so far as to have Donovan attend parties in the house in Webster Groves. Sherwood suspected something was amiss, but he could never prove anything and, still unwilling to fly, he had very few chances to get the drop on the pair. Moreover, he could hardly claim moral high ground when he began a dalliance of his own with a maid who'd been hired to look after the house and kids while Phyllis was on the road.

As her marriage fell apart, her career continued to soar: a continual cycle of club dates, TV game show and talk show and variety show bookings, paid endorsements for a number of consumer products, even the openings of banks and bowling alleys. And whatever she did, wherever she went, even when people weren't necessarily fans of her frantic stage manner, she got good press — in large part because she engendered it, taking time to drop in on local radio and TV shows, sit with newspaper columnists, drum up business for the venues that had hosted her in leaner days, even accept the keys to various cities. In June 1963, her launching pad, San Francisco, declared Phyllis Diller Day, and she gave a benefit performance at the Masonic Temple Auditorium. In November, she hosted the first of a planned series of variety specials for WABC television, the New York flagship of the national network, with guests including Warde Donovan, who sang two songs, and her son Peter, who played banjo. Recorded in advance, it had the misfortune to air on Thanksgiving night, November 23, the day after President John F. Kennedy was assassinated, hardly the sort of atmosphere in which audiences wanted laughs; the network declined to commission additional episodes.

The following year, WABC asked her to host *Show Street,* a Saturday-night variety program that featured up-and-coming talent. It offered early TV exposure to a number of notable acts, including singer Lainie Kazan and a musical comedy trio called Jim, Jake, and Joan (the Joan of which was an unknown named Joan Rivers, who was hired as a staff writer for the program a few weeks after appearing on it). But even at $10,000 per episode, Phyllis could barely afford to take time off the road to film her appearances on the show. She would fly in on a Sunday and tape two episodes worth of material, a breakneck schedule that she simply couldn't maintain. (She was, however, as almost everyone who knew her in her lengthy career seemed to attest, extremely decent to her staff. "She made it her business to know everybody's name and go over and say a word to them with no condescension in her voice," remembered Rivers years later. "She treated me as an equal, as a peer, as a professional in show business.") Loath to tell the station that she couldn't keep up the pace, she simply asked them for more money; they balked and let her go, and the show limped on for a handful of weeks before vanishing altogether.

She was so busy that she turned down offers to discuss possible Broadway appearances. She was simply making too much money in her proven routine of nightclubs, TV appearances, and one-off concert performances to try something else, even something that she might have dreamed of doing her whole life. In late 1965, however, she was finally lured off the road. Bob Hope offered her a feature role in his next picture, a marital farce about literally crossed wires entitled *Boy, Did I Get a Wrong Number!,* with an option for further movie roles later on. Barely a decade into her professional career, feature films were a frontier she was ready to explore. In addition to her cameo in *Splendor in the Grass* a few years earlier, she had a full movie role under her belt, having spent part of the summer of 1965 in Florida making *The Fat Spy,* a low-budget spy movie spoof that starred comedian Jack E. Leonard (Buddy Howe's old stage partner). It did no business, but she was keen to follow it up.

For all its studio pedigree, there wasn't much right about *Wrong Number.* Hope played an unhappily married real estate agent who, through the mix-up of a telephone operator, winds up involved with a diva-ish Swedish movie star (Elke Sommer). Phyllis plays his maid, with whom he has a relationship built on salty, antagonistic banter that feels more like a real relationship than Hope's character has with anyone else in the film. She's introduced through her cackle — heard from another room as Hope returns from a day's work — and sports pop art outfits throughout. When the picture debuted in

1966, reviews were mixed. The *New York Times* called it "a many-hued package of obvious and largely unfunny situations," the *Los Angeles Times,* rather more amused, said "it fairly bubbles with gags," and *Variety* split the difference: "If the action sometimes seems to get out of hand, it really doesn't matter." All three had praise for Phyllis, though, even complaining that she didn't get enough opportunity to do her usual thing. And audiences, still drawn by Hope after thirty years, made it a small hit, forking over almost $9 million to see it.[*]

The chance to make a picture with Hope kept her offstage for most of late 1965, costing her, Hollywood trade papers estimated, some $100,000 (she was said to be earning $10,000 per week for live appearances[†] — a huge sum, but chump change for Hope who paid his staff of comedy writers multiples of that sum each week). It might have been just as well, as there had been an even bigger change in her life. In July of that year, she announced that she was seeking a divorce from Sherwood after some twenty-five years of unhappy marriage. He hinted to reporters

[*] Approximately $72 million in 2022.

[†] She did another film that year, providing the voice for a Bride of Frankenstein–like character in the animated comedy *Mad Monster Party?,* which wouldn't be released until 1967.

that "there could be a reconciliation." But she was firm in her decision: "There's no chance of that as far as I'm concerned." She filed a divorce suit in Missouri, citing "incompatibility" and "general indignities," which Sherwood denied. He did not, however, oppose her action, and in early September they were legally split. There was no public accounting of the division of the considerable assets that she had generated in the preceding decade, but to give a sense of things, Sherwood agreed to pay child support for the four minor children amounting to one dollar per month total.*

That was the end of her connection to the Dillers of Bluffton but for one remaining legal matter. In the wake of the divorce, Sherwood and his mother and sister filed suit against Phyllis to stop her telling jokes about Fang, Moby Dick, and Captain Bligh, claiming that they themselves were the bases of these characters and therefore owned the rights to them. They sued her for $100,000 for defamation, and their attorneys contacted nightclubs and TV networks to tell them that they, too, could be subject to legal action if they allowed Phyllis to malign them in their venues. In January 1966, Phyllis countersued for $50,000, claiming "intentional interference" with her work. A year later, the case

* Approximately $8.25 in 2022.

was settled, with Phyllis paying the Dillers $6,000 to leave her alone, grateful to see their backs, still able to tell her jokes about her "husband" and his family.

She put Sherwood behind her almost immediately. Some six weeks after her divorce, she married Warde Donovan, who'd been widowed the previous year, in Southern California. To give them a place to live together with their kids — her four, his two — she bought a house in the Brentwood section of Los Angeles. At twenty-two rooms and ten thousand square feet, with formal gardens, it was known as "Rosewall" and had once been owned by a U.S. senator; at the time Phyllis acquired it, it belonged to the heiress, philanthropist, and socialite Marjorie Merriweather Post. Phyllis paid $200,000 for it, plus another $50,000 for most of the art and furniture.[*] (One of the items not in the estimable Ms. Post's collection was a full-size oil painting of Bob Hope, whom Phyllis regarded as her most important inspiration and ally, in a room known, inevitably, as the Bob Hope Room, which she used to entertain guests over cocktails and, presumably, one-liners.)

[*] Some $2 million total in 2022, though given the inflation of the Southern California real estate market, the home's worth is likely closer to $17 million.

There was no honeymoon, as in a trip: Phyllis was in production on *Wrong Number*. But there was also no honeymoon, as in a period of connubial bliss following the wedding, either. Although her current situation might have seemed the ultimate manifestation of the dreams she'd been pursuing for the past decade, it quickly soured — and for a reason that had nagged at her, if only subconsciously, for some time. Throughout their years of trysting and courtship, Phyllis had begun to suspect that Warde, over whom she rhapsodized as a lover, was cheating on her with men. There were strange gaps in his days when they were on the road together, there were his chummy exchanges with overly friendly waiters and bellhops, there were some old friends whom he never wanted to socialize with when she was around, often choosing their company over hers. One of these men even moved in with the newly blended family, occasionally disappearing for hours with Warde behind the locked door of the master bedroom. After three months, Phyllis tossed Warde from Rosewall, filing for divorce, and announcing in the press that her "twenty-minute marriage" was over. But, as she learned, California law then required a couple to have been married for one year for a divorce to be possible. She almost made it, but near the end of the year's cooling-off period, Warde reached out to her by telegram, asking if he could come by the house to talk things over, and, well, as she later put it, "Does the word *stupid* spring to mind? . . . My problem was the physical attraction. It was so strong. I couldn't resist." There would be other times when his promiscuity resulted in his banishment from the house, but the reconciliation took, more or less, and he even continued to perform as a featured guest in her stage and television appearances.

If her married life resembled a soap opera, her professional career soared into places she couldn't have imagined, even with the tools of positive thinking. In 1966, she released a book, *Phyllis Diller's Housekeeping Hints,* a compendium of one-liners, jokes, and tall tales about her domestic disasters. It sold hundreds of thousands of copies. At the time, Phyllis shared freely the fact that she was able to generate so much material because she was buying jokes from professional gag writers *and* from her public. She literally solicited fans to send her jokes, offering five bucks for every one she accepted; the outpouring was so great that she had to hire a small staff of secretaries to sort through the mail for promising stuff. Her favorite contributor was Mary McBride, a housewife from Janesville, Wisconsin, whom she put on retainer. Over time, between herself, her staff, and her public contributors, she amassed tens of thousands of jokes, which she filed away on index cards in binders, and a card catalog that held more than fifty thousand items was eventually donated to the Smithsonian.

For all that, she was very particular about jokes, able to expound at great length about what she thought was funny, what rhythms and sounds made for a good setup and punch line, and, of course, how to deliver gags for maximum impact. From the mid-1960s to the mid-2000s, she would happily discourse on comedy theory with interviewers for hours. She was, as she had always hoped to be, the fastest joke gun anywhere. By 1968, doing an extended riff on old age, she could literally rattle off a dozen one-liners in sixty-two seconds, leaving her audience breathless. And she could explain her approach to the craft of her act with the exactitude of a Talmudic scholar:

I always have . . . these little phrases . . . one word, three words, four words, that at the end of each line is a laugh. Now, I'm building to a big punch, or maybe I've given 'em a big punch, and I add, add, add, add, add, topper, topper, topper, topper, top-per. . . . Let me give you an example. I have a line where I'm talking about my mother-in-law, Moby Dick . . . I'd say the only way that I can describe her is "Jell-O with a belt." [A writer] said, "Why don't you say 'Jello-O with hair'?" Do you hear the difference? It doesn't work. . . . "Jell-O with a belt": belt is a *pow* word. "Jell-O with hair" is soft and lovely — it lets you down. . . . I only want boff, boff, boff, boff! I don't want giggles. I don't want twitters, because I can get that on the street with my clothes.

Whether the jokes had come to her from her own mind, from professional writers, or from her network of housewife fans, her standards were exacting, and she tinkered until she got the material exactly right for her patented delivery and style.

In the summer of 1966, she was back in business with ABC television, this time cast as the star of a sitcom, *The Pruitts of Southampton.* Based on a novel by Patrick Dennis, who wrote *Auntie Mame,* and produced and written by some of the people behind *The Addams Family* and *The Beverly Hillbillies,* it seemed tailor-made for Phyllis, who played the matriarch of a once-wealthy family that has gone flat broke but must continue to act out the pretense of high living in their Long Island mansion until the IRS can figure out a way to evict them. ("The Dillers of Bluffton," anyone?)

Even before the premiere episode aired, Phyllis sensed trouble. She groused to an interviewer, "Imagine four guys giving me their opinions on the show! And I'm the one who knows. If I'd listened to four guys, I wouldn't be where I am today." True to her intuition, the show was greeted by savage reviews when it debuted in September: "a forlorn item in every particular" (*New York Times*); a "puerile parade of primitive japes" (*Philadelphia Inquirer*); "predictable but hopefully forgettable" (*Los Angeles Herald-Examiner*); "atrociously executed" (*New York Daily News*); and, most painfully, the *Washington Post,* which offered this backhanded praise: "The show does have some powerful canned laughter and this occasionally drowns out the dialogue." Weeks of poor ratings prompted the network to give it a complete makeover, reshaping the mansion as a boardinghouse, moving in new characters played by comic actors John Astin, Paul Lynde, and Marty Ingalls, and retitling it *The Phyllis Diller Show.*

None of it helped. The show ran one season — thirty episodes in all — and died quietly.

It was a disappointment, her second canceled show in barely two years, but one that she could live with. In late 1966, she filmed a second picture with Bob Hope and George Marshall, *Eight on the Lam,* another tired comedy. It opened the following spring, and proved less of a box office draw than *Boy, Did I Get a Wrong Number!* By then, Phyllis and

Hope were widely seen as a team. She appeared on several of his TV specials and joined him in the winter of 1966–67 in a USO-sponsored performance tour to military bases in Vietnam, Thailand, Guam, and the Philippines. She had two sons of approximately draft age — Peter was twenty-six, Perry sixteen — and she greatly respected the sacrifice of the young men who were sent overseas. It was a grab bag of a revue, featuring singers Vic Damone and Anita Bryant, singer-dancer Joey Heatherton, the reigning Miss World, dancing girls, and a full big band. They played more than a dozen performances. Phyllis performed her act, and she and Hope did some skits in the roles of bickering spouses. She was generous with her time, visiting hospitals and talking with scores of servicemen, and she was cited as their favorite entertainer in a poll; a photo of her wearing a fantastically garish green dress (with matching gloves and boots) and entertaining troops in Cam Ranh Bay shows her smiling before a massive crowd of servicemen who are, to a one, smiling back.[*]

In a little over ten years, she had completely remade her life. Just as Claude Bristol promised, she was living what she had imagined.

[*] That dress, too, would eventually find its way to the Smithsonian.

She was one of the nation's highest-paid live entertainers, filling nightclubs coast to coast, playing single-night shows in large auditoriums at upwards of $10,000 a pop, touring state fairs and outdoor amphitheaters in the summer as headliner of an extravaganza that featured singers, dancers, and variety acts. She published a second book, this one on the theme of marriage, and launched a line of canned chicken chili based on a recipe of her mother's. She was in talks to buy a TV station in Las Vegas (she was eventually outbid). It was literally a dream come true.

At around this time, *Playboy* publisher Hugh Hefner, whom Phyllis had come to know through visits to his Chicago mansion and in appearances on his *Playboy After Dark* TV show, thought it would make a great gag to have Phyllis pose in boudoir shots in his magazine. The magazine had already run some sexy photos of Mama Cass Elliot, the famously plus-sized singing star, and Phyllis would, Hefner reckoned, provide another (cruelly) comic contrast to the parade of airbrushed playmates in his pages. Phyllis, roughly fifty years old, agreed to the shoot, showed up, and went through all the steps, only to hear back from the magazine's editors that she was, um, *too attractive.* Specifically, as she recalled, her full breasts, contrasted with her otherwise slender body, made her appear too conventionally sexy for the stunt to provoke laughs. They shot her again, this time trying to create a comic mood with exaggerated lighting effects, but, again, the results were deemed too pretty. They scrapped the project, but she boasted about her "failure" for the rest of her life.[*]

She appeared once again as the main character's screeching nemesis in a Bob Hope film, *The Private Navy of Sgt. O'Farrell,* an anemic World War II comedy. And she had a film of her own in the pipeline, that is, *an actual Phyllis Diller movie,* written for and starring her, a comedy set in the Old West entitled *Did You Hear the One About the Traveling Saleslady?* ("You'll wish you hadn't," sighed a typical review in the *Los Angeles Times.*) She even had a straight dramatic role in another picture, *The Adding Machine,* a British adaptation of a 1923 play about machines replacing humans in the workforce.

Even with all this work, they were throwing more at her. In late 1967, NBC gave her a variety special, *The Phyllis Diller Happening,* in which she performed doing stand-up and skits and which included appearances by Bob

[*] In June 1973, she *did* appear in the centerfold of a national magazine, the hunting and fishing bible *Field & Stream,* which featured her posed in a green gown, full stage makeup and jewelry, and shiny gold boots that could have passed for waders.

Hope, Sonny and Cher, trumpeter Hugh Masekela, and TV host and singer Mike Douglas. It fared well enough that the network offered her a weekly variety series. The producers and writers included a promising rookie, a Canadian comedy writer named Lorne Michaels, who would go on to write for *Rowan & Martin's Laugh-In* and eventually create *Saturday Night Live* (both of which, incidentally, would feature significant roles for women comedians). It was a gigantic show, with a cast of house dancers, a litany of guest stars, even a sitdown session during which Phyllis planned to do straight interviews with notables and newsmakers such as (she hoped) shipping magnate Aristotle Onassis and Prince Margaret of England.

Entitled *The Beautiful Phyllis Diller Show,* it debuted on Sunday, September 15, 1968, in a deadly spot, against CBS's top-rated thriller series *Mission: Impossible* and a movie of the week on ABC. The guests for that premiere included such NBC colleagues as *Tonight Show* host Johnny Carson and the comedy team of Rowan and Martin (the first interview subjects), as well as Sonny and Cher, comedian Norm Crosby, and an all-girl jazz band. Phyllis told jokes, sang, danced with the troupe ("I shouldn't dance!" she objected to producers, to no avail), and played the eager hostess to the hilt.

But the thing simply didn't click. Critics

tended to acknowledge Phyllis: "a novel and strangely appealing emcee" (*Variety*); "a refreshing new chapter in her career" (*New York Times*); "she'll please most of the people most of the time" (*New York Daily News*). But the show itself was deemed overly familiar, old-fashioned, and, inevitably, doomed against its competition. The show drew poorer ratings each week, and NBC finally pulled the plug in November, with fewer than a dozen episodes aired.

With *Show Street* and *The Pruitts of South-ampton,* she was now 0-for-3 on television, which was curious, since she was always a popular guest on talk shows and variety shows and in occasional cameos on sitcoms. It may simply have been that the intensity of her stage persona was too much for the medium. Per the media theorist Marshall McLuhan, television is a cool medium, that is, one best suited to easygoing personalities, the sort of folks you want to sit with in your living room or at your bedside, people like Johnny Carson or Dean Martin who soothe rather than ignite you. Phyllis, like, among others, Jerry Lewis, was an explosive person-ality whom people seemed to prefer in their homes — and, perhaps, their *heads* — in smaller or at least more contained doses. It was one thing to buy a ticket to see her know-ing that you'd have a raucous time, rather like attending a rock concert. It was another to have her over to the house every Sunday night just as you were trying to get to sleep before the rigors of the workweek commenced once again. Whether or not it was a conscious response, American TV audiences simply seemed to find a full meal of her to be too much. They liked her just fine; they just didn't want her moving in with them. She would continue to be a major star onstage and a welcome guest on TV for decades. But she would never get another TV series of her own.

She was in her early fifties, and she was known all over the world, quite literally. She toured Australia and the United Kingdom semi-regularly, appearing on TV in her accustomed role as guest on variety bills and talk shows. She was wealthy — having investments in real estate all over the country and selling her name, likeness, and considerable energy for promotion to a chain of franchised plant shops — Phyllis Diller Exotic Plants — with initial locations in Manhattan (three stores), Philadelphia, and Houston. She was perennially making improvements and additions to her Brentwood home,* she owned a

* In 1971, the town would appoint her honorary mayor in a corny bit of publicity that she simply adored and crowed about.

smaller home in Las Vegas, where she appeared for multi-week engagements several times each year. She was a grandmother, her daughter Suzanne having borne a son in 1968. It was a full life, with no signs of slowing down.

Yes, there were those who found her grating and always would, but, as she had since she first opened the pages of *The Magic of Believing,* she simply let negativity slide off her. She never tired of quoting the book or gifting it to acquaintances, whether fans or journalists or fellow show folk or people who delivered packages to her home. Her generosity went far beyond that relatively small gesture. She appeared dozens of times each year at charity events. She met Moms Mabley and was so enchanted by her that she commissioned a wardrobe for her fellow comedy pioneer from her own personal dressmaker. Unsolicited, she made a gift of $5,000 to a pit musician in one of her shows who had lost his home. She was a beloved figure, both in the popular culture and in the world of show business.

But there were still horizons to reach and conquer. In late 1969, it was announced that she would take over the role of the title character in the long-running Broadway musical *Hello, Dolly!* — the part originated by Carol Channing and subsequently played by such stars as Ginger Rogers, Martha Raye,

Betty Grable, and, most recently, Pearl Bailey in an all-Black production of the show. Phyllis, of course, had a background in serious music and training as a singer; in 1968, she even released an album of straight vocals, *Born to Sing,* on which she covered such standards as "My Man" and "The Man I Love" and such novelties as the Rolling Stones' "(I Can't Get No) Satisfaction." Broadway would require another level of discipline, though, and she was up to the task, committing to four weeks of rehearsals and vocal training. She debuted in the role in December 1969, and she made a credible impression — even though she had moments of unintentional comedy ("She was miked for performances," remembered her son, Perry, "and on opening night during a big dance number you could hear her say, 'Where the hell do I go?' ") Even the curmudgeonly critic Clive Barnes of the *New York Times,* who confessed that she was "an acquired taste that . . . I have never acquired," admitted that "she sings a lot better than I feared a cabaret artist might, [and] she mugs affectionately to her audience and keeps the thing going." She played the role through March, and it was something of a small triumph.

She managed, however, to one-up even that coup the following year. Contacted by a representative of the Pittsburgh Pops Orches-

367

tra to see if she would appear with them, she assumed they wanted her to play music. Actually, it turned out that they wanted Phyllis the comedian — they had no idea that she had once studied music. But in the course of negotiations, her representatives were able to get them to give her a shot. She rehearsed for months and then, in May 1971, debuted.

The show was billed as an evening with Phyllis Diller, but she didn't appear onstage until after intermission. Then, introduced as Dame Illya Dillya, she entered the stage in a gaudy-even-for-her ball-gown and spent several minutes wordlessly clowning in the manner of a grand but inept diva. She approached the piano warily, struggled to get her seat right, took note of the crowd through opera glasses, spent an eternity struggling to remove her overlong gloves, and, finally, started to play, startling an audience with her genuine, if not exactly virtuosic, ability with Beethoven (the C Major Piano Concerto) and Bach (selected pieces for solo piano). It was, inconceivably, a success. Not only did she blend comedy and classical music in a way that made audiences averse to one or the other appreciate *both,* but she could actually play — even critics admitted as much.

Dame Illya Dillya appeared more than one hundred times over the next eleven years with professional symphony orchestras all over the United States and Canada, and there is no doubt that she created an appetite for high-brow music among a public that had come to see comedy. (There was plenty of that, too, in the act: whenever she flubbed a passage and the other players stopped to wait for her, Phyllis would look to the audience and remark, referring to the orchestra, "*They've got music!*") In time, the show came to include straight vocal renditions of tunes from *Hello, Dolly!* and other Broadway shows. She had to cap her musical appearances at about ten per year: unlike her usual gigs, these performances required that she practice for two hours a day. Eventually, the strain of maintaining her piano technique was too taxing. Dame Illya performed her last show in 1982, her creator, Phyllis Driver of Lima, Ohio, having fulfilled her mother's vision of her playing beautiful music on a stage before an appreciative crowd.

Anyone watching Dame Illya with their own opera glasses in those years might have noticed that Phyllis looked a little different — a little, shall we say, *fresher* than she ordinarily appeared. It wasn't a trick of lighting. In the early seventies, Phyllis had very publicly begun to undergo plastic surgery, addressing her sagging neck, which she had apprehended in horror one night at home while watching herself on TV. She consulted with surgeons and decided, while she was at it, to have the lines around her eyes smoothed and, what the hell, finally address that long, skinny, broken nose. Soon she had her breasts reduced as well. In the coming years she would have some seventeen cosmetic surgeries in all, succumbing, in effect, to normative standards of beauty that she had mocked for her entire career yet nevertheless felt compelled somewhere inside her to adhere to.

What she *never* did, to her credit, was ignore the subject of the work she had done. In fact, she bragged about it, speaking openly on TV shows and making jokes about it in her act. Indeed, because she had become so famous by distorting and mocking her own looks, she could still crack wise about being ghastly because that was who the public thought she was. She could even get away with one-liners about her plastic surgeons having failed her, even though, in her heart of hearts, she would believe from the start of her journey into cosmetic surgery that "the result was all that I could have hoped for. I loved it. I'd been given a pretty face."

Along with her old looks, she decided that she would be better off without her inconstant husband. She had endured Warde Donovan's cheating, lies, and boozing since virtually the day they were wed, but by the early seventies, his career almost entirely finished, he started to become more assertive in his opinions

370

about *her* career. He quarreled with her management and with the managers of various venues in which she appeared, making it increasingly necessary to manage *him*. They separated officially in 1972, and this time she managed to ignore his entreaties to take him back. The divorce decree went through in 1975, and though she dated over the next decade, she never came close to marrying again. In 1985, she met an attorney named Robert Hastings, whom she came to consider the love of her life. They shared eleven years of travel, socializing, and romance before he died of heart failure, after which she never again entertained the thought of having a life partner.

She never really left the public eye. Her career, naturally, slowed and evolved as she reached her sixties and seventies. She still toured, but most of her engagements were not too far from her Brentwood home — Las Vegas and Tahoe, especially. At home *and* on the road, she passed hours by painting, often in manic bursts during which she produced dozens of canvases in a week, many of which she donated to charitable causes for auction. (Others she sold to visitors to her home: "There were literally hundreds of paintings on the wall all throughout Phyllis's house, each with a price tag," recalled pianist Thomas Lauderdale. "You would take whatever paintings you wanted off the wall, and at the end of the night you would get tallied up, Phyllis would sign them, you would give her a check and off you would go.") She took on small roles in films — particularly providing voices for animated movies, for which her cartoonish affect was perfect — and she turned up perhaps three or four times a year on popular sitcoms. She was still a regular on talk shows and variety shows, but the latter genre largely disappeared by the end of the 1970s, depriving her of one of her most favored platforms. Still, she was a regular pop culture presence for decades, appearing in scores of TV shows and films, including such memorable turns as voicing a major character in the Pixar animated feature *A Bug's Life* and making a string of some eighteen appearances on the soap opera *The Bold and the Beautiful,* of which she was a dedicated fan. (And, of course, she both pranked and was admitted to the Friars Club.)

Family life increasingly dominated her days. There were more grandchildren, blessings; but there were losses, too. Her oldest son, Peter, from whom she had been estranged for some years, died of cancer in 1998 without ever having reconciled with his family. Her daughter Stephanie died of a stroke just four years later.

Her own health was generally robust if not perfect. In 1999, she started to experience symptoms of heart failure, necessitating the installation of a pacemaker and a lengthy convalescence. Three years later, at the age of eighty-five, she retired from stage performances, bowing out with a show in Las Vegas that was filmed for posterity. She continued to appear on-screen or, most commonly, as a vocal performer, but she was done with the grind of the road. "I don't miss the travel," she told an interviewer a few years later. "I miss the laughter. I do miss the actual hour. I don't want to sound like I'm on dope, but that hour is a high: It's as good as you can feel."

In 2005 she wrote it all down — her earliest memories, her school days, her painful marriage, the germ of her career, her rise to her fame, her heartbreaks, her joys — in a candid if not always precisely verifiable autobiography, *Like a Lampshade in a Whorehouse: My Life in Comedy,* which she concluded with the words of a hymn she recalled singing in a small Ohio church: "Brighten the corner where you are!" As she put it, "I bought that. And I sold it."

Seven years later, on August 20, 2012, at age ninety-five, she died in her sleep, leaving behind two children, four grandchildren, a great-grandchild, and an estate estimated at some $15 million. Her passing was marked by appreciations in major newspapers, the airing of old clips on television, and an outpouring by her fellow comedians, particularly the women who followed her onto the comedy stage. "She was there, she was doing it, she was filling rooms, and that's what made her such a great role model for someone like me starting out," Joan Rivers said. "Phyllis came out, and she talked, and she was funny, and she got off — and that was a big revelation in those days."

She had learned to believe in herself so completely and so purely that she created her own world, her own future, her own fortune, her own luck. Her body, the object of so many of her jokes over the decades, had succumbed. But her spirit, her verve, her example, and even her signature cackle: those seemed likely never to pass away.

Her last public performance, recorded just a few months before her death, was an absolutely perfect coda. Pink Martini pianist Thomas Lauderdale came to her home with a recording team and accompanied her while she sang every comedian's favorite ballad, "Smile," whose melody was written by no less than Charlie Chaplin. In her personal music room, at the end of nearly sixty years of entertaining audiences, her voice strong in some phrases and crackling with age in others, she sounded utterly confident, utterly plausible, and utterly convincing sharing simple words of hope and wisdom, words she practiced and embodied through her entire remarkable life:

You'll find that life is still worthwhile
If you just smile.

Six:
The Perfectionist

There's always some idiot who will come up to you and say, "You're just great for a girl. You think exactly like a man." For Chrissake, I always thought intelligence was neuter.

— 1970

In the strictest sense, Elaine May was never a stand-up comedian. Though she did occasional monologues, they were never purely solo; there was always at least one other performer on hand to play off of her or (more often) chase after her, sometimes a whole troupe. And even if one agrees to consider her days as a comic performer in theaters and nightclubs and on TV and record albums to be a form of stand-up, they barely lasted five years, easily the shortest time span of any of the women in this book.

But Elaine was indisputably a major instigator of a revolution in comedy the impact of which is still being felt today. She brought it to arguably its highest level of perfection and acclaim within a few years of its invention, and she walked away from it while the fires that forged it were still smoking, making it almost inevitable that her contribution to comedy would become legendary and widely imitated. And then, almost as if in retaliation for her decision to turn out the lights after her brilliant debut, when she tried to build a second act for herself, one equivalent to the career of the man she had worked alongside, she was battered down by a system that seemed bent on giving her opportunities and then making her suffer for the impertinence of availing herself of them.

Elaine wasn't only the first woman to become a star in the branch of modern comedy known as improv, she helped to create the "rules," such as they were, for what constituted an improv scene or act or show, and, with her partner Mike Nichols (whom contemporary observers, while admiring, often thought of as her second banana), she turned it into a nationwide sensation at a time when there were probably fewer than twenty people anywhere capable of performing it. She was a beguiling and mercurial and inventive and unattainable and deeply hilarious wild card, legendary for both her successes *and* her failures. It would be a measure of her impact and allure that more than sixty years after her meteoric arrival in the world's pop consciousness her name would still carry a frisson of mystery, possibility, and wonder.

Saturday, October 8, 1960.

American voters digest the previous night's debate between presidential candidates John Kennedy and Richard Nixon. The New York Yankees take a 2–1 lead in the World Series against the Pittsburgh Pirates. The United Nations rejects the People's Republic of China for the tenth time. In Antarctica, Belgian explorers discover a new mountain group, which they name for their monarch, Queen Fabiola.

And, unnoted in headlines, a nagging mother lays a guilt trip on her rocket scientist son; a frustrated public telephone user cannot get his dime back from a truculent operator; a fatuous radio DJ interviews an equally fatuous starlet; two teenagers chat and neck while parked in a lover's lane; a pair of office colleagues discuss the events of the day at a water cooler; married couples in France, England, and the United States deal in their own culturally tinted fashions with the shock of adultery; a weedy southern author is introduced at a lecture by a pompous chairlady; and new lovers coo over art, music, and literature while smoking postcoital cigarettes.

These ordinary events might not have ranked with the other happenings of the day. But they resonated broadly, especially considering that they all took place in a single room — the auditorium of the Golden Theatre on West Forty-Fifth Street in Manhattan — and that, in all cases, the people in question were embodied by the writers and performers solely responsible for their existence: Elaine May and Mike Nichols, both twenty-eight years old, both making their Broadway debuts, and, as a team, responsible for one of the most invigorating revolutions to hit show business in decades.

Nichols and May had surfaced in New York cabarets not three years before, with a half hour of semi-improvised sketches based on work they originally conceived and workshopped at experimental theaters in Chicago and St. Louis. Within weeks, they performed on TV to rapturous reviews and generated explosive business in a small Upper East Side cabaret. More TV work followed, along with record albums and radio spots and sold-out nightclub gigs in San Francisco, Chicago, and Hollywood. They did bits on the Emmy broadcast two years running; they wrote and performed prize-winning advertisements on radio and television. They appeared in a solo show at New York's Town Hall, selling the house out in an unprecedented success for a comedy team.

Now they were conquering Broadway. Their show, *An Evening with Mike Nichols and Elaine May,* would become one of the hottest tickets in town, even with the likes of Laurence Olivier and Bette Davis appearing on nearby stages. And they were doing it all with comedy sketches of their own devising, never repeating the material exactly from one performance to the next, and outright improvising the final scene of every show from scratch and happenstance.

For American audiences accustomed to the rat-a-tat one-liners of Milton Berle and Bob Hope and the polished, rehearsed sitcom shenanigans of Lucille Ball and Jackie Gleason, watching Nichols and May was like watching people walk a tightrope blindfolded — and, it seemed, without a tightrope. The pair were gossiped about, hungered for, imitated. People came to see them again and again, marveling at their facility for refashioning bits they'd performed dozens of times.[*] They were celebrated in newspapers and magazines and on TV, and a small cottage industry of boy-girl comedy acts rose in the wake of their success. As much as Marilyn Monroe, Mickey Mantle, and the Twist, Nichols and May embodied the moment.

Sixty years on, the things that Nichols and

* Literary poo-bah Edmund Wilson wrote in his diary that he saw them on Broadway four times and had multiple copies of their LPs on hand to give away to dinner guests for whom he played them.

May did together seem familiar, even if their act, captured on sound recordings and clips on the internet, can still provoke deep laughter. What they did was simplicity itself: two well-dressed young people sitting on stools, usually without props, playing characters who interacted with each other spontaneously, albeit within preconceived scaffolding. From night to night, show to show, line to line, there were variations and inventions, but the general shape of the bits more or less stayed true: improv but not anarchy.

That in itself was novel, an outgrowth of the experimental theater scene in which they first met in Chicago and which hadn't yet spread as far as New York or Los Angeles, much less into the popular cultural mainstream. But, too, Nichols and May were, alongside comic performers like Mort Sahl, Lenny Bruce, and Tom Lehrer, focused on contemporary cultural mores, deflating the pompous, the trendy, and the comfortable by turning a mirror on them and skewing things *just slightly.* Playing to so-called sophisticated crowds in New York, Chicago, San Francisco, and Los Angeles, even on Broadway, they made fun of the very people who were paying to see them: educated neurotics who read weekly news magazines, attended the most talked-about films, and adopted "serious" positions on political and cultural issues.

Every Nichols and May show was different.

But there were pieces they carried with them the entirety of their relatively brief career as a team, and they remain comedy standards.

Radio DJ: Of course, there's Albert Einstein's theory of relativity.

Starlet: Oh, you mean Al. A great dancer. Love his hair.

DJ: But of course he had to leave Germany because of Hitler.

Starlet: Oh, that Dolphie. He was a riot. I used to call him Cuddles.

DJ: Good God!

Starlet: Oh, him: a close personal friend of mine.

Teenage girl: It's just suicidally beautiful tonight. That lake out there. It's just a lot of little water and then, bang, all together it's a lake. That just kills me. You know, like, have you, for example, have you ever gone into your kitchen or your bathroom — you have, of course — and you turn the faucet on and water comes out of it into your glass and did you ever stop to realize that that water is that lake? It just knocks me out . . .

Teenage boy: I go right along witcha. That whole deal is very rough.

Nagging mother: Listen to me. You're very young. Someday you'll get married, and you'll have children of your own. And honey, when you do, I only pray that they make you suffer the way you're making me. That's all I want. That's a mother's prayer. I hope I didn't make you feel bad.

Rocket scientist: Are you kidding? I feel awful!

Mother: Oh honey. If I could believe that I'd be the happiest mother in the world!

And somehow, even when they went out of the way to bite the hands that were feeding them, they still managed not to wear out their welcome. Mostly. In May 1959, still ascending to what would be the height of their fame, they were asked to appear on the Emmy Awards broadcast. Elaine came out onstage and said,

There will be a lot said tonight about excellence. And the creative, the artistic, and the skillful will all be recognized and rewarded. But what of the others in this industry? (*Pause for a laugh.*) Seriously, there are men in the industry who go on, year in and year out, quietly and unassumingly producing garbage. (*Pause for an even bigger laugh.*)

The audience in the auditorium loved it. But the network — and the sponsors — did not. The show aired live on the East Coast, but the bit was cut from the taped West Coast feed.[*]

For all the glorious accolades the pair garnered, it was Elaine who was especially singled out for attention. Nichols, seen as the straight man, was respected for his quick wit, his intellect, his ability to sink into types. But Elaine simply dazzled critics and audiences alike. Time and again she was singled out as the sharper and more versatile comic, as the true novelty in the act. There were boy-girl comedy teams in show business previously — George Burns and Gracie Allen, Desi Arnaz and Lucille Ball — and the woman was often the one who got the laughs.[†] But those

[*] This wasn't their only affront to sponsors. They were preemptively cut from the *following* year's Emmy show because their proposed sketch was a parody of hair care products, one of which was running ads throughout the broadcast. Another ad spoof nixed from TV involved the two of them standing in front of a refrigerator; as Nichols described it, "I come out and say, 'This product has some very nice features,' and Elaine says, 'Yeah? Name one,' and I slap her.' "

[†] Worth mentioning here as well is the comedy team of Dean Martin and Jerry Lewis, the two-act that caused the biggest sensation in show business prior to Nichols and May. Dean was the nonplussed straight man — the *man*-man — and Jerry, the feral,

women were stuck in a single persona: the dumb blonde, the ditzy redhead. Elaine was a chameleon, capable of playing a sexy starlet, a nagging Jewish mother, a pompous PTA chairlady, a little girl, or an urban sophisticate in lightning-quick changes. As Edmund Wilson noted in his diary after spending some time with her, "Elaine is perhaps something of a genius. She transforms herself so completely in her various roles that until I saw her off the stage I had no real idea how she looked." And when people, men especially, did get to know the "real" Elaine, they were almost invariably smitten. "In love with Elaine?" recalled one acquaintance. "You'd have to be stupid not to have been."

She was, by all accounts, a new type of woman, certainly in the circles of comedy and show business. She dressed and behaved like a bohemian, unconcerned with the fashions or proprieties of the moment. She ate a diet of junk food, smoked constantly (cigarettes *and* cigars), went through boyfriends with little apparent care. She was, according to her theatrical colleagues and May

---

unpredictable one. In their films, several of which were remakes of screwball comedies, Jerry was often cast in what had originally been female roles. Roughly speaking, Jerry was Elaine to Dean's Nichols.

herself, the inventor of much of their material, coming up with scenarios and characters faster than they could be fashioned into useful bits. And she seemed utterly unconcerned with the business side of show business. As Jack Rollins, who managed Nichols and May to fame, put it, she was "completely disconnected from the practical world, and surely one of the most gifted artists with whom I have ever worked."

That estimation of her personality never wavered. For more than sixty years, Elaine May constituted such a strange and alluring presence in popular culture that it seemed almost impossible that she should have been born and raised and had a childhood like anyone else. But, in fact, she did — *kind of.*

Although it seemed to one colleague, who was only half kidding, that it happened in "a car trunk in Brazil or Argentina," Elaine Iva Berlin came into the world in Philadelphia on April 21, 1932, the second child of a pair of Yiddish theater troupers: Jack Berlin, an actor sometimes billed as "The Clown," and Ida Berlin, née Ida Aaron, who occasionally performed with her husband and more often worked backstage as a kind of manager/troubleshooter, looking after the money, costumes, and props, while also raising her oldest child, Louis. Jack's career, which spanned homey melodramas, knockabout comedies, and spectacles with casts of fifty-plus, frequently found him billed opposite actress Molly Cohen in such entertainments as *Yankele Sheigetz, Her Child's Wedding Night, The Rabbi's Grandchild, Divorced in Sing Sing, Itzik Seeks a Bride,* and *The Child of Sin.* As might be expected of show people, the little family moved constantly. Between 1929 and 1941, Berlin performed multiple times in cities throughout the Northeast and Midwest, in Los Angeles, and once, just before the outbreak of World War II, in Buenos Aires — anywhere, apparently, that Jewish populations were large enough to make performing in front of them at least modestly profitable.

Since baby Elaine was along with them anyhow, the Berlins put her to work. Bearing in mind that Elaine herself would claim that her childhood didn't unfold precisely as it has been reported, *not even by her,* she apparently took the stage with her father as early as age three and performed on the radio with him in a series of comic shorts built around a character named Baby Noodnik (an obvious riff on Fanny Brice's Baby Snooks persona). She further said that he was once abducted by the legendary Yiddish actor Aaron Lebedeff (to ends that she never specified) and that she spent a few years onstage playing a boy named Benny in one of her dad's stock dramas, a role that dried up for her when she turned eleven and started to mature physically. ("Our people do not

387

believe in breast-binding," she drolly explained.)

Jack Berlin died in 1944, and Ida kept the family moving, first to Chicago, where she had a brother in the restaurant business, and, a year or two later, to Los Angeles. There, she pursued a number of means of supporting herself — "My mother's a good businessman," Elaine later said — including founding a record label, Constellation Recordings, which put out a single disc by the Lind Brothers, three sons of a Detroit cantor.

Ida hoped her daughter would have a conventional education in their new home. Elaine had started school late — at age eight, she later recalled — and had already attended, by her count, more than forty schools before she arrived at Hollywood High.* Bored by classes, uninterested in social activities, she simply stopped going, staying home, ducking truant officers, reading books of mythology and fairy tales. (She *perhaps* spent some time at the Young Actors Company, a school/troupe created by Viola Spolin, who is widely credited with introducing improvisation to the American stage through a series of "Theater Games" that she taught to her young charges, including her son, Paul Sills.)

* Also walking the halls of the school at that time were future stars Stuart Whitman, Sheree North, and Marni Nixon.

At sixteen, in one of the out-of-the-blue choices typical of her, Elaine married. Marvin May, three years her senior, was a budding engineer/inventor who would go on to create a number of well-known toys and games, including the popular Eldon Bowl-a-Matic. The youthful marriage didn't take. They parted by 1950, not long after their daughter, Jeannie Brette May,* was born, and they formally divorced a few years after that.

Elaine chose to keep her husband's surname and to continue exploring opportunities as an actor, as well as pursuing an oddball variety of careers including writing advertising copy and working on stakeouts for a private eye trying to catch adulterers. She spent some time studying the Stanislavskian system of acting — "the Method" — with the Russian actress Maria Ouspenskaya, who had learned it from the inventor of the system himself and had opened a school in Hollywood. But asked to enact the life of a seed that sprouts into a tree and then buds with leaves, Elaine froze. "I couldn't bud to save my life," she admitted later. "I knew I wasn't a tree." She considered giving formal education another try. She had heard that the University of Chicago didn't require a high

* As a teen and thereafter, the girl would take her maternal grandparents' name and be known as Jeannie Berlin.

school diploma or college entrance exams of incoming students, and so, leaving Jeannie in the care of her mother, she made her way to Chicago.

Consider her situation: a single mother, in her early twenties, with little formal education, no particular skills, no obvious direction, arriving in a big city by herself in the early 1950s. She was gifted with beauty and a sharp, if uncultivated, intellect. But she wasn't particularly keen to play on those assets to find a man to help her make her way in the world. Indeed, she had a chip on her shoulder. She favored bohemian clothing and hairstyles, she suffered fools not a whit, she proclaimed her disdains and distastes readily, and she had a famously quick and wicked tongue. Followed down a street by a pair of men catcalling her, she asked, "What's the matter? Tired of each other?" When one retorted, "Fuck you!" she replied, "With what?" Another day, another victim: A young man of her acquaintance chanced upon her on a windy afternoon, noted the disheveled, witchy state of her hair, and asked, playfully, "Hi, Elaine, did you bring your broomstick?" "Why?" she immediately replied. "Do you want something up your ass?" ("Generally," said Mike Nichols, "it was unwise for people to start trouble with her.")

Traditional schooling still held no allure for

her. She may not even have officially enrolled in the university. But she drifted in and out of classes, often making her presence known with sarcastic comments at the expense of instructors and students. She became something of a notorious figure on campus. Men, especially, found her unforgettable. But even as she was surrounded by potential suitors, she intimidated the hell out of many of them. "A kind of scarifying lady," said the theatrical director Tom O'Horgan. "A potential black widow," recalled the actor/writer Omar Shapli. (Women, predictably, saw something more human: Annette Hankin, who acted with Elaine, opined, "I think she saw love in a cruel light and all things as trade-offs. It was a terrible, awesome vision, that of a person who has survived an emotional holocaust." She was, Hankin continued, "one of these women who likes to think they're very vulnerable. In fact, she was one of the toughest women I ever knew, a real tough cookie.")

Almost inevitably, she gravitated toward the stage. Among her fellow theater rats was a fellow Angelino, Paul Sills, who was involved in several groups determined to shake up the university's relatively staid theater world. Sills and a wispy, evangelical fellow from back east named David Shepherd staged avant-garde plays and used some of the improvisational techniques taught by Sills's mother, Viola Spolin. Elaine was swept into the activity, joining Sills in a student-run troupe known as "Tonight at 8:30." When campus authorities shut that group down for fire code violations, Sills and Shepherd rebuilt it in a former Chinese restaurant nearby, launching it as the Playwrights Theatre Club in the summer of 1953.

Elaine was a keen participant in the Club (thus named because it was, in fact, an actual club with paying members). "I got all the parts that called for a girl who could wear a trench coat and a beret," she remembered. But she also appeared in productions of Shakespeare, Ibsen, Chekhov, and T. S. Eliot, wrote an adaptation of Rumpelstiltskin for the group's children's theater, directed a number of plays, and led workshops in improvisational techniques. The theater put on more than two dozen shows, including the Chicago premiere of *The Threepenny Opera,* and it attracted some impressive young talents: actresses Barbara Harris and Zohra Lampert and actor Ed Asner, who not only performed onstage but was in charge of cleaning the theater. In time, the group moved into a larger space, a former photographer's studio with two hundred seats. But, again, fire marshals shut the doors.

Sills and Shepherd launched a new enterprise meant to exemplify Viola Spolin's improvisatory techniques. A friend had recently taken ownership of a bar and the empty storefront adjacent to it and let the new acting troupe rebuild the vacant space as a small theater. On July 5, 1955, the Compass Theater — thus named to imply that its work would point to wherever society was heading — debuted. Among the performers on opening night was Elaine.

The Compass changed the world. Not immediately, not so that everyone saw it at once, but definitively and permanently. It was the first theater devoted entirely to comic improvisation, and together with its next incarnation, launched four years later as the Second City, it would serve as a training ground for some of the greatest comedy performers and writers of the latter decades of the twentieth century: Mike Nichols and Elaine May, Shelley Berman, Alan Arkin, Jerry Stiller and Anne Meara, Joan Rivers, Robert Klein, and dozens of cast members of *Saturday Night Live* and *SCTV,* among them John Belushi, Dan Aykroyd, Bill Murray, Martin Short, Catherine O'Hara, Gilda Radner, and Tina Fey. Comedy was changing rapidly at the end of the 1950s, with social satirists and quasi-confessional monologists increasingly taking the spotlight and alternative performance spaces popping up in the form of semi-underground nightclubs in New York, San Francisco, and a select few other big cities. But one of the most important new streams of comedy, for decades to come, had its headwaters at the tiny Chicago storefront theater that Sills and Shepherd opened that summer.

Prior to the Compass, a large part of what America consumed as comedy took the shape of funnymen (and, very rarely, funnywomen) delivering one-liners, usually created by paid gag writers, or playing scripted sketches (again, written by others). With the Compass, the emphasis shifted definitively to performers developing their own material in improvisatory exercises, creating characters that could inhabit various comic situations. It wasn't necessary to have a fully realized concept, fully human characters, a story with a beginning and end, or even, strictly speaking, *jokes.* The idea was to create lived-in vignettes that opened to bigger and further explorations — of humor, of pathos, of human behavior, of social foibles.

There was a similarity to the Stanislavskian school of method acting, in that performers were being asked to inhabit a specific moment and a specific persona or situation and then react instinctively. But the emphasis at the Compass was comedy, not the soul baring associated with method actors like Marlon Brando and James Dean. The Compass hoped to enlighten with a tickle, not a branding iron. And, strictly speaking, there were no scripts. Method actors strove to behave with lifelike instinct within the prescribed lines of a play or film. Compass performers approached every night as one of Viola Spolin's theater games, improvising off a rough blueprint, a thrilling (and potentially disastrous) proposition that, when it worked, yielded sensational entertainment and real epiphanies.

The Compass staggered in its earliest steps. It suffered from the sort of money problems, personnel issues, and human dramas to which such gaggles of young aesthetes can be prone. Within three months of opening, the struggling enterprise moved to a new home farther from the University of Chicago campus, and Paul Sills went to England on a Fulbright scholarship. Elaine was put in charge of the improv workshops. And a handful of new cast members appeared, including a tart actor named Shelley Berman and an aloof former University of Chicago student named Mike Nichols.

In many crucial ways, Nichols and Elaine couldn't have been more different. He was a born director, with the big picture always in his mind's eye; she was a natural writer and performer, too agitated and inventive to hold to the same course twice. He was businesslike and organized and prompt; she was scattershot and untidy and always, but *always,* late. He was materialistic; she had to be convinced to spend money on nice things. But they had a lot in common: creative restlessness and cruel tongues and an interest in theater and more ambition than they may have cared to admit. They were both perennial outsiders, starving for acceptance in some ways but sufficiently confident, as well, in their superiority to feel no need to belong to even an elite clique.

For Elaine, that sense of outsiderness stemmed from her vagabond upbringing and her independence of mind. For Nichols, it was a matter of intelligence, too, but also of literal alienation. May might have been born to a Yiddish-speaking family *named* Berlin; Nichols was actually born *in* Berlin, as Mikhail Igor Peschkowsky,[*] on November 6, 1931, to a physician named Pavel Nikolaevich Peschkowsky and his wife, Brigitte. Both sides of the family were Jewish, intellectual, and well off. As the Peschkowsky family of Berlin grew — Mikhail was followed in 1935 by a brother, Robert — it became clear that Germany was no longer safe for them. In late 1938, Pavel made his way to New York, where he Americanized his name to Paul Nichols. The following spring, Brigitte put her two boys on a boat to New York, where they were

[*] It has been suggested by Nichols's biographer Mark Harris that his name was possibly Igor Mikhail.

taken in by a foster family. She herself made her way the following year, and the four were reunited.

Mikhail, henceforth Michael, arrived in America knowing only two sentences in the language being spoken all around him: "I don't speak English" and "Please don't kiss me" (his parents legitimately feared communicable diseases). Additionally, he was painfully self-conscious because an inoculation he had received for whooping cough at age four had caused him to lose all the hair on his body permanently; he would wear wigs and false eyebrows for virtually his entire life. Moreover, Paul and Brigitte were both hard on their eldest son, he severely critical of the boy's intellect and accomplishments, she emitting an almost stereotypical litany of Jewish-mother guilt. You couldn't create a more perfect recipe for a thin-skinned outsider.

Financially, they were secure. Paul worked as a doctor in a union hall upon his arrival, X-raying workers for lung disease. Later, he opened a private practice and made enough money for a home near Central Park on the Upper West Side and private educations for his sons. But all that time around X-ray machines proved deadly; he developed leukemia and died in 1944 at age forty-four.

The Nichols household finances crumbled, but Mike was in sufficient academic standing to continue attending school on scholarship. When he finally graduated, though, he had no idea what was next. He was interested in the theater, so he investigated New York University but backed away, opting instead to work full-time. When *that* proved soul-sucking, he became aware of the relatively lax admission policies of the University of Chicago. So off he went.

On his very first day on campus, Nichols found himself in line at the registrar's office behind a darkly beautiful, terrifically intelligent young woman from California named . . . Susan Sontag. The two struck up a conversation and became fast friends, but where she had genuine interest in scholarship, Nichols was a dilettante, appearing in classes more like a visiting guest than a serious student. He found work as an announcer on classical music radio station WFMT and reveled in the bohemian squalor of his life, making enemies with his sharp tongue and behaving, an acquaintance said, not kindly, like "a princeling deprived of his rightful fortune."

He found his calling in student theatricals, acting in and directing a number of plays. Inevitably, he encountered Paul Sills and, soon after, just as inevitably, *another* dark, beautiful, intelligent girl from California.

They met cute, if by "cute" you meant

"under a veil of barely disguised hostility." Elaine was invited by Sills to attend the opening night of a campus production of Strindberg's *Miss Julie,* and, as Nichols, one of the leads, remembered, she sat in the front row laughing aloud at moments meant to be dramatic and regarding the entire enterprise with a "look of utter contempt." As he remembered, "I sensed her out there. In a dark brown trench coat. Hostile." The performance was reviewed favorably in the *Chicago Daily News,* and Nichols, a copy of the paper in hand, chanced upon Sills and "this evil, hostile girl" on campus. He showed them the review, which she took a look at and, walking away, summarized in one word: "Ha!" (He claimed that he brushed this insult off, but, she insisted, "He wept.")

Nichols couldn't forget being insulted so gratuitously ("My insults were not gratuitous," she recalled to his face), but he did agree that "we loathed one another at first sight." Yet there was a connection, too, if more Benedick and Beatrice than Romeo and Juliet; Nichols later admitted that he hated Elaine immediately because "I knew she knew [the play] was shit, and there was no way I could let her know that I knew it also." And there was the repeated assurance of mutual friends that they were just like one another. As Sills had told Elaine when inviting her to the play, "I want you to meet the only person at the University of Chicago who is as hostile as you."

A few weeks after that first gnarly encounter, Nichols was commuting to his radio job when he chanced upon that withering girl sitting, with a predictably unapproachable aura, on a bench in a train station near campus. He approached her, adopting a Mitteleuropean accent.

"May I seet down, pliz?"

She was game.

"Eeef you vish."

"Do you haff a light?"

"Yes, zertainly."

"I hed a lighter but . . . (*voice lowered conspiratorially*) I lost it on Fifty-Seventh Street."

"Oh! So you must be . . . Agent X-9."

And off they went.

(It was such a good bit that they would do variations on it for years as part of their professional act.)

It *wasn't* the start of a romance. In the coming years, many onlookers assumed that Nichols and Elaine were a couple, or at least *had been* one at some time. In part it was to do with the palpable chemistry and even intimacy between them that excluded others and *seemed* like a love affair: "People are always telling us they feel left out," Elaine remarked. Like everyone, Nichols lusted after Elaine: "Everybody wanted Elaine, and the

400

people who got her couldn't keep her," he remembered. In fact, many of them wound up burnt and skewered. But Nichols had an instinct that she wouldn't turn her vicious wit on him. "We were safe from everyone else when we were with each other," he said, "and also safe from each other. I knew somehow that she would not do to me the things she'd done to other guys." There were some hints that *perhaps* he spent a few nights at her squalidly appointed apartment; one colleague even noticed that there was a brief period when their improvs made reference to the Kama Sutra. But if it happened, and it's not clear that it did, it was over with quickly. Their romance was meant for the stage, their intimacy to be conducted through the masks of the characters they invented. Ever after, Nichols would only ever allow that *perhaps* they'd been romantic for one brief spell, and Elaine was even cagier. Decades on, asked outright, "Were you lovers or not?" She declared, conclusively: "I will answer that. We were lovers or not." Whatever the case, they were allied, if perhaps uneasily, from that encounter on.

A few months after falling in with Elaine, Nichols returned to New York to pursue an acting career. Always blessed with a sharp insight, though, he quickly discerned that he was nowhere near the level of the talent around him. In 1955, a rescue boat of sorts appeared. Paul Sills came through New York looking for new players for the Compass, and Nichols grabbed at the chance to return to Chicago. Even though he knew almost nothing of the improvisatory techniques the troupe employed, he decided he was ready to join.

Nichols's arrival at the Compass may have seemed a slight, even humble business — he later recalled that he'd "slunk back to Chicago." But there was some electricity in the air when he came face to face with his frenemy, Elaine. One witness to their reunion recalled the two of them facing off in a back room of the theater, sitting on stools, sizing each other up, "doing these routines, testing each other's ad-lib ability and spontaneity. Everybody was watching."

Everything that eventually made Nichols and May such a great comedy team was already there on those stools. Their minds delighted equally in wordplay, musicality, irony. "We both thought the same things were funny," she recalled. "We found each other hilarious." She was a consummate innovator; he had the ability to see patterns in the chaos of play and shape a coherent structure from it. He created a gallery of nebbishes, mediocrities, and insipid sophisticates, and she immediately invented shrews, martinets, and airheads to play off them. When they began performing their pieces for audiences, he could remember from night to night which lines and plot twists had worked and which hadn't, imposing some order, while she, ever restless, would ad-lib and improvise hilariously. Beneath this was a tension that could threaten to tear them apart: he was ambitious, materialistic, fearful of tumult; she was indifferent to success, money, and acclaim, always wanting to push toward innovation or deeper truths. But in the first flush of their partnership at the Compass, none of that was evident. What was clear was that two gunslingers had formed a team that had the potential to be bigger than the stage they were sharing with the rest of the troupe.

Otherwise, though, Nichols had trouble fitting in. It wasn't unheard of for newcomers to need a while to find their sea legs in this still-emerging theatrical form. What was unique with Nichols was that he was blocked with everyone *except* Elaine. With her, he said, he felt "a certain connection" and could sense "a certain mad gleam in either her or my eyes when we knew something was starting." And, he claimed, he could only generate this facility when working with *her*. "She could do it with several people. I could always do it only with her. I never did a good scene of any kind with anybody else."

For her part, Elaine still intimidated the snot out of many of her fellow Compass players. Her wit was too quick and sharp, her instincts too primal, her patience too thin. She sat around the theater in rumpled clothes, chain-smoking, eating apples, cores and all, with a cloud of suitors buzzing around her like drone bees. She literally had ideas for new scenes falling out of her pockets and the baby buggy that she pushed around in lieu of a purse. On top of fear, she also commanded respect — many of her colleagues would matter-of-factly refer to her "genius." But she was often treated with chauvinistic condescension. When she shared her ideas for new work, her fellow players would often act as if imposed upon. "I don't think anyone ever said it was good," remembered director Mark Gordon. "Every time she came in with material, it was, 'Oh my God, it's awful. It will never work'. . . . Then someone would kind of grudgingly say, 'OK, we'll try it.' Then we'd do it for people at night and the audience would be hysterical loving it. . . . But there was never a recognition that Elaine's stuff was fantastic." For Roger Bowen, another writer and actor in the group, the reason was obvious: "We, being men, just ignored her." (Compass co-founder David Shepherd would, years later, say that Elaine "broke through the psychological restrictions of playing comedy as a woman," apparently incapable of realizing that those psychological restrictions were not *hers* but *his* — and those of his male colleagues.)

Together at the Compass, Nichols and May developed the pieces that would become their bread and butter for years to come: the teenagers necking in the parked car; the parade of international couples reacting to the news of adultery; the name-dropping radio DJ and starlet; the pompous PTA lady and the drunken, poetic author. Their most exciting creation was an extended number they called "Pirandello." The radical piece started with them playing a pair of children interacting in imitation of their parents; they seamlessly segued into teendom, intensifying their mock-adult dialogue with an increasingly hostile edge; and finally they achieved adulthood and their banter morphed into outright anger bordering on violence; when the tension felt unbearably thick, almost as if the real Mike and Elaine were having a real fight as their real selves, they would suddenly break character, turn to the audience, and shout, "Pirandello!," revealing the whole thing as an elaborate game.

In the overheated atmosphere of the Compass, where people could be at one another's throats daily, the onstage friction of "Pirandello" could easily be mistaken for the real thing. "I thought Mike and Elaine had flipped and were really taking out some backstage venom," recalled Compass player Eugene Troobnick. "Of course, at the end I realized I had been taken in." Nichols and May would do "Pirandello" for years, often fooling people with the intensity of the thing, more often dazzling people with its sheer originality. They not-so-secretly relished the effect that the piece had on audiences and even their fellow players. But at least once over the years of performing it, something genuinely awful emerged. "The fight got away from us," Nichols recalled. "I must have blacked out because I suddenly found that I had her by the front of the shirt, and I had been hitting her back and forth for a long time, and my chest was pouring blood from where she had clawed it open. And they brought down the curtain and we cried a lot. It never happened again. But that one time, it suddenly actually did take us over."

That frightening incident seemed of a piece with the intimacy, immediacy, and depth of their rapport. Even the most talented and, eventually, famous of their peers couldn't penetrate their circle. Shelley Berman was a serious actor originally from Chicago whom Paul Sills had discovered on the same trip to New York during which he recruited Nichols. Berman was one of Elaine's best collaborators, creating scenarios with her that would long outlive their time as fellow players. She wasn't exactly an *easygoing* partner — "The next time you fuck me up onstage, I will pull your zipper and pull out your dick," she once told him. But she was able to move past such incidents to focus on the work. Nichols, though, was cold and even hostile to Berman. Berman tried to put his personal feelings aside and continued to conceive scenarios that the three of them could perform together. He even went so far as to propose that they officially form an act and set out on their own, but Nichols and May rejected the idea in their characteristic fashions. When Berman declared, "After all, we're a trio," Nichols withered him with, "What trio?" And to his suggestion that they might call themselves "Two Wigs and a Wag," Elaine shot back that a better name would be "Two Cocksuckers and Elaine."*

While Nichols and May nurtured the partnership that would make them famous, the Compass moved its home base again, settling further yet from the bohemian comforts of the University of Chicago community. There the troupe proved popular with a new crowd, a clientele that struck many of the players as

---

* Berman would go on to tremendous success as a comic monologist if not quite a stand-up comedian, with three massive hit LPs high on the charts simultaneously in 1959 and 1960, the most famous of which, *Inside Shelley Berman,* would become the first album to win a Grammy for a nonmusical recording.

the sort of people they should have been satirizing: well-to-do, suburban, entitled, *comfortable.*

Elaine was particularly unhappy with this turn in the company's fortunes. She hated being the hip flavor of the month. "Elaine didn't give a shit if the audience didn't like her work," remembered Mark Gordon. "She worried when the audience liked it too much." But Nichols actually thrived in an environment of good press and well-heeled patrons. He had taken the role of Lucky in the Chicago debut of *Waiting for Godot* and had begun a romance with Patricia Scot, a jazz singer and rising local celebrity. Scot had come to see the Compass several times and had touted them in her radio and TV appearances. The two married in early 1957; at the celebratory breakfast, Elaine remarked to another guest, "Isn't it a beautiful first wedding?"

Paul Sills had returned from Europe with the idea of expanding the Compass to other cities — New York, in particular. He began traveling back east in search of financial support and potential locations. At the same time, a new member of the circle, Ted Flicker, was granted permission to open a satellite troupe of the Compass in St. Louis, where they'd been offered a theater to perform in and an actual mansion where they could live.

In April 1957, the satellite version of the

Compass began appearing at the Crystal Palace, a cabaret built by the bohemian Landesman brothers of St. Louis. That first seedling group consisted of Flicker, a strange, talented young actor named Del Close, and the actresses Jo Henderson and Nancy Ponder. Within a month, Nichols and Elaine, who were still waiting for the New York Compass to come to fruition, visited St. Louis, unannounced, and declared their intention to return and join the company, which they did the following month.

As before, Elaine became the focus of the men in their new circle. "She was sitting on the floor," Flicker recalled, "and said, 'Where does a girl get laid around here?' I thought, 'Oh no, not me.' " She had a romance with Close, a volatile character prone to excess but a brilliant natural improviser. She and Nichols continued to work most productively in tandem, but she was fully immersed in the life of the Compass, regularly coming up with new scenarios for the troupe, creating, in partnership with Flicker, a set of "rules" for improvisatory performance, and conducting workshops to inculcate these precepts into her colleagues and any new arrivals to the troupe.

Nichols, on the other hand, considered St. Louis a step backward. He seemed more interested in the New York Compass, which was still only a theoretical entity. And his unhappiness was infecting the whole company.

The story gets a little murky here.

According to one account, Nichols decided to go to New York and help Sills get *that* version of the Compass off the ground or, to hell with Compass, to start a new group of his own. When no prospects arose, he returned.

According to another account, Nichols convinced Elaine, Close, and Ponder to form a quartet and go to New York, where, he said, he had connections to get them started; the four pooled their resources, bought two round-trip tickets to New York, and Nichols and Elaine went off to meet a prospective agent, returning the following day.

In either case, once he was back in St. Louis, his New York beachhead still not established, Nichols attempted a mutiny of sorts, trying to wrest control of the Compass from Flicker. A series of dramas unfolded, with Elaine insisting that Flicker fire Nichols or risk watching her leave. Flicker gave Nichols the ax, and Nichols determined to go off to New York and a new career.

But he didn't intend to do it alone. Again, it would prove hard in later years for the principals to be clear about what happened next, and it wouldn't, ultimately, matter. Nichols and Elaine were in New York by the end of summer, 1957, and soon after that

410

scheduled an audition with Jack Rollins, a rising figure in the ranks of talent managers, who'd been recommended to Nichols by an actor friend. If nothing else, they were hopeful that Rollins would buy them lunch. Their money was running low, and no prospects were forthcoming.

The meeting was a coup. Rollins may only have had a few clients — singer Felicia Sanders, impressionist Will Jordan, comedian Tom Poston — but he was on his way to becoming a legend, the man who would discover and launch such icons as Woody Allen, Robin Williams, David Letterman, and Billy Crystal and help them sustain their careers. He was able to do it all in part because he genuinely had two qualities that very few other people in show biz did: he was ethical, and he was an innovator.

Born in Brooklyn in 1915 as Jacob Rabinowitz, the son of immigrants, Rollins graduated City College and served the U.S. Army in India during World War II, after which he returned to New York with an eye toward a career in show business. He was floundering as an aspiring Broadway producer and a junior agent at MCA when he hit on a novel concept: he would *manage* talent, not as an agent — that is, a representative who could negotiate deals and contracts — but as a *personal manager,* a combination of coach, confessor, idea man, and drum beater, a role that prior to his conceiving of it didn't really exist.

A number of successful entertainers had managers who were relatives or family friends or early boosters who worked for them in the role that Rollins envisioned — one of them, Milton Berle's mother, Sandra, was a notorious lioness in protecting her son's interests. But Rollins had in mind to make a profession of it, scouring nightclubs and tiny theaters for undiscovered talents who could benefit from his services and were needy enough to take a flier on him. When he found performers he thought had the goods, Rollins would almost literally nurture them toward stardom. He provided his clients (and he never had a very large roster) with such basics as food, lodging, spending money, clothes, transportation. He cosigned their loans, stood for them at their weddings, spent nights listening to their tales of broken hearts, attended their family events. And he worked with them to forge their acts, selecting material, choosing wardrobe, honing their stagecraft, finding the best lighting and sound settings, and so on. He was Henry Higgins, Dr. Frankenstein, and Broadway Danny Rose in one, remaking raw talent into something that could — and many times did — succeed on stage and screen. By the fall of 1957, he had offices on the seventeenth floor of the Plaza Hotel, in what had once been a maid's bedroom. That was the tiny aerie in which he met these unknown kids from Chicago . . . or was it St. Louis?

Later, Nichols would recall that the meeting took place in the famed Russian Tea Room, not far from the Plaza on West Fifty-Seventh Street. "We walked in and had a scoop of borscht," said Nichols two years later, "while wildly improvising a set of ad-libbed little skits we not only had never rehearsed but had never even thought of until that desperate minute."

Rollins, who had a more likely recollection of meeting the pair in his office and *then* taking them to lunch, had never heard of, much less laid eyes on a demonstration of this sort. "I'd never seen this technique before," he recalled. "I thought, 'My God, these are two people writing hilarious comedy on their feet!' " What was more, they were, as far as the jaded Rollins could tell, almost entirely *innocent:* "They were so un-show business they didn't know how to be scared. They were remarkable immediately. They were complete. I knew they had something odd and wonderful, but I didn't know whether to laugh or cry."

(They all agreed, in the end, that Nichols and Elaine were off the hook for the tab. "When the coffee came," Nichols said soon after, "I remember with some relief that he

413

not only signed us but also sprang for the lunch check. That had us pretty worried.")

At first, Rollins wasn't entirely sure what to do with this new discovery or even, really, what it was. Nichols and May had a modern technique but were funny in a primal, human way. They were sophisticated, but they also seemed connected to the all-American, midwestern birthing grounds of their act. They were a boy-girl act like Burns and Allen or Lucy and Desi, but they played multiple characters and did bits and jokes from genres of their own invention. Where did they belong?

He was inspired to get them an audition at the Blue Angel, where the intrepid Herman Jacoby booked them immediately, nearly on Rollins's word alone, as the opening act on a bill with singer-pianist Martha Davis and comedian Phil Leeds. The gig would start ten days later, but, as Nichols and Elaine were quick to point out, they were broke. Fortunately, Jacoby had a partner, Max Gordon, who operated another club, downtown, the Village Vanguard, which normally featured jazz and folk musicians but was currently dark. Straightaway, Gordon booked Mort Sahl, the reigning king of social satire comedy, for a week, with Nichols and May opening. Not much more than a month or so after arriving in town, they debuted.

Their set was just short of a half hour,

including a couple of bits that they would do for years: the teenagers making out in the car, and the vignettes of the varied faces of adultery in the United States, England, and France. As they would for almost their whole career, they ended with an improvised sketch based on opening and closing lines of dialogue and a literary style suggested by the audience.

It was a smash.

"Mike Nichols and Elaine May are hipsters' hipsters," declared *Variety* in its "New Acts" section. "Their thought patterns are Cloud No. 7 inspired and their comedic routines are really far out. It's an act that requires plenty of 'digging' on the aud's part. In a setting such as the Vanguard with its hip music policy, the duo is in a favorable environment. The comedy interlude makes for an interesting, if somewhat heady, change of pace."

Backstage, Gordon and his wife, Lorraine, looked on in amazement. They, too, had never seen such an act. "They were auditioning live," she remembered. "Max, my husband, he came up to me and said, 'Please don't laugh so loud. The agent is in the room and the price is going to go up.' "

Despite acknowledging the brilliance of the act, *Variety* felt a need to qualify its praise. As if confounded by the sheer novelty of what he'd seen, its critic implied that the material was too high-toned for the general public, describing it as having an "egghead approach" and surmising that "in average exposure spots [it] will have trouble finding its mark." But there was no denying Nichols and May's impact among the cognoscenti, even during the relatively brief run at the Vanguard. Sahl, famously thin-skinned and disagreeable, didn't care for the competition they represented. He would occasionally tell the house manager that he wanted to take the stage without a warm-up. "[He] would feel the crowd was ready and say, 'They're not going on tonight. I'll go right on,' " remembered Nichols. "We were very pissed with him because we'd be ready to go and he'd say, 'No, no. Skip them — I'm ready.' "

It was the last time anyone thought of skipping over Nichols and May. At the end of the month, after Jack Rollins had taken them shopping for proper stage attire, they debuted at the Blue Angel, the bottom act on an eclectic bill. Once again, *Variety* simultaneously appreciated them and damned them as excessively clever, admitting they were "a pair of promising players" but adding that they were "too much impressed with themselves" and "too precious at several stages in their act." Once again, cult status was all that the critic could imagine, claiming the pair "needs the intimacy of a small room and an audience of spirits kindred to theirs. . . . Without a broader common denominator, their horizons are limited."

At the end of December, they played another run at the Blue Angel, this time *fourth* billed. Again, *Variety* liked what they saw and, again, the critic couldn't see it going very far: "It still seems like a specialized and precious kind of humor whose spark of life would be destroyed if purveyed before mass audiences on the slum side of Park Ave."

Among the "specialized and precious" Manhattan cabaret-goers and hipsters, however, Nichols and May were a sensation, almost immediately, and the tiny Blue Angel was choked with business. "There were lines outside the club within two weeks," remembered Rollins. "They were the hottest thing in the city." (It was said that Milton Berle, one of the reigning gods of comedy, came to see them and was turned away *three times* for lack of space.) As Nichols put it, "We were nothing, absolutely nothing. And then, all of a sudden, we've got a career."

Their horizons were soon tested in the most visible way possible: Rollins started booking Nichols and May on television. They had a run at Jack Paar's *Tonight Show* in late 1957 — and flopped, not even passing their audition. Their timing seemed too slow for the rhythm of the show, maybe even of the medium itself; laughs that built gradually in a nightclub never reached full power in the lightning-quick environment imposed by TV.

Rollins got them another shot, on Steve Allen's Sunday-night variety show, and, adjusting to the format and pace of television, they got onto the air and fared well.

And then, in January 1958, the breakthrough of breakthroughs, on *Omnibus,* a highbrow magazine-format cultural program. It was a special edition of the show, airing on Tuesday in prime time rather than Sunday afternoon and hosted by funnyman Bert Lahr rather than the professorial Alistair Cooke. The subject of the hour was contemporary suburbia, and Nichols and May were given two extended segments to present set pieces from their nightclub act; they did the surefire necking teenagers bit and another sketch about a man on a public phone being tortured by an information operator.

The reviews were sensational, coast to coast. "Each item had style and freshness," said the *New York Times,* "and Miss May in particular is a comedienne of very great promise." "Two of the funniest, freshest comics ever to use TV as a stepping stone to national fame," said *Billboard,* adding that Nichols and May "wiped Bert Lahr & Company off the screen." There were positive notices in *Newsweek* and *Time* (again, "fresh" being the accolade of choice). Even *Variety* had nothing but praise for the, yes, "fresh and engaging humor put forth by Elaine May and Mike Nichols — especially by Miss May."

Now they were a juggernaut. Rollins booked them as the headliners for the opening of a new club, Down in the Depths, in a bar-room underneath the Hotel Duane on Madison Avenue in midtown. Another triumph. They returned to the Blue Angel, this time on top of the bill, and the *New York Journal-American* reported that the sidewalk outside the club on East Fifty-Fifth Street was jammed with people trying unsuccessfully to get into either of the evening's two performances.

That spring, they made their West Coast debut at Mocambo, the Sunset Strip night-club better known for musical acts, and they were, again, a smash. (On opening night, they were introduced, with very little in the way of commentary, by Milton Berle, *finally* able to catch their act.) They played a homecoming engagement of sorts in Chicago at the famed club Mister Kelly's, where they shattered box office records. They returned to New York and the Blue Angel, and continued to pack the club for every show.

In August, they appeared in front of a small crowd at a Manhattan recording studio and spent several hours working through a number of routines with the accompaniment of pianist Marty Rubenstein. A *Billboard* reporter who sat in on the session lamented that some of the funniest things that the pair did weren't recorded for the album: "They really ought to cut a wax session incorporating the long bits that come from simple remarks like 'What we need is a theremin,' and 'Why can't I say *gloryosky?*' " The LP that resulted from the day was released by Mercury Records as *Improvisations Set to Music* and proved a critical and commercial hit when it appeared in December. (For the liner notes, the performers were permitted to write their own biographies. Elaine's said, in its entirety: "miss may does not exist" [*sic*]).

Rollins booked them to do small, improvised interstitial bits for NBC Radio's weekend *Monitor* news magazine; during the run of that gig, they conceived and performed *hundreds* of impromptu routines, several of which were nurtured into more robust sketches for stage and television. By the fall of 1958, Rollins claimed that he was turning down as many as eight offers of TV work each week.* People were speculating that they would get their own series or start making movies. They continued to do turn-away

---

* He was also turning away people who wanted to write for the pair, explaining that they created their own material; one of these prospective gag men captured Rollins's imagination sufficiently that he asked the writer if he had ever considered performing his own act — guy by the name of Woody Allen, who was said, in his early days, to be so unsteady onstage that he could only perform if he did so in imitation of . . . Elaine May.

business at the Blue Angel, where they had essentially become the house act and were commanding the highest minimum-per-customer fees of any nightclub in New York — a whopping seven dollars on weekends.*

All this within a year, more or less, of their professional debut.

There were missteps: *Laugh Line,* a TV game show based on improvised sketches that costarred Dick Van Dyke, Dorothy Loudon, and Orson Bean and debuted with a thud, quickly vanishing; *The Red Mill,* a TV adaptation of a Victor Herbert operetta along with such unlikely costars as Donald O'Connor, Shirley Jones, and Harpo Marx; a ninety-minute TV play, *Journey to the Day,* in which they were cast in straight dramatic roles (Elaine quit the cast before taping; Nichols stuck it out, to awful reviews). But the successes and the raves, from critics and audiences alike, were far more numerous and greater and truly astounding, even to Nichols and May themselves. "We were so surprised," Nichols recalled. "What were they all carrying on about? We were so sort of dazed by it. . . . Neither of us could understand this . . . *thing.* And to this day, it's the only thing that either of us has done that has never been criticized at all by anyone."

Nichols was chuffed with their heady as-

* Approximately $61 in 2022.

cent, spending money on cars, clothes, a posh apartment, even horses, and palling around with swells. But Elaine was, characteristically, more chary and uneasy about it all. She genuinely preferred the work to the acclaim, and she seemed truly uncomfortable with the accoutrements of fame and fortune. "My ambitions are not connected with success," she told a reporter. "I perceive nothing operationally different in my life." She liked to brag about being able to live on twelve dollars a week, and she came to see that "the only reason you become shaky about money is because you're scared it will go away." She moved her mother and daughter to New York and rented an apartment for them all to share on West End Avenue on the Upper West Side, but she barely furnished it, using a ping-pong table as a dining table and giving antique dealers hell when they tried to interest her in this or that precious item: "You mean it's *second-hand*???!!!" she would shriek in mock ignorance.

In the spring of 1959, they appeared on the bill of a showcase of performers at the New York City Center, alongside the likes of singer Lotte Lenya, dancer Jacques d'Amboise, and comic actresses Tallulah Bankhead and Martha Raye. The warm reception they received inspired Rollins to build an entire evening around them at Town Hall, a comedy concert, in effect, in a larger room than had ever been dedicated to such a performance. They did several of their familiar bits, and they presented what was apparently the New York debut of "Pirandello" to predictable gasps and thunderous appreciation. The show closed, as did their nightclub acts, with a bit of improv suggested by the audience; on this occasion, it began with the line "Dear Anthony, I have a problem," proceeded in the style of Beat novelist Jack Kerouac, and ended with "It was better in the laundry."

It was — surprise, surprise — a hit. So much so that Rollins began to make plans for an even more audacious showcase. He cut a deal with producer Alexander Cohen to present them on Broadway, performing without any supporting acts, in a proper two-person concert to be called, with elegant simplicity and clarity, *An Evening with Mike Nichols and Elaine May.* With a budget estimated at $50,000,[*] Cohen planned to premiere the show in October 1960.

En route to Broadway, they had a bumpy test run at San Francisco's 1,550-seat Geary Theatre, after which Cohen hired a proper director, Arthur Penn, who refined the show with brief runs in Falmouth, Massachusetts, and Westport, Connecticut, breaking house records in both theaters. (During the first of

[*] Approximately $435,000 in 2022.

these, they recorded a number of routines for a second LP, which would be entitled *An Evening with Mike Nichols and Elaine May* and be released for sale in August, *before* their Broadway debut; like their first record, it was a major critical and commercial success and was nominated for a Grammy as Best Comedy Album; unlike its predecessor, it won.) On October 8, the curtain rose at the eight-hundred-seat John Golden Theatre.

They were received as the hottest, newest, hippest thing in town, but almost all of the set pieces they performed that night were things they originated back at the Compass: the necking teenagers; the pseudo-intellectual lovers; the southern author and the pompous hostess; the name-dropping DJ and starlet; the suffocating mother and the rocket scientist. They closed the first act with "Pirandello," which gave the crowd a jolt, and ended the evening, as ever, with an improvisation prompted by the audience. Instead of traditional curtain calls, they did a couple of short blackout sketches lifted from their radio work. And then they went off to wait for reviews at a party thrown by Cohen in Shubert Alley.

As ever, the notices were raves. "Without overpowering you, it sneaks under your guard," said the *New York Times*. "They are attractive comedians whose years in night clubs have not given them a hard sheen."

"Convulsing," raved *Variety,* "a hilarious show [that] should be a substantial hit on Broadway." "All of their material is hilarious and their performances are consistently brilliant," wrote *Billboard.* Every single one of New York's daily papers (then seven in all) gave the show a thumbs up, and even the *Observer* of London, in the person of the redoubtable Kenneth Tynan, had only praise to offer, calling their "delicate verbal surgery. . . . an unnerving display of mutual empathy [and] a tremendous hit."

They settled in for a spectacular streak, selling out show after show except for a handful of performances when Broadway theaters were brought to their knees by a blizzard. It was the pinnacle of what had been an unprecedented three-year run. "We never got a negative review," Nichols recalled. "We never had an empty seat. Everybody loved us. Everybody felt they had discovered us."

Initially, they were delighted, if a bit puzzled, by the acclaim: "Everyone thought we were so wonderful," Nichols recalled, "and we felt *nothing.* 'Cause it wasn't new." After eight months or so, Elaine grew frustrated with the repetitive nature of what they were doing. As Nichols said, "It wasn't hard on me at all, but it was strangely hard on Elaine. She had to do it over and over and over. And I'd think, 'What is she complaining for? It's less than two hours out of every twenty-four. It's the perfect job! Cute people want you, we're famous, we have money, we just do our old thing, and we can't do any wrong.' But, Elaine wanted to do more." She announced to Nichols, Cohen, and Rollins that she intended to move on.

In June 1961 they dedicated the proceeds of an evening's show — upwards of $30,000 — to the civil rights activists known as the Freedom Riders. A few weeks later, after 306 performances, *An Evening with Mike Nichols and Elaine May* closed, almost entirely at Elaine's request. They were contractually obliged to present the show in Toronto at the end of the year, which they did; at a press conference there they denied that they were splitting up, mentioning a few ongoing commitments they intended to fulfill as well as some future projects they had in mind. But there was no confusion: Nichols and May, as the world had come to know and love them in less than four years' time, seemed to be done.

On the one hand, observers were stunned by the decision: *An Evening* was continuing to do sell-out business, supported by the pair's work on television, radio, and LP records, all of which, like virtually everything else they did, met with acclaim. (They even won awards for their radio advertisements for Jax Beer, for Pete's sake!) Sure, they could move on to anything they wished, and probably make a hit of it. But *why change?*

The answer, predictably, was Elaine.

"We stopped," Nichols explained, "because Elaine said, 'I don't know if I want to go on with this.' "

And that was that.

But it wasn't.

In February 1962, they released a third LP, *Nichols and May Examine Doctors,* compiled from their radio broadcasts; it was a hit.

They appeared together in May 1962 at Madison Square Garden, on the bill of a gala birthday party for President John F. Kennedy, an evening that would become immortal for Marilyn Monroe's scintillating rendition of "Happy Birthday." That summer, they traveled to Seattle to perform at the Seattle World's Fair.

And they announced plans to return to Broadway, after a fashion.

During the run of *An Evening,* Elaine had busied herself by writing plays: a one-act entitled "Not Enough Rope," about a despondent young woman who needs to borrow twine from a neighbor in order to kill herself; and *A Matter of Position,* a full-length comedy about a man who wants nothing more than to please people and who, after a brutal day when everything he does misfires, climbs into his bed and refuses to get out.

The former work was staged once, only off

Broadway, and it was greeted as continued proof of the playwright's brilliance.

The latter, however, proved catastrophic.

Elaine was working alongside Fred Coe, the producer-director of *Journey to the Day,* the ill-fated 1958 TV drama that she had walked away from. Before she had quit that show, Coe had asked her to write something for TV, perhaps for her and Nichols to play, and when she submitted what she'd come up with, he suggested that it might work better onstage. The play, with a considerable budget of $125,000,* was scheduled to open at the Booth Theatre on Broadway in October 1962, after rehearsals in Philadelphia and tune-up runs there and in New Haven.

It all went as poorly as could be. For starters, the play had three full acts (the first performance clocked in at more than three hours), the last of which, according to everyone, the author included, was especially undercooked. Secondly, Elaine was frequently dissatisfied with what Nichols was doing in the role but chose to give him notes not personally but through the intermediation of Coe; indeed, Nichols would later say, there were times when she wouldn't speak to him at all. Thirdly, Elaine was reluctant to take suggestions about the script from the director and producers.

* $1.077 million in 2022.

And a fourth complication: Between the closing of *An Evening* and the first rehearsals of *Position,* Elaine went out and got married, in March 1962, to Sheldon Harnick, the prolific musical lyricist whose Pulitzer-winning *Fiorello!* was then a smash on Broadway and who was busily working on the show that would immortalize him, *Fiddler on the Roof.** Nichols somehow took this personally — "She got married," he remembered, "which threw me for a loop." And even though later on he was able to own up to his poor form — "It was not a pleasant experience. I behaved very badly toward Elaine" — he wasn't at all apologetic at the time, and things between them were edgier even than their first encounters back in Chicago.

They brought all of this to Philadelphia in September, and it proved too much. Elaine and Nichols didn't speak, or spoke only tersely. Elaine had a beef with Coe. And Harnick was nowhere in sight, seeing to the London premiere of *Fiorello!* Elaine, who gave great press when sitting alongside Nichols, the two of them riffing off each other, sat for an uncomfortable interview

* One can't help but wonder if his work adapting Sholem Aleichem's stories for the stage, which resulted in striking portraits of strong-minded young women, wasn't influenced by the spirit of his wife, a child, of course, of the Yiddish theater.

with the *New York Times,* a chat so taciturn and unhelpful that the journalist ran it in Q&A format, just to convey how like pulling teeth it was. (The climax: Q: "Thank you, Miss May." A: "Maybe you're welcome.")

The play finally had its Philadelphia premiere on September 30, and it was a complete flop: overlong, unfunny, unstructured. *Variety,* which tried hard to commend Elaine for the wit in the dialogue while conclusively damning the whole, reckoned that a third of the audience had left before the final curtain. (During one of the intermissions, Elaine overheard someone in the lobby say, "Who can I warn to stay away from this one?")

In the wake of this catastrophe, Coe and Cantor sat Elaine down and walked her through the changes they believed would make the play more coherent and audience friendly. She kicked at them. On October 9, the Broadway production was called off; *A Matter of Position* would die in Philadelphia after only seventeen performances.

Before the story hit the papers, Elaine called Jack Rollins with the news. She spoke, he said, "just long enough to tell me what happened from her point of view. She was emotionally tied up, and I didn't get the full story." Cantor blamed Elaine, saying she "refused to provide the cuts and revisions the producers felt necessary." Elaine was unapologetic in her account:

Cuts and revisions were made up to the point where they would change the nature of the material and emasculate the play. A play is more than a formula made up of words and jokes and scenes. Somewhere it must have something to do with the realities of human behavior. This has always been my premise for comedy. It was the premise on which I wrote the play. The director and producers did not seem to agree with it.[*]

And the bad news kept coming. Three days after running accounts of the death of her play, the New York newspapers reported the death of her marriage. Elaine and Harnick had separated in June, barely three months after their wedding; they had mutually agreed, during the time when he was in London and she in Philadelphia, to divorce. "We are still friends and able to discuss it," she said, "but there's no chance of reconciliation. It's not a question of any other person being involved with him or myself. It just didn't work out."

What had begun as a season of promise had turned to ashes, and she wasn't the sort to reach out to the world for succor. She lay

---

[*] *A Matter of Position* would be revived, in a shorter version, in 1968 at the Berkshire Theater Festival — its last appearance.

low, confiding only in friends, undergoing psychotherapy, making vague plans for future work.

She wrote a film script, an adaptation of Evelyn Waugh's satirical novel *The Loved One,* and the producers said they were delighted with it and fast-tracked it for production. But then they hired Tony Richardson to direct, and he wanted to turn it from a black comedy about the funeral business into a satire on the culture of Southern California. There were so many conflicts and revisions that Elaine pulled out of the project entirely, ceding credit for the finished screenplay to Terry Southern and Christopher Isherwood.

In 1963, she married once again, in something of a scandal. Her new husband was David L. Rubinfine, a Manhattan psychologist who was *her own therapist.* This time, the marriage took (it would last until his death in 1982), although she was, typically, cynical about it: "Why don't you just say I'm married to a doctor," she suggested to a reporter. "It'll make my mother happy." She and Rubinfine blended their families — he had three daughters — in a townhouse on the Upper East Side, but Elaine kept a place of her own on the Upper West Side, finding it impossible to write in a home teeming with kids, even when she planted herself behind a door with a sign on it reading "Don't bother mother under the penalty of death."

The breach with Nichols had been severe — "She had treated him abominably," he had told Edmund Wilson over dinner, and they "were hardly on speaking terms." But they had reconciled. In the fall of 1963, it was announced that Nichols and May would appear together, for the first time in more than two years, in the American version of *That Was the Week That Was,* the popular British satiric news program brought west with Henry Fonda as host. In a review of the premiere, the *New York Times* declared Nichols and May "the hit of the evening." It was the first significant work Elaine had been seen in since *An Evening With* had folded. Afterward, they traveled to London to appear on David Frost's variety/talk show and signed on to do six appearances on a new program hosted by Jack Paar. They performed together in January 1965 at the inaugural gala for Lyndon Johnson and two months later in Selma, Alabama, at a star-studded civil rights benefit. And then they just sort of stopped.

Nichols and May soared so high and so fast and vanished so abruptly that there was a genuine hunger in the popular culture for a sequel. A variety of boy-girl acts with modern sensibilities stepped up to try to fill the gap.

There were Jack Colvin and Yvonne Wilder, aka Colvin and Wilder, who essayed a genuinely appealing fresh blend of verbal and physical comedy, such as a much-loved takeoff on *Hamlet* in which Ophelia played the "Get thee to a nunnery" scene in modern argot and sensibility and endured a sea of slapstick jabs and whacks at the hands of the ham-handed prince. Colvin was lean-jawed and possessed of a hard gaze and patrician manner; Wilder (born Yvonne Othon) was spry and bubbly and could sing and dance and had even appeared in the film version of *West Side Story.*[*]

There were Dick Clair and Jenna McMahon — predictably, Clair and McMahon — also both primarily actors, who met in Hollywood in the early sixties and began writing and performing together a few years later, in such clubs as the Basin Street East in Manhattan and on TV shows hosted by Ed Sullivan, Dean Martin, Art Linkletter, and Merv Griffin. Their material wasn't as kinetic as that of Colvin and Wilder, and it's not

[*] They both went on to long careers as actors. He played villains and martinets in a number of films and TV series (he had a long run on the Bill Bixby/ Lou Ferrigno *Incredible Hulk* show) and taught at the Michael Chekhov School in Los Angeles. She appeared in comic roles in films and dozens of sitcoms. They turned up as a pair of bickering anthropologists on a 1986 episode of *Gimme a Break!* and were quite funny together, still able to slip into the rhythm of working as a team.

surprising that they soon made their longest-lasting marks as writers.*

And there were Hershey Horowitz and Mary Elizabeth Doyle, a Jewish guy and a Catholic girl who met via a computer date, fell in love, and made comic hay of the ups and downs of what was known at the time as a "mixed marriage." They didn't, technically, exist, but they very closely resembled — in cultural background and in personal temperament — the performers who invented them: Jerry Stiller and Anne Meara. Working largely with scenes and lines that she wrote (but which he, with his combination of natural humor and well-honed stagecraft, enhanced), Stiller and Meara were a mainstay of television and nightclubs, portraying a couple who seemed to have nothing in common except for a genuine bond of love. But such was the public affection for them that even after they stopped doing comedy to pursue the serious acting careers to which they always aspired,

* As a team, they wrote for *The Mary Tyler Moore Show* and, especially, *The Carol Burnett Show,* for which they helped create the Eunice and Mama characters, which spun off into the sitcom *Mama's House.* They also created the series *The Facts of Life,* ensuring them work and residuals for decades, and perhaps even longer in the case of Dick Clair, who died in 1988 but had his body cryogenically frozen for . . . whatever may come.

they spent another decade doing their boy-girl act in radio commercials and would reprise it again and again over the decades, warmly received every time that they chose to appear together in their familiar, bickering, affectionate brand of back-and-forth.

For approximately ten years, almost exactly corresponding to the decade of the 1960s, Stiller and Meara were one of the most popular comedy teams in show business, and deservedly so. Mismatched, talented, quick-witted, human, and lovable, the tall, brassy redhead and her short, excitable partner could, like Nichols and May, slip in and out of a number of characters: psychiatrist and patient; cleaning woman and NASA scientist; atheist and proselytizer; girl reporter and man who was swallowed by a whale; naive Adam and saucy Eve; and, of course, a variety of couples on dates, at work, having arguments, cooing on the morning after, and so on. Under the management of Robert Chartoff (who, in a later career as a film producer, made, among many others, *Rocky, Raging Bull,* and *The Right Stuff*), they played all the important comedy clubs and all the essential TV programs, appearing on the most important of them all, *The Ed Sullivan Show,* no fewer than *thirty-six* times.

They were actually well along into their career — and their lives as parents of two children — when they landed on the characters of Mary Elizabeth and Hershey, the inspiration that truly separated them from the pack of ersatz Nicholses and Mays. They had both been serious actors — she was a staple of off-Broadway work, and he was in the founding casts of the American Shakespeare Theater and Joseph Papp's Shakespeare in the Park productions. When they'd married and sought opportunities to work together, Jerry got them hired by the St. Louis edition of Compass Theater, where they arrived not long after Nichols and May had departed. In time, they continued doing comedy in a Chicago outfit (*not* the Second City), and when Anne was pregnant with their first child, they returned to New York and she started writing comedy bits for them to perform together in nightclubs, an act they debuted in Manhattan in 1962.

They had always worked from an aesthetic of honesty rather than mere gags. "Although we are naturally eager for laughs," Stiller said, "we never depend on mere gags or wisecracks. Our comedy grows out of characters or situations." They spent time every day batting around ideas, sharpening lines, working up new scenes. It struck them during one of these writing sessions that the fact of their separate faiths — something that people actually took note of at the time — would make excellent fodder for a routine. "We were doing simple boy-girl sketches," Meara remembered. "But then we decided, 'Look, you're Jewish and I'm Irish, let's do it that way.' It's a good source of humor, and people seem to like it, but we're not bound by it."

Years on, they couldn't recall precisely which was the first sketch. But there's a good chance it was the one in which they had been paired by a computer dating service only to discover 1) that they were mismatched by religious and cultural upbringing, *and* 2) that they lived on the same New York City block and had never laid eyes on each other. A typical exchange, from one of their earliest routines, went like this:

Her: They're having a dance tonight at my sodality.
Him: At your *what*?
Her: My sodality.
Him: What's that?
Her: Well, it's a girls' organization in my parish.
Him: You mean like Hadassah?
Her: What's that?
Him: It's a girls' organization in *my* parish.

At the height of their fame as a team, they became almost synonymous with their creations, which, given their genuine artistic inclinations, also meant that they felt somewhat trapped by them. And so they simply walked away from the act. In the early seventies, Stiller and Meara, the act, more or less retired to, of all places, radio, where they were the voices of a number of highly popular ad campaigns, none more successful than the prize-winning one for Blue Nun wine, which ran for a decade or so. But they never performed in clubs again as a pair, aiming themselves at rich and varied careers as actors on Broadway, on TV, and in films, watching their children's careers flourish (especially that of their son, Ben Stiller), and remaining together, one of the great show-biz couples of their epoch, until Anne's death in 2015, sixty-one years after they first laid eyes on each other.

If the world was still hungry for Nichols and May, it would have to make do with these substitutes, if for no other reason than the fact that Mike Nichols was exceedingly busy, with a new wife and an entirely independent career. He hadn't seen it coming. In fact, he didn't know what, if anything, lay before him after *An Evening with Mike Nichols and Elaine May* closed. "It was in a way the worst time in my life," he said, "because not only had I lost my best friend, I lost my work. I was half of something. . . . I was Elaine-less."

And then a funny thing happened: Neil Simon, a TV writer who had switched to full-time playwriting had written a romantic comedy about a pair of newlyweds, and someone asked Nichols to direct it. In October 1963, the play, starring the virtually unknown pair of Elizabeth Ashley and Robert Redford, premiered as *Barefoot in the Park,* a stupendous hit that would run more than fifteen hundred performances and win Nichols a Tony Award as Best Director. The following year saw him open two new plays: Murray Schisgal's *Luv,* starring Alan Arkin, Anne Jackson, and Eli Wallach (more than nine hundred performances), and Neil Simon's next play, *The Odd Couple,* starring Walter Matthau and Art Carney (also nine-hundred-plus performances). He won a second Best Director Tony, for the *pair* of them. Hollywood called. He signed to direct an adaptation of Edward Albee's *Who's Afraid of Virginia Woolf?* starring no less than Elizabeth Taylor and Richard Burton, for which he would eventually be nominated for an Oscar as Best Director. He was in talks for a second film, a screen version of Charles Webb's novel *The Graduate* — for which he would *win* that Oscar. He was, by any reasonable measure, the hottest young director on Broadway *and* in Hollywood. The magazine *Paris Match* dubbed him "Monsieur Success."

And Elaine? Elaine floundered.

In the spring of 1963 she began work writing a TV pilot, called *Halfway House* (and, later, *Welcome, Convict!*) concerning two elderly ladies who operate a residence for

440

newly released parolees; it wasn't filmed. The following spring, she organized an off-Broadway improv revue called *The Third Ear* along the lines of the Compass. She created scenarios for it, directed it, and conducted workshops with the cast, which included such unknowns as Peter Boyle and Louise Lasser; it died after just a few weeks. That summer, she revised her Playwrights Theater Club script of Rumpelstiltskin at the Westport Country Playhouse; it began and ended life there.

She moved to Los Angeles for a time, living at the famed Chateau Marmont hotel and staring out glumly at the city that was once her home. It wasn't her scene — and she wasn't getting work, anyhow. (Nichols saw it coming: "Elaine is going to suffer in Hollywood," he said. "She must have complete control of a given situation. Out there she will be at the mercy of many people.") She returned to New York and the stage, where director Jerome Robbins cast her in *The Office,* a comedy by avant-garde playwright Maria Irene Fornes about a secretary unable to adjust to a modern workplace. The play went into previews in April 1966 at the Henry Miller Theatre, and the audience at the first night actually booed it at the curtain. It closed after ten performances, before ever officially premiering.

And then, opportunity: Columbia Pictures

hired her, strictly as an actress, for two roles. The first one to be filmed was *Enter Laughing,* a tale of a wide-eyed show business hopeful that Carl Reiner, himself formerly one-half of a comedy duo (with Mel Brooks), was adapting from his own popular, semi-autobiographical play in his debut as a film director. May was cast as a sex-hungry actress preying on the naive lead (Reni Santoni playing the part originated onstage by Alan Arkin). The film didn't make much of an impression, but May was well received — the *New York Times* appreciated her "charmingly genteel burlesque" and Reiner was especially full of praise, calling her "either the sexiest funny woman I ever saw or the funniest sexy woman," adding, admiringly, "She thinks only in curves."

The other role was in the film adaptation of *Luv,* with Jack Lemmon playing a schnook ready to jump off a bridge only to be talked out of it by an old school chum (Peter Falk) who happens to be passing by and gets the idea that his buddy would make a perfect match for the obnoxious wife (Elaine), whom he wishes to be rid of. The film was not, of course, directed by Mike Nichols, and, maybe not coincidentally, it flopped, Elaine receiving lukewarm notices for her work.

Through these struggles, Elaine retained a reputation for being a brilliant comic and for being a perfectionist — that is, for being *difficult.* She still loathed doing interviews, which was part of the gig, like it or not. Pressed by the *New York Times* to grant them some words in advance of her film debut, she "interviewed" herself, pretending to be a (male) journalist visiting her bungalow at the Sunset Marquis Hotel; she presented herself as hostile and suspicious ("Who told you I found working with Carl Reiner 'enjoyable'?") and claimed to be at work on a screen adaptation of Jean-Paul Sartre's *No Exit.* The editors, bless them, actually ran the thing under the pseudonymous byline "Kevin M. Johnson."

She still captivated people, she was still admired and even feared as a wit, she could still get meetings with producers and directors, she still had a name, she even seemed to have found some semblance of a happy personal life. But she wasn't doing the sorts of work that she was capable of. Six years after the final performance of *An Evening with Mike Nichols and Elaine May,* Nichols had four shows running on Broadway, multiple Tonys as Best Director, a hit film and Oscar nomination, and an even bigger hit film in the can. Elaine, on the other hand, was the subject of an article in *Life* entitled "Whatever Happened to Elaine May?" A sympathetic but somewhat damning account of her life and career, it ended with these poignant words, attributed to "a friend who knows her well":

> I feel sad for Elaine. She could sell out — write gag plays like Jean Kerr and make a fortune and be on magazine covers like Mike Nichols. She could take pratfalls and be funnier than Lucille Ball. She could hole up somewhere and write tragedies blacker than Lillian Hellman's. Hell, she could teach philosophy at Radcliffe. She has so many things going for her that, in a curious sort of way, I don't think she'll ever be happy.

She kept banging away. She was hired to write a script from Robert Gover's novel *The One Hundred Dollar Misunderstanding.* It never reached the screen. She wrote a new one-act play, *Adaptation,* a story about a TV game show in which the contestant is forced to pass through awkward and inane social situations. It made its way around New York with the idea that it could be yoked to another one-acter, or maybe two, and she would direct. In early 1969, when it finally opened, to glowing reviews, a literal blizzard shut the city down and nobody came. Thankfully, business picked up after the thaw, and the show enjoyed a modest run. (Ironically, the big off-Broadway hit of the season, Kenneth Tynan's revue *Oh, Calcutta,* included some material contributed by Elaine without credit.)

It seemed as if she was truly snakebit, meant to be one of those talents whom the public (and, indeed, the biz) never quite cottoned to. And then she landed a big one. In 1968, Elaine sold a script to Paramount, *A New Leaf,* an adaptation of a Jack Ritchie short story about an upper-crust ne'er-do-well who falls into debt and marries an awkward, spinsterish botanist with an eye toward killing her and making off with her fortune. Walter Matthau, a bona fide movie star, would play the lead, Elaine herself would play opposite him. And she would be allowed to direct in what the producer, Howard Koch, called, perhaps while tapping wood, "an exercise in Elaine May."

Elaine hadn't intended to put herself behind the camera. But as she recalled, her agent explained that although the studio wouldn't give her approval over directors it would allow *her* to do it if she wanted to. She called Nichols for advice, and he urged her to take the plunge.*

And boy did she.

Armed with a budget of $1.8 million (she was herself paid only $50,000), she went to work in August 1969, and quickly found herself in over her head. She shot scenes ten,

_____

* Cannily, her agent demanded a poison pill clause in the contract, requiring the studio to pay her $200,000 if she was replaced.

twenty, even thirty times, as if working on improv sketches back at the Compass. She went through staff with similar profligacy, firing two assistant directors as well as a couple of experts on the lives and habits of the super-rich whom she'd hired as advisers. She rewrote the script virtually constantly. Paramount producers, sensing a hot potato, passed the film off to one another; none could put the brakes on the thing. ("She's a fucking maniac," one of them told the studio.)

They certainly got their money's worth out of her. She put in heroically long days: sleeping, when she did, in her clothes, just as she had once joked was her wont; eating her few, scant meals during meetings and on set; smoking little cigars; gulping down endless cups of coffee; showing up every morning, first to report, with new script pages falling out of her arms; attempting to oversee every aspect of the production. "Elaine May makes Hitler look like a little librarian," said Matthau, intending a compliment.

She overshot the forty-two-day schedule by forty days and blasted through the budget, more than doubling it to over $4 million. When it came to editing, the *real* trouble began. Elaine was drowning in footage, in choices, in confusion. Nichols consulted, but he couldn't move her process along. Months passed — ten of them — and she still hadn't found her final cut. And while that wasn't an entirely egregious amount of time, the studio was concerned that Elaine's version of the film, *if* she could even arrive at one, might be three hours long, well beyond the length that a comedy could sustain. Studio boss Robert Evans took the footage away from her and recut it substantially, changing key plot points and tacking on a happy ending.

They showed her the new cut early in 1971, and she pitched a fit. She demanded that the studio restore her version. When that failed, she demanded that her name be taken off the film, at least as writer and director. When *that* failed, she hired attorney Martin Garbus to file suit enjoining the studio from releasing the film at all, in any version, with *any* name on it.

She lost on all counts. The studio cut of *A New Leaf* premiered in July 1971, nearly two years after the first day of shooting. It was well received. In the *Chicago Sun-Times*, Roger Ebert called it "one of the funniest movies of our unfunny age. . . . hilarious, and cock-eyed, and warm"; Vincent Canby of the *New York Times* also found it "beautiful and gently cockeyed. . . . touched by a fine and knowing madness"; and *Variety* called it "sophisticated and funny and adroitly put together." But its writer-director-star disavowed it, and she did no press to publicize it. (She may have been right: there are gems of comedy in the film, mostly generated by

Matthau, but it plays very stiffly at a half century's remove and the inanity and passivity of Elaine's character feel uncomfortably of another day.)

If she couldn't take her name off of *A New Leaf,* she could deny Paramount the benefit of her imprimatur on another film. In late 1971, she pulled her credit from the script of Otto Preminger's *Such Good Friends,* which she had, in fact, written, and assigned it to one Esther Dale, an actual woman who had achieved a mite of fame as a dowdy character actress, perhaps most famously as Shirley Temple's aunt in *Curly Top.* Dale had died in 1961 without ever having written or, to anyone's knowledge, attempted a screenplay, but there she was, getting credit for the adaptation of a novel written nine years after her passing.

Elaine's next bit of revenge was even sweeter. She was hired by Palomar Pictures International, an independent production company that had enjoyed a smash with Woody Allen's *Take the Money and Run,* to direct — not write, not appear in — *The Heartbreak Kid,* which no less a writer than Neil Simon had adapted from a novel by Bruce Jay Friedman. Almost as dark as *A New Leaf,* it concerned a callow New York man who, while honeymooning with his nebbishy bride in Miami, meets a young blond goddess and abandons his brand-new marriage to follow her to Minnesota. (It plays a little bit like a perverse variation on *The Graduate,* with Charles Grodin, who was nearly cast by Mike Nichols in that film, tooling around in a tiny sports car, scheming his way into a family which doesn't necessarily want him, and, upon succeeding, wondering whether his efforts were worth anything at all.)

Elaine shot and edited the picture in barely a year, and it appeared to critical and commercial success. Reviewers delighted in it: "a first-class American comedy. . . . behind the laughs there is, for a change, a real understanding of character. . . . an unequivocal hit" (Vincent Canby, *New York Times*); "The movie has a way of making us laugh while it hurts. . . . It's a comedy, but there's more in it than that; it's a movie about the ways we pursue, possess, and consume each other as sad commodities" (Roger Ebert, *Chicago Sun-Times*); "bright, amusing" (*Variety*). (Again, the male critics of the day didn't seem to notice or mind the film's objectification of women as sex partners or trophies, a subtext no less disturbing for Elaine's having cast her own daughter, Jeannie Berlin, as the abandoned newlywed in a role more or less analogous to the one she herself played in *A New Leaf.*) To top it off, it garnered two nominations for supporting actor Oscars, one

449

for Eddie Albert as the WASP girl's father, and one for Jeannie. Best of all? The picture was released by 20th Century Fox. Paramount could do nothing but look on enviously.

And so, seeing someone else succeed, Paramount executives did something they had probably sworn they never would: they green-lit Elaine's next film, *Mikey and Nicky,* a drama about a night in the life of two Philadelphia gangsters, childhood friends, one in trouble with his bosses, the other attempting to lure him out of hiding so he can be killed. Elaine had been mulling the project since she arrived in Chicago almost twenty years prior; it was based on a story she'd heard from her older brother, Louis, who had run with shady characters under the street name Johnny Fogarty. She had revived the idea and been tinkering with the script for at least five years; it was a pet project, a true labor of love. Like *A New Leaf* and *The Heartbreak Kid,* it was a tale of trust and betrayal, of soured friendship and misplaced loyalty, and its title eerily echoed the names "Mike Nichols" and "Nichols and May." Whatever the subtexts, it was a sufficiently promising project that it attracted Peter Falk and John Cassavetes to play the leads and was funded by Paramount to the tune of $1.8 million.

Well, any lessons about the management of

time, money, and the patience of movie executives that Elaine might have learned while making *The Heartbreak Kid* didn't stick. She began shooting *Mikey and Nicky* in May 1973, and she finished a full ten months later, a long shoot for what is effectively a two-character story. Some of the delay was caused by Falk's obligations to his *Columbo* TV series, but most of it was caused by May. She often employed three cameras, so as to catch her stars' spontaneous improvisations, and she reacted angrily when a camera operator, noticing all three still filming some minutes after the actors left the set, shouted, "Cut." (She allegedly admonished him: "They might come back!") She shot *1.4 million feet* of film — more than three times the amount that was expended on *Gone with the Wind.* She would watch the crew spend hours setting up a location only to demand that it be scrapped before filming a frame of footage on it. And, of course, there were constant rewrites. The budget more than doubled, edging toward $5 million.

When she finally got the thing in the can — so many cans! — she once again spent an unreasonable amount of time editing: upwards of a year, with nothing remotely resembling a releasable cut to show the studio. She was more than twelve months late on her contractual delivery date. Paramount demanded a movie, and she countered by demanding more money and time to finish it. Out came the lawyers, the threats, the suits and countersuits; much of 1975 was spent in courts and deposition rooms. And then, a bit of business worthy of a movie of its own: facing a writ of seizure for the still-unfinished film, Elaine and her husband snuck two reels out of one of the editing suites she was using in New York and hid them in a friend's barn in Connecticut, a brazen act for which Paramount sought to have criminal charges proffered against the pair. (The reels were returned after Warren Beatty offered his services as a liaison between Elaine and studio boss Barry Diller; no ransom was involved.)

Mikey and Nicky, cut by a hand other than Elaine's, would finally premiere at the end of 1976, a full four years after being green-lit by studio bosses who had since been replaced. It appeared in theaters for the contractually required minimal release, then was yanked unceremoniously. It's a sweaty, nerve-jangling, unsettling film with two virtuosic actors splashing emotions around like Jackson Pollack would a can of paint. Cassavetes and Falk, frequent collaborators in the former's intense, semi-improvised dramas, are intensely physical, raw, and intimate — truly electric. The film is spiced with Elaine's now characteristic use of lifelike sets and extras, her intense fascination with bonding and betrayal, her adoration of her cast. It's a movie like no other (saving, maybe, Martin Scorsese's *Mean Streets*), and, upon rediscovery, it clearly stands as one of the most daring experiments any Hollywood studio attempted at the time.

But in its day, it didn't so much get released by the studio as escape. They opened the film in a handful of markets at Christmas-time, 1976, and didn't, apparently, make it available in advance for reviewers in many cities. (It didn't even play some big towns, judging from the complete absence of contemporary reviews or references in newspapers in Chicago, Boston, and Washington, D.C.) And those critics who *did* manage to see and review it didn't seem to know how to respond: "[It is] told in such insistently claustrophobic detail that to watch it is to risk an artificially induced anxiety attack. It's nearly two hours of being locked in a telephone booth with a couple of method actors who won't stop talking, though they have nothing of interest to say, and who won't stop jiggling around, though they plainly aren't going anywhere" (the *New York Times*); "It suckers an audience into allocating sympathies and then, wham, you wind up getting kicked in the gut" (*Variety*); "You are not apt to find more intelligence and good acting expended on a lost cause" (*Los Angeles Times*).

Never mind that all three of the films she

had made in the face of titanic obstacles — many, to be fair, of her own devising — had been fascinating, this one included. It would be more than a decade before she would be allowed to direct again, and that film would become, unfairly, synonymous with Hollywood excess, ego, and mediocrity: 1989's *Ishtar.*

But that would be another megillah, for another time. Better to favor the higher notes. Elaine continued to vex and delight in a career as far-ranging as her mind. She appeared on screen in Herb Ross's adaptation of Neil Simon's *Plaza Suite* in 1978, then twelve years later in *In the Spirit,* a film written by and costarring her daughter, then ten years after that in Woody Allen's *Small Time Crooks.* She worked extensively as a screenwriter, most notably in 1978 on Warren Beatty's *Heaven Can Wait,* for which she received an Oscar nomination; then — usually without credit, at her request — as a script doctor on such films as *Reds, Tootsie,* and *Labyrinth;* and then, after *Ishtar,* on two films directed by Mike Nichols: *The Birdcage* and *Primary Colors,* accepting credit both times.

Elaine and Nichols saw one another socially over the years and after a time did something remarkable together, taking on the roles of Martha and George in a 1980 stage revival of

Who's Afraid of Virginia Woolf? in New Haven (critics weren't invited, but those who managed to sneak a look filed positive notices, despite which the production closed there). They reunited twice for live performances as Nichols and May: a sketch at a Comic Relief benefit in 1985 and a full-length show on Broadway in 1992, a single night to benefit Friends in Deed, a charity Nichols had helped found to assist people terminally ill with AIDS. And in 1986, Elaine directed an episode of PBS's *American Masters* series about a subject she knew uniquely: Mike Nichols.

Elaine was active in the theater most of all, writing more than a half dozen plays and one-acts that were produced on and off Broadway throughout the 1990s and 2000s. It was her time. In her eighties, she was feted in retrospectives and appreciative essays. In July 2013, she received a National Medal of Arts from President Barack Obama, among a cohort that included director George Lucas, musicians Allen Toussaint and Herb Alpert, and painter Ellsworth Kelly, an amazing acknowledgment of a singular career filled with estimable achievements but nevertheless haunted by might-have-beens.

More personally, having been widowed by David Rubinfine's passing in 1982, she found a life partner of varied talents equal to hers: Stanley Donen, the veteran Hollywood director of *On the Town, Singin' in the Rain, Funny Face,* and *Charade.* Eight years her senior, he had five divorces on his résumé when they began dating in 1999. Together they attended shows and dinners and awards events and the like, keeping homes in upstate New York and on Central Park West, and never marrying. They collaborated on a screenplay in 2013 that Donen was planning to direct with Mike Nichols producing; a table reading of the script was held with Christopher Walken, Charles Grodin, and Jeannie Berlin on hand. But the project died with Nichols's passing the following year.

In 2018, she took on her first proper acting role on Broadway in a revival of Kenneth Lonergan's *The Waverly Gallery,* playing an art dealer suffering from Alzheimer's. Her work won her unanimous praise. But the triumph was mingled with pain. A few months into the production, she lost Donen, who died at age ninety-four, still in possession of an ID tag she had given him that read, "Stanley Donen: If found please return to Elaine May."

The following spring, she won a Tony Award as Best Actress in a Drama. As she took the stage to accept it, amid a standing ovation, there was a bit of a thrill in the air: What would she say? As it turned out, it was grace itself. Eighty-seven years old, a singular career behind her, standing before a deeply admiring and even loving crowd, she started hesitatingly, then roused:

> I um . . . thank you. I . . . I . . . I've never won a nomination for acting before. So, uh, I wanna tell you how I did it. I got in a play written by Kenneth Lonergan. It was about his family. I played his grandmother. And my director was Lila Neugebauer. My producer was Scott Rudin. My family was played by everyone you ever wanted to be on stage with. Joan Allen was my daughter. Lucas Hedges was my grandson. David Cromer was my son-in-law. And Michael Cera was my only friend. And, at the end of the play, I died. Now, my death was described on stage by Lucas Hedges so brilliantly. And he described the death, my death, he described it so heartbreakingly, it was so touching, that watching from the wings, I thought, "I'm gonna win this guy's Tony."

Big laugh, thunderous applause, quiet exit. Elaine May had surprised and won them over once again.

SEVEN:
THE SONGBIRD

There was discrimination, yes. But what are you going to do? Cry about it or go out and beat it down? I don't want to get into competition with men. I just want to do what I do. Anyone who can do the job is entitled to the money.

— 1975

The singer had the pipes, sure, but she wasn't exactly wowing the crowd at the tiny nightclub on Revere Beach, outside of Boston. She was endearing: early twenties, tiny (five feet, maybe less, even in heels), a winning smile. And her voice was oversized, with a surprisingly deep quality, and she put it out with real energy and verve. It was charming when the material was right. But when she got into the love songs, the crowd somehow didn't buy it. You could feel them holding back. Hell, *she* could feel it.

"The crowd would begin laughing as soon as they heard me sing," she remembered. "They seemed amused by my husky voice."

458

She had been singing in clubs for a few years already, ever since her school days, and she had recently learned to get the audience to appreciate her act more by making little jokes about herself, self-deprecatory one-liners that won the crowd over just that smidgen, just enough to put her over. And then she would get on with her singing, and she'd usually get a nice hand when she finished. Still, something was missing.

Backstage, the comedian on the bill noticed what was happening, and he thought he could help. Even though she was supposed to be singing straight, he told her how she could make her jokes sharper and win the crowd over that little bit more. She replied that *she* knew what was funny better than *he* did, and to prove it she would do *his* act, which she'd seen plenty, at the next show. And she did, and she got bigger laughs than he ever got with the exact same material. And they realized a few things: she maybe was better suited to comedy than to singing, and she maybe was better suited to comedy than *he* was, and they maybe were interested in each other more than just as fellow performers.

His name was Georgie Johnston — George William Johnston Jr., actually. Hers was Totie Fields, or, rather, that was the name she had cobbled together for herself over the years. She'd been born Sophie Feldman, in Hartford, Connecticut, on May 7, 1927,* the fifth and final child, some four and a half years younger than her nearest sibling, of Russian immigrants Max and Fannie. While Sophie was still a toddler, the family had taken to calling her "Totie," which was how she mispronounced her given name. It was a perfect moniker for a sparkly, mischievous kid: "How much harm," she would joke in later years, "could a 'Totie' do?"

It wasn't the only way her family doted on her. She was a born performer, and her parents and siblings let her do her thing from the first time she let them know she was so inclined. "I was sort of a toy," she said. "I remember, when I was four or five years old, my brothers putting colored paper over the lights to make a stage, and they would say, 'Here she is!' and I would come out and sing for my sister and her friends. Imagine, teenagers were having to sit and listen to a kid sing! You know, they must have hated me."

In retrospect, that first barely patient audience would be excellent training for a career in comedy, though as a youngster Totie was

* Her official biography would shave three years off her age, but she appeared in the 1930 federal census as a child two years and ten months old. At age fifteen, when she went to work, she actually *added* two years to her age, applying, falsely, for a Social Security card as a seventeen-year-old.

all about singing. She sang throughout her school days, always with a dream of one day becoming a star, no matter how unlikely an ambition that seemed. Even when the household was shattered by Fannie's sudden death in October 1935, Totie maintained her determination. If she was ever given discouraging advice, she didn't hear it. "I always knew I would make it big, ever since my mind started functioning," she said. When she had free time in elementary school, she would practice signing autographs. She was, she knew, bound to be a star.

Max Feldman — a machinist, a practical man — wasn't so keen on the idea. Fannie's death fed his protective side. He wed again within a few years, to Sophie Taubman, a woman his own age who had never married and had no children. But he trusted much of Totie's care to her sister Rachel, known as Raye in the family, who was some eight years older than her baby sister. And he kept a strict eye on his kids, ensuring they got their schooling and went into good jobs.

Totie, though, was star-struck. "Even as a kid I wanted to go into show business," she remembered. "But my father was bitterly opposed. He figured only gypsies entered that field." Still, Max let her take voice and dance lessons through her teens, even when the payoff seemed unlikely. At Weaver High School, she auditioned for every play and

461

never got a part, and she failed to make the glee club (she did participate in the school choir). At the same time, she was enough of a go-getter to pursue any chance she could get to sing in public, often without pay, on weekends, during school holidays, in the summer. Max imposed some conditions, she recalled: "He wouldn't let me play a date unless he or some other member of the family went right along with me." (When she was once on a bill with Sally Rand, the celebrated, scandalous fan dancer, he yanked her after two nights.)

She graduated from high school in 1945, and her class yearbook, in which she was identified as Totie, recalled her as "a musically inclined girl . . . Weaver's Ethel Merman . . . nice dresser . . . a flirtatious manner and a roving eye." Like all the Feldman kids, she went to work, first as a salesgirl at the Gay Modern Dress Shop, and then at the Travelers Insurance Company, where her sister Raye was already working.

But she kept singing, backed by a couple of Hartford booking agents, Jack and Rhea Gordon, and got gigs around town: Club Ferdinando, the Lobster Restaurant, the Old Town Hall Inn. It was small potatoes — maybe $7.50 a night — but it was work. She created a stage name for herself, morphing from Feldman to Fields — "strictly a show business gesture," she explained of the very common practice of performers rinsing themselves of the spoor of Jewish heritage.

As Totie Fields, she began to get noticed in the press; the *Hartford Courant*'s nightlife columnist, M. Oakley Stafford, began writing little bits about her regularly. She developed a boy-girl act with a local comic, Dody Krivitz (whom she would forever credit with teaching her a number of tricks of professional stagecraft). She was billed as "That Little Miss with the Great Voice." And she started to get work out of town, which made her — and Max — feel that she really did have a legitimate shot at a career. "When I made a big hit in a New London club," she recalled, "I wired my boss at Travelers that I wouldn't be back."

By 1950, she was starting to receive offers from further afield, particularly from the Boston area, where she was being offered an audition for the out-of-town preview run of a show that had hopes of moving on to Broadway. If nothing else, there would be more and better-paid nightclub work in the bigger city, with much more potential upside; she asked Max's permission to move there. He agreed — provided that she live with her older brother, Edward, who had started a family in suburban Natick.

"That move changed my life," she recalled. She didn't mean the work. Yes, she was getting bookings and making a living. But mainly it was that gig at Revere Beach, the one where she met the boy comic who turned her head both professionally and romantically.

It wasn't an overnight thing, her transformation from singer to comic. During the several months that they worked at Revere Beach, Totie kept belting out songs, sprinkling her set with one-liners, and George Johnston kept at his jokes, and they kept meeting after the show to compare notes about what worked for her and what didn't. Little by little, they realized that the more she presented herself as a comic, the bigger the hit she was *and* the more she could get away with singing a song, her genuine musical ability surprising audiences that were enjoying her jokes. As she put it, "There were plenty of girl singers around, but not many good comediennes." Her act gradually evolved until the balance of it was comedy. "I went into this small club as a singer, and I came out a full-fledged comedian after playing there for more than a year," she said.

There was even more to it than that, in fact. Together, she and Johnston came to a pair of decisions that were really one decision: they would marry, and he would step away from the microphone and stick beside her as a combination of bandleader (he had some musical talent of his own) and straight man.

This decision, she confessed, was really more hers than his: "I proposed to him just as fast as was reasonable. He accepted — the doll — and we were married eight weeks later" — on May 22, 1951. A few hours after a civil wedding ceremony, they were back onstage.

It was a fantasy come to life for Totie. "The things I wanted in life were a home, children, and to be in show business, and I wanted them in that order," she later reflected. "I had to find somebody who would let me have all of it, and so I knew it would have to be somebody in show business. . . . The day I met Georgie, I called home and told my father that I'd met the boy I was going to marry."

Even still, to conceive of having a career as a comedian was a real leap of faith. If she and Johnston could name a woman comedian at all, it would have been Jean Carroll, who was pointedly elegant, a former dancer with poise and style, and who occasionally joked about diets that, to look at her, she didn't really need to be on. Totie Fields was another sort of creature altogether, not quite fully a comedian but no longer just a straight singer, either — brassy and sassy, a fireplug to the eye, a bullhorn to the ear.

Johnston believed in her, but before they could see whether anyone else did, in late 1951, they faced another choice. Totie was pregnant. A career as a comedian who sang was one thing; piling motherhood on top of that and show biz would seem impossible. She used to crack that as a newlywed she told her husband: "This house has a kitchen, a living room, and a bedroom. I can't excel in all of them. Pick a room. And so we got a maid and a cook." It was a joke, but there was truth to it. They had already decided to combine marriage and an act; why not a *family* and an act? They had two daughters — Jody, in 1952, and Debbie, two years later — and in between they bought a house in Boston. Whatever it was they were doing, they were all in on it.

For a few years, Totie was dedicated, by necessity, to her family, contenting herself with very occasional gigs. When she performed, in town or out, she invariably had a baby along with her, sometimes watched by a babysitter, sometimes by her sister, Raye. "We find taking the baby along presents no problem," she told M. Oakley Stafford during a gig in Hartford when Jody was only a few months old, "or relatively no problem compared to the loneliness of not having her with us."

She began to see that she had no choice: she was devoted to her family *and* her career. As she later put it, "I realized I could only be a good wife and a mother if I worked, too. I can't manage just staying here and doing domestic things every day — my God, I'd go bananas." And so, not long after her daughters began school, Totie was back on track trying to become famous. Not to have a way to keep from going crazy: To. Become. Famous. As she put it, "I wanted to make it, I knew I could make it, and I never, never doubted that I would eventually make it."

As previously, she started at a really low rung: one-night stands in tiny clubs out in the boroughs and the suburbs, the occasional slot at a smaller Catskills hotel, and even (pace Max Feldman) in strip clubs. She honed her comedy chops, which increasingly included material of the sort Georgie Johnston could never perform. Her pregnancies had left her thirty or so pounds heavier. "That's when I got fat," she said. "It comes from being happy with your husband, your family, from contentment."

Her most famous jokes had to do with her figure: "I've been on a diet for two weeks, and all I've lost is two weeks"; "I have an eighteen-inch waist. . . . through the center"; "Yesterday I got dressed in green, from my head to my toes, and I went to a big department store, and someone tried to trim me"; "Look at how thin my fingers are!"; "An Italian knit gives a little, but what I'm about to ask this dress to do is ridiculous!"; "Do you think it's easy pushing these fat Jewish feet into thin Italian shoes?" She joked about herself right from the start of her act, taking the potential bludgeon out of the audience's hand and using it, playfully, against herself as a way of winning them over and breaking the ice. It was a savvy bit of craft that was to become the foundation of her entire comic persona and career. "I come right out and say, 'I'm fat!,' " she explained. "This deprives the wise alecks from mouthing loud asides all night: 'Gosh, she's fat,' as they glimpse me in a tent dress. They're left with nothing to say."

Perhaps unknowingly, Totie had hit on a trope long practiced by women comedians before her, but she performed it with a twist. Like Fanny Brice, Moms Mabley, Minnie Pearl, and Phyllis Diller, she explicitly eliminated traditional comeliness from her persona, creating a safe, sexless guise from which to make jokes, often at her own expense. But unlike them, she wasn't wearing a mask. She didn't pretend to be a child or an old lady or a rube or some wild woman. She was exactly what you saw in front of you: a housewife like your own missus or your mother or your sister or your neighbor, a real person, albeit one with an outsized personality. Like Jean Carroll, her act made comedy of the foibles, frustrations, and drives that befell any woman: housework, feckless husbands, bratty kids, problems with salespeople and tradesmen. But she placed more emphasis than Carroll ever did on self-deprecating humor. And that, even more than her everywoman quality, evoked her audiences' goodwill: She could make fun of herself quicker than you or anyone else could — and then make fun of you while you were still laughing at that first joke: "I bought stockings yesterday: fifty pair for ten dollars! The seams go up the front, but for twenty cents a pair I can learn to walk backwards"; "Look at this face! There are only two things I use: Silly Putty and sandpaper." As she explained, "I make sure that the premise of my material is honest. People believe me. And no one in the audience can get offended at what I do because I'm the butt."

The other tradition that she relied on, although with a sense of whimsy, was Sophie Tucker's Red Hot Mama personality. Yes, she was big, but that meant that she had a big appetite for *everything,* including sex. She wasn't bawdy or naughty or explicit. She didn't, like Sophie, insinuate that she was on the make. Indeed, she spoke lovingly, if not without mockery, of her home life and, in later years, of her musical director/husband. But she stood brazenly as a big, beautiful woman who considered herself sexy — and had a husband and daughters to prove it. She would flounce around the stage singing the praises of her allure, describing herself as "adorable," and then zero in on some man laughing stageside: "You're dying to touch me, aren't you, you animal?" and "Look: He can't keep his eyes off me!" It wasn't revolutionary, it was still based in self-derision (and, at that, particularly male-defined self-derision), but it was assertive and unexpected and, at its best, truly funny. She frequently erased the threat entirely in the last bit of her act, when she would perform a familiar song straight, without mockery, or even, especially when playing a resort, getting the audience to sing along with her. Even at her most raw, she was still approachable.

That was the comic persona that Totie started to craft in the late fifties, when she was scrapping away, willing to do whatever it took and go wherever she had to to make a success of herself. "I didn't get a decent job for a long time," she remembered. "I guess I played every toilet in this country. But even during the hard times, I didn't sit around feeling sorry for myself or hating my family for turning me on to show business." She showed up, did her act, got laughs, got paid, then returned home every night and did the things expected of a wife and mother. She rarely performed farther from home than a long drive, and when she did it was with the family in tow. She kept making phone calls and knocking on doors, unsolicited, looking for help in the form of a manager or agent who could help propel her forward.

In 1960, she was working at one of her

semi-regular stops, the Golden Slipper night-club in Glen Cove on Long Island, and she implored the personal manager Howard Hinderstein, then building a client list of singers and comedians, to catch her show. He drove out to have a look. "She called and asked me to come out and see her act," he recalled, "and to be truthful, I doubt that I would have if she hadn't noodged me so much. On the night I went out, though, I came home and I told my wife I had just seen the funniest woman I ever saw in my life."

Hinderstein signed her straight away, and he set about sharpening and honing her act and getting her the sort of bookings and exposure he felt she needed in order to progress. Encouraged by his enthusiasm, Totie and Johnston decided to move to New York, where the real pay dirt was. In 1961, they took an apartment in Forest Hills, Queens, bringing along her sister Raye, who quit Travelers Insurance to manage Totie's household and take care of her nieces.

One of Hinderstein's innovations was to book Totie more frequently in the show rooms of Catskills resorts, where her riotous but essentially clean act and her everywoman qualities seemed an especially apt fit for audiences of vacationing families. The famed Catskills resorts — the Borscht Belt — had roots in the late nineteenth century, when Jewish populations of big northeastern cities began to seek some respite from their often overcrowded and even diseased urban neighborhoods. In addition to outdoor activities, these resorts frequently provided entertainment: traveling professionals, amateur theatricals, staff talent shows, open mics for guests who fancied themselves gifted. One of the most common items on the entertainment menu was a tummler, a house clown who may have had other duties such as bellboy or dishwasher but whose *real* job was to keep guests' spirits up as emcee of the evening's shows, as merrymaker on rainy days, or whenever an antic inspiration struck.

After World War II, the Catskills resorts expanded into massive hotels, often quite luxurious and appointed with top-class amenities: golf courses, tennis courts, Olympic-sized pools, and, of course, the best entertainment. Such varied stars as Danny Kaye, Sid Caesar, Jerry Lewis, and Mel Brooks had cut their professional teeth as tummlers in the Catskills, and more were rising all the time: Alan King, Lenny Bruce, Jackie Mason. The highest-wattage Catskills hotels — Grossinger's, the Concord, Kutsher's, Fleischmann's — became prime hunting grounds for talent scouts and bookers representing big-city nightclubs. Women comedians, even those who could legitimately sing, were still a rarity, and there were *never* women tummlers. But the homey confines of a Catskills show room seemed like a natural setting to introduce the world to someone like Totie Fields, who felt as familiar as your brassy sister, cousin, or daughter and who, in the context of a roomful of urbanites on self-indulgent vacations, could be as raucous and rude as she wished.

In addition to the Borscht Belt, Hinderstein booked Totie into resorts on the Jersey Shore, most propitiously at the Chateau Monterey, a nightclub in Wildwood by the Sea run by former speakeasy operator Lou (short for Louisa) Booth. Totie played Booth's club throughout the summer of 1960, and Booth proved something of a mother figure for her, advising her on business matters, on dealing with men in the entertainment world, on the finer points of working a crowd. During the weeks-long gig, Eddie Suez, who ran a talent booking service out of Philadelphia, cut a deal with Hinderstein to book Totie in markets throughout Pennsylvania.

In December 1960, she debuted at the Town House nightclub in Pittsburgh, and received her first review in *Variety:* "She is fast, clever, and gets big yocks from her one-liners and bits. Her singing is in the Roberta Sherwood style. There may be more expensive comediennes in the country but there are few funnier." It's a tiny review, but there's a lot in it. The comparison to Sherwood, a melodra-

473

matic torch singer known for having risen from obscurity as a forty-three-year-old mother of three, gives a sense not only of Totie's style as a singer, which is to say tear-jerky and booming, but of the impression she made, which is to say homey and domestic, like your mom (even though she was only thirty-three years old). As for there being "more expensive comediennes," it would be worth noting that there were really only *two* women doing straight stand-up in mainstream show business at the time — Jean Carroll and Phyllis Diller — so the reference was surely to other singing comediennes such as Sophie Tucker, whose shadow would figure in Totie's story for some time to come.

Through the winter of 1960–61, Totie bounced between Pittsburgh, Philadelphia, and New York, honing her responses to varied audiences and to the ups and downs that beset anyone trying to make a living by getting people to forget their lives and laugh. The summer found her back in the Catskills and doing the best-yet work of her still-evolving career. At the end of the season, the bookers of Borscht Belt resorts had pegged her as the top comic of the year, and the bookings available to her began to open up.

In November, she debuted at the Boulevard nightclub in Rego Park in Queens, not a mile from her home in Forest Hills. *Variety* was there again, and, for the second time, opined on her performance in its "New Acts" column, commenting, not at all kindly, on her body:

> A short and heavy girl, she makes the most of her looks by pinning the butt of the comedics on this peg. It's all done with a fat girl's good humor. . . . Miss Fields asks and gives no quarter. She works like many of her male contemporaries, punching out lines in a thoroughly professional manner. Much of her material is simple and direct, with little subtlety involved.

That last caveat was echoed throughout the review, which noted deficiencies in the act but conceded as well that she had the talent to overcome them:

> Her material still needs a lot of attention. . . . It would seem that she has wider horizons. . . . She should look for a higher material plane on which to settle. She can make the grade in legit, and later in some of the flossier cafes, and certainly in tele situation comedies.

In the spring of 1962, she played Chicago for the first time, opening for Tony Bennett at the Living Room, where she was a hit: "a brash, brassy, and hefty singer-comedienne from the east. . . . It's a raucous and at times rowdy turn, but just right for this show." After another season in the Catskills and at clubs in New York, New Jersey, and Pennsylvania, two things were clear to Hinderstein and Totie: she was ready for a bigger spotlight, and she would need an even better act.

Variety had noted that Totie's act at the moment consisted of her jokes about her weight, a series of impressions of more famous singers, and "My Fat Lady," a parody of the biggest hit then on Broadway, a bit she cowrote with Johnston and delivered with more verve and quality than the actual material merited.

To bolster her act, Hinderstein enlisted experienced comedy writers and musical composers. Marvin Marx had been writing *Honeymooners* sketches and episodes for Jackie Gleason for nearly a decade, and he was called in to shape Totie's comedic persona, a task to which he had an obvious answer, namely, *inevitably,* her shape. She was overweight, he told Hinderstein, and she should make greater use of it. It wasn't exactly a revelation — Totie had been making comedy out of her appearance for some time — but Marx provided some fresh jokes. Further material, including original songs and parodic lyrics to some standards, was provided by the team of Lyn Duddy and Jerry Bresler, who wrote revues and stage shows and had created nightclub acts for performers as varied as Sophie Tucker and Robert

Goulet. Hinderstein wanted some new music from them, and he got it, but he also got advice similar to Marx's (which, of course, echoed Totie's native sense): "She's a charming little butterball," Duddy told the *New York Times,* "and we have her come right out and say, 'You know, I have no weight problem. I have a height problem. For my weight I should be 12 feet 7 inches tall.' "

Totie might have taken umbrage at having her jokes — and, indeed, her body — mansplained to her, but she allowed Hinderstein to refine her act further, taking vocal coaching from Marty Lawrence and having custom gowns made for her by Felix De Masi. Before long, she got the first truly plum engagement of her career: opening for Jackie Wilson at the Copacabana, the most exclusive and prestigious nightclub in New York, on March 11, 1963.

She did her usual schtick, making fun of herself, making passes at the men in the room, joking about diets and clothes and shopping. And she debuted some of the new comedic songs and set pieces that Marx, Duddy, and Bresler had crafted for her: "Sexy Me," "I'm Perfect," and "It's a Shame to Take the Money." In all, she was onstage for thirty minutes, and it was a complete and utter triumph. Just as the cliché would have it, almost fifteen years after she left home to make it in show business, she was an "overnight sensation."

Earl Wilson, the influential columnist of the *New York Post,* raved, "This fat gal's fantastic . . . a female Jackie Gleason!" And *Variety* opined (once again under the heading "New Acts"),

There always have been comediennes who knew how to turn a physical deficit into a performing plus. Miss Fields' deficit is glamour (an Elizabeth Taylor she ain't), so it's easy to laugh at her as she laughs at herself. She's short and beefy with a rag-mop coif and she deftly turns these femme handicaps into comedic attributes. Bouncing around the Copa floor, she looks like somebody's maiden aunt at a family reunion loosened up by one tipple too many. Her passes and sexy winks at the male ringsiders are funny because you know that this gal just isn't going to make out in that department. . . . It's not a sophisticated turn, by far. But who needs it? After all, she doesn't expect to play Lincoln Center.

There was a lot of left hand in these raves. Even if Totie was brash onstage about her size and appearance, it couldn't have been a pain-free experience for her to read so much snark about her physique under the bylines of male writers. Fortunately, she was not only born with tough skin, she had a crucial vote

478

of confidence from a model and a mentor. On her opening night at the Copa, Sophie Tucker herself was in attendance and came backstage to congratulate and counsel the newcomer. According to Totie, the great star "sat me down for two hours and told me what I should and shouldn't do. The main thing she said was that you should take every penny you have and put it on your back." She obediently invested even more in her wardrobe. When Tucker next saw her perform and, smiling, deemed her appearance "perfect," Totie admitted that "I cried like a baby" at her hero's approval.

Tucker wasn't the only big shot who noticed. The William Morris Agency signed Totie as a client, a tremendous boost that paid dividends almost immediately: on March 24, not quite two weeks after her debut at the Copa, she made her television debut on *The Ed Sullivan Show,* the first of three times she would appear that year alone on the nation's most popular variety show. Sullivan truly enjoyed her broad-stroke comedy. "This gal has a wonderful sense of humor, a wonderful delivery," he said. "She'll be around as long as she doesn't go on a diet." He backed up his words with bookings: Totie graced his stage some twenty times before the show ceased production in 1971.

On the strength of her successful Copa and Sullivan gigs, Totie was in demand all over the country. In the coming year, she would play all the towns where she'd previously appeared, plus such new spots as Houston, Miami, Atlantic City, and Dallas. She debuted in L.A. to a *Variety* review that was as laudatory as it was unintentionally condescending: "Pound for pound, two-ton Totie . . . gets a lot of comic calories into the one fatty gag and manages to get off quickly before it wears too thin." She had return engagements in Chicago, where she headlined at Mister Kelly's, the city's premier showcase for comedians, and in New York at the Copacabana, where she was once again well received, this time as the opening act for Bobby Rydell. She continued to spend summers playing the Catskills and the Jersey Shore. She worked nightclubs all around the New York and Philadelphia markets (the Latin Quarter in the former and the Latin Casino in the latter became regular stopping points). She started appearing at show rooms in Las Vegas, Reno, and Lake Tahoe, and then at resorts in Puerto Rico and the Bahamas. And she would squeeze in lucrative one-night stands as the featured entertainer at business conventions or other seasonal events — in many cases playing to her largest live audiences of a given year.

Crowds reliably loved her. The critics were almost always positive, pointing out that her humor was naughty and rowdy but never dirty and that she played especially well to conventioneers and good-timers. It was also noted, regularly, that she should be given a shot on TV or on Broadway; she could sing, after all, even if she had all but forsaken straight material for parodies and novelty songs about her sexual allure. But her TV appearances through the coming years were limited to variety shows and talk shows. Apart from Sullivan, she began popping up on programs hosted by Joey Bishop (nine times over the years), Merv Griffin (an eventual fifty times), Mike Douglas (more than seventy times, including hosting gigs), and Johnny Carson (upwards of ten times). Almost always, her stand-up routines focused on self-deprecation: "I have the same measurements as Elizabeth Taylor. Her living room is nine-by-twelve, and so is mine!"; "I'm so sick of being everybody's buddy. Just to pick up a paper once and read, 'Totie Fields raped in an alley.' I put on new underwear every night just to get ready"; "I'm a flanken: a good hunk of Jewish meat." But she was an apt hand at sketch comedy, which she performed on variety shows hosted by the likes of Jerry Lewis, Sammy Davis Jr., and Bob Hope. She seemed ubiquitous, Hurricane Totie, a gale-force joke machine, bounding onto stages and TV sets all across the country, mocking herself, breaking up hosts and bandleaders, often ending with a song — a charming, brassy, essentially harmless good-time gal whom everybody seemed to love.

But there was something *not quite* about it all. Yes, she was playing the best venues, but frequently she was the opener: for Ray Charles, Trini Lopez, Bobby Vinton, Charles Aznavour, Enzo Stuarti. She didn't headline a big New York club until late 1966, and then it was atop a kind of vaudeville bill at the Latin Quarter, with, among other acts, a Hungarian juggler who worked with her feet and a troupe of singing and dancing "gypsies." She was the star, yes, but of what, exactly?

As if to reframe her brand before she became cemented in the public mind as a kind of sideshow or novelty act, her management team embarked on a public relations blitz. She'd never been shy about speaking out to the press or, least of all, saying her mind about *anything,* but in the winter of 1966–67 she appeared in feature stories in a variety of New York newspapers (with, of course, syndication in scores of out-of-town markets) discussing her career, her private life, her ambitions.

"At last I'm headlining," she boasted to the *New York World Journal Tribune.* "No more second-act billing for me. I'm a bona-fide star. Nobody's billed over me."

She told the *New York Sunday News* about

her $200,000 per year income,[*] her new Lincoln Continental, her "azurine" mink coat, and her fame: "I'm recognized everywhere I go. I'm like a dachshund. Once you see one, you never forget it."

For *Newsday,* she allowed a reporter to follow her around for a few days, dine with her, and speak with her management. When it came time to chat, she made a point of differentiating herself from other female comedians such as the "cerebral" Joan Rivers ("Comedy you have to sit and think about isn't my line. It's gotta be funny right away or it isn't.") and shared such harmless confidences as "My career is very important to me, but I'll tell you something: I never let my work interfere with my home life."

The Totie Fields who had emerged since turning to comedy on Revere Beach didn't cater to a sophisticated aesthetic. She shied away from topical humor ("I'd hate," she explained, "to come up with something strong only to find out that the audience hasn't read the paper"), and she didn't try to find a way, as, say, Phyllis Diller did, to emulate the aggressive delivery or subject matter of male comics ("You can't be hostile and expect the audience to like you," she said). But she was, as Joan Rivers put it, "a

[*] Approximately $1.55 million in 2022 terms.

throwback to the tough, vulgar Catskills comics. . . . a brilliant comic, singing a couple of songs, talking, doing routines about pantyhose, about her husband, George, about being fat. She came out of the lowest levels of show business, from toilets, a fat girl doing strip joints. And she was a total professional who knew how to work an audience, how to sell a joke."

Totie's act, at the apogee of her career, might consist of her coming onstage and praising her own praise-filled introduction ("Did you hear him say, 'The Star of the Show'? I get goosebumps every night."), lavishing affection on her own appearance ("I used to be heavy. That's hard to believe. I was obese. But this is the new Totie Fields. Adorable. I look like a pregnant bouquet in this dress."), and then singing a version of "Sexy Me":

> You're gonna see lips
> Like you've never seen before.
> You're gonna see hips
> You'll remember ever more.

But she occasionally dropped the comic edge and talked about her sexuality and desirability in a way that you couldn't really hold against her: "Nineteen years with the same guy. I must be doing something right. My old man smiles a lot"; "You show me a woman busy in the kitchen all day, I'll show you a guy fooling around with one that isn't. Let the Girl Scouts push the cookies." Her self-confidence, coming out of a woman who didn't look like the culture's ideal of a beauty, was so infectious that most couldn't resist its appeal.

By 1969, Totie was regularly seen on TV talk shows, game shows, and variety shows, and she was earning as much as $30,000 per week[*] appearing in nightclubs, Catskills show rooms, casinos, and other live venues. She and George and their girls were living comfortably in a new home in Las Vegas, and she could work as many weeks a year as she wished. She was a household name, if not quite an A-list superstar, and she enjoyed the perks that came with her fame, such as demanding twelve cups of coffee in her dressing room before every show, not because she was a caffeine junky but rather because she wanted to wipe away all memories of the days when she played dives and couldn't get a single cup of coffee from management.

But her ambition to do more, to be bigger, to conquer never seemed satisfied. Somewhere just out of her reach was a brass ring that she strove for. She constantly pushed Howard Hinderstein into carving out new opportunities. She started singing straight

[*] Approximately $213,000 in 2022.

again during her live shows, as if to let the world know she had other tricks up her sleeve. She appeared in a summer-season production of *Bye Bye Birdie* that toured outdoor amphitheaters around Ohio. She released an LP, *Totie Fields Live,* that captured her in performance at the Riviera Hotel on the Vegas Strip, where she had an exclusive three-year contract to appear twelve weeks per year. She turned up in made-for-TV comedy movies, novelties such as *Decisions! Decisions!* which let an in-studio audience choose the direction of the plot, and *Fol-de-Rol,* in which she played several roles opposite Sid and Marty Krofft's troupe of puppets. She signed a contract to "write" a "book," a slim little curiosity (and minor bestseller) entitled *I Think I'll Start on Monday: The Official 8 1/2 oz. Mashed Potato Diet.* She even became available for TV commercials, her agents assuring potential clients that her "style of humor would be a great asset to many advertisers."

She'd become a fixture in the popular culture, the highest-ranked female comedian in the annual "Q Study" that assessed performers according to their familiarity and favorability with audiences. A drag queen name Brian Marshall began impersonating her, and Totie was so flattered that she gifted him with $12,000 of gowns that she no longer wore.

The *Merv Griffin Show,* on which she was a regular, held an ongoing "Totie Fields Look-alike Contest" in which ordinary women competed over who resembled her the most, with the winner getting a chance to meet her.

She continued banging away, with dozens of weeks on the road every year and constant TV appearances alongside the likes of Carol Burnett, Glen Campbell, Dean Martin, Joey Bishop, Tony Orlando and Dawn, and Jerry Lewis, on whose annual Muscular Dystrophy Association Telethon her regular appearances were touted as a highlight. In late 1973, she landed a lucrative new deal at the Sahara Hotel on the Vegas Strip, calling for her to appear for fewer weeks a year than she had been performing at the Riviera but with a bigger salary. And in late 1975, she landed a dramatic role on TV's long-running *Medical Center.* She was celebrated on an episode of *This Is Your Life.* She talked of starting a line of clothes for larger women with the sizes deliberately marked low — say, 3, 5, and 7 — arguing that "mentally it will make us feel better." Some joker named a *racehorse* after her. Such was her ubiquity that off-Broadway producers could confidently invoke her image in a casting call in *Back Stage,* trying to fill a role by describing it as a "disturbed Jewish female type, cross between Totie Fields and Susan Hayward" (adding, helpfully, "no nudity").

She was generally known to be good company, a hale-gal-well-met, who could laugh easily at the goings on around her, who was quick with an ad-libbed quip, and who, according to her husband, "broke up at other comedians, no matter who they were." But she was also fierce and had a powerful memory for a slight. Over the years, gossip columnists hinted that she had fallings-out with fellow Vegas entertainers Shecky Green and Wayne Newton. And Joan Rivers recalled her shock at learning just how protective Totie was of her turf on the tiny island of women comedians:

> Totie was a gutter fighter who must have been contemptuous of this earnest college graduate with a circle pin and a small delivery, this comedy parvenue who she thought had never paid any real dues in comedy, never done three shows a night in Sheboygan — and was coming into her territory. I could not understand why certain major clubs around the country refused to book me, and I learned later that Totie Fields was spreading the word that I was dirty and vicious and not funny.

That alleged animus, perhaps born of the struggle to dominate the small bit of turf allowed women comedians, wasn't to prove long-lived. But the events that would put it to rest were impossible to foresee.

In many ways, she had reached the pinnacle of the success she'd been working so hard to achieve. And yet, somehow, it still wasn't enough. "I made them give me a suite facing the front so I could see my name on the sign all day long," she remembered of her Sahara debut. "I would sit up all night just staring at the sign. And I thought about Revere Beach, which was my first good job, and finally I turned to Georgie, and I said, 'It's the same thing as Revere Beach — it's just nicer drapes.' "

Perhaps she was having an existential insight about the nature of ambition or the yearning for material things. Or perhaps she was so used to scrapping and clawing that she felt a kind of emptiness when there was no immediate reason to keep at it. Either way, she was restless with what she had, and she kept pushing, with, it turned out, dire results.

Maybe because Phyllis Diller had done it and made so much comic hay of it, or maybe because, approaching fifty, she began to feel some real vanity beneath all her jokes about her weight and appearance, Totie began to think about plastic surgery. In late March 1976, after consulting with her physicians in Las Vegas, she checked into St. Joseph Hospital in Stamford, Connecticut, to have Dr. William T. Keavy do some work around her eyes. It was an elective procedure, but routine. Totie was set to open at the Sahara on April 22, another of her very popular $75,000 a week[*] engagements at the casino.

On April 21, though, the Sahara announced that the Smothers Brothers would be replacing Totie due to complications following what they called a "throat operation." The casino's PR department may have been protecting Totie's privacy by misstating the nature of her surgery and declaring that she was facing "recovery setbacks" in Connecticut. In fact, she was at Columbia-Presbyterian Hospital in New York, where, as a shocked world learned two days later, doctors had amputated her left leg above the knee.

The story was awful: Totie, suffering from diabetes and circulatory problems related to her weight, was something less than an ideal candidate for elective surgery, but she had been counseled that rest and proper diet in advance of the procedure would increase her chances of normal recovery. In fact, she worked almost until the day she checked into the hospital, completing an engagement at the Latin Casino in Cherry Hill, New Jersey, on March 29. After the operation, she suffered phlebitis in her left leg and had two heart attacks. When she was stabilized, she

[*] Approximately $341,000 in 2022 terms.

was transferred to New York, where doctors performed vascular surgery in an effort to save her leg. It failed. The limb became gangrenous, and the amputation was necessary to keep the infection from spreading. It would be late May before she was deemed stable enough to be discharged and sent to California to be fitted with a prosthetic leg and adjust to a new normal. In the meantime, she made one significant appearance, at the wedding of her oldest daughter, Jody, which she insisted go on as planned despite her weakened condition.

In October, she held a press conference in Beverly Hills, flanked by comedian Jan Murray and singer-emcee Burt Convy, to tell the world she was on the mend and ready for a comeback. Some seventy pounds lighter than when she was last seen, flashing a new haircut, a smart outfit, lots of bling, and, of course, an artificial leg, she joked about finally not being overweight and about using her jewelry as a form of mental therapy: "The minute I put the rings back on, I knew I was well. I don't care if I lost a leg: I've got my fingers." To celebrate her recovery, she gave herself a new nickname: the Bionic Yenta.

The following month, she appeared at a banquet at the Century Plaza Hotel, where Frank Sinatra, who was extremely solicitous and supportive of her during her convalescence, was being honored by the American

Friends of the Hebrew University of Jerusalem. Seated in the audience, Totie was acknowledged from the dais and received a lengthy standing ovation.

But despite her repeated assurances and those of her management, Totie did not resume performing until March 1977, when she appeared for a week at the Sunrise Theatre in Fort Lauderdale, a kind of warm-up for a full comeback. The following month, she made her "official" return, opening at the Sahara Hotel in Las Vegas before a crowd packed with her celebrity friends, her family, her entertainment world colleagues, even her doctors. Wheeled out onstage by Bert Convy, who had opened and who introduced her, she beamed broadly as the audience rose to a lengthy ovation. When she was finally able to speak, she delivered a line that took almost three decades and an unimaginable misfortune to produce, the joke of a lifetime, really: "I finally weigh less than Elizabeth Taylor!"

She sang (including new material written for the occasion by Lyn Duddy and Jerry Bresler, still working with her after seventeen years) and made lots of jokes about her condition and her care: "They sent me a psychiatrist immediately following the surgery. It took three or four days, but I finally straightened out his problems."

But quite a bit of the evening was more

serious and emotional. She spoke about her love for her daughters and for George Johnston, who, as usual, conducted the orchestra. And she opened up at length about the great support she received from the public and from many of those in attendance in Las Vegas that night: "I want you to know something. I have never been happier in my whole life to be anywhere. I am so ready to go back to work and all because of you, and it's so wonderful to know that people love you that much — your wires, your flowers, and, most of all, your prayers." The performance was filmed by HBO, which aired it in June as *Totie Returns.* Reviewing it for the *New York Times,* John J. O'Connor called it a "portrait of a resilient and determined performer," and was especially taken with the interviews of Totie offstage, where she spoke with emotion about her family.

She seemed, indeed, to be blessed with tremendous confidence. "I didn't lose my talent," she told *People* magazine, "I didn't lose my sense of humor, I just lost a leg." She added, "I never had good legs anyway. You never heard people say, 'Geez, what a pair of gams that Totie Fields has!' " And, more seriously, she said, "I never thought I wouldn't work again — and I never, ever thought I would die."

She appeared before appreciative crowds at

the Sahara for a couple of weeks; she and George even renewed their wedding vows at the hotel, calling in a rabbi to do the honors twenty-seven years after they were married in a civil ceremony back in Boston. But in early May, she began to cancel shows because, as she told Joan Rivers in a private chat, she was having trouble with her left eye. Doctors at Stanford University Hospital determined that her poor circulation meant that she required a vitrectomy, a procedure meant to seal the blood vessels in the eye to prevent hemorrhage and blindness. Fortunately, this operation went smoothly, and she recuperated according to schedule. By July, she was performing at the Sahara again but, cautioned against air travel, she canceled most of her schedule of summer appearances around the country.

She was dogged, though, and, it would appear, she had softened, even with people with whom she had once felt a rivalry. One night that summer at the MGM Grand in Las Vegas, Joan Rivers was unwinding from a performance when there was a knock at her dressing room door. "It was Totie," she remembered, "alone, a hundred pounds lighter, limping badly, going blind, and brave, brave, brave." Totie had been in the audience and wanted to tell Joan how much she'd enjoyed the show. "We talked for an hour," Rivers said, "muted and soft . . . about jokes

— what works and what doesn't work — about club owners we knew, funny things that had happened, and where comedy was going. This night was a rite of passage for me and, I hope, for her, too. I adored Totie in that hour."

By late August she was back in public, fulfilling a few dates in the Catskills. On September 28, her return to work was celebrated with a milestone luncheon hosted by the Friars Club. A packed ballroom at the New York Hilton was entertained by the likes of Milton Berle, Henny Youngman, Soupy Sales, and Norm Crosby, who all told relatively sanitized jokes (the ordinary Friars obscenities having been prohibited because ladies were in attendance). Sarah Vaughn and the duo of Marilyn McCoo and Billy Davis Jr. performed familiar songs with lyrics rewritten in Totie's honor by lyricist Sammy Cahn. New York mayor Abe Beame presented her with a Certificate of Appreciation, and Friars dean Buddy Howe gave her a watch. ("It doesn't have a diamond in it!" she shrieked in mock complaint.)

The following night, she opened an engagement at the Westbury Music Fair in suburban New York. Wheeled onstage in a golf cart festooned with flowers and ribbons, she stood for a lengthy ovation and then sat on a stool to deliver her act, making fun of her lighter body, her artificial leg, and her seemingly endless skein of medical woes. "If you're not funny with two legs," she told the crowd, "you won't be funny with one leg. And if you're not funny with one, you won't be funny with two, either."

She moved on from Long Island to Valley Forge, Pennsylvania, where she performed a series of shows to yet more enthusiastic embraces from the audience. And she promised the press that she had a full slate of projects planned: an ABC television Movie of the Week, an appearance at the Palladium in London, and a full-scale Broadway show scheduled to open in the spring. "I guarantee you one thing," she told the *Philadelphia Inquirer,* "no one leaves my show saying, 'Oh, that poor girl.' They come, and if anyone is uneasy at first, before long all you hear from them is rocking laughter. There's certainly no pity."

But the blows kept coming. Before she could continue her come-back tour, she was admitted to a hospital in Los Angeles for a modified radical mastectomy of her right breast, where cancer had been discovered. This time she recovered in private, without any chipper phone calls to newspaper columnists or ambitious talk about a touring schedule. She was resilient, but this was a relentless torrent of life-threatening conditions and medical procedures. No matter how determined she was to become a big star and to stay a big star, she had been overwhelmed.

Through it all, she relied on George to help her through the awful run of ill health. In the fall, she had told a reporter, "The one thing I can't stress strongly enough is the support I get from my husband. We've been married for 26 years, and if I have strength, it's because I got it from George."

As she recuperated yet again, she began to seek legal redress from the plastic surgeon whom she believed had kicked off her awful string of health issues with that ill-fated procedure on her eyes. In 1977, a year of depositions and behind-the-scenes negotiations began in Connecticut that would result in a $2 million malpractice suit against Dr. William Keavy and St. Joseph Hospital. Details were few, but the public evidence of what had happened was widely known and, at least to the untrained eye, fairly damning.[*]

In the coming months, Totie was presented with awards, feted at fundraisers, celebrated for her courage. But she wanted, more than anything, to get back to work. That was the

[*] The matter would finally approach trial in the spring of 1984, and the likes of Eydie Gormé, Steve Lawrence, and Merv Griffin were poised to testify to their observation of Totie's ordeal. Days prior to the trial, though, Dr. Keavy settled for a reported $850,000.

main source of her sense of well-being, of feeling loved, of being alive. She had a series of bookings in place for the spring and summer of 1978. But before they began, a diversion: Frank Sinatra invited her to join him on a star-filled trip to Israel to be in attendance at the opening of a student center at the Hebrew University of Jerusalem that would be named in his honor.

Not long after returning, she was back on the road performing: Cleveland, Cherry Hill, Nanuet, the Concord Hotel in the Catskills. She taped a ninety-minute visit with Merv Griffin in which she discussed her health battles and had four of her doctors appear along with her. According to Griffin, "The show is funny, sad, terribly dramatic, and, at times, shocking. Totie reveals things we've never known and often refers to death in a joking way."

Indeed, that was who she was. At every appearance, she was raucous and rowdy and made fun of herself and her ailments. Greeted at the Concord with a standing ovation, she chastised the audience: "Sit down! You're making fools of yourselves! I haven't done anything yet!" She told columnist Earl Wilson that she was in the pink: "Never felt better. I weigh 117, and I'm so pretty." She bragged of a new book she was working on and a movie about her life that was in the works. And, once again, she joked about her mortality: "I told the kids, 'If I croak, don't look for the money. I spent it all.' "

Three weeks later, she was gone.

It was a heart attack, at home in Las Vegas, on August 2 — her third cardiac episode in total, and one clout too many for her battered system to withstand. Her family found her in distress at around seven a.m. and called paramedics, who tried to revive her at home and then at a nearby hospital, to no avail.

Word spread through Totie's tribe quickly. Among the many who expressed grief was Joan Rivers, who conceded that without Totie's determined groundbreaking, "I would not be around, Lily Tomlin wouldn't be around, Carol Burnett wouldn't be around." Across the nation, dozens of performers canceled their engagements so that they could be present at the funeral in Las Vegas, which, in Jewish tradition, was held speedily, just two days after her passing.

For weeks, there was a pall around the fact of her passing. Merv Griffin televised the long final interview she'd done, all ninety minutes of it, and it had an eerie quality, as if she were making light of her own mortality from beyond the grave.

Her family continued to feel as if they'd been robbed of her. In June, George Johnston filed a second malpractice suit against the two Las Vegas doctors who had advised Totie that she was healthy enough to undergo that cosmetic surgery procedure that seemed to precipitate all her woes; the suit was eventually settled behind closed doors.

In the years that followed, as the roar of her voice and the laughter it occasioned faded, Totie Fields's figure began to diminish in the popular mind. A biopic with the working title *You've Got Everything* was floated in the Hollywood trades but never realized. Her TV appearances, via reruns, became less and less commonly seen. And her specific style — somewhere between the singing bawds like Sophie Tucker and Belle Barth and the gonzo Vegas comics such as Shecky Greene and Buddy Hackett — wasn't really practiced by anyone else in the business, let alone any of the women working in comedy. Her art, like her name and her voice, seemed to be of another time.

In the early nineties, cabaret performer Nancy Timpanaro wrote and appeared in a one-woman musical comedy entitled *Totie,* which she performed dozens of times throughout the decade, at first with the blessing of George Johnston, who allowed her to use his late wife's monologues, then, when he had a change of mind, without. A decade or so later, Totie's spirit and persona were resurrected again in *Sophie, Totie, and Belle,* another musical comedy in which she was

500

teamed, in a fashion, with her sisters in merriment, Misses Tucker and Barth; it, too, enjoyed a brief and modestly popular run.

But in other important ways, Totie was, unfairly, forgotten. She would literally be reduced to a footnote in various histories of stand-up comedy (even *histories of women in stand-up*). And, having never quite gained a cult audience or struck a particular chord with younger sensibilities, she receded in a way that seemed impossible when she was dominating nightclub and TV stages all across the country, commanding huge salaries, willing laughter out of audiences, pushing herself further and harder, determined to win everyone over, dead set on a stardom that she finally achieved only to see it stolen away in a succession of cruel and unfair blows. She had been persistent, resilient, tireless — dancing, singing saucy songs, making jokes about herself, willing audiences to love her. If her comedy was of a certain era, her spirit, infectious, was timeless. That little girl from Hartford who'd been born to steal the show did it again and again, and the tiny stage her siblings built for her in the backyard came, eventually, to be shared with a whole world.

EIGHT:
THE SCRAPPER

I don't want to be the kooky girl. I'm not a kooky clown, and I don't want to be a "character." But if you're a girl and a comedian, either you're expected to be the dumb blonde, or a sexy thing who says double entendres, or you come on and make faces and do pratfalls. They don't really know what I'm doing yet.

— 1965

In Joan Rivers, all the streams that women comedians had been working in previously came together in one quicksilver, five-foot-two-inch package of nerves, angles, jabs, and jokes. Declaring herself in the public mind in one fell swoop on a single night on national television, she was something like the Beatles of her chosen field. She bore at least some portion of the gifts of almost every woman who preceded her in the business: the wit, the determination, the thick skin, the hunger, the pugnacity, the ambition, the courage.

Joan emerged at just the moment when

American popular culture was ready to accept that a woman could be a stand-up comedy star. She had to fight her parents, the show business establishment, some colleagues, some critics, and a mountain of prejudices against women to become that. But even more than Phyllis Diller she achieved it *as* a woman. Phyllis did a masculine-style act almost as if in drag, punching the audience with jokes; Joan, especially in the early part of her career, expressed herself, almost apologetically, as an ordinary girl who was denied ordinary victories — love, beauty, marriage, domestic bliss. Phyllis presented herself as bizarre, a zany; Joan presented herself as the (neurotic, needy, self-deprecating) girl next door.

Perhaps that was why so many of her early audiences — showbiz professionals and critics, especially (all of them, predictably, men) — found Joan shrill and irritating. She wasn't a cartoon of a woman making fun of her own failings; she was someone you could imagine knowing (or *being*), whose frank bouts of self-doubt and even self-loathing were uncomfortably credible. When she joked about her parents' dislike of her, of their failed efforts to marry her off, of her busted romances, of her futile efforts to attain culturally prescribed standards of beauty, there was a palpable sense that she wasn't the only woman in the room battling those demons.

Like the "sick" comedians of the late 1950s, she spoke her inner truths, with wit and pungency and great technical craft and significant daring. And as she built her career, she pushed forward relentlessly: she would host a TV talk show (multiple times, in fact), write and star in a Broadway play (twice), write and direct a feature film, create successful lines of merchandise, even play herself in a TV film about her own life's struggles. She would become famous — notorious — for her savage insult humor. But she was always her own most blistering critic. And as acidic as her tongue could be, she was proud enough and confident enough in her achievement to serve as a mentor, even mother figure, to young women who, whether emulating her or not, came up in her wake.

Joan Alexandra Molinsky was born on June 8, 1933, to Dr. Meyer Molinsky and his wife, Beatrice, whose other daughter, Barbara, was three. The Molinskys lived in the Crown Heights section of Brooklyn, on New York Avenue, about a block and a half north of Eastern Parkway, a wide thoroughfare with a park-like promenade running down its center. The portion of the boulevard where the Molinskys made their home was known as Doctors Row, and — outwardly, at least — they fit right in. Meyer dressed formally every day in order to tend to patients at his street-level office, while Beatrice oversaw her house help, which included a maid and a governess, tending house immaculately, entertaining formally, and dressing the girls in matching outfits like a pair of store-bought dolls — "her little flowers," as she called them.

It was a grand show, but it was a facade. Meyer Molinsky was well regarded as a general practitioner, but he believed it was more important to treat patients than to profit off them. He had spent time as a young physician working for a free clinic in the relatively impoverished Brownsville section of Brooklyn, and he believed that medical care should be available to all who needed it, regardless of ability to pay. Even after he had married, become a father, and moved into a series of increasingly expensive homes, he never abandoned that mentality, behaving like a small-town, old-world doctor, treating patients according to their need. This made him beloved in his community, but it also meant that he was never as well off as his fellow practitioners.

This laudably communitarian ethos didn't compute for Beatrice, who had been raised to expect a fine life and was determined to have it, even if she had to defy her husband, the credit managers of luxurious stores, and simple common sense to do so. Beatrice was born in 1906, one of four children of Boris Cushman, a merchant with ties to the Czar's armies, and his wife, Hannah. They lived in a grand dacha outside of Odessa, but the storms of revolution and war forced them to flee to New York. There, the oldest son, Alex, put himself through dental school and managed to reconstitute a semblance of the family's former life of opulence in an apartment on Manhattan's Upper West Side, where they bore themselves as upper-class emigres.

Meyer Molinsky, too, had come from Odessa, where he was born in 1900 in the city's Jewish ghetto, one of four children of a widowed fruit peddler. She, too, was able to migrate to America, where Meyer attended medical school, paying his tuition by working nights as a subway conductor.

Meyer and Beatrice met in 1928 and had a whirlwind courtship of mere weeks before marrying. On the face of things, *he* was the catch: tall and smart, educated, a professional. But Meyer had already decided that his work would be based on the model of the clinic, not some tony Park Avenue practice. That didn't stop Beatrice from comporting herself as if she was still in her brother's apartment — or, indeed, her father's dacha. No sooner did Meyer bring home a dollar than she spent it. She insisted on grander and grander homes, working up toward that townhouse on Eastern Parkway; she bought furniture, jewelry, furs, fine clothes; she took on household help. And she regularly paid the tax of Meyer's fury when he learned of each new purchase and indulgence.

Joan and Barbara grew up hiding in their rooms as their parents fought over some outlandish expense their mother had incurred. A $2,000 mink provoked an especially memorable row that climaxed with Beatrice brutally reminding Meyer of the different classes from which their families had emerged: "You come from kikes!" Whenever her husband stopped the spigot and her favorite stores would no longer extend her credit, Beatrice would visit pawn shops, where she would borrow against her jewelry so as to make payments against her accounts and resume shopping.

Beatrice's focus on propriety, formality, etiquette and appearances was, finally, stronger than Meyer's native caution. If nothing else, at least in the algebra of society as she understood it, Beatrice had two daughters to raise and marry into worthy matches, a goal that she was set on accomplishing virtually from their birth: the precious matched outfits, the governesses, the lessons in etiquette and piano, and, when they were old enough, private educations.

The Molinsky girls attended the elite Jewish Ethical Culture School on Prospect Park West. In that, as so often, Beatrice's reach exceeded her grasp, and Joan would remember awful days when she delivered her tuition check to the headmaster and asked him not to deposit it until a bit of time had passed. The household anxiety about money thus followed her to school, where she sensed all of her classmates were better off than her *and knew it.* Throughout her school years, Joan felt like an outsider, like she was ducking under laser beams of harsh scrutiny, like she was passing, barely, for something she was not.

As she recalled it, she escaped those sensations only once: when she appeared as a kitty cat in a classroom play — as a prekindergartner — and received the acclaim of a tiny audience. Other than that, as she said for the rest of her life, she lived in a veil of shame beset by self-doubt, self-punishment, and the sense that she was a disappointment to her parents and an unwelcome presence among her peers.

To look at pictures of her in those years is to see an ordinary girl. Nevertheless, Joan had become absolutely crippled by her belief that she was fat and ugly. Years later, she would turn her distorted self-image into comic hay: "I was so fat that at camp I was my own buddy"; "in my class picture I was the front row"; "I had more chins than the Chinese phone book"; "I retreated into my-*selves.*" That sort of thing was the stuff of her profession. But her childhood dysmorphia had continual serious impacts on her throughout her life: bouts of bulimia, countless plastic surgery procedures, and, even when she was ensconced in the top rungs of her field, the sense that it was all a charade, that she was still the chubby, unliked girl who was always on the verge of being exposed as a fraud.

To fight off her insecurities and find her way into the center of things, she resorted, predictably, to wisecracking, talking loudly to draw attention to herself, even, according to one early report card, a "tendency toward bribery in order to win friends." She could be "extremely sensitive to criticism," observed another teacher. But she was invariably recognized by her teachers for her intelligence, her creativity, and her attention to schoolwork. She was never *not* bright or active or creative, but she was never the shining star among her classmates that she so longed to be.

After Brooklyn Ethical, Joan followed her sister to Adelphi Academy, a college preparatory school in the Bay Ridge section of Brooklyn. There she shed her babyfat, if not her self-sabotaging ways. She still pined, to no avail, to be among the in-group, and, now that she had reached an age of sexual awakening, to be courted by a boy, neither of which happened. But she was a funny, sharp, engaged student who contributed prose and cartoons to the school newspaper, worked on the yearbook, belonged to a number of clubs, and was recognized by classmates for her "ready wit."

Her chief interest was dramatics: anything resembling a performance at Adelphi, she was in on it. Somewhere along the way, she'd developed the idea of becoming an actress. She stole a book on breaking into show business from the public library and read it religiously. She slipped a professional photograph of herself out of its frame in the living room and sent it off to MGM, then spent weeks waiting for the phone call or letter that would announce that she had been discovered. She gobbled up movie star magazines, held jealous grudges against such young actresses as Margaret O'Brien, Natalie Wood, and Elizabeth Taylor, and imagined being romanced by her screen ideals Farley Granger and Richard Conte. She even fashioned a stage name for herself: J. Sondra Meredith.

Her efforts at Adelphi gained her a smidgen of renown. In 1950, the *Brooklyn Eagle* newspaper ran a feature story about a variety show that Joan and her classmates mounted. *Cavalcade of 2150,* which Joan cowrote, codirected, and starred in, was a revue loosely based on the girls' idea of what the future might make of the twentieth century. Chatting with the reporter, Joan called herself a "stage door Jane," talked of taking acting classes at a private studio near New York University, and spoke of her parents' dismay when they learned of her theatrical ambitions. They thought she was "joking" at first, she said, but "now they're resigned to it."

And that appears to have been true. Beatrice, who had forced the girls to take piano, voice, and dance lessons as part of their education as wives-to-be, was surprisingly encouraging of Joan's mania, allowing her to take acting classes in Manhattan and then, more impressively, permitting her to skip school so as to appear as an extra in *Mr. Universe,* a B movie about pro wrestling starring Vince Edwards.

Joan graduated Adelphi in the spring of 1950, just shy, precociously, of her seventeenth birthday. Rather than a school where her theatrical ambitions could be nourished, her parents sent her, again in Barbara's wake, to Connecticut College for Women, a straitlaced and tradition-bound institution perceived as a likely place for women to receive, even more than education, introductions to young men attending Ivy League colleges, which is to say, future husbands. Not entirely coincidentally, in the months before Joan's matriculation, the family moved from Brooklyn to Larchmont, a leafy suburb in Westchester County, and a Tudor-style house on Oxford Road, a perfect frame, Beatrice thought, in which to exhibit her daughters as suitable prospects for comfortable marriages. J. Sondra Meredith may have had designs on the stage and a great career, but in her mother's eyes, Joan Molinsky was strictly a future missus.

And that made the experience of a New England women's college in the early 1950s simply awful. Every weekend, the dorms would empty as girls went off to Cambridge, New Haven, Manhattan — wherever their beaux were in school. But Joan, who had no suitors, despite writing letters to every unattached boy she could think of, stayed alone, a spinster at seventeen.[*] For Barbara, Connecticut College was a perfect setting for focusing on schoolwork in preparation for acceptance as a law student at Columbia University. But Joan agonized for two years until she asked her parents to let her follow her sister yet again, by transferring to Barnard College, the women's adjunct to Columbia. If nothing else, she explained, they would save on room and board because she could live at home. They agreed.

It was a transformative choice. Joan was

---

[*] She wasn't *entirely* spurned. The *Brooklyn Eagle* reported in March 1952 that she attended the Yale Junior Prom as the date of Samuel Antupit of West Hartford, Connecticut — prompting one to wonder just how exactly they might have known that.

suddenly in a world filled with ideas about books, theater, art, and politics — and the whole of New York City in which to indulge her mind. She appeared in key roles in campus productions — at both Barnard and Columbia — of *Juno and the Paycock, Mourning Becomes Electra,* and *Othello.* She studied classical theater and, with a new group of friends she had fallen among with heartening ease, caught the latest Broadway and Off-Broadway sensations. For the first time, she was part of a big, encouraging group, and she felt that she was on the path to realizing her dreams.

She graduated Barnard in June 1954, a week shy of her twenty-first birthday (and *not* Phi Beta Kappa, as she claimed to the press and in her official publicity biographies for decades),* ready to launch a great theatrical career. She got her parents' permission to spend the summer in a real theater, and she

* Her 1986 autobiography *Enter Laughing,* cowritten with the journalist Richard Meryman, marked virtually the first place where she *didn't* claim this status. In addition to conferring this honor on herself illegitimately, she also sowed a great deal of confusion about her major, claiming in various interviews that it was social anthropology (she *had* taken a class with Margaret Mead), philosophy, theater, and English lit, the last of which was, in fact, the case, per her class yearbook.

applied for and was granted an internship at the Westport Playhouse in Connecticut, one of the finest regional theaters in the country. She packed a trunk and shipped it off, but on the day appointed for her departure, she lay in bed crying, frightened. Eventually, she resigned her position and had Beatrice phone the Playhouse to get her things sent back.

Thus began the career of Joan Molinsky, retail fashion big shot. She got a job at the Lord & Taylor department store in Manhattan, and she went at it with zeal, working in the publicity department, as a buyer, and as a junior in the executive training program. Before long, she was hired as a fashion coordinator at Bond Stores, for both the men's and women's lines. At twenty-two years old, she had a big title, a secretary/assistant, and a salary of $150 a week.[*]

And there was another perk: the attentions of James Bennat Sanger, whose father, Maurie Sanger, was a vice president of Bond. The younger Sanger was a Coast Guard veteran who had served in the Korean War and was enrolled at Columbia. After a mere three weeks of acquaintance, he proposed, she accepted, and a marriage was immediately scheduled. On August 12, 1956, a small notice in the *New York Times* declared "Student Is Fiance of Joan Molinsky," and on

[*] Approximately $1,400 in 2022.

September 20, an account of their wedding, held the previous day at the Park Avenue home of Beatrice's sister, appeared, complete with a photo of the bride. On the receiving line, under the influence of a tranquilizer, Joan met the eyes of her beloved cousin Allan Thenen and blurted out, "Can you believe I'm doing this?"

The marriage was a catastrophe. To avoid appearances of nepotism, Joan left Bond and started working at another clothing store. But Sanger didn't want his wife working *at all.* After several weeks of bickering, they began marriage counseling and then underwent a trial separation. Joan returned to Larchmont; they reconciled; finally, some six months after it began, the marriage was annulled on the (spurious) grounds that the groom had failed to tell the bride that he didn't want children.*

It was, Joan realized, the end of the chimerical notion that she could be satisfied being an adjunct to a man, that she could fit into a "normal" woman's role. Having made a genuine effort at living the sort of life her parents deemed appropriate, she would recoup her dream and aim at a career onstage. Living, once again, in Larchmont, she

* Decades later, his ex-wife a bona fide superstar, Sanger phoned her Beverly Hills home and left a message with the maid who answered: "Tell Joan that I'm proud."

took the train into Manhattan and started to make the rounds of agents' offices. Earning her keep with temp jobs, haunting the coffee shops favored by other young up-and-comers, chasing after every wisp of an audition, she put her mind toward becoming a working actress.

It was a truly epic quest. In the coming eight years, Joan trudged from office to office, audition to audition, rejection to rejection, lugging headshots and ginned-up résumés (some under the name Joan Perry) that gave her credit for performing onstage in cities she'd never visited, in commercials that never aired, and even in such films as Alfred Hitchcock's *North by Northwest* and Cecil B. DeMille's *The Ten Commandments* (she *was* Jewish, and there *were* a lot of extras, but, no). She made friends among the aspiring actors who haunted the B & G coffee shop on Seventh Avenue, but she made no headway in finding work or even an agent.

In the winter of 1958–59, her cousin Allan introduced her to an actor who was involved with a showcase (that is, unpaid) production of a new play in an attic theater on East Forty-Ninth Street. The play, called *Driftwood,* was an amateur production in every aspect, not least of which was that appearing in the cast was contingent on selling a certain number of tickets. Among those who made the quota was a teenage girl from Erasmus High School in Brooklyn, one Barbara Streisand, as she then spelled it. Despite the presence of two legends-in-the-making, *Driftwood* was a catastrophe, garnering a single review that dismissed it as rubbish and bolstering the impression of the Molinskys, who attended the first of the show's dozen or so performances, that their daughter was wasting her life.

The handful of people who seemed to think that Joan had any shot at a career in show business were the receptionists at the various talent agencies she regularly visited. Joan had taken to doing little bits of schtick when dropping off her résumés and headshots, and because she was naturally funny, a couple of secretaries mentioned that she should try comedy. Up to then, she had scorned the aspiring comedians who hung around Hanson's Drug Store, just down the street from her preferred B & G. But she ran into an old acquaintance from Bond Stores who revealed that her husband worked as a comedian at a nightclub on Long Island and was making forty dollars a night for four shows. Joan went out to the Golden Slipper in Glen Cove* to catch his act, and found him to be the picture

* Where Totie Fields would be discovered not long after. Remarkable to consider that the two so nearly missed each other.

of what she considered a pro: ruffled shirt, mohair jacket. They chatted, and he encouraged her to try her luck, even allowing her to steal his act, which, he confessed, he'd mostly cribbed from other comics.

And so she decided to have a go, if only as a means of making money while she built her career as an actress. The wrinkle was that comedians tended to have *two* representatives — a manager, who helped shape and guide their careers, and an agent, who got them bookings and oversaw contracts. This gave her a whole new category of professional to whom she could pitch herself. It was a wearying business, but she had a strange confidence about it: in fact, while she didn't know for sure if she had the stuff of a great actress in her, she'd known for years that she was funny — funnier, she was certain, than the slick wannabes she saw in clubs or on TV.

She began filling notebooks with gags — a good number of them stolen from TV and radio (her early files had a few Jean Carroll bits in them) or from hackneyed joke books that, ever the diligent student, she had gone out and bought. (To wit, seriously: "The doctor told me to go home and drink a glass of orange juice after a hot bath. Next day he asked me, 'Did you drink that orange juice?' And I said, 'I'm still drinking the hot bath!' ") And she began to pop into the nightclubs and coffeehouses dotting Greenwich Village to take her chances on open mic nights. She put her native relentlessness to the task, pushing herself to meet every important manager and agent in the comedy business. She even got an audience with the great Jack Rollins, who was marginally encouraging, refusing to represent her but assuring her that she'd "make it in three years."

Eventually, she did find a manager, one Harry Brent, a former musician who had been representing singers, comedians, and novelty performers for some fifteen years in New York and Miami. In an office-cum-apartment just off Times Square, straight out of *Sweet Smell of Success* or *Broadway Danny Rose.* Brent told Joan that he believed that there was room in the business for a girl comedian. He took her on, helped her develop material, told her how to dress and pose for photos and stage appearances, and, in his most inspired moment, gave her a new name and a slogan. Henceforth, Joan Molinsky would be billed as *Pepper January: Comedy with Spice!* This was hardly on a par with J. Sondra Meredith, thespian, but as she confessed, "I was willing to do *anything,* no matter how absurd. . . . All my career I have been a snob who has sold out a thousand times."

True to his word, Brent found his new protégé work. In December 1958, Pepper

January was booked as emcee and comedian at the Show Bar, a strip joint in Boston's notorious Combat Zone, at the rate of $125 for one week, two shows per night. And perhaps someone who truly could live with that ridiculous moniker could've made a go of it. But Joan Molinsky of Larchmont and Barnard College absolutely could not. The hotel where she was lodged was a flea pit. She barely had the means to pay for meals. The venue itself was small and ratty. Naively, Joan brought an entire wardrobe and makeup kit to the dressing room, which turned out to be a glorified closet that she had to share with the resident ecdysiasts, one of whom had actually attended Connecticut College not long before Joan. When she took the stage and started doing the schtick in which Harry Brent had coached her — including lathering up and shaving herself while she told jokes — the men in the audience predictably hooted and booed and rained profanities on her; worse, she believed that she recognized one of the gawkers seated up front as a guy from Yale she'd once dated. She staggered through her act, reappearing after each dancer's turn to introduce the next girl and tell a few jokes; each time the audience responded with greater hostility. She got through the show and told the manager that she was headed to her hotel room to regroup. "Don't bother," he told her. "You're fired."

Glumly, she returned to New York, where Harry Brent explained that had she done a second show her pay would have been guaranteed under American Guild of Variety Artist bylaws. He booked her into another strip joint, this one in Springfield, Massachusetts. Once again, catastrophe. This time, she managed to dodge the hook and take the stage a second time *before* being fired. When she insisted to the owner that AGVA rules required she get paid, he replied, "Ask AGVA if you can work with two broken legs."

Back in New York, she told Harry Brent she'd no longer work with him. He understood, but he insisted that she waive claims to his intellectual property, to wit the name and phrase *Pepper January: Comedy with Spice.* She agreed, but she recognized, too, how low she had sunk: "When you are not even Pepper January then you are *truly* nothing."

Could this be the bottom? Or could there have been an even deeper bottom that she could only feel if she stretched her tippy toes? If nothing else, she was fortunate to be in a good place at a good time. The slick Borscht Belt shtarkers with their monogrammed shirts and French cuffs were being pushed aside by a new breed of comedian — young and hip and funny and topical and satiric, with Mort Sahl (on whom Joan harbored a crush), Lenny Bruce, and Nichols and May in the vanguard. Joan Molinsky's larval comedy act may have been cribbed from the old school, but her instincts as a person — and, in truth, her situation as a woman trying to break into the business — made her feel more at home among the upstarts. She started hanging out with a new group of performers and writers of satiric songs and comedy sketches. She formed a special bond with Treva Silverman, a Bennington College grad from suburban Cedarhurst, Long Island, who worked as a proofreader at *Esquire,* performed at piano bars, and had aspirations toward writing for the stage. They became part of a clique of brilliant young things who fancied themselves another Algonquin Round Table over cheap meals, endless cups of coffee, and carafes of house red.

During yet another cold call on a small-time agent, one Tony Rivers, her life changed, or was at least tweaked. "I can't send you out as Joan Molinsky," he told her. "You've got to change your name." "Okay," she said, "I'll be Joan Rivers." It was more than just a stage name. It was an alter ego, a skin she could wear in order to disassociate herself from the deflating rigors and situations of her path. "Joan Rivers was like a party dress I put on," she explained. "She was only the tiniest part of me, and Joan Molinsky was still frightened and confused and bewildered."

Even as Joan Rivers, she continued to scratch away with dispiriting results. In Bridgeport, Connecticut, she got fired over the loudspeaker *while performing her act.* In Montreal, working as an assistant to a magician, she got the ax for mugging and making jokes while he was supposedly sawing her in half. She arranged to entertain her parents and their friends at their country club, the Riviera Shore Club in New Rochelle, and she bombed so completely that Beatrice and Meyer felt compelled to slink out the back door.

After that debacle, her parents sat her down in the pink kitchen and insisted that she face reality and give up the chimera of a career in entertainment. Meyer, in particular, had always been extremely suspicious of his daughter's chosen path. "When I went to medical school," he recalled years later, "whenever I had time to kill, I schlepped down to Magistrate's Court to watch trials. Through the side door would come a policeman with a hooker to be arraigned. Always, after name, age, address, they asked the occupation. And always they answered, 'Show business.' " Now, his daughter was doing something that only whores would admit to, *and* he had seen with his own eyes that she wasn't any good at it.

The conversation devolved into shouts, recriminations, banging on tables, stomping on floors, and when it was over, Joan drove angrily away from her parents' suburban home to the YWCA on West Sixty-Third Street and months of hardscrabble existence: staying in cheap hotels and sneaking out without paying the bills, which often included room service; crashing with friends; subsisting on coffee and luncheonette sandwiches; working temp jobs and scrambling off on her lunch hour to hound agents; spending nights at open mics. There was a romance — a well-to-do acquaintance from Westchester who collected modern art and attended cultural events and with whom she had a spark . . . until she suggested that he front her some money, as a backer, in effect, of her ambitions, say $10,000 in exchange for 50 percent of her income for the rest of her life. He laughed off what was, in her mind, a serious proposal, and they didn't see each other again for nearly a decade.

The litany of rejection became too much, and she moved back to Larchmont, where her parents, sobered by her enervated state, stopped harassing her about her choices. In their eyes, she was twenty-six, divorced, unhappy, even delusional. They must have pitied her.

As luck would have it, though, Joan was, almost accidentally, pointed in a direction in which she would soon flourish. She was cast in a showcase, *Talent '60,* which got her a few nice words in the *New York Post.* She got a job as an assistant to an agent, Irvin Arthur, whom she had been begging to represent her for years. Most promisingly, she was on the ground floor of a burgeoning craze for comedy revues — shows that combined comic sketches, musical bits, monologues, and a lot of hey-kids-let's-put-on-a-show gusto. These revues, popular staples of such clubs as Upstairs at the Downstairs, Phase 2, One Fifth, Cafe Society, and such higher-profile spots as the Blue Angel and Bon Soir, were fueled by the energy of young singers, comedians, comedy writers, and composers, the tribe of young creatives, in short, that Joan had already fallen in with.

In this atmosphere, she gradually evolved into a modern comedian. Working with Treva Silverman, she put together a one-woman show entitled *The Diary of Joan Rivers,* in which she thumbed through a big prop diary and told stories, some set to music, about the ups and downs of a young single woman trying to make it in show business. (One of these, about a bride-to-be who gets on a plane on the morning of her wedding and winds up in the wrong city, was part of her act for several years.) The show got booked at the Cherry Grove Hotel on Fire Island, the beach community well known for its gay population. Playing a thinly disguised version of herself — a neurotic who could never get the man, the job, the spotlight — she was a hit with the audience, who connected with her campy manner and her tales of big-city woe. She would always feel grateful to the gay men who first embraced her: "the most loving, the most generous, the most forgiving, the most loyal."

This small success got *The Diary of Joan Rivers* booked into Phase 2, a coffeehouse/club on Bleecker Street in Greenwich Village. The Village was teeming with clubs where unknown jazz musicians, folk artists, singers, and comedians could work: the Bitter End, the Cafe Wha?, the Gaslight, the Showplace, the Cafe Bizarre. Some of these performers had already signed with agents and even appeared on TV, but they could nevertheless be seen wandering from club to club in the Village, working on their material, honing their acts and their personae. It wasn't necessarily a world of riches — at Phase 2, as at virtually all of the clubs on the Village scene, Joan worked without a salary and was paid with what she got from the audience, among whom she passed a hat (well, a basket) after the show.

Phase 2 owner Dave Gordon wasn't a fan of Joan's — he called her "a clumsy, clumpy girl who hadn't made it as an actress and probably wouldn't make it as a comic either."[*] The most prominent print review *Diary* got was equally scornful: "Her material is tired and her delivery is frenetic," said *Off Broadway Reviews.* "She strains hard to put it over, as if her bright energy could somehow embellish the skeletal comedy. But her frantic and strained efforts are only nerve-racking and do not disguise, but rather point up, the material's essential aridity."

And, to be fair, the traces of her act that remain from those days make for pretty thin comedy: "Ladies and gentlemen, word has just come over the radio that the police have a definite lead on the maniac that has been stalking men in the Bronx. Apparently, this evening, while trying to accost a Mr. James Kenna in a deserted parking lot, the fiend was badly cut on the left hand (AT THIS MOMENT SHOW HAND WITH KERCHIEF AROUND IT)."

There was, however, real life in the act, and some seeds of what would become Joan's essential voice, which may have been why the bookers for NBC's *Jack Paar Show* — one of the most prominent early iterations of the venerable *Tonight Show* — decided in August 1960 to have her in and see if she was ready

[*] To be fair, he also couldn't stand Bob Dylan, whom he'd let go for performing "depressing songs" and considered "one of the worst who ever came through."

527

for a slot on national TV. This was a major coup, but also a potential minefield. Since his first flush of success, during which time he had introduced the world to, among others, Phyllis Diller, Paar's essential prickliness had become more pronounced. In several cases, he had turned suddenly cold on the oddball acts he had discovered, and earlier that very year he had famously broken down in tears on the air and walked off his own show because NBC censors had forbidden him to make reference to a "water closet." But he retained his well-deserved reputation for plucking "kooky" young talents from the fringes of show business, women especially, and turning them into national names. A shot on Paar was like rising to the penthouse via helicopter rather than climbing the stairs. Joan didn't even have a regular agent or manager, but she suddenly had a raffle ticket, a chance for the big time.

Came the big night, and she took the stage to chat with the great man. She told some of her stock jokes, about how she and her sister stood in for each other at temp jobs, about how she stole stamps from the office and sold them to friends to pay her bills, and about how she was dating a man whose father was in the Mafia. Paar looked at her with big eyes. "Do you really think there's a Mafia?" he asked. She did, she said, and she told a joke about how there are no gay Italians because if a boy seems to be heading that way they send him to the convent. The audience laughed, but Paar kept his poker face and said, "Do you realize there are Italian people watching this show?" She thought he was kidding, but when they found themselves in the elevator together after the show, he stared at the doors in silence, freezing her out.

It should have been a crowning achievement, but it was a slap-down. Even Meyer Molinsky, who'd rarely shown support for his daughter's ambitions, was affronted, writing a letter to Paar, whose show he watched regularly, to point out that the in-studio audience laughed at her jokes. He never heard back, and the Paar show was taboo at 6 Oxford Road in Larchmont ever after.

There had to be moments when she wanted to quit. But she was always forward focused, always certain in her doggedness. As she reflected later on, "Even in the fall of 1960, I knew instinctively that my insane drive was my most valuable asset. And, in a strange way, maybe that is why I always hugged the negative side of everything. If I ever believed something good was permanent, maybe I would relax." She never did.

In October 1960, she got a spot in a USO show that spent twelve weeks touring American military installations in Asia and the Pacific. It went well enough that a second outing was planned for the following February: five weeks in the North Atlantic. Before that, she endured a second disappointment on *The Jack Paar Show*. In late January, when Paar was in Washington to take part in John F. Kennedy's inaugural gala, the amiable Hugh Downs sat in as host, and Joan was granted a second shot as a kind of recompense from the staff for Paar's brusqueness. It was almost just as bad: she told jokes, and Downs, as if he'd never heard there was such a thing as a comedian, dimly asked her to explain them. The air simply bled out of the spot. She would never be asked back to Jack Paar's *Tonight Show.*

Throughout the remainder of 1961, she appeared regularly in Greenwich Village at the Duplex, a night spot operated by Jan Wallman, a quintessential New Yorker born, naturally, in Montana. A club owner from 1959 on, Wallman was brassy and bossy but also motherly, taking a foster interest in the unknown acts who performed on her stage and helping them craft their acts and personae. She was especially eager to promote funny women: Jorie Remus, Linda Lavin, Anne Meara (with, of course, Jerry Stiller), and, later, the likes of Jo Anne Worley, Lily Tomlin, Ruth Buzzi, and Marcia Lewis. At the Duplex, Joan polished her act sufficiently to step up in class to a booking at the nearby Bon Soir, the club that had helped launch

Phyllis Diller. She didn't get a marquee slot, but it was a serious solo gig in a serious New York nightclub. It was *big . . .* ish. Big enough, anyhow, to gain her the aura of being an up-and-comer. (But not big enough for Jack Rollins, who caught the show and, buttonholed afterwards by the ever-eager Joan, assured her, "In three *more* years you'll be very big.")

In late 1961, she auditioned for Second City, the already-famous Chicago improv troupe that was looking for a woman to replace Barbara Harris, someone whose name would always rank highly among the troupe's celebrated alumni. Joan spent almost five hours cooling her heels in the waiting room. By the time she finally got in front of the men who would evaluate her, she was in a proper snit, and they exacerbated her poor mood by asking her to improvise rather than giving her a script to read and *then* by taking phone calls. She chewed them out for their rudeness and left convinced that she would never see them again. The next day, she was genuinely shocked to learn that she'd been hired. Of all the women they'd seen, she had most impressed them. She was off to Chicago to become part of a legendary show.

Joan Rivers's experience of Second City was a mixed affair. Although Second City was aligned with satire and sketch comedy and with some performers who went on to be comedians rather than comic actors, stand-up was actually looked down upon by the purists in the troupe: "Too jokey," they would often tell her when she adlibbed. Plus, she didn't have either experience with or patience for the improv games that were fundamental to Second City's praxis. She was well paid, she was in a truly legendary outfit that was one of the cultural jewels of a big city, and she was surrounded by talents from whom there was a lot to learn: Del Close, Avery Schrieber, Melinda Dillon, Zohra Lampert, and Anthony Holland. But she was, according to a semi-official history of the troupe, "never really happy at Second City," and she always remembered being alienated from her fellow players both onstage and off. "It was a very closed and cliquish group," she said. "I watched the show three nights before I joined them onstage, and during that time nobody spoke to me because I was an outsider. . . . Nobody was generous in that company."

In time, though, she created scenes, especially with Holland, and took bits that Harris had performed and made them her own. Indeed, in many ways, she flourished in Chicago. She was dazzled when celebrities came by the tiny Second City playhouse, the likes of playwright Tennessee Williams, actors Anthony Quinn and Melvyn Douglas, and comics Godfrey Cambridge and (her crush) Mort Sahl. She spent a few off nights doing stand-up at the famed nightclub Gate of

Horn. She hosted her parents and sister on a wintertime holiday in the city, complete with fancy meals, theater tickets, and shopping sprees. (She delighted when random folks recognized her as a member of Second City in the presence of her family.) And she found that by forcing her way into the shows, by learning how to adapt to changing stage conditions, she was maturing and emerging as a performer. She barely lasted the winter, but she acknowledged how crucial those few months were to her growth: "I finally in Chicago came to *believe,* totally — for the first time in my life — that my personal, private sense of humor, my view of the world, could make smart adults laugh," she remembered. "I felt a comedy ego beginning to grow, which gave me the courage to begin tentatively looking into myself for comedy I was really born as a comedian at Second City. I owe it my career. No Second City, no Joan Rivers."

Actually, it was a little deeper than that. During the months she was trying to prove herself at Second City, Joan, already working within the "party dress" of her stage name, conceived of yet another alter ego, a comic mask through which she could channel her sensibility and do a variety of jokes about her shortcomings and disappointments — childhood, school, dating, work — to which audiences seemed to relate. "Rita," she named this new entity through which she had begun to speak, "the loser girl who cannot get married . . . my stand-up comedy persona . . . the secret of my success. She works because people recognize insecurity and respond to it, because everybody is like me, just a lot cooler than I am about their self-consciousness, their certainty that they will be found out at any moment."

Almost simultaneously, she found the wardrobe that would allow her to embody Rita onstage: a black cocktail dress, a string of pearls, and a wig, a blonde fall. In her new stage attire, she looked rather like what she really was, a Jewish Seven Sisters alumna from the New York area on a professional treadmill and looking for a guy. But when she opened her mouth, well, she might say anything, no matter how conventional she appeared. She was still buying and "borrowing" material from other comics, in part because she still didn't trust her instincts and wit sufficiently, but in part, too, because she couldn't name any other women out there, with the exception of Phyllis Diller, who were working successfully in stand-up comedy.

She had dropped the music from her act after Jan Wallman, who had moved from the Duplex to a club called the Showplace, convinced her that she was no singer: "It's not your forte. You're using it as a crutch."

534

Even more, Wallman told her that she needed to stop relying on hired jokes: "You're far funnier than any of the material you buy from others. Use your own stuff."

She began to tape her sets, lugging an old reel-to-reel tape recorder through the night and then studying what worked and what didn't long after the clubs had closed. Wallman was impressed. "She had the *fastest* comic mind I'd ever seen," she recalled. "She worked hard. If she was stopped in one direction, she moved in another. She just wouldn't take no for an answer."

Her material sharpened, *slightly:* "This girl was such a bad singer, she even talked off-key"; "This hotel was so exclusive that even room service had an unlisted number"; "In the old days, there were no psychiatrists; everyone just told their troubles to bartenders, and by the end of the evening they had a solution . . . or they just didn't care." It was *her* stuff, but it was still impersonal. Without a real internal connection to the words, her jokes could have been told by *anyone* — which meant she was selling herself rather than her wit.

She was heartened by the sight of other comedians around the city making headway with acts that were just as iconoclastic as hers, none more than Lenny Bruce, who'd spent a decade honing a personality built of fearlessness, frankness, wild imagination, and

535

a willingness to push every boundary that show business and, indeed, *society* might put in front of him. Unlike all the comics she saw, who were either spritzing one-liners or working from personae that were unlike themselves, Bruce was working from his own gut, saying what he wanted to, putting himself on the line as a way of making his audience imagine *it*self similarly exposed. (Years later, Joan was fond of a story about Bruce encouraging her, after he witnessed her bombing at a Village nightclub, by sending a note backstage reading, "You're right, they're wrong." True or not, it demonstrated the effect his courageous example had on her.)

She spent 1962 and 1963 scrambling: playing the clubs in the Village and, when she could get a gig in one, uptown; joining the cast of a comedy record, *At Home with That Other Family,* a Cold War spoof of the Khrushchev family in the vein of Vaughn Meader's megahit LP spoof of the Kennedys, *First Family;* appearing, briefly, in the New York contingent of Second City; venturing to the Catskills, where she felt unappreciated and misunderstood. She wasn't mentioned as a performer in *Variety,* not even in club listings, between January 1962 and June 1964, but she was establishing herself as a club staple, and she started to draw solid reviews. In 1963, *Cue*'s Eugene Boe called her "a very funny femme in search of an act" and declared her material to be "some of the sharpest, smartest talk to proceed out of the mouth of a babe since Elaine May." And then, almost as if to renege on his kind words, Boe continued, "Female comics are usually horrors who de-sex themselves for a laugh. But Miss R. remains visibly — and unalterably — a girl throughout her stream-of-consciousness script." That was kind, though, compared to what *Back Stage* said of her at around the same time. Sheldon Landwehr, reviewing her at the Cafe Society, called her "The major disaster for the evening," adding, "this girl just can't deteriorate any further as a performer. Rarely has more vulgar material been presented as ineptly and tastelessly."

As these reviews indicated, her act was edging toward something more contemporary than previously: jokes about her Jewish background, about her schooling, about her (fictional) best friend and hairdresser, Mr. Phyllis ("I said to him, 'I'm looking for a style that will drive men crazy,' and he said, 'That's funny! So am I!' "). She was working up a longish bit about a (true) incident in which she dropped her hairpiece on the street and watched in horror as it was run over by a passing car that screeched to a stop, the driver thinking he had just killed someone's dog. She even crafted a signature line for herself: during a run at the Bitter End, arguably the premier club in Greenwich Village, she closed with the declaration, "If you liked me and know any agents, please remember: My name is Joan Rivers, and I put out!"

The Bitter End's owner and booker, Fred Weintraub, saw something in her. Weintraub often took a managerial interest in the performers he presented, and he had an idea for a new act in which he thought Joan would fit: a trio — two guys and a girl — who would perform comedy sketches and light musical numbers. In late 1963, he teamed Joan with singer-songwriter Jake Holmes and comedian/comedy writer Jim Connell in an act called, cleverly, Jim, Jake, and Joan. It wasn't a merry union. "We all hated each other," she later recalled. "It was the unhappiest time of my life." Joan and Connell didn't have well-matched comedy sensibilities; Holmes, who was suffering the emotional wounds of a failed marriage, wanted to write more introspective material than the act called for; and they were launching just as the beatniky fad of coffeehouses and folk acts was giving way to the rock and roll revolution heralded by the Beatles. They all knew it was a bad scene — "There was no joy *ever* in that act," she said — but they sallied forward, teeth clenched.

They debuted in April 1964, opening at the Bitter End for a folk duo consisting of singing siblings Carly and Lucy Simon. By June, they were headlining at the club, and *Variety* found them trying too hard and, at twenty-five relatively brief minutes, wearing out their welcome. There were nice words for Joan — "a pert blonde with a mobile face" — but the gist of the notice was that their material was weak. They played Mister Kelly's in Chicago that summer and the Playboy Club in Miami in the early fall. They appeared on TV in July (*Kaleidoscope,* a new-talent showcase on NBC's New York flagship station) and September (*Show Street,* a similar program on ABC's flagship, hosted by Phyllis Diller), both times to tepid reviews. They even turned up in a movie, *Once Upon a Coffee House,* an insipid little independent film shot in Miami. Rereleased decades later as *Hootenanny-a-Go-Go,* it features a short set by Jim, Jake, and Joan that showcases their highly stylized act, in which little musical interludes gave way to very brief comedy sketches about current events; Joan, in perhaps the oldest surviving footage of her performing, was completely recognizable as herself, with her scratchy voice, her energetic, puppet-like mugging, and her self-deprecatory jokes.

No movie or TV show or high-profile gig was going to make this act a hit — it was never exactly inspired, there were the personality issues, and its cultural moment had passed. Nevertheless, Weintraub kept supporting it, even when Joan announced to him at the end of the year that she was quitting. "Fine," he told her, "we'll get another girl."[*] When Joan added that she was going back to performing on her own and asked if he was interested in managing her comedy career, his response was brusque and final: "I don't see you ever making it as a single."

She went back to lugging her tape deck night after night among the clubs, in particular the Duplex, where, as before, Jan Wallman gave her a semi-regular home. She had a plan, though. Weintraub wasn't the only manager connected to the Bitter End. Roy Silver, who had been one of his original partner/investors in the club, had, like Weintraub, metamorphosed into a talent manager, both on his own and in cooperation with Weintraub. As a team, the pair had managed Bob Dylan, Cass Elliott, and the lightweight folkies the Serendipity Singers. When they split up, Silver took Dylan and, before long, lost him. Barely missing a stride, he began to manage Bill Cosby, helping turn him from one of the fastest rising comedians in the Greenwich Village scene into a national star. Having been rebuffed by Weintraub, Joan savvily approached Silver and asked him to see her at the Duplex. He

[*] And he did, booking Jim, Jake, and Joan (no matter the new girl's real name) on the coffeehouse and college circuit well into 1966.

did, and he was impressed, but also wary. Why didn't she already have representation? He phoned an agent at William Morris and asked why Joan was unsigned. "Everyone has seen her" was the answer. "There's absolutely no interest in her anywhere." Rising to a challenge, he decided he would take her on as a client and prove that his instincts about her were correct.

Silver helped shape her stage presence and her act further, cutting the groovy bits designed to amuse her chums and focusing on her best asset, which was *herself.* He made her see that the audience could be a partner in the personal travails of which she made such comic hay, that by opening herself up and being less self-protecting and less eager to please, she would be truer to herself *and* be funnier. (Years later, her "Can we talk?" catchphrase emerged as a means of treating the audience as confidants and making them feel as if she was sharing something personal and private — which, of course, she was.)

He also helped her develop as a comedy writer, like Treva Silverman, and he began getting her gigs. She had begun in that direction earlier that year, when a friend was offered a chance to write scripts for Topo Gigio, the puppet mouse from Italy who made the first of some fifty-plus sickly, sentimental episodes on *The Ed Sullivan Show* in April

1963.* Her friend wanted nothing to do with the gig, but Joan leapt at the chance for paid work: "I was born corrupt," she recalled. "I said, '*I'll* do it! *I'll* do it!" and they split the money for scripts submitted under his name. Soon after, Silver got her a job writing for *Show Street,* the variety show hosted by Phyllis Diller. The most successful woman in stand-up comedy, Phyllis was a marvel to Joan, who watched in awe as the star marched into the studio right before her call time, just in from Hollywood, wearing a mink coat and trailed by an assistant who toted a gigantic book of jokes indexed by subject.

Alas, *Show Street* was a brief job, and the next gig Silver landed for her was hellish. The hidden-camera prank show *Candid Camera* had been on television since 1948, virtually as long as there was such a thing as televised entertainment, and it was old even then, having been spun off of *Candid Microphone,* a radio show with the same premise: unsuspecting randos taken in by some sort of practical joke — "punked" or "trolled" in the modern parlance. Allen Funt, creator, producer, and

---

* Topo Gigio, voiced with a thick Italian accent, would appear in sketches with Sullivan that invariably ended with the little fellow's tag line, "Kees-a-me goo' night, Eddie," which Sullivan obligingly did. The mouse was wildly popular, but he provided nightmare fuel as much as he did laughter.

presenter of the program, was notoriously hotheaded, berating and firing employees regularly and, according to Joan, often holding staff meetings dressed in only a bathrobe, which would occasionally slip off and reveal him in all his . . . candor.

She hated the work, and so she continued to push herself vigorously to be able to leave it forever.* Among the gigs she most coveted, along with every other comedian in the business, was a spot on *The Tonight Show*. Jack Paar had left in March 1962, and a permanent replacement, the sly, clean-cut, quickwitted former magician and game show host Johnny Carson, was named that fall. Under Carson's cool guidance, the show soared higher in the ratings and, indeed, in the national consciousness, than ever. For comedians in particular, a booking on the show — and the even rarer chance to sit on the couch next to the host after performing — was considered a star-making turn.

Joan had auditioned for Carson's *Tonight Show* at least three times. But staffers always explained that her material wasn't right for them or, worse, that she wasn't right for TV. Roy Silver managed another tryout for her

---

* At this time, she and fellow aspiring stand-up Dick Cavett thought about doing a Nichols and May–type act and even recorded some demos, since lost, alas.

through a ruse, saying he was sending Joan Molinsky over for their scrutiny. They weren't amused, but they could only get *so* upset with him, as he represented Bill Cosby.

In mid-February 1965, Silver watched as a comedian he'd never heard of bombed terribly on *The Tonight Show,* and he lambasted his contacts there for giving *that* guy an opportunity while stiff-arming Joan. He had an inspiration: Don't put her on as a comedian, he said, put her on as a *comedy writer,* and give her the "death slot," as the final ten minutes of the show were known. As it happened, a guest had pulled out of that very night's show; they consented to let Joan fill the vacant time.

Silver called her at home in Larchmont with the news, and she was instantly a ball of nerves. She called in sick to *Candid Camera,* got out her black dress, pearls, wig, and, for some reason, a pink boa, and drove to Rockefeller Center to prepare. Auspiciously, someone whom she considered a friend, comedian Milt Kamen, was also on the bill that night, and his presence helped put her at ease. She sat in the greenroom as the show began taping at 7:30, waiting until almost 9:00 before being led to the spot behind the curtain. And then her name was called.

It's a truism of show business that a performer dubbed an "overnight sensation" has often spent years in the trenches before being granted the opportunity, the one moment of magic, that turns him or her into a star. Well, on Wednesday, February 17, 1965, in the final minutes of *The Tonight Show,* Joan Rivers, who, at the age of thirty-one, had a full decade of experience, found herself in just that situation, and she filled it and seized it and wrung every drop out of it and, son of a gun, transformed herself forever, right there on TV, in front of a nation.

She and Carson had an immediate rapport, his cool and relaxed mien tempering and sanding smooth her frazzled, frantic energy. He asked leading questions about Larchmont, about dating, about her struggles with beauty, about, well, being Joan Rivers, and she knocked each softball out of the park, with Milt Kamen beside her on the couch breaking up just as hard as Carson was behind his desk. She did the bit about the wig being run over by the car, which, by then, she had written into a little symphony of well-honed beats and riffs. When her ten or so minutes were up, Carson, wiping a tear of laughter from his eye, beamed and said, "God, you're funny! You're going to be a star!"

She didn't hear him. She was too frayed, too enervated, too tired from so many years of struggling so hard. She'd had shots before, and they'd fizzled. She was banking on exactly *nothing* to be true. She made her way through the congratulatory knot of performers and show staffers backstage and drove home to Larchmont to watch the taped show with her parents. She saw that she'd done well, and she heard Carson's words of anointment. But she was inured to disappointment. It was one a.m. at the end of a long, emotional day, and she had to report to the *Candid Camera* set early the next morning. She went to bed.

Funny how the mind can work. She thought that, at best, *maybe* they might want her back on the show sometime. It seemed to go well enough, after all. But she almost didn't dare hope. She had been hungry — famished — for success for so long, and she had failed to attain it so regularly, that she got up, went to work, and waited hours before she called Roy Silver to find out what they'd said about her.

"Jesus Christ!" he shouted. "Where have you been? The phone has been ringing off the hook. . . . You'll never make under $300 a week for the rest of your life, I guarantee it."

He told her to go out and find a *New York Journal-American,* in which columnist Jack O'Brian had written, "Johnny Carson struck gleeful gold again last night with Joan Rivers . . . an absolute hilarious delight. . . . Her seemingly offhand anecdotal clowning was a

546

heady and bubbly proof of her lightly superb comic acting; she's a gem."

Silver told her that she had indeed been invited back to *The Tonight Show* — in two weeks, in fact — and he wanted her to come in, immediately, if not sooner, to sort through the dozens of opportunities that suddenly lay before her. She quit *Candid Camera.* She called home to share the good news, and she learned from her mother that *their* phone had been ringing all day with well-wishes. (Meyer proudly told one and all, "Of course, we always knew. . . .") And she headed out into the light of day and the future that she had scrapped so hard for so long to build for herself.

"It was all over," she realized. "Thirty-one years of people saying 'no'. . . . Ten minutes on television and it was all over."

Roy Silver wasn't exaggerating when he said there were more offers for Joan's services than he knew what to do with. In the coming weeks, he got her a proper agent at General Artists Corporation (home, of course, of super-agent Buddy Howe and comedians Jean Carroll, and, for a while, Phyllis Diller). He arranged a lucrative multiweek residency for Joan to headline at the hungry i in San Francisco and a similar gig at Mister Kelly's in Chicago, as well as stints in Pittsburgh and Dayton and one-night stands on the college and nightclub circuit all over the country. He got her a deal with Warner Bros. to record a live LP that would be stitched together from her shows in San Francisco and in New York, where Fred Weintraub was keen to feature her at the Bitter End. He booked her for a number of high-profile TV slots, including a fresh chance with Jack Paar, who had his own chat/variety show in prime time (Joan's welcome was assured by having Silver's top client, Bill Cosby, on the same episode). He got her a first-look deal at NBC to develop comedy shows (none were ever realized). And he made her a regular on *The Tonight Show,* where she and Johnny Carson honed their improvisatory rapport on five more install-ments before the summer ended.

And in a truly stunning instance of kismet, of wish fulfillment, of having it all, those ap-pearances alongside Carson led her to, of all things, a husband.

Edgar Rosenberg was a publicist and pro-ducer working for an arm of the United Na-tions, and he needed a comedy writer to rework a script he was developing as a feature film to star Jack Lemmon.[*] In June 1965, he contacted an acquaintance at *The Tonight*

[*] In her 1986 autobiography, in which she misre-membered the title of the play *Driftwood,* Joan identi-fied the star as Peter Sellers, but she said that it was Lemmon in a TV appearance in 1967.

Show and asked if there was an appropriate writer on staff for such a job. His friend mentioned that funny comedy writer they'd been featuring recently, Joan Rivers. Rosenberg invited Joan and Roy Silver to dinner at a French restaurant. He sent a limousine, which picked Joan up from her new apartment above the Stage Deli on Seventh Avenue.

Rosenberg was everything Joan's mother had raised her to admire in a man: educated, well mannered, impeccably dressed, gracious, apparently wealthy — *classy,* in a phrase — *and* a lifelong bachelor. He was born in Germany in 1925 to a prosperous Jewish butcher and his wife, and his family had fled, via Copenhagen, to Cape Town, South Africa, where he was raised, a loner who read books voraciously and was housebound with a case of tuberculosis (a disease that so shamed him that Joan didn't learn he'd once had it until she'd known him for some twenty years). He attended Rugby School and the University of Cambridge in England, then came to America in the late 1940s, working as a bookstore clerk and a functionary at an advertising agency before entering show business, first as a budget supervisor at NBC and then as a producer of public service films for the network. From there, he moved to the public relations firm headed by Anna Rosenberg (no relation), whose company helped such entities as governments, corporations, politicians, and, most notably, the United Nations express their purposes to the world. Edgar produced promotional films and televised events for the firm, and in the course of his work, he made the acquaintance of scores of major players in the entertainment industry. His prospective Jack Lemmon movie was an outgrowth of those relationships, a first foray into independent film production.

The dinner went splendidly. Not only was Joan enticed by the chance to write a feature film for Lemmon, but she was intrigued by this formal, cultured man with the British accent who seemed so worldly and connected. A few days later, Joan and her soon-to-be boss had a second dinner, without her manager, at the super-exclusive Four Seasons. The evening confirmed her initial impression: she *was* interested.

The deal was signed, and Rosenberg suggested that Joan join him, her co-screenwriter, novelist Eugene Burdick (*Fail Safe, The Ugly American*), and Lemmon himself in Jamaica for a getaway conference at which they'd rewrite the script. If it was a setup by Rosenberg, it was an elaborate one. The party, which also included another producer, Christopher Mankiewicz, and his wife, was to be housed in bungalows at the posh Round Hill resort near Montego Bay. En route from the airport, they learned that Burdick would not be coming and that Lemmon would be delayed.

Joan was on guard: "I did not want to be a date. I wanted to be a professional screenwriter," she recalled. But Rosenberg was a perfect gentleman, never once suggesting anything other than professionalism and friendliness. And then the Mankiewiczes left, and Joan and Rosenberg were alone, with no work to do and no one to distract them. Joan phoned Treva Silverman in New York and begged her to come down and serve as, in effect, a chaperone. But before Treva could arrive, the seemingly inevitable happened. Joan went off for a swim, and when she returned, "there was Edgar, standing in the doorway. Suddenly, when I saw him, I had a deep sense of well-being, of coming home, a certainty that he was what I had been looking for, that this was absolutely right." They made love, and as they lay together afterward, he proposed, and she accepted.[*]

They were at once an odd couple and a good match: he gave her breeding and re-

---

[*] It is possible — *possible* — that one outside factor figured in Joan's acceptance of this hasty proposal of marriage: just the previous month, her older sister, Barbara, the successful attorney, had wed a cardiologist named Edward Waxler. The once-divorced, thirty-something Joan might well have felt her old insecurities about her desirability rise in her.

spectability, she gave him vitality and humor. They both came from places of privilege yet felt underestimated by the world around them. They believed that their show business talents and aspirations could mesh. They were a good physical match, the tiny Joan not remotely threatening to overshadow her short husband-to-be, even in heels. Yes, he could be stiff and cool and awkward, and she could be strident and needy and neurotic. But those qualities seemed to link them, like teeth in a set of gears. They barely knew each other, but they felt like kindred.

When they returned to New York, Joan moved in with her new fiancé. Three days later, on July 15, at a courthouse in the Bronx filled with Filipino sailors and their new brides ("the first and last time that Edgar and I were the tallest people anywhere," she said), they were married. They had known each other less than a month. And that night, Joan worked: two sets at the Bitter End, where Fred Weintraub refused to give her the night of her wedding off unless she could get Woody Allen or Bill Cosby to sub for her. As a bonus, she had a new font of material: "I married Edgar right after I met him. I figured I didn't have long until he got sober. . . . My honeymoon was a disaster. He wanted to have sex twelve times. I said, 'Edgar, please be reasonable. We can't afford that many hookers!' "

■ ■ ■ ■

If she felt that she was on top of the world, the world seemed happy to remind her that she was still a girl trying to make her way in a man's business. Just two days before her wedding, the *New York Times*'s Robert Alden wrote about her in a profile that read as the most backhanded heap of compliments imaginable. It was the paper's first-ever article about her or her work, and it began:

> Women comedians like women shot-putters come to their profession with a certain handicap. Traditionally, women are supposed to be beautiful, seductive, gentle and fair — not funny or muscular. But through the years and despite the handicap that these metiers do not come naturally to them, women shot-putters like women comedians have existed and thrived.

After this appalling lead, Alden continued on, offering what was, essentially, a favorable opinion in a nonetheless barbaric tenor: "a new comedienne of ripening promise . . . an unusually bright girl who is overcoming the handicap of a woman comic, looks pretty and blonde and bright and yet manages to make people laugh. . . . Her humor is bright and pointed. . . . Miss Rivers is quick-witted and inventive. . . . She improvises with assurance."

But, clearly, the point was made: A woman comedian was, more or less, a freak in the eyes of this one man. Joan might've been a *promising* freak, an *attractive* freak, but she was no less freakish for the fact.

Joan continued to rise under Silver's sure hand, abetted by General Artists' clout. By late 1965, her Warner Brothers LP, *Mr. Phyllis and Other Funny Stories,* had been released to modest success, she was under contract to *The Tonight Show* for a string of appearances, she had shown up on several TV game, talk, and variety shows, and she had appeared in a lucrative nightclub engagement at the Basin Street East, a tony uptown joint where she drew a salary of $2,000 a week[*] as the opening act for Mel Tormé and the Duke Ellington Orchestra.

It was exactly what she had wanted, but, just as Phyllis Diller felt when *she* signed with GAC, Joan had the sense that she was getting too big too fast. "My agents pushed me toward money deals," she remembered years later, "rather than the correct moves for *my* career. . . . I was quickly being destroyed." As if to prove her point, Roy Silver told the press that he planned to get her into a salary range between $100,000 and $200,000 per year and turn her into "the next Lucille Ball."

Joan asked Silver to slacken the pace and

[*] Approximately $16,500 in 2022.

let her continue to develop her material and her skills in the low-profile, intimate settings that she'd been accustomed to. He told her she was just feeling the nerves one feels when one rockets to fame: "Don't worry, baby, it's all in your head. You can do it. You've got to. This is the big time." She talked it over with Edgar, and he agreed with her. In the fall, her contract with Silver expired, and she didn't renew it.

Instead, she signed with Jack Rollins, who *finally* agreed that she was ready for his services as manager. He booked her into a setting where she truly could shine: Downstairs at the Upstairs, a club on West Fifty-Sixth Street and Fifth Avenue that had the bohemian feel of a Greenwich Village spot. It was, as the name indicated, two clubs, with the Downstairs given over to showcase acts, and the Upstairs, the larger room, set aside for multiperformer musical revues. On the Upstairs stage, the promising likes of Madeline Kahn and Lily Tomlin, among any number of still-unknown singers, comic performers, and cabaret artists, made some of their first notable impressions.[*] Downstairs was more like a private club, a space not unlike the ones in the Village where Joan was so comfortable. For several years, singer Mabel

[*] One of these, the piano accompanist Barry Manilow, played regularly before and after Joan's sets.

Mercer had been the chief attraction Downstairs, but Joan gradually made it her own room. She would appear for weeks at a time, testing out new material, polishing her onstage presence, and then taking her act on the road. The intimate room drew a sophisticated crowd — Phyllis Diller came, and laughed louder and harder than anyone; *Jacqueline Kennedy Onassis* came, and ducked her head when Joan scanned the crowd for a woman with whom to launch into some schtick. It was a small enough space for her to work off the crowd but a financial step up from the Village scene and a significant booking in the eyes of TV and film executives.

Rollins, following Roy Silver, convinced Joan that she needed to sharpen her act. She was still given to making esoteric jokes about highbrow culture, her gay friends, her Jewish roots. These were crutches, in Rollins's eyes, and he taught her that material of that sort had a floor (that is, a certain portion of the audience would *always* laugh at it) but also a ceiling (that is, *only* a certain portion would ever laugh at it). She admitted that settling into a new, broader sort of comedy wasn't yet a natural choice for her. "Two years ago," she said, "if I had two jokes and one was very hip — I hate the term — and one was very commercial, I would have chosen the hip joke. Now, I choose the commercial joke, because it's funny to me."

Under Rollins's guidance, she developed her talent to its full potential. She used to spew one-liners that often had nothing to do with her life. After working closely with Rollins, she could go for several minutes, building a theme and creating paragraphs, even mini-essays, about, say, getting married later in life than she (or, more to the point, her mother) thought she might:

> The whole society is not for single girls. Single men, yes. They're so lucky. A boy on a date, all he has to be is clean and able to pick up the check and he's a winner. But a girl: When you go on a date, the girl has to be well dressed, the face has to be nice, the hair has to be in good shape; the girl has to be bright and witty and a good sport — "Howard Johnson's again! Hooray, hooray!" A girl, thirty years old, you're not married, you're an old maid. A man, he's ninety years old, he's not married — he's a catch! . . . My mother had two of us at home that weren't, as the expression goes, "moving". . . . The neighbors would come over and say, "How's Joan? Still not married?" And my mother would say, "If she were alive!" And I was sitting right there! When I was twenty-one, my mother said, "Only a doctor for you." When I was twenty-two, she said, "All right, a lawyer, a CPA." At twenty-four she said, "We'll grab a dentist." Twenty-

six, she said: "Anything!" Anyone who came to the door was good enough: "Oh Joan! There's an attractive young man down here with a mask and a gun!" . . . Catholic mothers have an excuse: "She wants to be a nun! What can I do?" A Jewish mother would be walking around with a bag over her face.

It was a tumultuous working relationship — the breezy, gentle Rollins and the volatile, emotionally needy Rivers — and it wouldn't last long. But with his help she well and truly found her voice, her calling, during those years doggedly working on her act and, indeed, her very *presence* on the Downstairs stage.[*]

Rollins got her some plum gigs. She was cast in a small role in *The Swimmer,* director Frank Perry's adaptation of a John Cheever story about a man who decides to swim his way across his Connecticut suburb by taking laps in the pools of various neighbors and acquaintances. Burt Lancaster, still as fit as

---

[*] Ironically, now that she was doing so much nationally visible work, she needed new material at a greater rate than ever before, so she started hiring comedians to write with her. One of her best collaborators was Rodney Dangerfield, still largely unknown, who would come to her apartment and type as the two of them riffed off each other.

in his days as an acrobat, would play the protagonist, Ned Merrill. Joan was cast as a woman whom he meets at a raucous party. She's there on a date but chats him up until someone whispers to her that Merrill's social stock has bottomed out, and she walks away.

The film premiered in the spring of 1968. Joan's scene is brief: she has about eight lines — and she gets no close-ups. But she still makes an impact, especially with the vulnerable way she asks, "You, uh, married?" — shrugging and looking away as she says it, but peeking hopefully out from underneath her hair-sprayed coif and false eyelashes, the eternal bachelorette always ready to be disappointed. The film was well reviewed but didn't do a lot of business. In the *New York Times*, Vincent Canby mentioned Joan among the several cast members whom he found "especially interesting." But that wasn't enough to yield any other film offers.

By then, though, it might not have been possible for her to entertain them. As 1966 ended, Joan had appeared on *The Tonight Show* some twenty times and was making her Las Vegas debut, at the Flamingo, opening for the French singer Charles Aznavour. She felt entirely unprepared: "I didn't even have a dress," she recalled. "I had a plain black dress, and I went out and bought sequins and sewed them on it!" She was still most comfortable in more modest venues, and she always came home to Downstairs at the Upstairs, her small playground, where she packed the house regularly and got the immediate feedback that was so crucial to her not only in developing her craft but in helping her to feel comfortable inside her own skin. She had been so discouraged over the years — by her parents, by dismissive agents and managers, by her own nagging insecurities — that she had come to trust only her internal voice and, now, too, the voice of Edgar. While Joan battled her demons, wrote jokes, performed, networked, and battled her demons some more, she turned to Edgar for reassurance and to see that all the details were handled — a combination of spiritual confessor and hard-nosed producer. Their partnership allowed her to retract her claws and be the genial, agreeable talent, while he took — indeed, *relished* — the role of the aggressive, demanding overseer of his client/wife.

Even on familiar turf — the nightclub stages and TV shows where she plied her trade — Joan could still be considered an iconoclast and a danger. She finally got the nod from *The Ed Sullivan Show,* arguably the only entertainment outlet that carried as much prestige as *The Tonight Show,* and she was convinced that it was an accident. "He was a little foggy sometimes," she said of the host. "Right before the show, they had been pitching singer Johnny Rivers to him, and he went out and said, 'Next week, Joan Rivers!' " Having accidentally booked her, Sullivan insisted that he see her act first, and he had her come to his apartment at the Delmonico Hotel on Park Avenue and perform it for him and his wife, Sylvia. She was put through the ordeal, she felt, for one reason: "I wasn't risque at all in those days, but he was very worried about me because I was a woman." She got the gig, and she did well, and she was invited back several times. Even Edgar found a place in Sullivan's head, if a mistaken one. "He somehow decided," Joan recalled, "that Edgar was a doctor, and so for the rest of our relationship he would say, 'Hi, Doctor, nice to see you Doctor.' "

Joan's unsteady rapport with Sullivan would be tested not long after when she was scheduled for a return visit and happened to be eight months pregnant. Being so driven in her career, she had never thought much about motherhood. But she started to feel differently as she hit her mid-thirties and started taking note of other women and their babies. Joan had been on the pill, but she stopped taking it in early 1967, and by April she was pregnant.* Being a neurotic who

* Again, it might only be a coincidence, but her

shared everything and turned it into comedy, she immediately began making jokes about her condition and how she got that way: "I have no sex appeal. If my husband didn't toss and turn in his sleep, we'd never have had the kid." But Sullivan wouldn't allow her to broach the subject on his stage. In fact, he wouldn't even let her use the word *pregnant*. Instead, she was forced to stand there, visibly with child, and declare, "I'll soon be hearing the pitter-patter of little feet."

It wasn't often that she compromised. Pregnant though she was, she kept doggedly working. On the night of January 19, 1968, she was onstage at the Downstairs when she started to feel contractions. She finished her set, sat for an interview with a newspaper reporter, went home, and went to bed. The next day, she woke at noon and went to the hospital, where she delivered her baby, Melissa Warburg Rosenberg,[*] after only a couple of hours of labor.

It was yet another episode of wish fulfill-

---

older sister, Barbara, had become pregnant three months prior.

[*] The Warburg was for Edgar's mother's family; by some accounts, Melissa's middle name was Frida, which was Edgar's mother's name. Professionally, of course, Melissa has always gone by her mother's surname, as Melissa Rivers.

ment for the doctor's daughter from Larchmont: career, husband, and now a child. She had achieved a state that had eluded her for more than a decade. Not, of course, that she was above making jokes about it: "Having my daughter, I screamed and yelled for twenty-three hours straight. And that was just during the conception!"

By all accounts, Joan was a doting mother from the start. With Melissa, she finally had someone whom she could hug and kiss and love and pamper whenever she felt like it, someone who could return her love in just the way she wanted, which is to say, without judgment, unconditionally. The bond was deep and rich and lifelong.* But, being who she was, her life as a mother was never without jokes. Indeed, she had new comic territory to mine — she suddenly had a baby and a postpartum body to make fun of — and she never mined it more sensationally than some months before Melissa's first birthday.

At the time, she was riding the crest of a true coup: Jack Rollins and the William Morris Agency, which had replaced GAC as her agents, had negotiated for her to star in a

* Not for nothing, but you should know that the Santa Monica Chapter of Hadassah named her Mother of the Year in 1973.

syndicated daytime talk show, entitled *That Show,* that was budgeted at $2.5 million* for a projected two-year run. Taping before a live audience just downstairs from the *Tonight Show* studio, the thirty-minute program had a familiar shape: Joan would open with a comedy monologue and then get behind a desk to jabber with guests.

That Show launched with great promise in September 1968; independent stations in more than twenty-five markets signed on to air it. The premiere featured the King of Late Night himself, Johnny Carson, as the sole guest. It was an unheard-of gesture: the biggest star of network talk shows appearing on a syndicated daytime show simply because the host asked. As Joan recalled, "He just said, 'When and where do you want me?' No retinue, he came alone. . . . At the time, he was in the midst of contract negotiations with NBC. The president of the network threatened him, told him he'd be in violation of his contract if he appeared with me, because I was primarily on CBS stations. He said, 'I gave my word. You can sue me, but I'm going to do it.' And you know the nicest part? He never even told me about it. I heard about it from his secretary ten days later."

Well, Joan had been raised to believe that such a gesture needed to be marked with a

* Approximately $18.7 million in 2022.

gift. A few days after Carson's appearance on *That Show,* a nurse in a cape and bonnet appeared at the *Tonight Show* offices carrying a basket with a note attached to it. She was led to a production meeting where Carson was at work with his staff and handed him the basket. Inside, he was startled to discover, was a live human baby. He read the note: "Dear Mr. Carson, My parents don't know how to thank you for what you did for my mother, so they wanted to give you something they really love, and that's me. My name is Melissa Rosenberg. I weigh 12 pounds. I eat very little. Please bring me up Jewish." Carson and his people just about died laughing, and he took Melissa out of the basket and played with her until Joan showed up to relieve the nurse and fetch her daughter.

This sort of confident, inspired wit was evident to the viewers of *That Show.* Jack Gould, writing about the program in the *New York Times,* called Joan "quite possibly the most intuitively funny woman alive" (though still with the qualifying "woman") and noted her "vitality and sense of humor." He gushed:

If there is a comedienne who can think and talk faster than Miss Rivers — the name does not immediately come to mind. . . . Her spirit of fun is totally contagious. The words come tumbling out, but her observant quips and her upside-down perspective survive most enjoyably. Moreover, her great asset with guests is that she particularly thrives on topics with a trace of substance and manages to deal with them in the framework of humor.

In the coming months, a galaxy of talents graced the show: Joel Grey, Dionne Warwick, Jerry Lewis, Rita Moreno, Ed Sullivan, Jacqueline Susann, Bob Fosse, Julie Harris, James Earl Jones, and Lily Tomlin, among dozens. Joan taped every week's slate of shows in a single day, in addition to filming promotional spots. The ratings were solid, and new stations were regularly coming online. But advertising revenue wasn't following, and, besides, she was burning out on the pace she'd set for herself. She was still doing two shows a night at Downstairs at the Upstairs, she was still appearing in periodic one-offs at various locations around the country, and she had even taken a few turns behind the desk as guest host of *The Tonight Show* when Johnny had the night off. (And, of course, she still had an infant daughter at home, having reclaimed Melissa from Carson.) Eleven months into this tireless grind, production of *That Show* ceased, with some two hundred episodes to show for its brief but vivid life.

Again, though, as with the lack of a film

career after *The Swimmer,* the cancellation of *That Show* seemed almost no setback at all. Joan continued to be a big attraction onstage and as a guest on TV talk shows and game shows. In November 1969, she made her second "debut" in Las Vegas, opening for singer John Davidson at the Riviera, and this time she was ready. It was by some measure the largest live audience she had played to in several years, but, as *Variety* saw it, she was more than up to the task:

> The redoubtable Miss Rivers . . . sails right in and on, grabbing rapt attention immediately and extending her net until enthusiastic closing plaudits. Ringsiders are pelted with direct assaults, generally on sexual references, fashion, marriage, and babies. Although heavily oriented toward femmes, her spanking twits tickle male ribs as well.

Other reviewers were equally effusive. "She destroyed the audience," said columnist Joe Delaney in the *Las Vegas Sun,* adding, obnoxiously, "She has that rare commodity among femme comics — class." The *Hollywood Reporter* declared that she "wraps herself in new, hilarious glory." *Billboard* called her "one of the brightest and most delightful comediennes around." And the *Los Angeles Herald-Examiner* gave her the highest of insulting compliments, saying she "easily matches the best male comic around today."

From then on, she would always have a home somewhere on the Vegas Strip, which for her symbolized yet another of the peaks that she had determined to conquer and bend to her will. As she put it a few years later, "I don't break in new stuff here, and I'm always amazed when someone says they are. I use my golden oldies because this is *it* for entertainment, this is *the* town. Do you realize what people have to turn down when they're deciding on your show? It's an incredible buffet of talent. You can delude yourself when you walk into an SRO house in — let's say, Milwaukee. But here in Vegas you know exactly where you're placed in the echelon. It keeps you very humble."

Humility didn't keep her from pushing. In January 1970, she hosted *The Tonight Show* for an entire week. Then she set out touring the country: Miami; Syracuse; Windsor, Ontario; suburban New York; Cherry Hill, New Jersey; multiple appearances in Chicago, Las Vegas, Reno, and Manhattan; a guest stint on *Love, American Style;* more appearances on *The Tonight Show* and other TV venues. In October, she made her debut at the absolute pinnacle of New York nightclubs, the Copacabana, where she not only wowed the press and the audience as headliner but did so under the threat of an abscess developing in her mouth, her dentist standing in the wings in case she needed treatment. It wasn't her only medical scare of the year: in Boston that April, she was briefly hospitalized for what was reported as emergency abdominal surgery but may in fact have been a failed pregnancy; years later, Joan reported that after Melissa she suffered two miscarriages and an ectopic pregnancy before giving up on having a second child.

She had reached a previously unrealized level of confidence in herself — at the Copa, her scripted introduction, read over the PA, declared her "a fine American, a wonderful mother, and an animal in bed." But at the same time, she wasn't remotely content to rest. Her unremitting drive was apparent to everyone; *Variety* even published a short feature describing a jam-packed but ordinary day in her life. It all derived, she readily admitted, from that childhood sense of insecurity and insufficiency. She still insisted, even at her relatively high and ever-rising station in show business, on getting paid in cash after each show or gig, a vestige of her hardscrabble days, when she was sometimes fired or stiffed before being fully compensated. As she put it years later, "Our business loves to destroy you — and then maybe bring you back if you're lucky. There's no security in it. . . . You have to recoup yourself every day."

With that mentality, she tackled something seemingly impossible: she would cowrite (with Edgar and writer Lester Colodny) a comedy for the Broadway stage, and she herself would star in it. The Rosenbergs and Colodny conceived a story, clearly inspired by the spectacularly popular comedies of Neil Simon, about a Manhattan woman so dedicated to political activism that she has neglected her boyfriend, a violinist in the Radio City Music Hall orchestra. Throughout any number of rewrites (Joan estimated that there were seven versions), the trio made no particular effort to hide their inspiration: Joan joked that the working title was *The New Neil Simon Play.*

The understanding was that Edgar, of course, would produce alongside whoever could help them bring the project to the stage; but he had never done anything remotely like it. The project eventually came to Alexander Cohen, the veteran producer who had, among other coups, brought Nichols and May to Broadway. Renaming the show *Fun City* and ditching Edgar, Cohen hired the versatile Jerry Adler to direct and polish it and brought it to Washington, D.C., in late November 1971 for a tryout and additional tinkering. Joan played the lead (although there was a casting call for the part as late as that September); Gabriel Dell, the one-time Dead End Kid, was cast as her fella; Rose Marie, formerly of TV's *Dick Van Dyke Show,* played her mother.

In Washington, the reviews were tepid but kind, noting the unmistakable influence of Simon, particularly *The Prisoner of Second Avenue,* which, in a painful twist of fate, had beat *Fun City* to the stage by a matter of weeks. *Variety* conceded that "the play has its laughs" but delicately concluded, "the most charitable judgment is that [*it*] needs a lot of work." Whether or not that work was ever successfully done would remain a mystery. Cohen had already booked the Morosco Theatre for early January, and that would be where Joan Molinsky of *Driftwood* would finally make her Broadway debut on the night of January 2, 1972. It was, alas, a you-had-to-be-there event, because *Fun City* came and went in a flash, closing after a mere eight performances.

Joan was always proud that reviewers gave her serious consideration as an actress and that none dismissed her as merely a stand-up comedian trying to be taken seriously. "I am, in fact, a trained actress who chose comedy," she said soon afterward. But the fact that *Fun City* fared so poorly with critics and audiences was still, she added, "an open wound."

The hurt was deepened, perhaps, by a secret that she didn't share for years: she had carried on an affair with Gabe Dell during the show's out-of-town warm-up, and she and Edgar had separated briefly as a result.

It wasn't the last rift that would open between them, but it seemed to inspire them to save their marriage by shaking it up. They were New Yorkers in their bones; other than her couple of months at Second City, Joan had never lived farther from Times Square than the dorms of Connecticut College for Women. But Johnny Carson had recently announced his intention to move *The Tonight Show,* one of Joan's chief gigs, to the West Coast, and the Rosenbergs believed that there would be more work for Joan if they, too, lived out there. In April 1972, they left Manhattan and moved into a rental house in L.A.'s Coldwater Canyon. Joan Molinsky had always fantasized about going to Hollywood. Now, through the unlikely path of stand-up comedy, Joan Rivers was fulfilling that dream.

Right away, she landed hot. She wrote a TV film, *The Girl Most Likely To . . . ,* a dark comedy about a homely woman who is transformed into a beauty after an automobile accident requires her to undergo plastic surgery; pursued by the men who once scorned her, she lures them into traps to take her revenge, going as far as murder. Starring

Stockard Channing as the heroine and Ed Asner as the detective on her trail, it appeared on ABC's Movie of the Week in November 1973 and scored highly with critics and audiences. (On the strength of it, CBS commissioned Joan to write a pilot for a sitcom; entitled *Husbands, Wives & Lovers,* it was never picked up or, apparently, aired.)

At the same time, Joan was headlining in Las Vegas, having secured a three-year deal at the Desert Inn. In addition to her ceaseless touring gigs all around the country, she had taken up periodic residency in Los Angeles at Ye Olde Pub, a tiny Santa Monica club where she honed new material in front of small crowds, keeping up the practice she'd developed at the Downstairs at the Upstairs. She wrote a book about motherhood, *Having a Baby Can Be a Scream,* which sold nicely. She and Edgar still endured struggles in their marriage — there was a second separation in their early years in Los Angeles — but they reconciled and bought a permanent home, a twelve-room "bastard colonial," in Joan's phrase, on Ambazac Way in Bel Air. Boasting a balconied two-story entryway that made her heart leap on her first sight of it, it was a "micro-Tara" that they bought for $325,000,[*]

[*] Approximately $1.88 million in 2022 — but, given the hyperinflated Southern California real estate market, closer to $14 million in value.

and it became the centerpiece of a lifestyle that expanded on Beatrice Molinsky's blunted dreams of material opulence. Joan and Edgar filled the house, which they dubbed "Ambazac," with dark wood, thick carpets and drapes, European and Asian antiques, a formal library. They created a traditional English rose garden and entertained lavishly and formally, with liveried house help hired for special occasions.

Sadly, not long after she started building this embodiment of her mother's ideals of propriety and class, Joan lost her. In October 1975, Beatrice died suddenly of a heart attack in her home in Larchmont. She was sixty-nine. As awful as the shock of the news was the fact that Joan's last conversation with her mother was a quarrel — Joan wanted Beatrice to hire a full-time nurse for Meyer, who was recovering from a heart attack of his own. The words that passed between them were, apparently, sharp; journalist and PR consultant Sue Cameron, who was working closely with Joan at the time, recalled that "Joan never got to rectify it, and she felt terrible guilt."

She continued to break new ground in the years that followed. In 1977, she cowrote and directed a feature film, *Rabbit Test,* about the world's first pregnant man (played by Billy Crystal in his movie debut), making her only the second woman comedian, after Elaine May, to write and direct a Hollywood studio film. Edgar served as producer, and he and Joan cut all sorts of corners in budgeting the movie, determining that they could shoot it on videotape and then transfer the finished product to celluloid for release. When no financiers showed up to back the project, they put their home on the line — and even took out a second mortgage on Meyer Molinsky's house — to fund it.

The picture opened in February 1978, and it got shredded by critics. "Whenever one does laugh, it's in spite of the movie, rather than because of it," said Janet Maslin of the *New York Times;* "Sure to be among the year's worst," said Kevin Thomas in the *Los Angeles Times,* adding, "It isn't just the rabbit who dies"; Roger Ebert of the *Chicago Sun-Times* gave the picture one star out of four; his colleague Gene Siskel, of the *Chicago Tribune,* more generously awarded it one and a half. It is a painfully inept film: while Joan must be commended for her achievement in getting it made, it's impossible to overlook the fact that she was no filmmaker, and that it wasn't, sin of sins, even a little bit funny. But it was marketed with savvy — Joan gave many interviews wearing a T-shirt that read "director Person" — and it found a niche with audiences, grossing $12 million at the domestic box office by the end of the year. Even still, Joan never got another shot behind the camera.

And truth to tell, she may not have needed the headache. At the same time that she was trying to conquer every popular medium in show business, she was more successful than ever as a stand-up. As a comic, she had evolved yet again. No longer the desperate single girl or the incompetent wife and mother, she refashioned herself into an insult comic, turning her acid tongue — which, to be fair, she still turned most frequently and savagely on herself — to zingers about the appearance and personal travails of celebrities: Elizabeth Taylor, in particular, but also Liza Minnelli, Bo Derek, Jacqueline Kennedy Onassis, Michael Jackson, and Queen Elizabeth. She had always been judgmental about her own flaws and issues. But by the early eighties, she was shooting not at herself but outward, with her shocking and funny but often gratuitous barbs.

Perhaps it was a sign of changing times. In the reign of Richard Pryor and Eddie Murphy, clever jokes about hairdressers or blind dates seemed toothless and passé, and Joan was always determined to be neither. Indeed, the meaner she got, the more famous, even *notorious,* she got. She defended her caustic barbs on the grounds that she was always punching *up,* at the rich and famous, and not down. She insisted that the people she insulted could take the heat of a few one-liners, and while some may have been hurt, many of her targets realized that the jokes were, in a twisted way, compliments, potshots from an insecure woman jealous of the position, wealth, and glory of the icons at which she aimed.

She was famously brutal toward Taylor, compiling more than eight hundred jokes in her files about how her onetime screen idol had let herself go: "She puts mayo on aspirin"; "She had her ears pierced and gravy came out"; "She has a bumper sticker that says 'Save the Whales' and in small print 'for appetizers' "; and on and on. It was a cottage industry, a calling card, a gauntlet — and, of course, schtick. Nevertheless, she got a good, humbling measure of just where her jokes about famous women being fat, dumb, tacky, and promiscuous got her during one of her formal dinner parties. Among her invited guests was actor George Hamilton, who asked to bring a date. On the appointed night, Hamilton showed up with . . . Elizabeth Taylor, who had lost much of the excess weight that Joan had been telling fat-shaming jokes about for years.

Edgar, answering the door, went pale when he saw whom Hamilton had brought along, and Joan, too, was fazed, clucking around Taylor like a starstruck adolescent, deeply uncomfortable in her own skin and home. For her part, Taylor, rather than make mention of her host's many, many put-downs, lorded it over the evening with dignity, oozing charm and class as if she had no reason at all to act offended. It was a superb lesson in both civility *and* one-upsmanship, Hamilton recalled. Joan behaved as if, he said, she'd been hit with "an animal tranquilizer dart. . . . It was done so deftly that Joan felt more humiliated than Elizabeth ever felt."

If her comedy persona was fixed permanently when she turned toward mocking celebrities, she would nonetheless continue to evolve and change and reach and grow, sometimes sensationally.

In the summer of 1983, after more than a decade of regularly subbing behind the desk of *The Tonight Show* when Johnny Carson had the night off, she was named the show's permanent guest host, contracted to appear for at least eight weeks per year. It was widely assumed that this was a semi-coronation, a sign that when Johnny finally stopped coming in altogether — and he seemed to have lost much of his appetite for the work — Joan would ascend, queen, finally, of all she surveyed.

But life got in the way.

In late October 1984, not long after his fifty-ninth birthday, Edgar suffered a heart attack at home at Ambazac, requiring emergency quadruple bypass surgery. He had never been the picture of vitality or fitness, but the episode sapped him of energy and acuity.

Just three months later, Meyer Molinsky died at home in New Rochelle. In the nine years since he had lost Beatrice, he had married Anna Ludner, who, like him, had been born in Europe, emigrated to the United States as a child, married, raised a family, and been widowed in her seventies. Meyer and Anna lived together in the house on Oxford Road in which Joan had found so much drama and comfort during her collegiate and early career years, but Meyer was buried alongside Beatrice when he passed.

Joan turned fifty-three in 1986, and for all that she had done and that had happened to her in the previous half century, it would turn out that the drama was just getting started. In April, she released *Enter Talking,* a thoughtful and intelligent (if not exactly *verifiable*) autobiography that spent its 370-plus pages working up to the night in 1965 when her first appearance on *The Tonight Show* changed her life. Such was her reverence for that moment that the book had two dedicatees: "Edgar, who made this book happen" and "Johnny Carson, who made it *all* happen." She showed up on *The Tonight Show* to promote the book, only to be taken aback when she realized that not only hadn't Carson *read* it, he didn't even know that the book was dedicated to him. That was who he was, she knew — aloof, remote, hard to fathom. But she herself was sentimental: that night she even wore the same dress and string of pearls and boa that she wore on her first visit to the show twenty-one years prior. Carson, she noted, seemed to have only a vague memory of the occasion.

But then she too was also holding something back. Earlier that year, two things had happened that triggered her lifelong sense that she was unwanted and unappreciated. One was that NBC had renewed Carson's massively lucrative contract for two years but had only renewed *her* pact as his permanent guest host for a *single* year. The other was that she had been given access to a memo — which may or may not have been authentic — that had circulated among NBC executives listing possible replacements for Carson should he step down at the end of his newest deal (something he had not so much as hinted at). It was a list of *men;* she wasn't on it.

This was the sort of thing Joan and Edgar had always anticipated, that it was the two of them against the world, that nobody in the business could be trusted to have their backs, not even the man to whom they had once (briefly, in jest) gifted their only child. But this was not Pepper January or J. Sondra Meredith or the Joan of Jim, Jake, and Joan who was being rebuffed. This was Joan Rivers, one of the most successful women in the history of American comedy. She was not without resources or recourse or, for that matter, options.

Not long before these shocks, Joan had been approached, almost as if in a spy movie, by representatives of a new TV network that was being started by media tycoon Rupert Murdoch and Barry Diller, chairman and CEO of 20th Century Fox. The network, to be called Fox, was seeking to declare its intention to rank alongside NBC, ABC, and CBS, and its creators determined that a late-night talk show significant enough to pose a challenge to *The Tonight Show* was the way to do it. Obviously they couldn't get Johnny Carson to host the show, so why not ask the person whom Carson trusted most when he was away?

When this proposal first arose, Joan wasn't interested. But when she began to believe that NBC didn't take her seriously as the future permanent host of *The Tonight Show,* she entertained an offer and struck a deal. She and Edgar, named as a producer, would have approval over staff, guests, and the format of the new show; the production resources would be equivalent to Carson's; and Joan would be paid $5 million per year for the three years of the contract.[*]

And so, on the night she went on *The Tonight Show* to promote her autobiography, in her good-luck dress and pearls, when she was wounded upon realizing that Carson hadn't read her book, she had already made the deal to go into business against him with her own show on a rival network. And she was under strict orders from Fox to keep the news to herself; she was forbidden from telling Carson what she had done.

She came back to *The Tonight Show* the following week as guest host and taped those shows as if with a time bomb ticking beneath her seat. Her last show would air on a Friday; the press conference announcing her new job would be held the following Tuesday. Over the weekend, word of her new gig started leaking around Hollywood, and Carson heard it. She reached out to him; he wouldn't take the calls. She kept trying: his offices, his staffers' offices, his home. Finally, her secretary managed to get him on the line and handed Joan the phone. She was ready to apologize for not telling him the news, for not consulting with him, for not seeking his blessing, ready to express her gratitude, even her love, to him.

"Johnny, I . . ."

He hung up.

[*] Approximately $11.9 million in 2022.

They never spoke again.

The Late Show Starring Joan Rivers debuted on the new Fox network at eleven p.m. on Thursday, October 9, 1986, with a very mid-eighties roster of superstar guests: Cher, Elton John, Pee-wee Herman, David Lee Roth. The appearance of so many big names was a particular coup, as Carson's staff had made it clear that anyone who showed up on Joan's show would face blacklisting from theirs. (Johnny's guests that same night were Richard Pryor, Sean Penn, and Kenny G.) The reviews for Joan's premiere were middling: "Overwhelmingly nervous," said *Variety* about the first episode, noting that the hour was so poorly planned that Joan had to skip doing a monologue and, thus, "left the program almost totally devoid of her distinctive brand of humor, which was sorely missed." In *Newsday,* Marvin Kitman called the show by a number of unflattering names — *"The New Joan Rivers Without Johnny Carson Show . . . The New Unimproved Joan Rivers Show."* Howard Rosenberg of the *Los Angeles Times* called the show "futzy and klutzy, more glitz than ritz, more razzle than dazzle." And John O'Connor in the *New York Times* sighed, "This may have been the first hour in the history of television that begged for a stiff tranquilizer."

At the outset, the reviews didn't seem to

matter. The show's ratings were competitive with — if inevitably second to — *The Tonight Show.* But the show soon found a regular place in the pecking order well behind Carson — and further, with each week, from the center of the public mind. Worse, Edgar and Barry Diller fought regularly about the management, promotion, and content of the show.

What Joan and Edgar seemed not to realize, or be willing to admit, was that once *The Late Show with Joan Rivers* launched to massive publicity, Fox executives no longer needed it, or *them.* The purpose of drawing attention to the new network had been served. Joan had been a herald for the venture, but she wasn't essential to its survival. After seven months of lagging ratings and behind-the-scenes drama, Fox pulled the plug on her, replacing her as host with Arsenio Hall. They ultimately settled her contract for $2 million, scant compensation for what she had suffered in humiliation: the biggest, most publicized enterprise she had ever embarked upon, and it didn't last as long as *That Show.*

And that wasn't, by a large margin, the worst news of the year. The pressures of mounting, maintaining, and, finally, burying the show had taken a brutal toll on Edgar, who became chilly, remote, quick-tempered. Joan suggested they visit a therapist, but he refused. She watched him slip into depression and anger and spoke openly with intimate friends about her exasperation: "I can't stand this anymore," she told one. She gave him an ultimatum: Get psychiatric help, or I will leave you.

He agreed, but before he began therapy he had some business to tend to, he said. In mid-August, he flew to Philadelphia to look into a land development deal: a mini-Hollywood, in fact, with residential and commercial tracts built around modern soundstages. His closest friend lived there, and the two spent three days going over the proposed venture and compiling a comprehensive account of all of Edgar and Joan's holdings, investments, and financial affairs. Throughout the trip, Joan kept in regular touch with Edgar on the telephone. He was in a parlous state. "I'm so depressed," he told her at one point, "I'm going to kill myself." She made a joke, reminding him that she had a liposuction procedure planned: "Don't do it till Friday, because Thursday I'm going under anesthesia." To his friend, he made a sobering confession: "Pride can kill a man, and that's all I have left." His friend and Joan both urged him to hospitalize himself for counseling and care when he got home to Los Angeles. He agreed and said he would be home on Friday.

On Thursday afternoon, his business in

Philadelphia done, he went to a barber shop to have his beard shaved off, bought a cassette recorder and some blank tapes, and returned to his room at the Four Seasons Hotel. He recorded messages on three separate tapes: one for Joan, one for Melissa, and one for his friend. He took the hotel stationery out of the desk in his room, and put each tape in an envelope, labeling each with a recipient's name and slipping his Rolex and money clip into the one addressed to his daughter. He filled other envelopes with tips for the hotel staff. He compiled business papers and instructions about his financial affairs in a large manila envelope and addressed it to Joan. He unlocked the door to his room. He put a picture of his wife and daughter on the nightstand. And he swallowed a handful of pills — Valium and Librium — washing them down with liquor from the minibar.

The next morning, when he missed a breakfast appointment, hotel security checked on him. They found him on the floor, dead, with a bruise on his head that was apparently caused by a fall. There would be an autopsy, but it was obvious that he had taken his own life. Melissa, home for the summer from college[*] and alone in the house while Joan

[*] Painfully, she attended the University of Pennsylvania, not two miles from Edgar's hotel.

convalesced from her procedure, took the devastating call. It was left to her to tell her mother the news.

Joan was destroyed. She wanted to respond the only way she knew — by working, even that very night. But she was obviously in no condition, and no one in the world would let her do it, anyway.

Funeral arrangements, a whirlwind of phone calls, visits, a week of shiva at Ambazac, meetings with advisers, nightmares, emotional breakdowns, the funeral itself — and all amid the glare of headlines and speculation and horrible Hollywood gossip. Edgar's effects were returned by the authorities in Philadelphia, and Joan stared at the tape recording he made for her for weeks, unable to listen to it, finally, for two full years. She heard from all of show business, it seemed, even Elizabeth Taylor. But there wasn't so much as a syllable from Johnny Carson — a snub that reopened the unhealed wound of their rift of just a year before.

She was without Edgar, without Carson, without a regular job, cruelly and publicly exposed in her work and in her marriage. Friends and colleagues had rallied around her, yes. But when the commotion settled, it was just her and Melissa alone in a world that seemed always ready to rebuff her. She was fifty-four years old and a veteran of thirty years in show business, and she felt just as raw and scared and unsteady and unwanted as on those awful nights when she was Pepper January.

And so she did what she always did when she felt that her parents or other kids or blind dates or show-biz executives had no interest in her: she showed up, did the work, made a place for herself. By November, she was back onstage, telling jokes about Edgar's death: "My husband said in his will that I should cremate him and scatter his ashes in Neiman Marcus, that way he knew he would see me five days a week." When audiences gasped or seemed uncomfortable, she would chide them: "Oh, grow up!" She had made a career out of oversharing, of shocking, of going where no comedian — let alone a woman — had dared. If nothing else, her willingness to make comedy of her husband's suicide ("It was my fault! We were making love, and I took the bag off my head!") proved that she walked the walk of her comic persona. It wasn't always pretty, but it was truthful, and it took guts.

And that was more or less what she did for the next three decades: stand in the public eye and tell jokes, sometimes unthinkable, often hilarious jokes; make a spectacle and even a punch line of herself; launch audacious gambits; take punches, get back up, and come back harder, more determined, with a belief in herself that she seemed born both with *and* without in equal measure.

She had, witness her liposuction procedure the day before Edgar's suicide, become a devotee of plastic surgery, undergoing countless procedures over the next decades, her face becoming smoother and more removed from its original appearance regularly. Like Phyllis Diller, she never hid the fact of the work she had done — and that would have been impossible, anyway — and instead made jokes about it and spoke of it encouragingly as a form of self-care and positivity.

In 1988, she left Ambazac and spent $1.6 million[*] on a penthouse apartment that had once been the ballroom of J. P. Morgan's mansion on the Upper East Side of Manhattan. As if to mark her return, she appeared on Broadway for three months in one of the lead roles in *Broadway Bound,* Neil Simon's autobiographical play about his youth, which had already been running for two years. In the straight role of the protagonist's mother, she received appreciative reviews.

There was another talk show, in the daytime, which aired from 1989 to 1993 and won her an Emmy as its host. She toured constantly, taped multiple comedy specials

[*] Approximately $3.5 million in 2022 dollars, but worth upward of $24 million on the real estate market.

for cable, and appeared regularly in voice-over gigs in movies and on TV, in cameos on sitcoms. She made scores of visits to talk shows — but never once, not until Jimmy Fallon broke Johnny Carson's embargo against her in 2014, nine years after Carson's death, did she visit *The Tonight Show.*

In 1994, she and Melissa, who had changed her name from Rosenberg to Rivers and begun her own career in show business, appeared *as themselves* in a TV movie, *Tears and Laughter: The Joan and Melissa Rivers Story,* an account of their relationship and trauma in the wake of Edgar's suicide. That same year, Joan returned to Broadway yet again, in the lead role of *Sally Marr . . . and Her Escorts,* a realization of her long-held ambition to tell the story of the mother of Lenny Bruce done up as, essentially, a one-woman show; critics admired Joan's pluck, energy, and humor, but the play, which she had cowritten, ran for only six weeks, even though Joan was nominated for a Tony in the lead role.

The following year, she began a two-decade gig selling costume and semiprecious-gem jewelry on cable TV's QVC network — run by the same Barry Diller who had fired her a decade prior from Fox. While that business, which would result in more than $1 billion in sales, soared, Joan and Melissa became twin fixtures of another type of pop TV, as fashion commentators, first on the red carpets of Hollywood awards shows, where they chatted with — and often mocked — passing celebrities. That gig morphed into *Fashion Police,* which Joan hosted and presided over as queen bee. And alongside *those* gigs, she became a staple of reality TV competition shows such as *I'm a Celebrity . . . Get Me Out of Here!* and *Celebrity Apprentice,* the second season of which she won, beginning a friendship with the host, whose work on the show convinced some people that he should be elected president of the United States.

In 2013, she marked her eightieth birthday, still performing regularly in Las Vegas, in concert dates around the United States and in England, and in tiny, sometimes unannounced dates at the Laurie Beechman Theatre, which sounded a lot grander than the tiny basement club on West Forty-Second Street that it actually was — another of the small rooms where, as throughout her career, she tried out new material before taking it to TV or bigger gigs.

She was there on the night of August 27, 2014, and was, by all accounts, in fine form, having spent the day doing press for a new book and warming up for a larger show the next night in New Jersey. She finished early — nine-thirty — because she had a medical appointment the following morning. Always known for her sandpaper voice, she had been bothered for a few weeks by an unusual rasp in her throat, and she was going to undergo a photographic examination of her upper digestive system to see if there were serious problems.

She arrived at Yorkville Endoscopy, a small clinic near her home, and signed consent forms for the procedure, which was to be performed by Dr. Lawrence Cohen, medical director of the clinic, assisted by anesthesiologist Dr. Renuka Bankulla, and joined, unusually, by Joan's personal ear, nose, and throat specialist, Dr. Gwen Korovin. Joan was sedated, as was standard for the procedure. But once she was under, Korovin took the occasion to perform a transnasal laryngoscopy on her, an examination of the throat and voice box, even though Joan had neither consented to nor known about the procedure, and even though Korovin was not authorized to perform *any* procedures in that clinic or *even to be present in the procedure room.* After the laryngoscopy, Cohen performed the endoscopy, and then Korovin performed a *second* laryngoscopy, also, obviously, unauthorized.

Bankulla kept pointing out that Joan's oxygen levels were getting lower and lower, indicating that the procedures had irritated and swollen her throat and larynx and that she was having difficulty inhaling. Cohen responded with jokes and rebuffs. Worse, according to legal papers filed later, he took at least one occasion to photograph himself and Korovin with their sedated patient — again, obviously, without her consent.

Joan's oxygen levels continued to dip, as did her heart rate. The anesthesiologist tried to administer oxygen through a mask, to no avail, and sounded an alert in the clinic, summoning additional clinic personnel but not, crucially, a crash cart, which had potentially life-saving medications and treatments on it. It became clear that Joan would need an emergency cricothyrotomy — a puncture in the throat to allow the insertion of a breathing tube — and Cohen wanted Korovin, a trained ENT physician, to perform the procedure. But Korovin had, according to court documents, left the clinic.

During this dithering, Joan slipped into cardiac and respiratory arrest. Only then — twelve full minutes after the emergency alert had sounded — was an ambulance summoned. Joan was taken to nearby Mount Sinai Hospital, where ICU doctors put her in a medically induced coma.

Melissa and various close friends stayed at her bedside around the clock. Finally, on September 4, told that there was no hope that her mother would recover, Melissa took Joan off life support and climbed into the hospital bed to hold her as she died.*

Per her wishes, Joan was cremated, and a funeral was held for her three days later at Temple Emanu-El, a mammoth Upper East Side synagogue with almost as many seats as Carnegie Hall. Crowds lined the street outside, snapping photos of the parade of famous faces arriving to pay their respects: Barbara Walters, Whoopi Goldberg, Sarah Jessica Parker and Matthew Broderick, Diane Sawyer, Barry Diller, Alan Cumming, Bernadette Peters, Joy Behar, Rosie O'Donnell, Margaret Cho, Kathy Griffin, and John Waters among them. The mourners were handed a program in which Joan's wishes for her send-off were printed: "I want my funeral to be a big showbiz affair with lights, cameras, action. I want paparazzi and I want publicists making a scene. I want it to be Hollywood all the way. I don't want some rabbi rambling on."

She got her wish: The ceremony rivaled an episode of her *Late Night* show. There were musical performances by Audra McDonald, Hugh Jackman, the New York City Gay Men's Chorus, and a pipe and drum band

* A lawsuit on behalf of Melissa against Yorkville Endoscopy, Cohen, Bankulla, and Kovorin was settled in the spring of 2016 for a reported multimillion-dollar payout, with the doctors formally accepting responsibility for Joan's death.

from the NYPD's Emerald Society. There were eulogies from TV host Deborah Norville, from a small, select group of friends, and from Melissa, who read aloud a letter to her mother and best friend.

Howard Stern, the radio personality who pushed edges like Joan and who viewed her as a "big sister" and "crazy aunt," was called upon to bat cleanup, as it were, and he did not disappoint. "Joan Rivers had a dry pussy," were his first words, and he went on, alternating shocking declarations about Joan's body with admiring comments about her tenacity, her wit, her courage. He was moved to tears several times, but he kept on in the groove in which he began, and ended with this final wish for his departed friend and role model: "I hope Joan is somewhere chasing Johnny Carson with a baseball bat."

Stern's eulogy was stunning in its profanity and its daring — more than one attendee shrugged apologetically at the synagogue's head rabbi as it continued — but it was absolutely the send-off Joan wanted. She had spent her whole life dedicated to making audiences laugh at her misfortunes and troubles. She had fought ceaselessly to be treated as an equal of any man in show business and as a singular star in her own right. She had given no quarter, not even to Edgar after his suicide, and she asked none from anyone. In turning her funeral into a Friars

Club roast, Stern was true to her wishes, to her spirit, and to her own patented brand of comedy.

Nothing was taboo for Joan Rivers, not even the death of Joan Rivers, as everyone in that synagogue knew in their bones. And that, more than anything she ever earned or achieved, may have been her most profound accomplishment. She rewrote the rules of comedy to suit her own fearless sensibility. And even her own death would be fair game for her. She attacked her life and her career like a prizefighter outmatched but unfazed by a stronger, faster, bigger opponent, and it was clear, on that bittersweet late-summer day, that she had won by a knockout.

CONCLUSION

In October 1970, NBC aired a Bob Hope comedy special in which the king of the one-liners pretended to have been dethroned by the ascent of women's lib and found himself living in a world dominated by women. In a series of sketches, seventeen women (including stand-up comedy heroes Phyllis Diller, Totie Fields, and Minnie Pearl, and comic actresses Imogene Coca, Martha Raye, Nanette Fabray, Kaye Ballard, and Nancy Walker) made a hash of Hope's world by assuming positions that society traditionally reserved for men: TV news anchors, taxi drivers, show-biz executives, stars of Western dramas, and so on (Phyllis's bit was to perform *as* Hope, doing his traditional schtick in the machine-gun style she'd originally cribbed from him). The point of the show, insofar as there seemed to be one, was that women had emerged to full social equality, and men could no longer count on the privileges that were formerly the perks of their gender.

But, of course, they were playing for laughs, right? I mean, a woman reporting the news or running a TV network, or *telling jokes as well as Bob Hope*??? And, unsurprisingly, the director, producer, and all *ten* writers were men. And, of course, none of the women were paid anything like Hope's salary for the gig. So: yeah.

Obviously, the battle for gender equality is still, half a century later, being waged in every corner and at every tier of our culture. And while the women in these pages certainly made it possible for other women to ascend to fame and glory in the world of stand-up comedy, the truth was that comedy did not become — and still has never been — a world in which women readily get the same shot accorded men. There has never been a comedy girls' club to rival the comedy boys' club, and the larger culture is still unable to wrap its mind around professional equality for women, even in a field such as show business in which there is ample evidence now that women are every bit as good — as funny, original, commercially viable — as any man.

Consider two more bits of evidence, some forty-six years apart.

In January 1970, when every single one of the women you've just read about was engaged in her career at a high level or had retired to enjoy the fruits of her work, the

New York Times ran an article about the new breed of young women in stand-up who were noteworthy because not only were they funny but they were — can you believe it? — *attractive*! Entitled, "The Funny Thing Is That They Are Still Feminine," it surveyed a variety of women comedians (including Joan Rivers, Lily Tomlin, and Madeline Kahn) for their thoughts on dating, fashion, and the business of comedy. The astounding last words came from the mouth of Jo Anne Worley, then a star of TV's *Rowan & Martin's Laugh-In,* who recalled the advice she got from comedian Jerry Lewis a decade prior, when she was barely in her twenties: "He told me a female comedian should never be unattractive and that a man should always want to take her in the next room and give her a big hug."[*]

The second data point comes from September 2016, when *Forbes* magazine published its annual list of the highest-earning comedians of the previous year. Finishing at number four in the list was Amy Schumer, who made $17 million over the preceding twelve months, much of it earned from the box office receipts of her hit feature film *Trainwreck,* but much, too, thanks to a massive book deal,

[*] I happen to have written a five-hundred-page biography of Lewis, and if he really said "give her a big hug," I will eat it, dust jacket and all.

a successful Comedy Central series (*Inside Amy Schumer*), and an ongoing career on the road as a stand-up. Schumer was ranked behind Kevin Hart ($87.5 million), Jerry Seinfeld ($43.5 million),* and ventriloquist Terry Fator ($21 million), and ahead of six others, including Dave Chappelle and Jim Gaffigan, each of whom earned less than $15 million. The truly notable thing wasn't where Schumer placed in the list but that she was on it *at all.* Sixteen years into the twenty-first century, and she was the *first woman ever* to land on the *Forbes* list. And that would continue to be the case for the next three years: she would finish at number five in 2017 (earning $37.5 million), she would fall off of the list in 2018, and she would return in 2019 in seventh place (with $21 million).† And she would *still,* at the time of this writing, be the only woman ever to claim a place on the list.

There it is, really.

Yes, in 2021 nobody was writing about whether a woman could be both attractive *and* funny (although Schumer once devoted an entire episode of her TV show to a spoof of *Twelve Angry Men* in which a jury deliber-

---

* It was the first time in more than a decade that Seinfeld didn't top this list.

† There would be no *Forbes* list in 2020 because of the COVID-19 pandemic's impact on the live comedy business.

ated over whether or not she herself was hot enough to be on TV).

And, yes, in 2021, one of the nation's most popular and celebrated television series, *The Marvelous Mrs. Maisel,* concerned a woman (and mother) trying to build a career in stand-up comedy in the late fifties and early sixties and offered an entertaining and enlightening look at the sort of professional and personal obstacles she faced (with the suggestion, surely unintended by the show's creators, that depicting those barriers as part of history might mean that they no longer exist).★

But the truth is that women are still struggling, more than a century after Moms Mabley and Jean Carroll began making audiences laugh, to be seen, to be accepted, and, crucially, to be *paid* as equals of men for a skill that, truly, knows no gender and that

---

★ I generally enjoy the series, despite my historian's gripes over factual (in)accuracy. One of my favorite descriptions of the show came up in conversation with the poet and novelist Brian Stephen Ellis, who called it "a Magical Realist version of the life of Joan Rivers." Pretty much, I'd say, but I nevertheless slightly prefer *Hacks,* set in the here-and-now, with a more on-the-nose Joan Rivers type dueling with a young woman hired to write modern comedy for her.

they demonstrably possess in at least equal measure.

In the late sixties, cracks in the glass ceiling, many formed by the incessant banging and kicking of the women in these pages, began to allow a new generation of younger women comedians to emerge.

In January 1968, *Rowan & Martin's Laugh-In,* a comedy-based variety-sketch show, debuted, and the cast of its first season featured Jo Anne Worley and Ruth Buzzi, veterans of the Manhattan cabaret/revue scene, as well as comic actresses Pamela Austin, Judy Carne, and Goldie Hawn. The show would last until 1973, and of this initial group only Buzzi stayed with it until the end. But arguably the great standout, male or female, to emerge from the show would be Lily Tomlin, another veteran of Manhattan's club scene (and lifelong Jean Carroll fan), who joined the cast in 1969 and introduced a gallery of characters that would make her famous, including the telephone operator Ernestine and the five-and-a-half-year-old moppet Edith Ann. Working within these skins, Tomlin more resembled a comic actress than a straight stand-up, but she went on to perform in clubs and arenas and, eventually, on Broadway in one-woman shows that were as successful as any comic performances by any woman of any era.

Yet another avenue of opportunity for women on the comedy stage opened in 1972 in Los Angeles, when comedian Sammy Shore and his wife, Mitzi, opened the city's first club dedicated strictly to comedy, the Comedy Store, in a spot on the Sunset Strip in West Hollywood that had once been the chichi Hollywood nightclub Ciro's. Mitzi would acquire the club outright two years later in the couple's divorce, and she would preside over a titanic revolution in stand-up, albeit made up mostly of men: Richard Pryor, Robin Williams, Steve Martin, Jay Leno, Albert Brooks, Andy Kaufman, and on and on through the years. Proportionally, very few women were able to take the stage at the Comedy Store, much less make an impact, though the formidable Elayne Boosler managed to carve out a space for herself at the club and then, later, as the first truly prominent woman stand-up to appear after 1970. Mitzi, as if to acknowledge the frat-house atmosphere around the Comedy Store, briefly opened a club-within-the-club, the Belly Room,[*] which was reserved for women performers only and barely lasted a year, but allowed such iconoclastic up-and-coming women comics as Lotus Weinstock and Sandra Bernhard a regular platform for their

[*] The space had, apparently, once actually been the site of a club for belly dancers.

emerging talents.

In the fall of 1975, yet another venue for women comedians debuted: *Saturday Night Live,* the weekly sketch comedy series on NBC that featured in its debut season Jane Curtin, Laraine Newman, and Gilda Radner, the latter of whom, especially, had a breakout career not unlike the one Lily Tomlin launched on *Laugh-In.* In its forty-six seasons on the air, *SNL* has given dozens of women the chance to prove themselves as comedians, whether in the cast or as hosts, but it has also been, notoriously, just as much of a boys' club as the Compass was when the men in the troupe perpetually dismissed the contributions of its most brilliant member, Elaine May. *SNL,* to its credit, eventually appointed Tina Fey as its head writer (and paired her, notably, with Amy Poehler on its Weekend Update news desk), but it took decades for that to happen, and only the most devoted of the show's scores of comic alumnae have claimed that they were treated as equals of the men alongside whom they worked. And all of this happened, remember, while many of the trailblazers in women's comedy were still active: Minnie Pearl, Rusty Warren, Phyllis Diller, Anne Meara, and Joan Rivers all performed into the 1990s and beyond, but only Joan ever got to host *SNL,* and only once, even though Phyllis had hired the show's creator, Lorne Michaels, when he was a struggling comedy writer just arrived from Canada.

The slights, indignities, and even crimes suffered by women in the business of stand-up comedy have been endless, just as prevalent in this age of #MeToo and #Times Up as they were in the days when most club-goers and critics assumed the girl at the microphone was there to sing. Even as recently as 2018, bona fide comedy superstar Amy Schumer had to endure the embarrassment of Netflix offering her *one half* the salary for a comedy special that it paid the likes of Chris Rock and Dave Chappelle. (Yes, that still puts her compensation in the range of eight figures, but it's a matter of equity, not dollars.) The many brilliant young women emerging in comedy today — Iliza Shlesinger, Nikki Glaser, Jenny Slate, Heather McMahan, Kelly Bachman, Jessica Williams, Cameron Esposito, Negin Farsad, Bridget Everett, and Fortune Feimster, to name but a tiny fraction of them — all seem to be doing a million things: podcasts, shows, TV series, films, writing staff positions, and so on; and no doubt they *must* hustle like crazy simply to reach some sort of parity, in pay and in stature, with the most ordinary male comedians working around them.

It's a despairing thing, but, then, compare the lot of today's rising comics to the place where Moms and Minnie and Jean Carroll were in, say, 1953, or where Elaine May, Phyllis Diller, Belle Barth, and Rusty Warren were, say, five years after that, or Totie Fields and Joan Rivers after yet *another* five years had passed. That remarkable group of women, born between 1897 and 1932, active, in several cases, a decade or more into the twenty-first century, laid out a path — rocky in some places, for sure — that future generations, right down to this day, could follow.

If a woman comedian wants to work inside the persona of a character, the model was laid out for her. If she wants to sing a little, that too. If she wants to work raunchy or hip, if she wants to work in improv or in sketches, if she wants to write a play or a movie, if she wants to perform in a nightclub, a theater, a casino — check, check, check: the women in these pages did it, often first, and usually well enough that there was at least *some* consideration given to the next funnywoman who came along and wanted a shot.

Take these two perspectives on the change, from women who are only fourteen years apart in age:

> I grew up in a time when women didn't really do comedy. You had to be homely, an old maid, all that. You had to play a stereotype, because women were not supposed to be funny.
>
> — LILY TOMLIN

I began comedy in Manhattan in 1980. Comedy clubs were in vogue, and the rule there was simple: you were either funny or not funny. It didn't matter if you were male, female, black, white, gay, straight. Were you funny?

— RITA RUDNER

That difference in the sense of possibilities, that cultural shift, is the result of the hard work — and thick skin — of the heroines of this book, who blazed a discernible trail where one never existed before. This isn't to say it's easy. Nobody hands anybody a career in comedy; it's as tough a buck as, oh, poetry or jazz or puppetry. But until the pioneers in these pages showed the world that it *could* be done, and well, in every possible forum, nobody in show business thought a woman was capable of it at all. So the next time you enjoy a set or a concert by Amy Schumer or Ali Wong or Leslie Jones or Mindy Kaling or Hannah Gadsby or whichever rising young woman comedian makes you snort your two-drink-minimum cocktail through your nose, have a thought for Moms and Hattie and Jean and Minnie and Belle and Pearl and Rusty and Jorie and Phyllis and Elaine and Anne and Totie and Joan. Their day may be past, their jokes may be out of fashion, but the things they did and said, and the paths they worked so tirelessly to blaze: those endure.

ACKNOWLEDGMENTS

My name is on the jacket of this book, but a thing like this is almost inevitably built on the effort and input of a cohort.

I am grateful to my editor, Yaniv Soha, for finding in the proposal for another book altogether the seed of the idea for this one. His patience, intelligence, and camaraderie have been essential.

Richard Pine, my agent and friend, was, as ever, crucial in helping shape the idea and unflagging in his encouragement as I executed it.

I am deeply, deeply indebted to the friends and families of the women whose lives and work I've explored and written about, in particular Melissa Rivers, who was gracious and frank in her support of my effort to cast a new light on her mother; Perry Diller, who shared stories of his mother and their lives together with enthusiasm and candor; and Susan Chatzky, who was forthright and helpful in guiding my thinking about her grandmother, Jean Carroll.

Several of the inheritors of the tradition forged by my subjects were kind enough to share their thoughts about their predecessors and about the lives of women in the world of comedy in general. I can't thank Nora Dunn, Kathy Griffin, Lisa Lampanelli, and Rita Rudner enough for their time and perspectives.

Some twenty-five years ago, when we were both ten years old, Jeff Abraham was part of my first journey as an author, and it was a treat to be able to call on his expertise as a historian of comedy to fill in holes on this one.

Grace Overbeke, whose dissertation on Jean Carroll is authoritative and comprehensive, shared some invaluable resources and pointers. She's at work on a full-scale biography of Jean, and it should be a significant work.

The holdings of a variety of institutions were essential to my ability to tell these stories: the Multnomah County Library (especially its Interlibrary Loan department), the Billy Rose Collection of the New York Public Library, the Margaret Herrick Library of the Academy of Motion Picture Arts and Sciences, the Knight Library of the University of Oregon, the Los Angeles Public Library, and the Pasadena Public Library. And though they don't necessarily qualify as research institutions, Powell's City of Books and Photofest were, as ever, troves of useful information. I am also, as a researcher in a time of quarantine, indebted to various Pro-Quest databases and the institutions, some named above, through which I was able to access them.

At Inkwell Management, I'm grateful to Eliza Rothstein who offered valuable commentary on the initial proposal. At Doubleday, I appreciate the contributions of Cara Reilly, who read the first drafts with great care and insight, Nora Reichard, who oversaw production editorial; Mike Windsor, for a dazzling design; and Rosalie Wieder, for a sharp-eyed and face-saving copy edit.

When conceiving and working on this book, I particularly had in my mind two women who have shaped so much of my thinking, not to mention my heart: my daughter, Paula Levy, and my partner, Shannon Brazil. I learn from them always; I laugh with them constantly; I love them immensely. Whatever is best in me, whatever is best in these pages, is inspired by and in honor of them.

NOTES

Introduction

"Women? There were no women": *New York Post,* August 21, 1983.

"A woman is feminine": *Rolling Stone,* March 22, 1979.

"A woman doing comedy": *Hollywood Reporter,* August 23, 2017.

"Why are women": *Vanity Fair,* January 2007.

"I don't like funny women": *Playboy,* August 8, 1981.

"Whenever someone says to me": Fey, *Bossypants,* p. 144.

"The only disadvantage": *Hollywood Reporter,* January 7, 2014.

Chapter One: The Philosopher

"When I look out in an audience": "Jackie 'Moms' Mabley Talks About Her Life and Career as a Comedian," part 2, Studs Terkel Radio Archive, June 13, 1961, https://studs

terkel.wfmt.com/programs/jackie-moms-mabley-talks-about-her-life-and-career-comedian-part-2.

"To tell the truth": "Jackie 'Moms' Mabley Talks About Her Life and Career as a Comedian," part 1, Studs Terkel Radio Archive, June 13, 1961, https://studs terkel.wfmt.com/programs/jackie-moms-mabley-talks-about-her-life-and-career-comedian-part-1.

"He had the only white barber shop": "Jackie 'Moms' Mabley Talks," part 1.

"I wasn't born": *Chicago Defender,* January 5, 1963.

"The mountains were very high": *Chicago Defender,* January 5, 1963.

"My great-grandmother": "Jackie 'Moms' Mabley Talks," part 1.

"My granny was a slave": *New York,* October 14, 1974.

"I loved that baby": "Jackie 'Moms' Mabley Talks," part 1.

"I was in Buffalo": "Jackie 'Moms' Mabley Talks," part 1.

"I got on my knees": "Jackie 'Moms' Mabley Talks," part 1.

"I used to star": *Washington Star-Times,* October 4, 1974.

"She asked me": *Los Angeles Times,* December 26, 1974.

"The first time I set foot": *Pittsburgh Courier,* March 14, 1964.

"I had those girls young": *Chicago Defender,* January 5, 1963.

"You're too much like me": *Chicago Defender,* January 5, 1963.

"It taught young people": "Jackie 'Moms' Mabley Talks," part 1.

"You talk about rehearsals": *Ebony,* January 1974.

"I had listened": "Jackie 'Moms' Mabley Talks," part 1.

"When I got raised": "Jackie 'Moms' Mabley Talks," part 1.

"a line of chatter": *Billboard,* August 26, 1922.

"We were going from Dallas": "Jackie 'Moms' Mabley Talks," part 1.

"I didn't know I was a comic": *Newsday,* undated clipping, New York Public Library.

"had to respond": *New York Amsterdam News,* July 27, 1927.

"Particular mention": *New York Amsterdam News,* October 26, 1927.

"Honey, when I was startin' ": *Pittsburgh Courier,* March 14, 1964.

"Jackie Mabley defies": *Inter-State Tattler,* October 17, 1930.

"Jackie Mabley back": *Inter-State Tattler,* November 21, 1930.

"She and I shared": *Moms Mabley: I Got Somethin' to Tell You,* HBO, 2013.

"Any man who was caught": "Jackie 'Moms' Mabley Talks," part 1.

"They just parted": *Baltimore Afro-American,* October 9, 1937.

"spotty": *Variety,* September 22, 1931.

"Most of the singing": *New York Times,* September 16, 1931.

"Twicetimes": *Baltimore Afro-American,* November 21, 1931.

"The people had written": *Washington Star-Times,* October 4, 1974.

"tells the dirtiest jokes": *Baltimore Afro-American,* January 23, 1932.

"Scallions to Jackie": *Baltimore Afro-American,* October 3, 1936.

"Jackie Mabley kept": *Baltimore Afro-American,* November 6, 1937.

"My audience helps me": *Baltimore Afro-American,* October 9, 1937.

"a vaudeville show": *New York Amsterdam News,* December 9, 1939.

"The show people gave me": "Jackie 'Moms' Mabley Talks," part 1.

"I just tell folks the truth": *Norfolk New Journal and Guard,* May 14, 1966.

"letting granny grow": *New York,* October 14, 1974.

"under the sheer weight": *New York Amsterdam News,* January 27, 1940.

"Put this jive": *Baltimore Afro-American,* January 31, 1942.

"I wish I could find": *Baltimore Afro-American,* December 7, 1940.

"Feeling wonderful": *New York Amsterdam News,* April 1, 1944.

"One of the greatest comedians": *New York Amsterdam News,* April 19, 1947.

"combine the technique": *Chicago Defender,* June 12, 1948.

"I am not opposed": *Baltimore Afro-American,* June 5, 1948.

"only a limited opportunity": *New York Amsterdam News,* August 7, 1948.

"Her patter routine": *Variety,* October 26, 1949.

"one of the most entertaining": *Billboard,* June 2, 1956.

"dominate[s] this waxing": *Pittsburgh Courier,* June 23, 1956.

"My best audiences": *Pittsburgh Courier,* March 24, 1964.

"She brought down the house": *New York Amsterdam News,* June 9, 1962.

"Man, I was so scared": *Philadelphia Tribune,* April 5, 1966.

"Everybody likes me": *Cleveland Call and Post,* February 6, 1971.

"her homebase": *Variety,* December 27, 1972.

"I told her, 'Moms' ": Perry Diller, author interview, 2020.

"I don't care if you could stand": *New York Post,* 1974, undated clipping, New York Public Library.

"The movie sort of shambles": *New York*

Times, November 2, 1974.

"patently — very, very patently": *Los Angeles Times,* September 27, 1974.

"rough sledding": *Variety,* July 17, 1974.

"a sluggish, unsatisfying": *New York Amsterdam News,* November 9, 1974.

"Moms will never retire": *Chicago Defender,* June 1, 1974.

"She was a consummate artist": *Chicago Defender,* May 29, 1975.

"She just finally lived": *Chicago Defender,* June 2, 1975.

"The other day": *New York Times,* June 2, 1975.

"She used to call me": *Jet,* August 14, 1975.

"I contend": *Norfolk New Journal and Guide,* June 23, 1962.

"take me home": *Pittsburgh Courier,* June 13, 1981.

Chapter Two: The Pro

"I didn't think of it": *Orlando Sun-Sentinel,* June 16, 1991.

"She was the only woman": *Orlando Sun-Sentinel,* June 16, 1991.

"If you couldn't do it": Susan Chatzky, author interview, 2019.

"Jean used to make them scream": *Orlando Sun-Sentinel,* June 16, 1991.

"Other women doing comedy": *New York Times,* November 5, 2006.

"I stole from everybody": *Orlando Sun-Sentinel,* June 16, 1991.

"He was a baker": Overbeke, *Forgotten Pioneer,* p. 53.

"If you brought home the pay": *Orlando Sun-Sentinel,* June 16, 1991.

"Oh no, oh no!": Overbeke, *Forgotten Pioneer,* p. 56.

"all the German bundts": Overbeke, p. 58.

"I said, 'No, you won't' ": Overbeke, p. 60.

"I went from age 11": *Orlando Sun-Sentinel,* June 16, 1991.

"petite ingenue": *Variety,* February 24, 1922, September 22, 1922.

"I'd tell the band": *New York Times,* November 5, 2006.

"Nothing shook me": Smith, *Vaudevillians,* p. 254.

"You know something": Smith, pp. 254–56 passim.

"I was so hurt": *New York Daily News,* August 31, 1958.

"Nothing was written": Smith, *Vaudevillians,* p. 256.

"a clever comedienne": *Billboard,* November 14, 1931.

"as comedienne and as hoofer": *Variety,* July 5, 1932.

"Good at Dumb Dora": *Billboard,* August 13, 1932.

"The Carroll line": *Variety,* June 6, 1933.

"A pretty lass": *Billboard,* June 24, 1933.

"Miss Carroll's chatterbox style": *Variety,* May 22, 1934.

"An ideally mated couple": *Billboard,* June 30, 1934.

"You worked by yourself": Overbeke, *Forgotten Pioneer,* p. 71.

"essay a comedy act": *Variety,* June 26, 1934.

"Apronmate of Marty May": *Billboard,* January 27, 1934.

"and how he can dance": Smith, *Vaudevillians,* p. 20.

"He made a comment": Overbeke, *Forgotten Pioneer,* p. 76.

"He was asserting": Overbeke, p. 76.

"My heart went": Smith, *Vaudevillians,* p. 256.

"He got up": Overbeke, *Forgotten Pioneer,* p. 76.

"Jean wrote us an act": Smith, *Vaudevillians,* p. 20.

"Jean could dance": Smith, p. 20.

"I was lucky": Smith, p. 21.

"Jean Carroll and Buddy Howe deuced": *Billboard,* February 16, 1935.

"Forte is comedy": *Billboard,* April 13, 1935.

"This is a new comedy team": *Variety,* May 20, 1936.

"a peach of a comedy": *Billboard,* July 11, 1936.

"Their chief appeal": *Stage,* July 16, 1936.

"Act is good": *Variety,* September 12, 1936.

"We were playing Loew's State": Smith, *Vaudevillians,* p. 21.

"If she wrote": Smith, p. 21.

"Most unusual": *Billboard,* December 27, 1941.

"in each town": *Billboard,* July 24, 1943.

"Their comedy turn": *Billboard,* July 17, 1943.

"I stood for hours": Overbeke, *Forgotten Pioneer,* p. 94.

"Jean Carroll is a singing comedienne": *Variety,* March 29, 1944.

"Miss Carroll sang": *Billboard,* April 1, 1944.

"Jean Carroll, now doing a single": *Variety,* May 10, 1944.

"Jean Carroll is a bit unusual": *Billboard,* February 16, 1946.

"Jean Carroll, femme raconteur": *Variety,* February 20, 1946.

"Jean was already doing": Smith, *Vaudevillians,* p. 21.

"He told me, 'I held you back' ": *Orlando Sun-Sentinel,* June 16, 1991.

"A sense of humor has no sex": *New York Herald-Tribune,* April 18, 1961.

"If the male comics": *New York Herald-Tribune,* March 5, 1952.

"There seems to be a subconscious": *New York Mirror,* undated clipping, New York Public Library.

"Men in the audience": *New York Journal-American,* January 31, 1956.

"The task is to get them": *New York Journal-American,* January 31, 1956.

"I usually pick out": *New York Herald-Tribune,* March 5, 1952.

"must be selected": *New York Journal-American,* June 21, 1959.

"I can joke about the foibles": *New York Herald-Tribune,* March 5, 1952.

"Unlike a male comic": *New York Journal-American,* June 21, 1959.

"Customers are accustomed": *Variety,* December 4, 1946.

"Perhaps it's the novelty": *Variety,* June 11, 1947.

"One of the few femme comics": *Variety,* June 9, 1948.

"Here's a comedienne": *Variety,* August 18, 1948.

"A solid five-minute laugh": Smith, *Vaudevillians,* p. 22.

"Jean Carroll scores": *Variety,* March 5, 1952.

"Jean Carroll is the best": *New York Daily Mirror,* undated clipping, New York Public Library.

"Miss Carroll does not hurt": *New York Times,* February 27, 1952.

"The hell I can't!": *Orlando Sun-Sentinel,* June 16, 1991.

"I'll never, never undertake": *New York Daily*

News, August 31, 1958.

"I was making much more": *New York Times,* November 5, 2006.

"He was my soul mate": *New York Times,* November 5, 2006.

"Their marriage was respectful": Susan Chatzky, author interview, 2019.

"Jean Carroll's reconciliation": *Washington Post and Times-Herald,* February 2, 1956.

"Just before I'd go on": *New York Times,* November 5, 2006.

"He really had no great sense": Nachman, *Right Here on Our Stage Tonight,* p. 227.

"I'll come to your house": Nachman, p. 225.

"I did my show": Nachman, p. 225.

"would finish cleaning": *Washington Post,* January 13, 2010.

"I am not desperate": Overbeke, *Forgotten Pioneer,* p. 170.

"I'm too much in love": Overbeke, p. 173.

"I used to have to go": *Orlando Sun-Sentinel,* June 16, 1991.

"I was making pots": *Orlando Sun-Sentinel,* June 16, 1991.

"You're cried out": *Orlando Sun-Sentinel,* June 16, 1991.

"People were legitimately afraid": Susan Chatzky, author interview, 2019.

"widely credited": *New York Times,* January 2, 2010.

"It was not lost on her": Susan Chatzky,

author interview, 2019.

"I had no idea": Overbeke, *Forgotten Pioneer,* 310.

Chapter Three: The Sunflower

"I didn't complain": Pearl, *Minnie Pearl,* p. 154.

"Right off Brother": Pearl, *Minnie Pearl's Diary,* unpaginated e-book.

"Minnie Pearl, *doyenne":* New York Times, July 28, 1957.

"Oh, Minnie Pearl!": Pearl, *Minnie Pearl,* p. 249.

"Minnie's never lost": *Washington Post,* December 1, 1980.

"Daddy was a yellow-dog": *Chicago Tribune,* November 18, 1984.

an unplanned surprise: Pearl, *Minnie Pearl,* p. 11.

"I thought, 'Oh, Lord' ": Pearl, p. 45.

"I perceive you've been given": Pearl, p. 81.

Ophelia took meals: Pearl, p. 119.

story about this fictional woman: Pearl, p. 122.

headed to a thrift store: Pearl, pp. 129–30.

"Most country music stars": Pearl, p. 136.

"I explained over and over": Pearl, p. 137.

On a November night: Pearl, p. 138.

"I realized I didn't have": *Chicago Tribune,* March 28, 1972.

"I was country": *Chicago Tribune,* March 12, 1989.

"When Minnie first started": Nash, *Behind Closed Doors,* p. 415.

"I still wasn't ready": Pearl, *Minnie Pearl,* p. 147.

"Now, why don't you": Pearl, p. 149.

"Those people from the William Esty": Nash, *Behind Closed Doors,* p. 415.

"I was a pretty normal old gal": *Chicago Tribune,* December 12, 1979.

"Baby, after the Lord": Pearl, *Minnie Pearl,* p. 192.

"Mrs. Colley": Pearl, p. 198.

"I am Sarah Cannon": *Chicago Tribune,* March 12, 1989.

"a good style": *Variety,* May 28, 1952.

"Each of the cornfed": *Variety,* June 18, 1952.

"I thought they were going to bypass": Nash, *Behind Closed Doors,* p. 405.

"no one exemplifies": Pearl, *Minnie Pearl,* p. 9.

Chapter Four: The Bawds

"I ain't afraid": *Variety,* December 24, 1969.

"glitter as I used": Tucker, *Some of These Days,* p. 104.

"committing an act": *Morning Oregonian,* November 6, 1910.

"I intend": *Morning Oregonian,* November 6, 1910.

"I was left sitting": Tucker, *Some of These*

Days, p. 104.

"special material": *Variety,* May 20, 1953.

"lewdness and immoral activity": *Variety,* August 2, 1961.

"if it's breaking the law": *Variety,* December 5, 1962.

"grievous mortification": *Variety,* February 17, 1971.

"I give the people": *Back Stage,* October 11, 1968.

"She worked at four": Kliph Nesteroff, "An Interview with Rusty Warren," Classic Television Showbiz, July 21, 2010, www .classicshowbiz.blogspot.com.

"You have to record the comic": *Billboard,* October 23, 1961.

"You have to record it live": *Billboard,* October 23, 1961.

"Women telling suggestive": *Billboard,* October 23, 1961.

"an expurgated edition": *Variety,* March 22, 1961.

"you could bring your 13-year-old": *Billboard,* March 27, 1961.

"took off many of the wraps": *Variety,* April 26, 1961.

"Miss Barth is not only": *Variety,* November 29, 1961.

"Her second show was spicier": *Variety,* March 6, 1963.

"one unkind and tasteless": *Variety,* October 23, 1963.

"Miss Barth is very much": *Variety,* April 13, 1966.

"spice-filled specialties": *Billboard,* January 11, 1941.

"smutty songs": *Variety,* November 5, 1941.

"she was nervous": *Billboard,* December 4, 1961.

"some of the bluest": *Variety,* September 4, 1963.

"It should . . . be kept": *Variety,* November 29, 1961.

"We all did totally": Nachman, *Seriously Funny,* p. 214.

"Something didn't satisfy me": Burt Kearns and Jeff Abraham, "Retro Icon Rusty Warren: The 'Knockers Up' Gal!," Please Kill Me, March 28, 2018, www.pleasekillme-.com.

"One of my bosses": "Knockers Up! Rusty Warren: The Shecky Interview," undated, www.sheckymagazine.com.

"I was scared": Nesteroff, "Interview with Rusty Warren."

"You're going to have to get up": Nesteroff, "Interview with Rusty Warren."

"scared to death": Nesteroff, "Interview with Rusty Warren."

"Miss Warren has only lately": *Variety,* March 11, 1959.

"She leaves absolutely nothing": *Fort Lauderdale News,* undated clip, 1959.

"She asked me to have lunch": Kearns and Abraham, "Retro Icon Rusty Warren."

"They said 'You wouldn't dare' ": Nesteroff, "Interview with Rusty Warren."

"I didn't talk dirty": Kearns and Abraham, "Retro Icon Rusty Warren."

"any place that had a drinking": "Knockers Up! Rusty Warren: The Shecky Interview."

"Comedians often specialize": *Time,* January 11, 1963.

"I could hardly believe it": Kliph Nesteroff, "The Life and Times of Rusty Warren," WFMU's Beware of the Blog, www .blog.wfmu.org, June 27, 2010.

"A woman doing material": Nesteroff, "Life and Times of Rusty Warren."

"Are these the things": Nesteroff, "Life and Times of Rusty Warren."

"I said, 'What?' ": Nesteroff, "Interview with Rusty Warren."

"We stayed over": Nesteroff, "Interview with Rusty Warren."

"becoming a nun": *New York Times,* September 14, 1968.

"Joan Rivers was always nice": Kearns and Abraham, "Retro Icon Rusty Warren."

"The one who did Phyllis": Nesteroff, "Interview with Rusty Warren."

Chapter Five: The Positive Thinker

"Being a woman": Wilde, *Great Comedians Talk About Comedy,* p. 207.

"Leave it in": Diller, *Like a Lampshade,* p. 6.

"She seemed to do the work": *National Enquirer,* October 14, 1973.

"State your business": *Village Voice,* August 15, 1989.

"She even played the piano": *National Enquirer,* October 14, 1973.

"I was an absolutely perfect": Wilde, *Great Comedians Talk About Comedy,* p. 204.

"the kind of face": *New York Mirror Magazine,* December 21, 1958.

"with their noses": Diller, *Like a Lampshade,* p. 48.

"boasting a terrific": Diller, p. 46.

"It was sort of a mating thing": *You Bet Your Life,* January 30, 1958.

"Before long": Diller, *Like a Lampshade,* p. 46.

"Almost as soon": Diller, p. 48.

"Sherwood was *lousy*": Diller, p. 57.

"I was very young": *West Side TV Shopper,* May 28, 1983.

"agoraphobic sex tyrant": Diller, *Like a Lampshade,* p. 100.

"It was too painful": Diller, p. 71.

"Thought is the original source": Bristol, *Magic of Believing.*

"because I didn't want to stick": Diller, *Like*

a Lampshade, p. 80.

"I sang seriously": Gavin, *Intimate Nights,* p. 136.

"Perched atop the piano": *The Unpredictable Jorie Remus* [audio recording, 1960], jacket notes, undated.

"If she could do it": Diller, *Like a Lampshade,* p. 87.

"My husband decided": *Toledo Blade,* February 23, 1958.

"There were times": *TV Guide,* February 25, 1967.

"He's always wanted a product": *Show,* March 1963.

"Lady, stop": Diller, *Like a Lampshade,* p. 90.

"When I went on stage": *Boston Globe,* February 6, 1959.

"these whites": Angelou, *Singin' and Swingin',* p. 85.

"You'll be a smashing": Angelou, p. 85.

"Di-vine, darling": Angelou, pp. 95–96 passim.

"a frowzy blond": Angelou, p. 100.

"When you've been pregnant": *Spotlight,* June 1989.

"I looked exactly": *Interview,* September 1986.

"You virtually needed": *Spotlight,* June 1989.

"I had only seventeen minutes": Gannett newspapers, September 10, 1982.

"I found that agents": *Boston Globe,* February 6, 1959.

"It was my grand affirmative": *New York Post,* September 1, 1963.

"I don't want a leave": Diller, *Like a Lampshade,* p. 92.

"I have five children": Diller, p. 105.

"I did anything": Diller, p. 97.

"When my material stopped": Wilde, *Great Comedians Talk About Comedy,* p. 208.

"a good figure": *Interview,* September 1986.

"I looked like a typical": Diller, *Like a Lampshade,* p. 113.

"I was always chic": *Interview,* September 1986.

"I used to have to laugh": *TV Guide,* February 25, 1967.

"a stand-up comedian who works": Diller, *Like a Lampshade,* p. 121.

"Trying to ensure": Diller, p. 114.

"My delivery didn't work": Diller, p. 123.

"She bombed": Gavin, *Intimate Nights,* p. 166.

"rather forced": *Variety,* March 12, 1958.

"above a liquor store": Perry Diller, author interview, 2020.

"Are you two having": Diller, *Like a Lampshade,* p. 111.

"the weirdest, wildest yet": *Chicago Tribune,* October 16, 1958, October 19, 1958.

" 'hip' and lunatic": *Chicago Tribune,* October 19, 1958.

"Hilarious isn't a good word": *Boston Daily Record,* December 15, 1958.

"called the Paar show": Phyllis Diller, unpublished interview by James Robert Parrish, 1971, New York Public Library.

"That's all it took": Diller, *Like a Lampshade,* p. 128.

"When it ended": Diller, p. 128.

"My screen test": Diller, Parrish interview.

"You're sensational": Diller, *Like a Lampshade,* p. 142.

"Her delivery is staccato": *New York Times,* March 13, 1961.

"I'm not big enough": November 1977, uncredited clipping, New York Public Library.

"Baby, we made it!": November 1977, uncredited clipping, New York Public Library.

"I'd had my one-night stands": Diller, *Like a Lampshade,* p. 163.

"Within a couple of days": Diller, p. 163.

"She made it her business": Rivers, *Enter Talking,* p. 349.

"a many-hued package": *New York Times,* June 9, 1966.

"it fairly bubbles": *Los Angeles Times,* June 15, 1966.

"If the action sometimes": *Variety,* June 8, 1966.

"there could be a reconciliation": *New York World Telegraph & Sun,* July 22, 1965.

"Does the word *stupid*": Diller, *Like a Lampshade,* p. 206.

"I always have . . . these little phrases": Wilde, *Great Comedians Talk About Comedy,* pp. 212–17 passim.

"Imagine four guys": *New York Daily News,* August 11, 1966.

"a forlorn item": These review quotes all appeared in *Broadcasting,* September 12, 1966.

"You'll wish you hadn't": *Los Angeles Times,* April 5, 1968.

"a novel and strangely appealing": *Variety,* September 18, 1968.

"a refreshing new chapter": *New York Times,* September 16, 1968.

"she'll please most": *New York Daily News,* September 16, 1968.

"She was miked": Perry Diller, author interview, 2020.

"an acquired taste": *New York Times,* January 25, 1970.

"the result was all": Diller, *Like a Lampshade,* p. 229.

"There were literally hundreds": "*Get Happy:* The Stories Behind the Songs," Pink Martini website, December 19, 2013, www.pinkmartini.com.

"I don't miss the travel": *New York Times,* August 21, 2012.

"Brighten the corner": Diller, *Like a Lampshade,* p. 266.

"She was there": *Los Angeles Times,* August 21, 2012.

Chapter Six: The Perfectionist

"There's always some idiot": *Look,* February 10, 1970.

"Elaine is perhaps": Wilson, *Sixties,* p. 36.

"In love with Elaine?": Coleman, *Compass,* p. 67.

"completely disconnected": Coleman, p. 272.

"a car trunk": Coleman, p. 38.

"Our people do not": *Life,* July 28, 1967.

"My mother's a good": Coleman, *Compass,* p. 39.

"I couldn't bud": *New Yorker,* April 8, 1961.

"What's the matter": Nachman, *Seriously Funny,* p. 331.

"Hi, Elaine": Sweet, *Something Wonderful Right Away,* p. 74.

"it was unwise": Sweet, p. 74.

she intimidated the hell: Coleman, *Compass,* pp. 66–67.

"I think she saw": Coleman, p. 111.

"I got all the parts": *New York Times,* May 24, 1959.

"a princeling deprived": Coleman, *Compass,* p. 18.

"look of utter contempt": *New Yorker,* April 8, 1961.

"I sensed her": *Life,* July 28, 1967.

"Ha!": *Playboy,* June 1966.

"My insults": *New York Post,* February 2, 1958.

"we loathed one another": *New York Times,*

May 24, 1959.

"I knew she knew": Sweet, *Something Wonderful,* p. 73.

"I want you to meet": Nachman, *Seriously Funny,* p. 324.

"People are always telling": Nachman, p. 329.

"Everybody wanted": *New Yorker,* February 13, 2000.

"I will answer": Nachman, *Seriously Funny,* p. 334.

"slunk back": Coleman, *Compass,* p. 120.

"doing these routines": Coleman, p. 128.

"We both thought": Harris, *Mike Nichols,* p. 71.

"a certain connection": Sweet, *Something Wonderful,* p. 78.

"I don't think anyone": Sweet, pp. 106–107.

"We, being men": Coleman, *Compass,* p. 109.

Elaine "broke through": Coleman, p. 120.

"I thought Mike and Elaine": Sweet, *Something Wonderful,* p. 191.

"The fight got away": Sweet, p. 80.

"The next time": Coleman, *Compass,* p. 164.

"After all, we're a trio": Coleman, p. 195.

"Elaine didn't give": Coleman, p. 146.

"Isn't it a beautiful": Coleman, p. 219.

"She was sitting": Nesteroff, *Comedians,* p. 169.

"We walked in": *New York Morning Telegraph,* undated 1959 clipping, New York Public

Library.

"I'd never seen": Nachman, *Seriously Funny,* p. 340.

"When the coffee came": *New York Morning Telegraph,* undated 1959 clipping.

"Their thought patterns": *Variety,* November 13, 1957.

"They were auditioning": Kohen, *We Killed,* p. 23.

"[He] would feel": *Vanity Fair,* January, 2013.

"It still seems": *Variety,* January 1, 1958.

"There were lines": Gavin, *Intimate Nights,* p. 162.

"Each item": *New York Times,* January 16, 1958.

"Two of the funniest": *Billboard,* January 20, 1958.

"fresh and engaging": *Variety,* January 22, 1958.

"They really ought to": *Billboard,* August 11, 1958.

"What were they all carrying": "Mike Nichols," *American Masters,* PBS, January 29, 2016.

"My ambitions": *New Yorker,* April 8, 1961.

"the only reason": *New York Post,* April 14, 1958.

"You mean it's *second-hand*": *New Yorker,* April 8, 1961.

"Without overpowering": *New York Times,* October 10, 1960.

"Convulsing": *Variety,* October 12, 1960.

"All of their material": *Billboard,* October 17, 1960.

"delicate verbal surgery": *Observer,* October 23, 1960.

"We never got a negative": Nachman, *Seriously Funny,* p. 350.

Initially, they were delighted: "Mike Nichols," *American Masters.*

"We stopped": "Mike Nichols," *American Masters.*

"She got married": "Mike Nichols," *American Masters.*

"It was not a pleasant": *Life,* July 28, 1967.

"Thank you, Miss May": *New York Times,* September 23, 1962.

"Who can I warn": *Life,* July 28, 1967.

"just long enough": *New York Post,* October 10, 1962.

"refused to provide the cuts": *New York Times,* October 10, 1962.

"We are still friends": *New York Mirror,* October 13, 1962.

"Why don't you just say": *New York,* July 22, 1967.

"She had treated him": Wilson, *Sixties,* p. 174.

"the hit of the evening": *New York Times,* November 11, 1963.

"Although we are naturally": *New York Sunday News,* January 29, 1967.

"We were doing simple": *New York Post,*

undated 1967 clipping, New York Public Library.

"It was in a way": quoted in *American Masters: Mike Nichols,* 2016.

"Elaine is going to suffer": *Life,* July 27, 1967.

"charmingly genteel": *New York Times,* August 1, 1967.

"either the sexiest": *Life,* July 27, 1967.

"Who told you": *New York Times,* January 1, 1967.

"I feel sad for Elaine": *Life,* July 27, 1967.

"She's a fucking maniac": *New York,* December 6, 1976.

"one of the funniest": *Chicago Sun-Times,* April 6, 1971.

"beautiful and gently": *New York Times,* March 12, 1971.

"sophisticated and funny": *Variety,* March 10, 1971.

"a first-class American": *New York Times,* December 1, 1972.

"The movie has a way": *Chicago Sun-Times,* January 1, 1973.

"bright, amusing": *Variety,* December 13, 1972.

"They might come back": *New York,* December 6, 1976.

"told in such insistently": *New York Times,* December 22, 1976.

"It suckers an audience": *Variety,* December 22, 1976.

"You are not apt": *Los Angeles Times,* December 25, 1976.

Chapter Seven: The Songbird

"There was discrimination": *Playgirl,* January 1975.

"The crowd would begin laughing": *New York Sunday News,* February 19, 1967.

"I was sort of a toy": *Playgirl,* January 1975.

"I always knew": *Hartford Courant,* June 26, 1966.

"Even as a kid": *New York Sunday News,* February 19, 1967.

"He wouldn't let me": *Hartford Courant,* June 26, 1966.

"strictly a show business": *New York Sunday News,* February 19, 1967.

"When I made a big hit": *Hartford Courant,* June 26, 1966.

"That move changed": *Hartford Courant,* June 26, 1966.

"There were plenty": *Hartford Courant,* June 26, 1966.

"I went into this small": *Newsday,* December 17, 1966.

"I proposed": *Hartford Courant,* June 26, 1966.

"The things I wanted": *Playgirl,* January 1975.

"We find taking": *Hartford Courant,* December 30, 1952.

"I realized I could only": *Playgirl,* January 1975.

"I wanted to make it": *Playgirl,* January 1975.

"That's when I got fat": *Hartford Courant,* June 26, 1966.

"I come right out": *New York Sunday News,* February 19, 1967.

"I make sure": *Hartford Courant,* April 5, 1964.

"I didn't get a decent": *Playgirl,* January 1975.

"She called and asked": *Newsday,* December 17, 1966.

"She is fast": *Variety,* December 7, 1960.

"a short and heavy": *Variety,* September 27, 1961.

"a brash, brassy": *Variety,* March 2, 1962.

"She's a charming": *New York Times,* July 2, 1964.

"There always have been": *Variety,* March 13, 1963.

to congratulate and counsel: *Newsday,* December 17, 1966.

"This gal": *Newsday,* December 17, 1966.

"Pound for pound": *Variety,* June 19, 1963.

"At last I'm headlining": *New York World Journal Tribune,* January 8, 1967.

"I'm recognized": *New York Sunday News,* February 19, 1967.

she allowed a reporter: *Newsday,* December 17, 1966.

The Totie Fields who had emerged: *Hartford*

Courant, April 5, 1964.

"a throwback": Rivers, *Still Talking,* pp. 51–52.

"mentally it will make": *New York Times,* August 3, 1978.

"broke up at other": *Variety,* August 9, 1978.

"Totie was a gutter fighter": Rivers, *Still Talking,* p. 52.

"I made them give me": *Playgirl,* January 1975..

"The minute I put": *Newsweek,* November 15, 1976

"portrait of a resilient": *New York Times,* June 24, 1977.

"I didn't lose": *People,* March 21, 1977.

"It was Totie": Rivers, *Still Talking,* p. 52.

"I guarantee you": *Philadelphia Inquirer,* October 2, 1977.

"The one thing I can't": *Philadelphia Inquirer,* October 2, 1977.

"The show is funny": *New York Daily News,* August 5, 1978.

"Never felt better": *New York Post,* July 10, 1978.

"I would not be around": *New York Daily News,* August 3, 1978.

Chapter Eight: The Scrapper

"I don't want to be": *New York Post,* June 20, 1965.

"her little flowers": Rivers, *Enter Talking,* p. 4.

"You come from": Rivers, p. 3.

"tendency toward bribery": Rivers, *Book of Joan,* pp. 83–85 passim.

"stage door Jane": *Brooklyn Eagle,* June 16, 1950.

"Can you believe": Rivers, *Enter Talking,* p. 68.

"make it in three years": Rivers, p. 119.

"I was willing to do": Rivers, p. 131.

"Ask AGVA": Rivers, p. 151.

"When you are not even": Rivers, p. 151.

"I can't send you out": Rivers, p. 164.

"Joan Rivers was like": Rivers, p. 164.

"When I went to medical": *New York Daily News,* April 9, 1978.

"the most loving": Rivers, *Enter Talking,* p. 227.

"a clumsy, clumpy": Rivers, p. 230.

"Her material is tired": Rivers, p. 231.

"Ladies and gentlemen": Rivers, *Joan Rivers Confidential,* p. 34.

"Even in the fall": Rivers, *Enter Talking,* pp. 241–42.

"In three *more* years": Rivers, p. 259.

"never really happy": Patinkin, *Second City,* p. 60.

"It was a very closed": Sweet, *Something Wonderful,* p. 287.

"I finally in Chicago": Rivers, *Enter Talking,* p. 274.

"the loser girl": Rivers, pp. 277–78.

"It's not your forte": *Cosmopolitan,* October 1965.

"She had the *fastest*": *Ms.,* October 1984.

"a very funny femme": Rivers, *Joan Rivers Confidential,* p. 46.

"The major disaster": *Back Stage,* March 29, 1963.

"We all hated": *New York Post,* June 20, 1965.

"There was no joy": *TV Guide,* August 10, 1968.

"a pert blonde": *Variety,* June 17, 1964.

"Fine," he told her: Rivers, *Enter Talking,* p. 334.

"Everyone has seen her": Rivers, p. 340.

"I was born corrupt": Rivers, p. 348.

"Jesus Christ": Rivers, p. 371.

"Johnny Carson struck": *New York Journal-American,* February 18, 1965.

"Of course, we always knew": Rivers, *Enter Talking,* p. 373.

"It was all over": Rivers, p. 373.

"I did not want to be a date": Rivers, *Still Talking,* p. 28.

"there was Edgar": Rivers, p. 31.

"the first and last time": Rivers, p. 32.

"Women comedians like women shot-putters": *New York Times,* July 13, 1965.

"My agents pushed me": *Theater Week,* September 5, 1988.

"the next Lucille Ball": *Newsday,* October 16, 1965.

"Don't worry, baby": Rivers, *Still Talking*, p. 41.

"Two years ago": *Newsday,* October 16, 1965.

"especially interesting": *New York Times,* May 16, 1968.

"I didn't even have a dress": *Theater Week,* September 5, 1988.

"He was a little foggy": Nachman, *Right Here,* p. 385.

"I wasn't risque": Nachman, p. 223.

"He somehow decided": Rivers, *Still Talking,* p. 58.

"He just said, 'When and where' ": *Los Angeles Times,* October 21, 1973.

"Dear Mr. Carson": Bennetts, *Last Girl Before Freeway,* pp. 87–88.

"quite possibly the most": *New York Times,* October 3, 1968.

"The redoubtable Miss Rivers": *Variety,* November 19, 1969.

"I don't break in new": *After Dark,* September 1975.

"Our business loves": *Theater Week,* September 5, 1988.

"the play has its laughs": *Variety,* December 1, 1971.

"I am, in fact": *Los Angeles Times,* February 4, 1973.

"bastard colonial": Rivers, *Still Talking,* p. 97.

"Joan never got": Bennetts, *Last Girl Before*

Freeway, p. 102.

"Whenever one does": *New York Times,* April 9, 1978.

"Sure to be": *Los Angeles Times,* April 8, 1978.

"an animal tranquilizer": Bennetts, *Last Girl Before Freeway,* p. 114.

"Overwhelmingly nervous": *Variety,* October 15, 1986.

"The New Joan Rivers Without": Newsday, October 11, 1986.

"futzy and klutzy": *Los Angeles Times,* October 11, 1986.

"This may have been the first": *New York Times,* October 13, 1986.

"I can't stand this": Bennetts, *Last Girl Before Freeway,* p. 178.

"I'm so depressed": Rivers, *Still Talking,* p. 248.

"Pride can kill": Rivers, p. 5.

Conclusion

"He told me a female comedian": *New York Times,* January 14, 1970.

"I grew up in a time": *Vulture,* March 19, 2013.

"I began comedy": Rita Rudner, author interview, 2020.

BIBLIOGRAPHY

Adams, Joey. *Here's to the Friars: The Heart of Show Business.* New York: Crown, 1976.

Angelou, Maya. *Singin' and Swingin' and Gettin' Merry Like Christmas.* New York: Random House, 1976.

Ballard, Kaye, with Jim Hesselman. *How I Lost 10 Pounds in 53 Years: A Memoir.* Boulder, CO: Argent Books, 2004.

Bennetts, Leslie. *Last Girl Before Freeway: The Life, Loves, Losses and Liberation of Joan Rivers.* New York: Little, Brown, 2016.

Bristol, Claude. *The Magic of Believing.* New York: Prentice-Hall, 1948.

Cohen, Sarah Blacher. *Jewish Wry: Essays on Jewish Humor.* Bloomington: Indiana University Press, 1987.

Coleman, Janet. *The Compass: The Improvisational Theatre That Revolutionized American Comedy.* Chicago: University of Chicago Press, 1990.

Diller, Phyllis. *Phyllis Diller's Housekeeping*

Hints. New York: Fawcett Crest, 1966.

———, with Richard Buskin. *Like a Lampshade in a Whorehouse: My Life in Comedy*. New York: Jeremy Tarcher, 2005.

Fey, Tina. *Bossypants*. New York: Little, Brown, 2011.

Fields, Anna. *The Girl in the Show: Three Generations of Comedy, Culture, and Feminism*. New York: Arcade, 2017.

Fields, Totie. *I Think I'll Start on Monday: The Official 8 1/2 oz. Mashed Potato Diet*. New York: Hawthorn Books, 1972.

Firestone, Ross. *Breaking It Up! The Best Routines of the Stand-Up Comics*. New York: Bantam, 1975.

Forbes, Camille F. *Introducing Bert Williams: Burnt Cork, Broadway, and the Story of America's First Black Star*. New York: Basic Civitas, 2008.

Franklin, Joe. *Joe Franklin's Encyclopedia of Comedians*. New York: Bell, 1979.

Gavin, James. *Intimate Nights: The Golden Age of New York Cabaret*. Revised edition. New York: Back Stage Books, 2006.

Green, Abel, and Joe Laurie Jr. *Show Biz: From Vaude to Video*. New York: Henry Holt, 1951.

Griggs, Jeff. *Guru: My Days with Del Close*. Chicago: Ivan R. Dee, 2005.

Harris, Mark. *Mike Nichols: A Life*. New York: Penguin Press, 2021.

Kanfer, Stefan. *A Summer World: The Attempt to Build a Jewish Eden in the Catskills, from the Days of the Ghetto to the Rise and Decline of the Borscht Belt.* New York: Farrar, Straus & Giroux, 1989.

Knoedelseder, William. *I'm Dying Up Here: Heartbreak and High Times in Stand-Up Comedy's Golden Era.* New York: PublicAffairs, 2009.

Kohen, Yael. *We Killed: The Rise of Women in American Comedy.* New York: Farrar, Straus & Giroux, 2012.

Maroulis, Athan. *Greetings from the Borscht Belt: The Best Broads of Comedy.* Fuel Label Group, 2012, compact disc.

Mazursky, Paul. *Show Me the Magic: My Adventures in Life and Hollywood.* New York: Simon & Schuster, 1999.

Mizejewski, Linda, and Victoria Sturtevant, eds. *Hysterical! Women in American Comedy.* Austin: University of Texas Press, 2017.

Nachman, Gerald. *Right Here on Our Stage Tonight! Ed Sullivan's America.* Berkeley: University of California Press, 2009.

————. *Seriously Funny: The Rebel Comedians of the 1950s and 1960s.* New York: Pantheon, 2003.

Nash, Alana. *Behind Closed Doors: Talking with the Legends of Country Music.* New York: Cooper Square Press, 2002.

Nesteroff, Kliph. *The Comedians: Drunks,*

Thieves, Scoundrels and the History of American Comedy. New York: Grove Press, 2016.

Overbeke, Grace. "The Forgotten Pioneer: Jean Carroll and the Jewish Female Origins of Stand-Up Comedy." PhD diss., Northwestern University, Evanston, IL, 2019.

Patinkin, Sheldon. *The Second City: Backstage at the World's Greatest Comedy Theater.* Naperville, IL: Sourcebooks, 2000.

Pearl, Minnie. *Minnie Pearl's Diary.* New York: Greenberg Publishing, 1953.

Pearl, Minnie, with Joan Dew. *Minnie Pearl: An Autobiography.* New York: Simon & Schuster, 1980.

Rivers, Joan, with Richard Meryman. *Enter Talking.* New York: Delacorte Press, 1986.

———. *Still Talking.* New York: Turtle Bay Books, 1991.

Rivers, Melissa. *The Book of Joan: Tales of Mirth, Mischief, and Manipulation.* New York: Crown Archetype, 2015.

Rivers, Melissa, with Scott Currie. *Joan Rivers Confidential: The Unseen Scrapbooks, Joke Cards, Personal Files and Photos of a Very Funny Woman Who Kept Everything.* New York: Abrams, 2017.

Shales, Tom, and James Andrew Miller. *Live from New York: An Uncensored History of 'Saturday Night Live' as Told by Its Stars, Writers and Guests.* New York: Little, Brown, 2002.

Shydner, Ritch, and Mark Schiff. *I Killed: True Stories of the Road from America's Top Comics.* New York: Crown, 2006.

Silverman, Stephen M. *Funny Ladies: 100 Years of Great Comediennes.* New York: Harry N. Abrams, 1999.

Skarloff, Lauren Rebecca. *Red Hot Mama: The Life of Sophie Tucker.* Austin: University of Texas Press, 2018.

Smith, Bill. *The Vaudevillians.* New York: Macmillan, 1976.

Sweet, Jeffrey. *Something Wonderful Right Away: An Oral History of the Second City and the Compass Players.* New York: Limelight, 1986.

Tafoya, Eddie. *The Legacy of the Wisecrack: Stand-up Comedy as the Great American Literary Form.* Boca Raton: Brown Walker Press, 2009.

Terkel, Studs. *The Spectator: Talk About Movies and Plays with Those Who Make Them.* New York: New Press, 1999.

Tucker, Sophie. *Some of These Days: The Autobiography of Sophie Tucker.* Garden City: Doubleday, Doran, 1945.

Unterbrink, Mary. *Funny Women: American Comediennes, 1860–1985.* Jefferson, NC: McFarland & Company, 1987.

Warren, Roz, ed. *Revolutionary Laughter: The World of Women Comics.* Freedom, CA: Crossing Press, 1995.

Watkins, Mel. *On the Real Side: Laughing, Lying, and Signifying: The Underground Tradition of African-American Humor That Transformed American Culture, from Slavery to Richard Pryor.* New York: Simon & Schuster, 1994.

Wilde, Larry. *The Great Comedians Talk About Comedy.* Mechanicsburg, PA: Executive Books, 2000.

Wilson, Edmund. *The Sixties.* New York: Farrar, Straus & Giroux, 1993.

Zoglin, Richard. *Comedy at the Edge: How Stand-Up in the 1970s Changed America.* New York: Bloomsbury, 2008.

ABOUT THE AUTHOR

Shawn Levy is the bestselling author of *The Castle on Sunset, Rat Pack Confidential, Paul Newman: A Life,* and *Dolce Vita Confidential.* His writing has appeared in *The New York Times, Los Angeles Times, The Guardian, The Hollywood Reporter, Sight and Sound, Film Comment,* and *American Film.* He jumps and claps and sings for victory in Portland, Oregon.

The employees of Thorndike Press hope you have enjoyed this Large Print book. All our Thorndike, Wheeler, and Kennebec Large Print titles are designed for easy reading, and all our books are made to last. Other Thorndike Press Large Print books are available at your library, through selected bookstores, or directly from us.

For information about titles, please call:
(800) 223-1244

or visit our website at:
gale.com/thorndike

To share your comments, please write:
Publisher
Thorndike Press
10 Water St., Suite 310
Waterville, ME 04901